M000266287

Fact and Fiction in Economics

Models, Realism, and Social Construction

Feb 2003

Cambridge, UK

There is an embarrassing polarization of opinions about the status of economics as an academic discipline, as reflected in epithets such as the "Dismal Science" and the "Queen of the Social Sciences." This collection brings together some of the leading figures in the methodology and philosophy of economics to provide a thoughtful and balanced overview of the current state of debate about the nature and limits of economic knowledge. Authors with partly rival and partly complementary perspectives examine how abstract models work and how they might connect with the real world, they look at the special nature of the facts about the economy, and they direct attention towards the academic institutions themselves and how they shape economic research. These issues are thus analyzed from the point of view of the methodology, semantics, ontology, rhetoric, sociology, and economics of science.

USKALI MÄKI is Professor of Philosophy at the Erasmus University of Rotterdam. He is Academic Director of the Erasmus Institute for Philosophy and Economics and an editor of the *Journal of Economic Methodology*. His recent publications include being an editor of and contributor to *The Handbook of Economic Methodology* (1998), *Economics and Methodology: Crossing Boundaries* (1998), and *The Economic World View: Studies in the Ontology of Economics* (2001).

Fact and Fiction in Economics

Models, Realism, and Social Construction

Edited by
USKALI MÄKI

PUBLISHED BY THE PRESS SYNDICATE OF THE UNIVERSITY OF CAMBRIDGE
The Pitt Building, Trumpington Street, Cambridge, United Kingdom

CAMBRIDGE UNIVERSITY PRESS
The Edinburgh Building, Cambridge CB2 2RU, UK
40 West 20th Street, New York, NY 10011-4211, USA
477 Williamstown Road, Port Melbourne, VIC 3207, Australia
Ruiz de Alarcón 13, 28014 Madrid, Spain
Dock House, The Waterfront, Cape Town 8001, South Africa

http://www.cambridge.org

© Cambridge University Press 2002

This book is in copyright. Subject to statutory exception
and to the provisions of relevant collective licensing agreements,
no reproduction of any part may take place without
the written permission of Cambridge University Press.

First published 2002

Printed in the United Kingdom at the University Press, Cambridge

Typeface Times 10/12 pt.   *System* LATEX 2$_\varepsilon$ [TB]

A catalogue record for this book is available from the British Library

ISBN 0 521 81117 1 hardback
ISBN 0 521 00957 X paperback

For EIPE

Contents

Contributors

Roger E. Backhouse is Professor of the History and Philosophy of Economics at the University of Birmingham, UK. His recent books include *The Penguin History of Economics* (Penguin, 2002), published in the USA as *The Ordinary Business of Life* (Princeton University Press, 2002), and *Truth and Progress in Economic Knowledge* (Edward Elgar, 1997). He has edited (with Jeff Biddle) *Toward a History of Applied Economics* (Duke University Press, 2001), (with Andrea Salanti) *Macroeconomics and the Real World* (Oxford University Press, 2000), and (with Roger Middleton) *Exemplary Economists* (Edward Elgar, 2000). He is an editor of the *Journal of Economic Methodology* and an associate editor of the *Journal of the History of Economic Thought*.

Wolfgang Balzer is Professor of Mathematical Logic and Philosophy of Science at the University of Munich. He habilitated on a new, 'structuralist' view of measurement and became a leading figure in the 'structuralist' group of philosophers of science. He has published widely on reconstructions of scientific theories, the general structure of scientific theories, their development, and their application, and on social institutions. He has recently worked together with Raimo Tuomela on belief structures and their applications. Among his books are *An Architectonic for Science* (together with Moulines and Sneed), and *Soziale Institutionen*.

Mark Blaug is Professor Emeritus of the University of London and Buckingham University, UK, and Visiting Professor of Economics at the University of Amsterdam and Erasmus University of Rotterdam, The Netherlands. He is a Fellow of the British Academy and a Foreign Honorary Member of the Royal Netherlands Academy of Arts and Sciences. His principal fields of interest are economic methodology and the history of economic thought. His publications include *Introduction to the Economics of Education* (1970), *The Methodology of Economics* (1980), *Great Economists since Keynes* (1985), *Economic History and the History of Economics* (1987), *The Economics of Education and the Education of an Economist* (1987), *Economic Theories:*

ix

True or False? (1990), *Not Only an Economist: Recent Essays* (1997), *Who's Who in Economics* (edited) (1999).

Bruce Caldwell is a Professor of Economics at the University of North Carolina at Greensboro, USA. During the 2000–2001 academic year he held the Ludwig M. Lachmann Research Fellowship in the Department of Philosophy, Logic and Scientific Method at the London School of Economics, where he worked on a book on the development of F. A. Hayek's methodological thought. He is a past president of the History of Economics Society, and has published extensively in the areas of history of thought and economic methodology. Caldwell is the author of *Beyond Positivism: Economic Methodology in the Twentieth Century*, and the editor of two volumes in *The Collected Works of F. A. Hayek* titled *Contra Keynes and Cambridge* and *Socialism and War.*

Nancy Cartwright is a Professor in the Department of Philosophy, Logic and Scientific Method at the London School of Economics, UK and at the Department of Philosophy at the University of California at San Diego, USA. She is a Fellow of the British Academy and of the American Academy of Arts and Science and has received the highly prized MacArthur Fellowship. Before coming to the LSE and UCSD she taught for two years at the University of Maryland, and then for most of her career at Stanford University; she has had visiting appointments at UCLA, Princeton, Pittsburgh, California Institute of Technology, and Oslo University, and has been a Fellow at the Institute for Advanced Studies in Berlin, the Centre for Interdisciplinary Research in Bielefeld, and the Pittsburgh Center for the Philosophy of Science. She has published three books, *How the Laws of Physics Lie* (Oxford University Press, 1983), *Nature's Capacities and their Measurement* (Oxford University Press, 1989), *The Dappled World: A Study of the Boundaries of Science* (Cambridge University Press, 2000) and a fourth co-authored with Jordi Cat, Lola Fleck, and Thomas Uebel, *Otto Neurath: Philosophy between Science and Politics* (Cambridge University Press, 1995).

Partha Dasgupta is the Frank Ramsey Professor of Economics at the University of Cambridge and Fellow of St. John's College, Cambridge, UK. A past President of the Royal Economic Society and the European Economic Association, Professor Dasgupta is a fellow of the British Academy, Member of the Pontifical Academy of Social Science, Foreign Member of the Royal Swedish Academy of Sciences, and Foreign Associate of the US National Academy of Sciences. His latest publication is *Human Well-Being and the Natural Environment* (Oxford University Press, 2001).

Neil De Marchi is Professor of Economics at Duke University, Durham, North Carolina, USA. He has published methodological and historical studies of David Ricardo, and James and John Stuart Mill, and his contribution to this volume is a continuation of a longstanding interest in J. S. Mill's reconciliation of the empirical and the *a priori* in economics. His recent work in the history of economic ideas, however, has mostly focused on the role of consumption in Adam Smith, and Smith's treatment of pleasure in consumption as the necessary complement to income growth as the measure of meterial achievement. Publications in the area of methodology include the edited volume *The Popperian Legacy in Economics* (Cambridge University Press, 1988), (with Abraham Hirsch) *Milton Friedman: Economics in Theory and Practice* (Wheatsheaf and Michigan, 1990), and (with Mark Blaug) *Appraising Economic Theories* (Edward Elgar, 1991). A growing research interest is the interplay of economic ideas, incentives, and constraints in the shaping of early modern art markets and visual culture, in collaboration with art historian colleague Hans Van Miegroet.

D. Wade Hands is Professor of Economics at the University of Puget Sound in Tacoma, Washington, USA. His research interests range broadly over a number of different subjects within the history and philosophy of economics. His recent books include *Reflection Without Rules: Economic Methodology and Contemporary Science Theory* (Cambridge University Press, 2001) and *The Handbook of Economic Methodology* (edited with John B. Davis and Uskali Mäki) (Edward Elgar, 1998).

Shaun P. Hargreaves Heap teaches at the University of East Anglia, UK. His research is in macroeconomics and in philosophy and economics. He is particularly interested in the role of rationality assumptions in economics and his most recent research is in the economics of the media. His publications include *Rationality and Economics* (1989), *The New Keynesian Macroeconomics* (1992), *Game Theory: A Critical Introduction* (with Y. Varoufakis, 1995), and articles in the *Economic Journal, Journal of Post-Keynesian Economics* and *Kyklos*.

Kevin D. Hoover is Professor of Economics at the University California, Davis, USA. He is the author of numerous articles in macroeconomics, monetary economics, economic methodology, and the philosophy of science. His most recent books are *Causality in Macroeconomics* and *The Methodology of Empirical Macroeconomics* (both Cambridge University Press, 2001). He is President-Elect of the History of Economics Society, immediate past Chair of the International Network for Economic Method, and an Editor of the *Journal of Economic Methodology*.

Deirdre N. McCloskey has been since 2000 UIC Distinguished Professor of Economics, History, and English at the University of Illinois at Chicago, USA, and is Tinbergen Professor (2002–2006) of Economics, Philosophy, and Art and Cultural Studies at Erasmus University of Rotterdam, The Netherlands. Trained at Harvard as an economist, she has written a dozen books and two hundred articles on economic theory, economic history, rhetoric, feminism, ethics, and law. She taught for twelve years in Economics at the University of Chicago, and describes herself now as a "postmodern free-market quantitative Christian feminist." Her latest books are *How to be Human* *Though an Economist* (University of Michigan Press, 2001) and *Measurement and Meaning in Economics* (S. Ziliak, ed., Edward Elgar, 2001). Specifically philosophical books include *The Rhetoric of Economics* (University of Wisconsin Press, 1st edn., 1985, 2nd edn., 1998), *If You're So Smart: The Narrative of Economic Expertise* (University of Chicago Press, 1990), and *Knowledge and Persuasion in Economics* (Cambridge University Press, 1994), which concern the maladies of social scientific positivism, the epistemological limits of a future social science, and the promise of a rhetorically sophisticated philosophy of science.

Uskali Mäki is currently Professor of Philosophy of Science at Erasmus University of Rotterdam and Academic Director of Erasmus Institute for Philosophy and Economics (EIPE), The Netherlands. Among his research interests are scientific realism, unrealistic assumptions, economic explanation, social ontology, the rhetoric and economics of economics, and the methodology of the new institutional economics. His recent publications include articles in economics and philosophy journals as well as *The Handbook of Economic Methodology* (edited with John Davis and D. Wade Hands, 1998), *Economics and Methodology: Crossing Boundaries* (edited with Roger E. Backhouse, Daniel Hausman, and Andrea Salanti, 1998), and *The Economic World View: Studies in the Ontology of Economics* (2001). He is an editor of the *Journal of Economic Methodology*.

Mary S. Morgan is Professor of History of Economics at the London School of Economics UK and Professor of History and Philosophy of Economics at the University of Amsterdam, The Netherlands. She has published on both the methodological and historical aspects of economics, including *Models as Mediators* (1999, with M. Morrison) and *Empirical Models and Policy Making: Interaction and Institutions* (2000, with F. den Butter). She has recently held a British Academy Research Readership to work on economics as a model-building and model-using science.

Ilkka Niiniluoto's doctoral dissertation in 1973 extended and applied Jaakko Hintikka's system of inductive logic to inferences involving scientific theories. In 1973–1977 Niiniluoto was Associated Professor of Mathematics (Foundations) at the University of Helsinki, and since 1977 Professor of Theoretical Philosophy. Since 1975 he has been the President of the Philosophical Society of Finland. He has written, in the spirit of scientific realism, on probability and induction, explanation, truth and verisimilitude, theory change, and scientific progress. His other interests include philosophical logic, epistemology, philosophy of technology, and philosophy of culture.

Niiniluoto's main works are *Is Science Progressive?* (1984), *Truthlikeness* (1987), and *Critical Scientific Realism* (1999).

Philip Pettit is Professor of Social and Political Theory at the Research School of Social Sciences, Australian National University. He is author of a number of books, including *Republicanism: A Theory of Freedom and Government* (Oxford University Press, 1997), *Three Methods of Ethics* (Routledge, 1997, with M. Baron and M. Slote), *The Common Mind: An Essay on Psychology, Society and Politics* (Oxford University Press, 1993), and *A Theory of Freedom: From the Psychology to the Politics of Agency* (Polity Press, UK and Oxford University Press, USA, 2001).

Robert Sugden is Leverhulme Research Professor at the University of East Anglia, Norwich, UK. His research uses a combination of theoretical, experimental, and philosophical methods to investigate issues in welfare economics, social choice, choice under uncertainty, the foundations of decision and game theory, and the evolution of social conventions. Recently he has also worked on issues of methodology. He is the author of several books, including *The Economics of Rights, Co-operation and Welfare* (one of the first applications of evolutionary game theory in social science), and of many articles in the scholarly journals of economics, philosophy, law, and political science.

Raimo Tuomela is Professor of Philosophy at the University of Helsinki, Finland. His main field of research is the philosophy of social action. He is a member of the editorial board of several journals and book series and a recipient of several grants and awards, including the von Humboldt Foundation Research Award. He has published extensively in philosophy journals. His recent books include *The Importance of Us: A Philosophical Study of Basic Social Notions* (Stanford University Press, 1995) and *Cooperation: A Philosophical Study* (Kluwer, 2000).

Jesús P. Zamora Bonilla is a PhD. in both philosophy and economics. He is currently Associate Professor at Universidad Carlos III, Madrid, Spain, where he teaches philosophy of science and economic methodology. He has worked extensively on the problem of scientific realism and approximation to the truth, having published some papers on this topic in international journals ("Verisimilitude, Structuralism and Scientific Knowledge," *Erkenntnis*, 1996, "Truthlikeness, Rationality and Scientific Method," *Synthèse*, 2000). He is also working on the economic approach to the production of scientific knowledge.

Preface

Fact or fiction —/
Fact and fiction

Fact or fiction? Is economics a respectable and useful reality-oriented discipline or just an intellectual game that economists play in their sandbox filled with imaginary toy models? Opinions diverge radically on this issue, which is quite embarrassing from both the scientific and the political point of view. The chapters in this volume, taken together, approach the issue in a manner that is more balanced and sophisticated than what one ordinarily encounters in popular – sometimes populist – statements about economics. Conceptual and argumentative sophistication in meta-analysis is needed to get to the facts of this matter, but few economists – regardless of how skillful they are in analyzing the economy – are trained to provide such analyses, and few philosophers are interested in looking at economics sufficiently closely. As soon as one looks more closely, what one starts seeing is fact *and* fiction, in a variety of combinatory incarnations. One also begins to appreciate both of them as necessary elements in a scientific study of the social world.

The chapters of the volume deal with the issue from three interrelated perspectives: those of economic models, the nature of the economy, and the social structure of the discipline itself. The three key questions are, respectively: How do economic models work in relation to reality? How does the world work in regard to its economically relevant aspects? How do the institutions of the discipline of economics work concerning its orientation toward facts and fictions? Many further questions can be raised about these issues and their interrelations. Given that both economic models and economic reality are socially constructed, is there a conceivable possibility that a model is true of the world? Under what conditions could such a possibility actualize?

Except for two (chapters 3 and 18, by Partha Dasgupta and Jesús Zamora Bonilla), the chapters in this volume are revisions (some of them revisions of revisions) of papers that were presented at the conference on 'Fact or Fiction? Perspectives on Realism and Economics' that took place at the Erasmus University of Rotterdam, November 14–15, 1997 at the time of my (somewhat delayed) inauguration. The invitation was sent to a selection of scholars who have contributed to shaping my thinking about economics and philosophy in the course of my intellectual career. Many more could have been invited, but constraints were imposed by the dismal fact of limited resources: time, space, and funding. Chapter 5 by Robert Sugden has since been published in the *Journal of Economic Methodology*. Earlier versions of Chapters 2, 6, 8, 11 and 17, by Mark Blaug, Nancy Cartwright, Mary Morgan, Philip Pettit, and D. Wade Hands, have been published in *Policy Options, Perspectives on Science, Journal of Economic Methodology*, and *Krisis*, respectively.

It was a great pleasure to host this intellectually alert group of first-rate scholars at the conference, and to work with them when preparing the volume for publication. Special thanks go to the Erasmus Institute for Philosophy and Economics, Loes van Dijk in particular, for excellent support in organizing the conference; to Eric van Damme, John Groenewegen, Arjo Klamer, Theo Kuipers, Maarten Janssen, Albert Jolink, and Jack Vromen for serving as discussants on the conference papers; and to Frank Hindriks, Jan Ravensbergen, and Judith de Putter for assistance in preparing the volume. Chris Harrison's support from Cambridge University Press has been indispensable. Financial support by the Trustfond Erasmus University of Rotterdam is acknowledged. Final touches were put to the project when I was a Fellow at the Netherlands Institute for Advanced Study, which I gratefully acknowledge.

Uskali Mäki, Wassenaar

Part I
Introduction

1   The dismal queen of the social sciences

Uskali Mäki

1   The factuality and fictionality of the "dismal queen"

Economics is a contested scientific discipline. Not only are its various theories and models and methods contested but, remarkably, what is contested is its *status as a science*. This becomes evident as soon as we think of some of the popular nicknames used of economics – such as "the dismal science" and "the queen of the social sciences."

Suppose we take one of the characteristics of science to be the capability of delivering relevant and reliable information about the world. Suppose furthermore that this is not just a capability, but also a major goal and actual achievement of whatever deserves to be called by the name of "science." How does economics do in this respect? This question is about as old as economics itself.

Many of those who are unimpressed think of economics as an arrogant and ignorant discipline, driven by methodological values that have little or nothing to do with the goal of delivering truthful information about the real world – values such as mathematical elegance and professional status. They might say that while economics may be the queen of the social sciences in regard to mathematical rigor, it is a failure in so far as its contact with the real world is concerned. Economics is largely a matter of formalized thin fiction and has little to do with the wonderful richness of the facts of the real world. It is the "dismal science," as Thomas Carlyle once put it.[1]

The expression "dismal science" seems to have grown in popularity – perhaps for reasons such as the new debates over the present and the future of economics, the current relaxed rhetorical atmosphere that favors fancy language, and, importantly, the ambiguity of the expression. The expression "dismal science" has many connotations. The most general and entirely useless one derives from its use as a tool for denouncing bad economic reasoning or an economic idea that one does not like. One of the more specific and familiar connotations relates to the Malthusian-type anticipations of a gloomy future, based on the presumed

3

fact of diminishing returns. Another relates to a depressing awareness of the "economic necessities" that govern social life in the form of budget constraints and trade-offs of various sorts. A related connotation refers to a heartless attitude towards human suffering, often attributed to the proponents of free market economics. Yet another relates to the narrow focus on calculative greed and its consequences as shaped by the values of money and the market, while being blind to social norms, customs, emotions, and the moral strings of personal relationships, thus missing major facts of economic reality. The final connotation is connected to the alleged impotence of the theoretically narrow and inward-looking academic economics in explaining, predicting, and controlling the functioning of the complex economic system – for example, in anticipating and helping prevent major economic crises. It is the last two connotations – economics missing important aspects of economic reality and its autistic impotence with respect to real-world issues – that are the most relevant to the main themes of this volume.

Can economics predict?

Other people, most notably many practicing economists, disagree on the pessimistic diagnosis of economics – or at least of their own favorite part of it – as "dismal." For them, economics is the queen of the social sciences, and this is so not only because of its superior mathematical rigor. They believe that the best of economics is driven by a keen interest in real-world issues and policy-relevance, and that it is capable of delivering insights and important information about economic reality: or at any rate more relevant and reliable information about economic issues than any other intellectual endeavor. These people – if they were methodologically enlightened – might say that it just appears as if economics deals only with fictions: the fictitiousness of economics is itself a fiction. In fact, economics – or at any rate a sufficiently large part of it – is very much a respectable fact-oriented scientific discipline. This fact about economics is easy to overlook, for the simple reason that the relationships between economic theory and reality are quite convoluted and hard to monitor: by necessity, reality is indefinitely complex, while theory is simple. Carlyle missed this because he did not understand that "all science is 'dismal' to the artist" as Schumpeter once put it (1954, 410).

The controversy around the "dismal queen" is old. In 1819, Simonde de Sismondi put forth a complaint that sounds very familiar today: "We see political economy adopting a more sententious language, enveloped in calculations increasingly difficult to follow, losing itself in abstractions and becoming, in every way, an occult science." One and a half centuries later, similar appraisals were put forward by many prominent economists. Indeed, the early 1970s witnessed a barrage of critical assessments from among the highest ranks of the economics profession: fellow economists were charged with "continued preoccupation with imaginary, hypothetical, rather than with observable reality" (Leontief 1970, 1) and for working with theories and models "built upon assumptions

Process of the model

[handwritten: Coase – blackboard economics]

about human behavior that are plucked from the air" (Phelps Brown 1972, 3). More specifically, the criticism was voiced that "these assumptions are frequently made for the convenience of mathematical manipulation, not for reasons of similarity to concrete reality" (Frisch 1970, 162). As a consequence, there "now exist whole branches of abstract economic theory which have no links with concrete facts and are almost indistinguishable from pure mathematics" (Worswick 1972, 78). These statements are manifestations of what Hutchison (1977) dubbed "the crisis of abstraction." *[handwritten: The crisis of abstraction]*

Ronald Coase's attack on what he calls "blackboard economics" is on largely similar lines. Coase suggests tracing this approach back to Joan Robinson's *The Economics of Imperfect Competition* (1933): "This new theoretical apparatus had the advantage that one could cover the blackboard with diagrams and fill the hour in one's lectures without the need to find out anything about what happened in the real world" (Coase 1993a, 51). Coase complains that "when economists find that they are unable to analyze what is happening in the real world, they invent an imaginary world which they are capable of handling" (1993a, 52), and summarizes his account like this: "What is studied is a system which lives in the minds of economists but not on earth. I have called the result 'blackboard economics'" (Coase 1993b, 229). Blackboard economics, so characterized, looks like sheer fiction and not in the least a factual enterprise. The famous discovery by Arjo Klamer and David Colander (1990, 18) appears to confirm Coase's worry: the economics students on the most prominent graduate programs at US American universities believe that being excellent in mathematics and skillful in puzzle-solving (on the blackboard, we might add) are important for success in economics, while having a thorough knowledge of the economy is regarded as unimportant for success.

In their discussion of what they call the "crisis of vision" in economics, Heilbroner and Milberg (1995) share these concerns. They argue that up to the post-Keynesian period – roughly up to 1970 – economics was characterized by analysis based on a vision of social reality and therefore by "its continuously visible concern with the connection between theory and 'reality.' By way of contrast, the mark of current economics is its extraordinary indifference to this problem. At its peaks, the 'high theorizing' of the present period attains a degree of unreality that can be matched only by medieval scholasticism" (1995, 3–4). Heilbroner and Milberg argue that, especially since the rational expectations revolution, there has been an "inward turn" away from real-world concerns and towards mere intellectual games amongst academic economists.

In this volume, the critical voice is Mark Blaug's (see also his earlier falsificationist account in Blaug 1980). In chapter 2, he laments the illness of formalism that he believes dominates economics and has turned it into a policy-irrelevant academic game. Special blame is put on general equilibrium microeconomics after the Arrow–Debreu proof in 1954, on the more recent fascination with

[handwritten: economics as a policy-irrelevant academic game]

game theory, and on New Classical macroeconomics. Economists have lost their interest in tackling real-world issues, and some of them find justification for their attitudes in postmodern meta-theories that question the sensibility of notions such as the real world and its theoretical representation. Realism is the advisable alternative to help reorient economics, maintains Blaug.

In response to charges of the above sort, some practicing economists have taken on the task of defending economics as a fact-oriented discipline while blaming the critics for being uninformed about what is going on. Some argue, in diametric opposition to the critics, that in the last thirty years or more, economics has become more, rather than less, fact-oriented. A few prominent and representative illustrations will suffice to highlight the major themes in these arguments.

With a long career behind him, Robert Solow (1997) explicitly denies that mainstream economics has lost touch with reality. He recognizes a major change in economics from 1940 to 1990, but his diagnosis is decisively more moderate than that of the more radical critics: economics has become "a self-consciously technical subject, no longer a fit occupation for the gentleman-scholar" (1997, 42). Solow suspects that this may have led some observers to adopt the misconception of a discipline unconnected to real-world issues. Here we should add that this conclusion may require another premise, namely the observation that economics is a discipline without popularizers who would bridge the gap, in the minds of the lay audience, between forefront technical research and the pressing economic issues of the day (Krugman 1998, 8). Solow admits that there is a small minority of "formalists" in the economics profession, and that they are mainly writing to one another. Most of economics is not a matter of formalist fiction but rather model-building, "which is an altogether different sort of activity" (Solow 1997, 43) – more on this in a moment. The crux of the matter is that economics has become *technical* rather than "formalistic, abstract, negligent of the real world . . . Far from being unworldly, modern model-builders are obsessed with data" (Solow 1997, 57). If there is a problem, it is that there is a shortage of relevant data, and that sometimes model-builders keep building their models without adequate evidential checks-ups.

Another recent defensive voice is that of William Baumol (2000). In his assessment of the achievements of the economics of the twentieth century, he argues that, throughout this period, economics has made significant progress in what it offers to practice: "advances in empirical work and application of theoretical concepts to concrete issues of reality are where one can find the most distinct advances beyond the state of knowledge at the beginning of our century" (2000, 10). Baumol acknowledges that this observation cannot be extracted from economics textbooks that to a large extent fail to reflect relevant developments in actual frontline research. In his view, these developments stress the importance of rigorous data analysis and the interdependence between theory and data: "we have grown increasingly uncomfortable with theory that provides no instruments for analysis of the facts and no opportunity for empirical testing" (2000, 26–27). The employment of sophisticated mathematical techniques and drastic theoretical simplifications promote, rather than hinder, success in applied research that endeavors to support practice. The basic image of economics Baumol is suggesting is one of a discipline responding, in a systematic and rigorous fashion, to demand based on concern with practical real-world issues. It is an image of a fact-oriented discipline. *Baumol — fact —*

Representative of a younger generation, David Kreps (1997) offers further *oriented* nuances to the largely optimistic picture. Kreps perceives a strong trend, in the *disciple* last thirty years or so, towards a broadening range of research issues that are tackled in an empirically sensitive fashion by economists who are increasingly willing to reconsider the assumptions of their theories. Like Solow and Baumol, Kreps points out that there is an increasing body of data available to economists, and that they are increasingly prepared to produce more data themselves, for example by way of experimentation. He also indicates the growth of two-way interaction across traditional disciplinary boundaries with biologists, sociologists, and psychologists whereby economists learn from these fields. In microeconomics, Kreps identifies two trends, one more radical than the other. The less radical trend consists in relaxing "contextual" assumptions such as large numbers and anonymity of agents, shared information, and static analysis, and replacing them by small numbers interaction, asymmetrical information, and nontrivial dynamics. This is the main current in the new microeconomics. The more radical trend consists in relaxing one or more of the "canonical" assumptions of far-sighted rationality, purposeful greed, and equilibrium. This trend is understandably weaker as it challenges the canon and meets with more resistance from the established paradigm. Even though the canon is admittedly empirically deficient, the move away from it will be impeded by the (still) relative shortage of adequate empirical data and the possibility of tweaking the true-to-the-canon models on the face of almost any evidence.[2] What emerges from this is a qualified optimism about economics as a factual discipline.

In chapter 3 of this volume, Partha Dasgupta joins the camp of those who have set out to defend economics, motivated by a sense of social responsibility to defend an unjustly criticized discipline. Just like Solow, Baumol, and Kreps, Dasgupta claims that, in the last quarter of a century, economics has become more rather than less factual. While Baumol warns against just looking at textbooks, Dasgupta warns against just listening to what economists say about their work: both recommend looking at what they do in their research. Dasgupta explicitly launches a counterattack against the version of discontent put forth by Heilbroner and Milberg. By citing a number of examples in recent research, he argues that economics has moved away from grand theoretical issues towards small and sharp applied issues, and that this has helped economics become increasingly factual.

I have listed just a small selection[3] of representative assessments of economics, and the clear picture that emerges is that there is no clear picture. Opinions diverge as to whether economics is on the right or wrong track, and, if on the wrong one, when exactly the sinning started: in the early 1930s, early 1950s, or early 1970s? Given the role and status of economics in university education, in policy, and in our culture at large, the radical disparity of these commentaries must be found very confusing, if not alarming. What to make of such striking differences in the assessments of economics? Whenever one comes across with such polarized claims, it is time for further questions and some conceptual scrutiny. This is where a little help from one's methodology friends is welcome, and this is where this volume sets out to offer some community service. Things will turn out to be much more complex than the most simplistic statements suggest.[4]

The first easy observation is that "economics" is a dangerously aggregated notion that hides a lot of variety and diversity behind it. One takes big risks by maintaining that economics is like this or economics is like that – for the simple reason that there is no one homogeneous "economics" about which one can justifiably make straightforward claims. A more differentiated approach is advisable. Statements should be made about particular branches of economics during particular spans of time being factual or fictional in carefully specified respects. Another obvious qualification is that the disjunctive "fact or fiction?" is misleading. The right configuration is the conjunctive "fact and fiction" – this latter serves as the title of this volume. *Any* scientific discipline combines fact and fiction, and there are many kinds and degrees of factuality and fictionality.[5] Finally, whenever one attributes fictionality or factuality to something, one has to be very clear about what exactly this something is – a concept, an assumption, a model, a framework, a piece of data, a metaphor, a graph – as well as what one means by "fact" and "fiction."

Philosophers have offered a number of rival accounts of both fact and fiction. Economists and others, on the other hand, use these notions without analyzing their precise meanings. In a volume like this, bringing together a variety of themes, approaches, and perspectives, there cannot be a precise account of the notions of fact and fiction, unifying the contributions. We need to be content with somewhat intuitive and simple ideas. These notions can be linked to the issue of realism (of which more will be said in chapter 4). One can be a realist about the world and about theories of that world. Take T to be a theory, model, or assumption related to chunk S of the world. One is a realist about S in relation to T if one believes that S exists independently of accepting, believing, or uttering T. One is a realist about T in relation to S if one thinks that T and its constituents refer to S or that T in addition truly represents or should truly represent S – where truth is likewise independent of whether T is accepted, believed, or "truth" vs. "fact"

uttered. These definition sketches imply that, for example, the observability of an object and the testability of a theory are conceptually unconnected to realism.

Facts are what is the case, they are what make true statements true. A true statement is true because it stands in a suitable relation (such as that of correspondence) to facts in the world. Many economists believe that it is a fact about inflation that it is a monetary phenomenon. The link between facthood and truth then suggests that to say, "it is a fact that inflation is a monetary phenomenon" is to say, "it is true that inflation is a monetary phenomenon" (which, the redundancy theorists of truth will controversially add, is nothing else but to say, "inflation is a monetary phenomenon"). On this view of facts, facts are objective features of the world that serve as the truth-makers of true statements: if "inflation is a monetary phenomenon" is a true statement, then what makes it true is the fact that inflation is a monetary phenomenon. Some philosophers are concerned about whether there is sufficient distance between fact and truth, but for our purposes it is enough if we just take facts of the economy to be objective features of social reality that are not constructed in the intellectual games economists play. What counts as a fact and what counts as true in a community of scholars is socially constructed, whereas what is a fact and what is true, is not. Such a simple distinction will satisfy some unqualified realist intuitions.

One can attribute fictionality both to objects and to representations. We may say that an object is fictional where its existence and the truths about it are dependent on particular descriptions of it. Just like Robinson Crusoe's existence and any truths about him are dependent on Daniel Defoe's descriptions, the existence of *homo oeconomicus* and truths about "him" may be dependent on the various assumptions used by economists to describe the economic actor. One may then regard a representation such as a model or its constituent assumptions as fictional if it is about such fictional objects. If one thinks there are nonfictional real objects in the world as well, one may call a representation fictional if it is not taken to refer to any real objects, thus is not used for making assertions or conjectures about the real world. It lacks factual truth-value altogether: it is factually neither true nor false because it is about nothing real. Another possibility is to consider a representation fictional because it is false or radically false when interpreted as an assertion or conjecture about the real world. One then proceeds to study the real object *as if* it were as represented. Both of these ideas seem to appear in the commentaries of economic models: these models are claimed to be fictional in being radically false or in lacking truth-value altogether.

* * *

These issues can be approached from at least three perspectives, from the point of view of three questions. (1) *How do economic models function*: How do economic models and theories relate to the world? This question, too, has many

How do economic models function?

[handwritten: How does the economy function? How does good econ. funct.?]

facets and thus falls within the semantics, epistemology, and methodology of economics, addressing questions of truth, knowledge, and methods of testing. (2) *How does the economy function*: What is there in the social world that will be causally or constitutively relevant to the functioning of the economy, or to the occurrence and shaping of economic phenomena? This is a question in the ontology of economics.[6] (3) *How does the academic discipline of economics function*: What is its structure of institutional constraints and behavioral incentives that shapes the endeavors of economists? How does the "industrial organisation" of economics enhance or hinder its fictionality and factuality? To answer these questions, one has to study the institutions of economics – the rhetoric, sociology, and economics of economics.

[handwritten margin notes: rhetoric, sociology, eco of econ]

In actual practice, these are not fully separate perspectives, but for the purposes of this volume, the chapters are arranged in these three categories. These three perspectives have been characteristic of my own work, and I am delighted that the invited contributions appear to fall within this scheme. The scene is set by raising some of the key issues in the three chapters in part II of the volume. The six chapters in part III address question (1), asking how models link with reality. Question (2) about the constitution of economic reality is addressed by the five chapters in part IV. Finally, question (3) about the institutions of economics is the theme of the last three chapters in part V of the book.

2 Economic models

To do economics is to do modeling. In assessing the truth of this claim one had better be attentive to the ambiguity of "model." On a narrow sense of "model" – a notion of model defined in terms of mathematics – the claim may have a great deal of truth in it, even though it may be taken to exaggerate with misleadingly restrictive implications (such as "you are not doing economics if you don't build mathematical models"). On a broader sense of "model" – model as selective representation – all of economics was, is, and will be, a matter of modeling; and there is nothing peculiar about economics in this respect, in comparison to cosmology, chemistry, criminology, and casuistry.

If there is a puzzle about modeling, it is that economists build models that depict model economies that may appear to bear little or no resemblance with the real world. For outsiders, such as journalists, beginning undergraduate students, and many other social scientists, it may appear as if economists are living in a dream world of their models, in an imaginary world of fiction that they themselves have designed. The challenge for economists and economic methodologists alike is to analyze the ways in which models could convey, or fail to convey, truthful information about the facts of real economies.

Above, I cited Solow's remark that economics is engaged in model-building that is an activity different from what "formalist" economists do. Indeed,

model-building at its best can be construed as fact-oriented activity that takes as
its objective to isolate key causal dependencies in reality: "The idea is to focus on
one or two causal or conditioning factors, exclude everything else, and hope to
understand how just these aspects of reality work and interact . . . modern mainstream economics consists of little else but examples of this process" (Solow
1997, 43). This is to say that modern economics is a matter of using the generic
method of isolation, of inclusion and exclusion, of focusing on key elements
and neutralizing the rest, of simplification and idealization. Models involve idealizing assumptions that are strictly false but serve the purpose of simplifying
the problem attacked by excluding or neutralizing many factors that might be
expected to have an impact on the outcome of an actual process. Such false
assumptions help isolate some key dependencies for closer inspection. While
laboratory experiments accomplish such isolations by way of causal manipulations of actual situations, the isolations of a model-builder take place in the
theoretical sphere as thought experiments. Models are (among) the economists'
laboratories. (See Mäki 1992a.) As Solow suggests, "A good model makes the
right strategic simplifications. In fact, a really good model is one that generates a lot of understanding from focusing on a very small number of causal
arrows" (Solow 1997, 46). A model isolates one or a few causal connections,
mechanisms, or processes, to the exclusion of other contributing or interfering
factors – while in the actual world, those other factors make their effects felt in
what actually happens. Models may seem true in the abstract, and are false in
the concrete. The key issue is about whether there is a bridge between the two,
the abstract and the concrete, such that a simple model can be relied on as a
source of relevantly truthful information about the complex reality.

Since realists are friends of truth, they want to have models that provide
truthful representations of economic reality. The challenge is to reconcile this
goal with the intrinsic feature of models that they contain a lot of falsehood.
This is too big an issue to be discussed here in any satisfactory detail and
comprehensiveness, but let me make a brief remark about the important notion
of representation. Virtually any objects can serve as models of something else,
and such objects can be of various kinds: models may be material, linguistic, and
abstract objects; they can take on the form of concrete analogues, graphs, experimental designs, idealized thought objects, systems of mathematical equations,
and so on. In each case, we may think of a model, M, as a simple system used
as a representation of something else, a more complex system, X, in two senses.
First, M represents X in that M is used as a representative of X. By studying
M instead of X directly, one hopes to learn about X. One manipulates M by
way of constructing, experimenting, calculating, and imagining, and so learns
about the properties of M. Second, M represents X by resembling it in relevant
respects and sufficient degrees relative to the use to which M is put. Thanks
to this resemblance, the examination of M will convey information about X.

We may say that the two aspects of representation are interdependent in that M earns its justification as a representative of X by resembling X, or corresponding to it. Resemblance is a matter of relevant respects and sufficient degrees, and these are relative to the many possible uses of models as representatives.

This is far from a complete account of models, but should give some clues as to the variety of aspects involved in the issue of how models relate to reality (other questions deal with how models relate to theories and data, for example; see Hausman 1992; Morgan and Morrison 1999; Mäki 2001b). The intuitions behind judgments of the familiar sort, "this model is (un)realistic," are unhelpful – vague and devoid of implications concerning the adequacy of the model – unless made explicit along the several dimensions that are involved. Chapters 5–10 in part III of this volume offer further illumination on selected aspects of this conundrum, discussing different kinds of models and various ways in which they might have something to tell us about social reality.

In chapter 5, Robert Sugden argues that abstract and unrealistic models are able to provide true and important information about the real world. Using Akerlof's "lemons" model and Schelling's checkerboard model of racial segregation as illustrations, Sugden develops an account of how the imagined world of the model connects with the real world. We may say that on this account, good economic models satisfy both aspects of representation. In the model world, a cause brings about an effect, such as a regularity, or could do so. Other causal factors and connections, active in the real world, are not considered. Sugden suggests that the move from the model world to the real world is an inductive inference from claiming a connection in a highly simplified case to claiming it in real-world cases under various contingencies. Our confidence in this inference is based on the belief that the model worlds – such as Schelling's checkerboard cities and Akerlof's used-car market – are possible, that they could be real given what we know about how the world works. Such a possibly real model world is a credible world, and such a simple credible world is not an isolation of a small set of elements from the rest of the actual real world, or so Sugden argues. He suggests that the credibility of a model is a matter of *coherence* – a harmonious relationship between the assumptions of the model, and between the model and what we know about the causal structure of the world. This is an intriguing account that offers a way of thinking of good economic models as truthful representations of matters of fact. It gives rise to further questions, such as how the suggested inductive inference relates to analogical reasoning, and how the idea that credible model worlds are constructed relates to the idea of theoretical isolation.

In line with an old scientific and philosophical tradition and her own earlier work, Nancy Cartwright argues in chapter 6 that laws – empirical regularities of stochastic or nonstochastic kind – are not free-standing features of the world, they rather require a background structure that generates them.

These underlying socio-economic structures or chance set-ups ("nomological machines" as Cartwright calls them) contain things equipped with causal powers or capacities to bring about definite effects. This is the traditional nonempiricist ontology behind her account of models. A model is about a nomological machine or causal mechanism under highly stringent conditions such that strict lawlike regularities arise. The problem with economic models is that those idealized conditions hardly ever materialize. In the actual world, many causal mechanisms interact in an uncontrolled manner and thus fail to generate strict empirical regularities. Economic models are constructed in terms of very concrete concepts, close to everyday experience, which is why the models do not have precise deductive implications (do not yield "results," as economists would put it) without being engineered in just right ways by "hyperfine-tuning" – by imposing stringent idealized constraints on the models. This, Cartwright believes, makes them fit only with very special situations in the world, thereby radically restricting their scope of applicability. Situations that would satisfy the idealized conditions of the models, while common in laboratory sciences, are rare or nonexistent in the economic world where strict manipulation of causal factors is impossible. This is the pessimistic conclusion of her local realism. (See also Cartwright 1999.)

Cartwright's conclusion is based on premises that one may challenge. One could raise questions about her ontological framework, including her (empiricist) notion of law; her implicit view, as it seems to me, of the primary function of idealizing assumptions as determining conditions of applicability; her methodological views about the standards of science; and her views about what econometrics and economic models are all about. Sugden's account is not about econometric models, but it includes a resource that could be used to question an element in Cartwright's account: the idea of inference from fine-tuned but credible model worlds to real-world situations that do not satisfy the idealized conditions of the models. In chapter 9, Backhouse takes issue with Cartwright's arguments by suggesting that her pessimism about econometrics is due to her general and overly strict standards of science, and defends instead field-specific standards: precise and stable quantitative relationships do not occur in the domain of economics and should not therefore be required. Kevin Hoover's chapter 7 makes a similar point by suggesting that precision on the one hand, and reliability and scope on the other, come in degrees and that there is a trade-off between them: more precision, less reliability, and smaller scope; less precision, more reliability, and broader scope.

Both Cartwright and Hoover look at econometrics from a realist point of view, but they draw different conclusions, because their understanding of econometrics is different. For Hoover, econometrics is neither about measuring strict universal regularities that could serve as covering laws (as in Tony Lawson's account), nor about characterizing the causal powers of socio-economic structures or nomological machines. Hoover's defense of econometric models is by way of being more modest about their goals. Econometrics is about observing nonobvious robust regularities. These regularities are not regarded as freestanding features of social reality, since they are believed to be generated by (and ultimately to be explained in terms of) causally powerful structures even though the econometric models do not describe these structures. In case more generality is claimed for the regularities, less precision will be imposed, while more specific models incorporating information about local circumstances can be used to make more precise claims. Hoover points out that while a theoretical model – highlighting perhaps just one mechanism – is highly fine-tuned, the corresponding empirical models incorporate the influences of several mechanisms and are more schematic, include vaguely defined variables, and are not tightly linked to the respective theoretical model. (See also Hoover 2001.)

Both Morgan and Backhouse emphasize the informal aspects of modeling. In chapter 8, Morgan argues that the use of models involves telling stories: one cannot fully describe and understand a model without understanding how it works, and narrative stories are integral elements in the working of a model. In particular, it is by means of these stories that models are linked with reality. This may be taken to imply the claim that one has to incorporate stories in one's account of models in order to avoid unnecessarily fictionalist views of economic models. Stories connect the abstract to the concrete by way of providing interpretations of mathematical formulas, explanatory questions and answers, supplementary causal chains, and other things. In his chapter, Backhouse argues that the term "story" as used by Morgan covers a number of distinct informal elements in the use of models and that more traditional terminology is better in capturing these elements – such as theory, interpretation, causal mechanism, problem, and its solution. Another issue has to do with what emerges from Morgan's account regarding the very concept of model. One may read Morgan's chapter as an account of the pragmatics of modeling – of the role stories play in the use of models for certain purposes. On the other hand, she also says stories are part of the identity of models. On the first reading, the uncontroversial point is implied that models don't *do* anything: models *are used to do* things. It is suggested that stories – or whatever one wants to call this heterogeneous set of items – are essential tools in using models. One can then raise questions about epistemic appraisal: for example, can a bad model be saved with a good story? On the second reading, stories are part of models, and models are indistinguishable from their use. In describing a model one describes its use which involves telling narratives. An obvious question to ask is how one is supposed to appraise the multitude of closely related but distinct models conceived as such conglomerates. Morgan's chapter is not unambiguous between these readings.

While acknowledging that economic models are not quite true, economists themselves frequently defend them as being close to the truth or as approximations to the truth. These are difficult notions that Karl Popper's doctrine of verisimilitude failed to analyze, but they have kept some analytical philosophers of science busy with a headache. In chapter 10, the leading expert on these notions, Ilkka Niiniluoto, discusses some of the key ideas (for a survey of some of the relevant philosophical literature, see Niiniluoto 1998). He focuses on the idea that models may be intended to highlight the key dependencies in the domain modeled, and discusses it in terms of truthlikeness, counterfactuals, idealizing assumptions and their relaxations, and reference. He defends a realist account of theories and models that involve false assumptions. Many of the insights suggested by Niiniluoto will be put on the research agenda to be exploited by philosophically minded students of economics.

The chapters dealing with economic models generously offer many examples of notions that can be used to enrich our instruments of assessing the factuality and fictionality of economics, and to do this in a manner that is more refined than what one encounters in most commentaries about the credentials of economics. The list would include concepts such as theoretical and empirical model, story, regularity, causal mechanism, causal power, precision, reliability, scope, robustness, counterfactual, idealization and its relaxation, horizontal and vertical isolation, and kinds of truthlikeness.

3   Economic ontology

If modeling were just a matter of a formal exercise with a goal of showing that a stylized fact can be derived from a set of premises, then economics would be an all-too-easy intellectual game. For any given stylized fact, there is an infinite number of possible models that entail it in a logically appropriate fashion. Drastic selection is required to sort out a tractable set of models that is regarded as worth the economists' attention. For a selection of a choice set of models, constraints are needed. Some such constraints are based on economists' and others' beliefs about the constitution of social reality. The imposition of such constraints will delimit the choice set, the range of minimally plausible models considered as candidates for further scrutiny.

We have entertained the possibility that good economic models are about economic reality and purportedly represent its properties, its structure, and its functioning. Obviously, the prospects of modeling are dependent not only on the properties of the models put forth by economists, but also on the properties of economic reality. Economists, other social scientists, philosophers, as well as business people and other economic actors hold (pre-model or extra-model) views about various fundamental properties of the economy. These views can be characterized as (rival and complementary) parts of economic ontology. Such ontological convictions characteristically remain imperfectly elaborated and they tend to be taken for granted without much or any explicit argument. Among such convictions are the individualist doctrine of the individual as the fundamental building block of society – as well as the anti-individualist views that

16   **Introduction**

dispute this idea; various "models of man" that constrain views of what counts as rational behavior; views about whether values and emotions are causally relevant factors in economic processes; implicit conceptions of the free will that shape views on, say, what counts as involuntary unemployment; the constitutive metaphors of the economy as a clockwork or as an organism; the range of types of institution one regards as playing major causal or constitutive roles in economic processes; the belief that the market is, or is not, a self-coordinating system; the related pre-analytic beliefs about the relative importance of market failure and government failure; the belief that there are, or are not, sufficiently robust macro regularities in the functioning of the economic system that can be used for controlling it by way of deliberate policy; conceptions of whether the society is a unified system governed by a small number of dominant principles; the view that statistical correlations are generated and sustained by socio-economic structures; the various views of lawlikeness as what regularly happens, as what would happen in certain conditions, and as what tends to happen.

Such ontological convictions held by economists and others appear at different levels of generality. Some social ontologies are about the constitution of society in general, raising and answering questions about the possibility and existence of social order (see Giddens 1984; Pettit 1993; Tuomela 1995). Some others are concerned with the economic realm more narrowly, dealing with the ontology of economic agency, the market mechanism, and economic aggregates, among other things. Such convictions function variously as constraints on acceptable economic theories and models and explanations. Sugden's suggestion that what makes a model world credible is coherence with what we know about the *way* the *world works* is in line with the "www constraint" on acceptable theories and models (Mäki 2001a). For example, one may hold the conviction of ontological individualism (only individuals are real, hold beliefs and goals, and act) and insist that all acceptable, non-ad hoc theories should be derivable from suitable microfoundations. One may also endorse a general causal process ontology and insist that it is a mark of good economic theories that they give an account of causal processes – rather than, say, just descriptions of states of equilibrium. Or one may hold a more specific view of a given economic order and require that acceptable theories be respectful for the fundamental characteristics of that order. The Heilbroner–Milberg (1995) thesis exemplifies this latter type of constraint. They argue that adequate economic theories are consistent with a specific vision of capitalism as a complex social system characterized by capital accumulation as the driving force; the market as the organisational mechanism of allocation; and the division between a private and a public sphere as the dominant administrative principle (1995, 106–109). They claim that much of current economics has lost touch with reality because it has lost connection with such a vision – or because it does not meet a specific "www constraint," as we may put it.

Economic ontology may be partly based on the models economists put forth. But it inevitably draws – explicitly or implicitly – from other sources as well, such as other social sciences, social actors' experience, religious convictions, and philosophical categories and arguments. Once an economic ontology is in place, it variously shapes the models economists build. It is not claimed that such a general economic world view – a system of general conceptions about the economic realm – uniquely determines the form and contents of economic models. There are two reasons why unique determination does not take place. One is the unavoidable slack between a general ontology and any specific economic model. The relationship between the two levels of generality can at most be one of constraining: economic ontology constrains a feasible set of economic models. The second reason is that even though sometimes specific economic models and a more general economic ontology are in harmony with one another in the sense of one meeting the constraints imposed by the other, at other times there is a tension between the two. In the latter case, the economist's deeper convictions may be in tension with the models she holds: for various reasons, such as the limitations of available formal techniques, the models built and held are not (yet) consistent with the general ontology. In both cases – the cases of harmony and disharmony – the role of economic ontology may be crucial. In the harmonious case, the form and contents of a set of models fit with the ontological convictions, thus giving assurance that the models are right. In the disharmonious case, the mismatch between models and ontology may function as a driving force behind a evolving sequence of models and modeling techniques: economists are inspired to look for more adequate techniques and seek to build models that cohere better with their underlying convictions about the constitution of economic reality.

Some commentators suspect that many economists are unconstrained by such deeper convictions, or at any rate by any such systematic ontological visions about the economy. Schumpeter (1954) referred to the "vision" of economics, together with economic "analysis" the history of which he set out to write. Heilbroner and Milberg (1995) adopt this distinction and argue that there is a crisis of vision in modern economics. Their notion of "vision" comes close to our idea of economic ontology: "By vision we mean the political hopes and fears, social stereotypes, and value judgments – all unarticulated, as we have said – that infuse all social thought, not through their illegal entry into an otherwise pristine realm, but as psychological, perhaps existential, necessities" (1995, 4). In comparison to the notion of economic ontology as used here, this formulation stresses the normative elements and perhaps underplays the descriptive convictions involved in a vision – while rightly emphasizing the implicitness and inescapability of such fundamental convictions. Heilbroner's and Milberg's worry about modern economics is "the widespread belief that economic analysis can exist as some kind of socially disembodied study" by which they mean analysis without vision (1995, 6). This, they argue, has led to "the extraordinary combination of arrogance and innocence with which mainstream economics has approached the problems of a nation that has experienced twenty years of declining real wages, forty percent of whose children live in 'absolute' poverty, and which has endured an unprecedented erosion of health, vacation, and pension benefits . . . Once the dismal science, it will become the irrelevant scholasticism" (1995, 6, 8).

It is not clear how exactly one should read such complaints. Let us suppose we can distinguish between the descriptive and normative aspects of a vision and of a model. Let us further suggest that the notion of real-world connection includes, among other things, the notions of *reliability* and *relevance*. In assessing analytical models, reliability is a property of the descriptive component, while some aspects of relevance are based on normative considerations such as those that concern the moral or political significance of the issues that are selected for attention. Assessments of reliability make claims about the descriptive performance of analytical models in regard to those selected issues. In these terms, what is the thesis of the crisis of vision and its harmful consequences for the real-world connection of economics? One may read it as the claim that, without the guidance of a vision, economists fail to tackle relevant real-world issues. Or one may read it as claiming that whatever issues are addressed, the information conveyed about them is not reliable. One may then try to combine the two claims by suggesting that if analytical modeling becomes unconstrained by considerations of relevance, it is inclined to become just an inward-looking academic game and lose touch with the real world and hence the ability to convey reliable information about it.

Unsurprisingly, ontological convictions or visionary views tend to be at least as contestable as the models that economists hold. James Buchanan (1999) agrees with Heilbroner and Milberg on the claim that economics has lost its vision, but he has a different conception of the contents of the appropriate vision. Buchanan believes there is a coherent explanatory vision of "the inclusive structure of social interaction . . . informed by an understanding of the principles of operation" (1999, 2–3). This vision can be traced to Adam Smith and other classics and their insight that people seek to better their own position and that there are mutual gains from trade. At the core of this vision is the notion of value arising from the exchange process in the market. Economics has taken the wrong turn "when value, in any meaningful economic sense, is presumed to exist independently of market evaluation through exchange processes . . . As the superficial analytical sophistication increased, the formal structure of neoclassical economics somehow lost its behavioral moorings" (1999, 6–7). While Heilbroner and Milberg believe that Keynes was on a relatively right track regarding visionary matters, what Buchanan calls the "Keynesian aberration" is based on misunderstanding this classical ontological vision.

Other disagreements about ontological visions may concern their degree of coherence or systematicity and the ways in which they are revised. One may argue that a systematic, unified vision is required for establishing a relevant real-world contact for models; someone else may hold a vision according to which the world itself is fragmented – a unified vision would be a distortion of the facts. One might also admit that there are occasional "crises of vision" but that this does not imply any serious deficiency of factual orientation: an economist may be deeply concerned about real-world issues, but believe that a new vision is needed and furthermore that the path to such a revised vision goes through fragmented models.

The properties attributed to economic actors are among the key elements in any economic ontology. As we know, *homo oeconomicus* has a long and varied history during which he (*sic*) has been equipped with a variety of objectives, epistemic and other capabilities, attitudes regarding others, and so on. Most economists have granted that real human beings are not quite like that, but argue that depicting them in those terms is scientifically justified. There seems to be a tension between the ontological convictions of economists and the assumptions of actors they employ. Some have sought to resolve the tension by adopting an instrumentalist position: *homo oeconomicus* is just a fiction, but it serves well the goals of inquiry such as the organization or manipulation of empirical facts. The interesting question is whether there is a realist interpretation of *homo oeconomicus*.

In chapter 11 in part IV, Philip Pettit argues that if we construe *homo oeconomicus* in terms of self-regarding desires, the resulting creature runs counter to commonsense experience that takes people to recognize loyalty and fair play, kindness, and honesty. It appears that there is an empty "black box" at the origin of economic behavior, with no mechanism inside it. Pettit argues this is an appearance only, but to see what is in the box, we need to have a more refined ontology. Self-regarding desires are real in a special sense – they are virtually real. People are ordinarily driven by culturally framed routines of friendship, obligation, and so on. Only in situations where an individual's interests are violated or served below some tolerable level of aspiration, will the self-regarding desires and deliberations become activated. On this ontology of social actors, self-regarding desires are not actual causes but rather "standby causes" or potential causes that are triggered in those special situations. Such virtually real standby causes have explanatory power of a certain limited kind: they explain the resilience or robustness of behavioral patterns. This is how the conventional economic assumptions can be aligned with commonsense beliefs about human behavior, even outside of the traditional economic realm. Pettit also shows that the same argument can be used to salvage functionalist theory, a popular target of individualist criticisms. The claim that functionalism is flawed in offering an empty "black box" devoid of any selection mechanism is not sensitive to the more refined ontology of virtual selection. A selection mechanism is virtually real and becomes activated in special situations and thus helps explain the resilience or modal persistence of certain important social institutions. As Pettit says, in both cases, the "black boxes" are empty in one sense and not empty in another. Fact *and* fiction.

Many proposals have been recently made to ascribe richer contents to the box of economic actors. In chapter 12, Shaun Hargreaves Heap suggests that judgments of self-worth are to be incorporated as ontological constraints on theories. The idea is that it is an important feature of social reality that people seek to make sense of their social lives: people give accounts of the reasons and worth of their social behavior. In this sense, the social reality encountered by an economist is pre-interpreted by social actors themselves (this view is sometimes called "existential hermeneutics" or "hermeneutical ontology"; see Lavoie 1991). Hargreaves Heap suggests that the standards of judgments of self-worth are shared by others, hence they form a common culture that is external to particular individuals. Such common cultures constrain the theories agents can use in interpreting their actions from the point of view of self-worth; for example, a problem with the preference satisfaction model is that preferences are not publicly accessible. A model with wealth-seeking will do better, in particular in contemporary Western culture, especially when supplemented with considerations of cooperation, fairness, shame, and embarrassment. Supposing one requires some sort of continuity between the theories the agents use and those that economists use, Hargreaves Heap turns out to have developed an ontological constraint on economic theories that will be welcome by hermeneuticists and realists alike – and that will avoid the hazards of relativism.

From a different angle, chapter 13 by Raimo Tuomela and Wolfgang Balzer pursues an account of collectivity and cooperation. Economics has not traditionally been strong on such notions, with manifestations of the prisoner's dilemma type. These notions also relate to the theme of social construction. There is an obvious sense in which social reality is constructed by people: we make the social world through our conceptualizations and interactions, attitudes, and acceptances. Yet, there are senses in which the social world is real. Tuomela and Balzer outline some aspects of a detailed account of how the social world is constructed (for a more comprehensive exposition, see Tuomela 1995). Collective acceptance is the key to the construction (including maintenance) of many social entities and properties. Squirrel fur counts as money in a society and a particular person counts as a CEO of a company because these things have been collectively accepted to be so. Collective acceptance can be, respectively, norm-based and agreement-based. Collective acceptance in the we-mode is by group members *qua* such members, while collective acceptance in the I-mode does not require such group orientation. Such distinctions give us different kinds and degrees of sociality or collectivity. The second section of the chapter compares the ensuing goal notions with the concepts of public good and club good as used by economists. In addition to Tuomela's, other accounts of sociality and collectivity include those of Gilbert (1989), Pettit (1993), and Searle (1995). This body of literature will serve as a resource in the search for a more genuinely *social* ontology, and thereby more factuality, for economic theories and models (see Sugden 2000).

Social institutions and arrangements are constructed and maintained, but they also change, sometimes in a piecemeal fashion, sometimes abruptly. Mainline economics has not been very strong on the theme of social change. The identity of Friedrich Hayek's theory of cultural evolution – evolution of traditions of rules and norms, moral precepts and practices – as an economic theory may be an issue, and so is its correctness, but it is worth a closer look as a source of ontological insight. In chapter 14, Bruce Caldwell takes on the task by considering three classes of criticisms against Hayek's account: his idea of group selection as a mechanism of cultural evolution is inconsistent with his professed individualism; his epistemological pessimism about people's ability to constructively shape social institutions recommends against attempting to improve the constitutional framework of society; and his explanation of how cultural evolution occurs is incomplete. In response to these criticisms, Caldwell shows, first, that if Hayek is taken to endorse an individualist outlook at all, his is a broad "non-neoclassical" version of individualism that is consistent with group selection. Second, he also points out Hayek's ambivalence about the need of the external imposition of constitutional rules in addition to the endogenous establishment of informal norms and moral rules, and considers possibilities of resolving the tension between constitutional political economy and Hayek's epistemologically pessimistic critique of "rationalist constructivism." Finally, Caldwell admits that Hayek's account of cultural evolution is very incomplete and unrefined, lacking detailed ideas of the units of selection and the mechanisms of variation and selection. But if Hayek's intuitions are on the right track, the incompleteness of his account serves as an invitation to others to join in an interdisciplinary project of developing them into a serious theory that would support an ontology that is not only social but also genuinely dynamic.

Chapter 15 by Neil De Marchi is a study of the notion of "facts in the concrete" in J.S. Mill's writings. The chapter is a piece of historical inquiry, but the topic is timeless and very relevant for today's concerns and debates about economic theory and method. De Marchi's study has an ontological aspect – dealing with the ontology of facts in the concrete – as well as an epistemological aspect – how theoretical reasoning should relate to such concrete facts (thus the chapter cuts across the first and the second themes of this volume). The problem with using facts in the concrete in economic theorizing stems from their ontology: they are mixtures of the effects of a multiplicity of causes. These causes are hard or impossible to access independently owing to the unavailability of effective experimentation. They cannot therefore be used as a secure basis for deriving general principles, nor for falsifying such principles. Mill wanted to ensure certitude for the statements of political economy as he thought this is required for its public credibility (this provides a link with the third theme of this volume). He believed the method appropriate for attaining this goal has to be some other than the use of history or experimental method. De Marchi traces Mill's development to the view of the *a priori* method of political economy. The solution is to start from the assumed laws of the human nature and to deduce their consequences for economic phenomena. The list of such "laws" relevant to the economic realm is short, as it isolates only a few of them from the full set: the desire for wealth and the capacity to judge the relative efficacy of the means to this end as well as the antagonizing principles of an aversion to effort and a preference for present enjoyment. This is not a complete list of factors driving real people, but it gives us an account that is closer to the truth about economic phenomena than any other equally simple alternative. And while experience of facts in the concrete cannot provide a secure source for general principles, it does constrain theories and explanations in important ways. We might say – and De Marchi might agree – that while sound economic theory does not capture facts in the concrete, it does capture facts in the abstract. Fact *and* fiction again. Phrased in various vocabularies, this line of thought is pursued by Cartwright, Sugden, myself, and others in the methodology of economics.

The chapters in part IV, devoted to economic ontology, highlight a variety of categories that are needed for expressing and refining the ontological convictions economists hold. These include virtual reality, standby cause, resilience, self-worth, common culture, kinds of collective acceptance, elements of cultural evolution, individualism, and facts in the concrete. Many more are needed to determine the complete set of ontological convictions that constrain and should constrain the theories and models accepted by economists.

4   The institutions of economics

The third perspective from which the issue of the fictionality and factuality of economics can and should be approached is the practice of research and communication by economists, and the ways in which this practice is conditioned by the institutions of economics. Such institutions are rules of the game: they consist of structures that relate to incentives and rewards, education and employment, publishing and expert consultation, agendas of topics, and standards of assessment. The institutions of economics shape the values and goals of practicing economists. Like other institutions, they are subject to change. The question here is about the direction to which the academic (or nonacademic) institutions at any given time and place guide model-building. Many of the critics of current economics are skeptical about the incentive structures within economics, Leontief's (1970, 1) being a classic statement: "Continued preoccupation with imaginary, hypothetical, rather than with observable reality has gradually led to a distortion of the informal valuation scale used in our academic community to assess and rank the scientific performance of its members." In chapter 3, Dasgupta expresses optimism about the presence of "internal checks and balances" and "incentives for constructive work" required for "a progressive republic of social science" (59).

All this relates to the theme of social construction. If it is an essential property of economic models that they are constructions by economists, it is just a small step from this observation to suggest that models are social constructions. Economics as a scientific discipline is, among other things, a matter of social interaction between economists, and between economists and other people, such as students, other social scientists, some natural scientists, university administrators, politicians, and the media. These interactions take place within a changing social structure, within the evolving institutions of economics. I find it almost trivial to claim that the models designed by economists are shaped by the institutions of economics. They are so shaped regardless of whether and how well they represent economic reality. Models are socially constructed.

The import and implications of this claim – that models and theories are socially constructed – have turned out to be hard to understand by its proponents and opponents alike. Some proponents of the social construction thesis appear to believe that the implications are radically anti-realist without being bothered by this: the social construction of a model entails a social construction of a portion of reality as well as the truth about that reality. Some opponents of the constructivist thesis are realists, believing in the nonconstructed objectivity of truth and reality. Some of them believe that this is why they have to oppose the social construction thesis. Both groups are mistaken. They are mistaken in sharing the belief that the social construction of economic models entails the social construction of what the models are about and of their truthlikeness. The difference between the two is that one group is, while the other is not, bothered by this implication. Those who are not bothered, accept the premise of the argument, while those who are, reject it. However, the error does not lie in the premise – the claim that economic models are socially constructed – but in the alleged entailment.

Chapters in part IV show that social reality is socially constructed, while chapters in part V show how the study of that reality is socially constructed. To deny the entailment presupposed in the two positions outlined above is to deny that the two processes of social construction are identical: it is to deny that to socially construct economic knowledge claims *is* to socially construct what those knowledge claims are about. The social construction of the inquiry of social reality is not identical with, nor does it entail, the social construction of that reality. These are two separate processes of social construction, even though they may interact with one another.

The recent conversation on the rhetoric of economics, and of inquiry more generally, is a special manifestation of the constructivist conundrum. There is a long tradition of contrasting rhetoric with knowledge, of seeing a conflict between fact-distorting persuasion and a genuine and unbiased interest in the way the real world is. This shows, for example, in the title of numerous books and articles that include as their component the words "rhetoric and reality" or some such, suggesting a contrast between the two: for example, *Rhetoric and Reality in Economics* (Bauer 1984). Among contemporary students of rhetoric, this contrast is no longer found persuasive. There are many ways of undermining the traditional contrast. The anti-realists seek to establish a connection between the rhetoric and reality by redefining reality: reality and truth are rhetorically constructed rather than independent of any persuasive practices of economists or others. Realists may try to accommodate rhetoric by incorporating it into one's notion of knowledge, by letting persuasion play a role in the construction of knowledge, while sticking to the view that reality and truth are not rhetorically constructed. In recent debates about the rhetoric of economics, Deirdre McCloskey has been closer to the former view, while I hold the latter viewpoint (see McCloskey 1994, 1995; Mäki 1995, 2000).

McCloskey's chapter 16 provides the latest statement on these issues. McCloskey argues for a few points. First, philosophers, even when arguing against rhetoric, are themselves rhetorical (with suitable specifications, a realist will agree). Second, knowledge is socially constructed. This may be taken to mean a number of different ideas, such as these: economists manage to establish factual claims only if they, among themselves, share the standards of assessing such claims; economists rely on the testimony of their fellow economists, thus building upon the work of others; and what passes for truth in a given context and community is all there is to truth. We need to distinguish between such different ideas in order to see that it is only the last one with which realists take issue: realists insist that truth does not reduce to what counts as true. McCloskey's example of the low yield of corn in the Middle Ages adds a complicating dimension of vagueness to the picture – the vagueness of the property of being low. A realist would agree that if there is a fact of the matter regarding whether the yield of corn was *low*, this is very much dependent on agreed-upon standards of what we take to be low. The important observation that McCloskey does not address is that there is a difference between there being a fact of the matter regarding what the yield of corn was, and there being a fact of the matter regarding whether a relevant body of people considers the yield to be low. McCloskey's third claim is that we are all realists of sorts – because we all want to make claims about what "really" is the case – but that this realism is ethical realism rather than realism of a more ordinary sort. "Ethical realism" seems to amount to a general idea in social epistemology that knowledge acquisition is a collective endeavor and that as members of collective cognitive endeavors we are obliged to hold certain beliefs. A challenge that McCloskey does not discuss but that social epistemology will have to meet is to provide an account of the possibility of collective error. Realists claim to be able to offer such an account, while McCloskey still needs to come up with her version. History of science offers examples of collective error, suggesting the possibility that whatever degree of consensus there is in economics at any given time on any given topic, it may get things wrong in the sense that the world is not as it is collectively believed to be. In insisting on this – however likely or unlikely – possibility, I might, I think, still really be a little bit more realist than McCloskey.

Another worry for realists comes from the radical wing of the sociology of scientific knowledge (SSK). One claim is that scientists do not pursue epistemic goals such as true information about the world, but rather seek their private or collective nonepistemic interests, such as prestige, credibility, fame and fortune, or status of the profession. The argument continues with the idea that the outcomes of such pursuits do not count as knowledge of a reality that is independent of this knowledge and these pursuits. Rather, it is by way of such pursuits that social construction takes place, not only of knowledge but of reality as well. Reality and scientific claims about it become functions of the social games scientists play. This is the anti-realist line. Realists may resist this reasoning by arguing that while knowledge claims are socially constructed (and it is an empirical question to determine the precise ways in which they are constructed), the truth of those claims and the reality that those claims are about, are not (see Mäki 1992b).

Chapter 17 by Wade Hands discusses an episode in this literature (Hands 2001 gives a more comprehensive overview). The episode is the so-called "epistemological chicken debate," and the special issue examined is about "social realism" or about the explanatory role of social factors in understanding science (Hands defines "social realism" as the view that social factors should play the most significant role in explaining social phenomena – a more accurate label might be "explanatory socialism" or "social explanationism"). In the course of the 1980s, the sociologists of scientific knowledge played the game of epistemological chicken in the sense that each move led to an increasingly radical relativism, thereby ultimately threatening to undermine the credibility of the SSK itself. The various streams of SSK have subsequently offered their respective responses to the conundrum by assigning various specific explanatory roles to social factors in scientific belief formation. They have also reraised questions about the role of "nature" and the individual scientist in explaining scientific beliefs. Some of these developments suggest employing economic metaphors like entrepreneurship, market, investment, and capital accumulation. The upshot is that traditional issues of social explanation are now argued to be relevant to understanding science in general, including physics, archaeology, and economics.

The issue Hands addresses is about which factors – society, individual, nature – and which conceptualizations to invoke in explaining the beliefs that scientists collectively hold. I would like to stress that it is important not to conflate this explanatory issue with the issue of whether those beliefs adequately represent reality – whether they are about facts or fictions. The question of whether beliefs held by a scientific community are true is separate from the question of how they were generated. Unfortunately, as long as knowledge is defined weakly and thinly just as collectively held belief, as in much of the SSK and in Hands' review of it, this difference will remain hidden. The concept of knowledge has to include that of truth in order for the difference to be visible. It is only with this traditional and richer notion of knowledge that we can entertain the idea that different constellations of belief-shaping social conditions have different likelihoods of generating true beliefs. This is a "realist version" of the idea that truth is socially constructed. It suggests that the institutions of economics have to be so designed as to maximize the likelihood that the economic models published in journals and textbooks help us attain maximum relevant truthlikeness in our beliefs about the way the economy works.

Recent developments in science studies suggest that perhaps economics can be employed in a meta-theoretical role to come to the rescue of realism. In its traditional domain, economics has shown how the self-seeking pursuits of individual agents can be transformed by the market mechanism into desirable collective outcomes. By an analogous argument, scientific activity can be depicted as self-seeking entrepreneurial scientists working under a division of intellectual labor, exchanging their products in the marketplace for ideas that transforms, as it were by the invisible hand of truth, the individual endeavors into epistemically desirable outcomes. Thus there is, or may be, an economic or quasi-economic mechanism in the social organization of science ensuring that factual rather than fictional beliefs win the day. If the mechanism is not in place, it has to be designed and established. This reasoning can be applied to economics itself, as a reflexive self-scrutiny in an economics of economics.

Some other economic considerations refer to the opposite direction, citing forces that appear to support fictional rather than factual tendencies. James Buchanan refers to the familiar observation that prospective participants in the professional discourse in economics must nowadays "make a substantial investment in the acquisition of technical proficiency, as such, leaving less time and energy for attention to or concern with the ultimate usefulness of the construction." The outcome is fortified by a biased self-selection process: "Persons who choose to become economists, at the century's end, are those who are attracted by the analytical properties of the models manipulated rather than by the success or failure of such models in offering improved understanding of economic reality" (1999, 9).

Solow makes similar observations that qualify his assessment of economics as summarized in the beginning of this chapter: "There is a tendency for theory to outrun data . . . Theory is cheap, and data are expensive" (Solow 1997, 57). This fact about the cognitive economy has implications for practice, including research, education, and employment – including, we should add, the analyses of economic models in this volume. A lengthy passage by Solow is worth citing as it puts the point so sharply:

In economics, model-builders' busy work is to refine their ideas to ask questions to which the available data cannot give the answer. Econometric theorists invent methods to estimate parameters about which the data have no information. And, of course, people are recruited whose talent is for just these activities, whose interest is more in method than in substance. As the models become more refined, the signal-to-noise ratio in the data becomes very attenuated. Since no empirical verdict is forthcoming, the student goes back to the drawing board – and refines the idea even more . . . Perhaps here we have the overeducated in pursuit of the unknowable. But it sure beats the alternatives. (1997, 57)

This suggests that, relative to theory, data in economics are expensive. If one further assumes that, relative to the situation in physics, data in economics are more expensive in relation to theory than are data in physics in relation to physical theory, one may try to use these presumed facts to explain the further fact that economists put less effort to empirically testing their theories than do physicists while more effort is put to refining theory in economics than in physics. The relative distribution of effort would be explained by the constraints economists and physicists face. As Zamora Bonilla (1999) has shown, this is consistent with assuming that physicists and economists have the same epistemic preferences in the sense that they both pursue a combined goal of plausibility and evidential confirmation and would thus satisfy some notion of factual orientation.[7]

One may extend the notion of cost to cover second-order transaction costs – the costs of the search, communication, monitoring, measurement, and assessment of scientific ideas and intellectual performance. By applying this notion to economics itself as an exercise in comparative institutional analysis, one may derive the conclusion that, *ceteris paribus*, "blackboard economics" is transaction cost efficient economics (Mäki 1999). On this picture, the economic forces contained in the institutions of economics would favor a discipline oriented to the study of fictions.

In chapter 18, the last in this volume, Jesús Zamora Bonilla provides an exercise in an economics of economics. Economists are depicted as self-interested economic agents who would not pursue truthful knowledge if it were not in their interests. Like politicians, they could as well be rent-seekers. Zamora

Bonilla outlines elements for a supply and demand model of economics where economists supply economic theories that are demanded by economic agents. The demand for theory T is assumed to be a function of the degree of consensus about T among economists, the popularity of T among the general public, consistency of T's predictions with lay intutions, and the perceived advantageousness of T's policy implications for the agent. On the supply side, economists are assumed to derive utility from having their theories accepted by their colleagues and the general public; they also prefer more income to less, and wish to see their theories put to practice (these latter two goals being dependent on the first). In seeking acceptance and recognition by their fellow economists, economists agree to subject their theory choices to some rules of the game, in exchange for other economists doing the same. A set of different kinds of constitutional norms arises as a result of a negotiation where each relevant party is driven, among other things, by expectations about its own favorite theory being accepted in terms of those norms. The key question then is whether these norms guide economists towards truth-seeking or rent-seeking behavior. Like many others, Zamora Bonilla has doubts about whether the institutions of economics are fully supportive of truth-seeking aspirations.

The institutions of economics have numerous aspects that can be approached from a variety of perspectives, using various conceptual tools. The set of economic perspectives alone is a broad family (see, e.g. Dasgupta and David 1994; Sent 1999). The key question is whether economics itself can help explain and justify the degree to which economics is factual and fictional. Can economics be employed to usefully refer to itself? If one is inclined to answer positively, then a further question arises: if a meta-economics is taken to explain and justify an object-economics, then how does one justify the use of that meta-economics for this purpose without circularity or infinite regress? How does one assess the use of economic principles in the study of scientific inquiry, economics itself included? Is economics of economics a feasible option? This is the standard reflexivity problem that awaits further scrutiny (see Mäki 1999).

* * *

We are back where we began. We started with distinguishing three themes that would organize the chapters of this volume: economic models, economic ontology, and the institutions of economics. We now see how intimately these perspectives are interrelated. We cannot answer questions about the institutions or industrial organisation of the discipline of economics without answering questions about the model–reality connection and about economic ontology. We have now been talking about economic models of economics, and about the discipline of economics itself possibly inhabiting the economic realm. We need to answer questions such as (1) How does an economic model of economics (such as Zamora Bonilla's) relate to what it is supposed to be about, namely economics? and (2) Is economics an economy in sufficiently significant respects and to sufficiently high degrees? in order to answer question (3) What is the structure of institutional constraints and behavioral incentives that shapes the endeavors of economists? Likewise, in order to answer questions about whether an economic model has the chance of being about facts or fictions, questions about the constitution of economic facts and about the constitution of the discipline of economics cannot be escaped. No one having a stake in the "dismal queen" – as a performer or as a spectator – should draw definite conclusions about its factuality and fictionality until satisfactory answers have been given to all three sets of questions.

Notes

1. For the anti-market and pro-hierarchy context of Carlyle's criticism of liberal political economy, see Persky (1990) and Levy (2000).
2. Kreps here invokes what economic methodologists would call a strong form of the Duhem–Quine thesis: empirical tests always involve a very large number of auxiliary assumptions, and in the case of a negative test result, one is unable to attribute the failure to any particular component in the total set of assumptions, and is therefore free to save the target hypothesis from refutation by way of adjustments elsewhere in the system.
3. From among the large number of commentaries that have appeared recently, let me just pick out Thomas Mayer's *Truth and Precision in Economics* (1993), David Colander's *Why Aren't Economists as Important as Garbagemen?* (1991), and Melvin Reder's *Economics: The Culture of a Controversial Science* (1999).
4. If most of the statements of the sort summarized in the foregoing are methodologically and philosophically unsophisticated, some of them even simplistic, this will not imply that there is not a great deal of truth in them. My call for sophistication is based on the conviction that without it, there is no way that we could ascertain in what respects and to what extent they are true – and in particular no way of generating sensible conversations about these issues between the opposing parties with any hope of mutual understanding and convergence of opinion. Therefore, I disagree on Dasgupta's dismissal of specialized methodological work in the beginning of his chapter. While I am the first to admit that some work in economic methodology is not in great shape – just as everybody agrees that some work in economics is far from perfection – there is an increasing body of methodological analysis that is both informed about what is going on in economics and that tackles some of the most relevant methodological issues in a skillful fashion. Lest a practicing economist does not want to be charged for the same flaw that he may attribute to a methodology specialist – being ignorant of the subject matter – he had better check sources such as the IEA volume devoted to case studies in economic methodology (Backhouse *et al.*, 1998), selected articles in the *Journal of Economic Methodology* and in *The Handbook of Economic Methodology* (Davis *et al.* 1998).
5. The conference that featured early versions of many of the chapters in this volume was originally provocatively entitled, "Fact or Fiction?" At the end of the conference, the participants agreed that the correct expression is "Fact and Fiction" – without a question mark.

6. The parallel volume, *The Economic World View: Studies in the Ontology of Economics* (Cambridge University Press 2001), is completely devoted to economic ontology.
7. This reasoning serves as another reminder of the fact that fictionality and factuality are highly ambiguous notions. Importantly, if one is intuitively tempted, as many seem to be, to consider empirical confirmation as a feature of factuality, then one should remember that truth and empirical confirmation (and the lack thereof) are different and independent dimensions of factuality and fictionality. For example, an apriorist may consistently seek factuality in the sense of truth while rejecting the requirement of empirical testing.

References

Backhouse, Roger, Daniel Hausman, Uskali Mäki, and Andrea Salanti (eds.) (1998). *Economics and Methodology. Crossing Boundaries*. London: Macmillan

Bauer, Peter (1984). *Reality and Rhetoric*. Cambridge, MA: Harvard University Press

Baumol, William J. (2000). What Marshall *didn't* know: on the twentieth century's contributions to economics, *Quarterly Journal of Economics*, 115, 1–44

Blaug, Mark (1980). *The Methodology of Economics*. Cambridge: Cambridge University Press

Buchanan, James (1999). *Has Economics Lost Its Way?* Fairfax, VA: Institute for Humane Studies

Cartwright, Nancy (1999). *The Dappled World: A Study of the Boundaries of Science*. Cambridge: Cambridge University Press

Coase, R.H. (1993a). The nature of the firm: meaning, in Oliver E. Williamson and Sidney G. Winter (eds.), *The Nature of the Firm. Origins: Evolution, and Development*. Oxford: Oxford University Press, 48–60

(1993b). The institutional structure of production, in Oliver E. Williamson and Sidney G. Winter (eds.), *The Nature of the Firm: Origins, Evolution, and Development*. Oxford: Oxford University Press, 227–235

Colander, David (1991). *Why Aren't Economists as Important as Garbagemen?* Armonk: M.E. Sharpe

Dasgupta, Partha and Paul A. David (1994). Toward a new economics of science, *Research Policy*, 23, 487–521

Davis, John, Wade D. Hands, and Uskali Mäki (eds.) (1998). *The Handbook of Economic Methodology*. Cheltenham: Edward Elgar

Frisch, Ragnar (1970). Econometrics in the world today, in W.A. Eltis, M.F. Scott, and J.N. Wolfe (eds.), *Induction, Growth and Trade: Essays in Honour of Sir Roy Harrod*.

Giddens, Anthony (1984). *The Constitution of Society* Cambridge: Polity

Gilbert, Margaret (1989). *On Social Facts*. London: Routledge

Hands, D. Wade (2001). *Reflection without Rules. Economic Methodology and Contemporary Science Theory*. Cambridge: Cambridge University Press

Hausman, Daniel (1992). *The Inexact and Separate Science of Economics*. Cambridge: Cambridge University Press

Heilbroner, Robert and William Milberg (1995). *The Crisis of Vision in Modern Economic Thought*. Cambridge: Cambridge University Press

Hoover, Kevin (2001). *Causality in Macroeconomics*. Cambridge: Cambridge University Press

Hutchison, Terence (1977). *Knowledge and Ignorance in Economics*. Oxford: Blackwell

Klamer, Arjo and David Colander (1990). *The Making of an Economist*. Boulder, Co: Westnew Press

Kreps, David M. (1997). Economics – the current position, *Daedalus*, 126, 59–85

Krugman, Paul (1998). *The Accidental Theorist: And Other Dispatches from the Dismal Science*. New York: W.W. Norton & Co.

Lavoie, Don (ed.) (1991). *Economics and Hermeneutics*. London: Routledge

Leontief, Wassily (1970). Theoretical assumptions and unobserved facts, *American Economic Review*, 61, 1–3

Levy, David M. (2000). How the dismal science got its name: debating racial quackery, *Journal of the History of Economic Thought*, 23, 5–35

McCloskey, D.N. (1994). *Knowledge and Persuasion in Economics*. Cambridge: Cambridge University Press

(1995) Modern epistemology against analytic philosophy: a reply to Mäki, *Journal of Economic Literature,* 33, 1319–1323

Mäki, Uskali (1992a). On the method of isolation in economics, *Poznán Studies in the Philosophy of the Sciences and the Humanities,* 26, 319–354

(1992b). Social conditioning of economics, in Neil De Marchi (ed.), *Post-Popperian Methodology of Economics*. Dordrecht: Kluwer, 65–104

(1995). Diagnosing McCloskey, *Journal of Economic Literature*, 33, 1300–1318

(1999). Science as a free market: a reflexivity test in an economics of economics, *Perspectives on Science*, 7, 486–509

(2000). Performance against dialogue, or answering and really answering: a participant observer's reflections on the McCloskey conversation, *Journal of Economic Issues*, 34, 43–59

(2001a). The way the world works (www): towards an ontology of theory choice, in Uskali Mäki (ed.), *The Economic World View. Studies in the Ontology of Economics*. Cambridge: Cambridge University Press

(2001b). Models, in Neil J. Smelser and Paul B. Baltes (eds.), *International Encyclopedia of the Social and Behavioral Sciences*, 15. Amsterdam: Elsevier, 9931–9937

Mayer, Thomas (1993). *Truth and Precision in Economics*. Aldershot: Edward Elgar

Morgan, Mary and Margaret Morrison (eds.) (1999). *Models as Mediators*. Cambridge: Cambridge University Press

Niiniluoto, Ilkka (1998). Verisimilitude: the third period, *British Journal for the Philosophy of Science*, 49, 1–29

Persky, Joseph (1990). A dismal romantic, *Journal of Economic Perspectives*, 4, 165–172

Pettit, Philip (1993). *The Common Mind*. Oxford: Oxford University Press

Phelps Brown, E.H. (1972). The underdevelopment of economics, *Economic Journal*, 82, 1–10

Reder, Melvin W. (1999). *Economics: The Culture of a Controversial Science*. Chicago: University of Chicago Press

Robinson, Joan (1933). *The Economics of Imperfect Competition*. London : Macmillan

Schumpeter, Joseph (1954). *History of Economic Analysis*. New York: Oxford University Press

Searle, John (1995). *The Construction of Social Reality*. New York: Free Press

Sent, Esther-Mirjam (1999). Economics of science: survey and suggestions, *Journal of Economic Methodology*, 6, 95–124

Solow, Robert M. (1997). How did economics get that way and what way did it get?, *Daedalus*, 126, 39–58

Sugden, Robert (2000). Team preferences, *Economics and Philosophy*, 16, 175–204

Tuomela, Raimo (1995). *The Importance of Us*. Stanford: University of Stanford Press

Worswick, G.D.N. (1972). Is progress in economic science possible?, *Economic Journal*, 82, 73–87

Zamora Bonilla, Jesús (1999). Verisimilitude and the scientific strategy of economic theory *Journal of Economic Methodology*, 6, 331–350

Part II
Setting the scene

2 Ugly currents in modern economics

Mark Blaug

1 Introduction

The last few years have seen an astonishing series of books and articles with titles like *The Decline of Economics* (Cassidy 1996), *The Crisis of Vision in Modern Economic Thought* (Heilbroner and Milberg 1996), *Against Economics* (Kanth 1996), *The End of Economics* (Perelman 1996), and even *The Death of Economics* (Omerod 1994).[1] A survey of graduate students in elite American universities by Arjo Klamer and David Colander (1987, 1990) revealed a striking lack of interest among young would-be economists either in the economy or in the literature of economics; success in the economics profession, they shrewdly perceived, came principally to those with a knowledge of mathematical economics and econometrics. The study sparked a chorus of complaints about the nature of economic research and training at top universities in the Western world and led in 1991 to a full-scale report of a Commission on Graduate Education in Economics (1991) sponsored by the American Economic Association. The commission included leading figures in the economics profession and, like all such reports, produced a blend of various views in which, however, one dominant note appeared repeatedly: economics as taught in graduate schools has become increasingly preoccupied with formal technique to the deliberate exclusion of historical and institutional understanding. More recently, John Hey (1997), the Managing Editor of *The Economic Journal*, the leading economics journal in the UK, looked back over ten years of his editorship and summed up his appraisal of the type of papers that were regularly submitted to the journal:

Many of the submissions do not appear to be written in order to further economic knowledge. Whilst I fully understand the pressure on authors, particularly young academics, it is still disheartening that so many economists seem to be playing the "journal game", i.e. producing variations on a theme that are uninteresting and which do not enlighten.

More specifically, he noted the overwhelming predominance of mathematical modeling in the investigation of economic problems:

It often appears that the model has been constructed for no other purpose than to produce a result which is a stylised fact observed by the author. That may be an interesting exercise but it needs to be supplemented with a discussion of whether this particular explanation for the stylised fact is useful and better than the alternative explanations. Simply producing a model that comes up with a desired result is a test of the cleverness of the author, not a test of the relevance of the theory.

Similarly, Edmond Malinvaud (1997), no mean mathematical theorist himself, conceded that too much weight in research was given to mathematical skill: "today much praise is given to building and solving models of disputable relevance: too little is given to good pieces of economics as long as they contain no mathematical model." We could go on all night piling up similar testimony from other leaders of the economics profession[2] but perhaps enough has been said to make my point: modern economics is sick; economics has increasingly become an intellectual game played for its own sake and not for its practical consequences; economists have gradually converted the subject into a sort of Social Mathematics in which analytical rigor as understood in math departments is everything and empirical relevance (as understood in physics departments) is nothing. If a topic cannot be tackled by formal modeling, it is simply consigned to the intellectual underworld; to pick up a copy these days of *The American Economic Review* or *The Economic Journal*, not to mention *Econometrica* or the *Review of Economic Studies*, is to wonder whether one has landed on a strange planet in which tedium is the deliberate objective of professional publication. Economics was condemned a century ago as the "dismal science" but the dismal science of yesterday was a lot less dismal than the soporific scholasticism of today. To paraphrase the title of a popular British musical: "No Reality, Please. We're Economists."

2   General equilibrium theory

It was not always so. If we can date the onset of the illness at all, it is the publication in 1954 of a famous paper by Nobel Laureates Kenneth Arrow and Gerard Debreu; it is this paper that marks the beginning of what has since become a cancerous growth in the very center of microeconomics.[3] The Arrow–Debreu paper provided a rigorous proof of the existence of multimarket equilibrium in a decentralized economy, a notion which Léon Walras had entertained eighty years earlier but which he had failed to establish convincingly. This proof was rigorous by mathematical standards but it required some assumptions which clearly violated economic reality; for example, that there are forward markets for every commodity and for all conceivable contingencies in all future periods and yet that no one holds money as a store of value for more than one period. Even so, Arrow and Debreu did not manage to prove that such a general equilibrium is stable in the sense that it is actually attained from whatever position at which we start. In short, the Arrow–Debreu proof had more to do with mathematical logic than with economics.

Unfortunately, this paper soon became a model of what economists ought to aim for as modern scientists. In the process, few readers realized that Arrow and Debreu had in fact abandoned the vision that had originally motivated Walras. For Walras, general equilibrium theory was intended to be an abstract but nevertheless realistic description of the functioning of a capitalist economy and he was therefore more concerned to show that markets will clear automatically via price adjustments in response to positive or negative excess demand – a property which he labelled "tâtonnement" – than to prove that an unique set of prices and quantities is capable of clearing all markets simultaneously.[4] By the time we get to Arrow and Debreu, however, general equilibrium theory has ceased to make any descriptive claim about actual economic systems and has become a purely formal apparatus about a virtual economy; it has become a perfect example of what Ronald Coase (1993b, 229) has called "blackboard economics," a model that can be written down on blackboards using economic terms like "prices," "quantities," "factors of production," etc. but which nevertheless is blatantly and even scandalously unrepresentative of any recognizable economic system.

To make things worse, the Arrow–Debreu model was soon augmented by the so-called Fundamental Theorems of Welfare Economics, namely, that every perfectly competitive economy in a state of general equilibrium is Pareto-optimal and, moreover, that any Pareto-optimal allocation of resources can be attained by means of perfectly competitive equilibrium once we make an appropriate redistribution of initial endowments. This is said to nail down precisely what Adam Smith perceived only dimly two hundred years ago: the "invisible hand" of competition secures the best of all possible worlds, an optimum allocation of resources in which no one can be made better off without making someone else worse off.

Alas, what a historical travesty is here! What Adam Smith meant is what the man-and-woman-in-the-street means when she applauds the competitive process. A competitive economy tends to produce the kind of goods people want at the lowest possible price because it encourages entrepreneurship and technical dynamism through a relentless struggle for advantage, a struggle that is not confined to price competition but includes nonprice variables, such as new goods, better old goods, better-serviced goods, more quickly delivered goods, etc. In other words, for Adam Smith and for the man-and-woman-in-the-street, competition is a type of behavior on the part of businessmen and not a market structure like "perfect competition," according to which business firms are purely passive "price-takers" rather than active "price-makers." This is what

Richard Lipsey (1997) calls the "informal defence" of competition in contrast to the "formal defense" enshrined in proofs of the Fundamental Theorems of Welfare Economics grounded in the concept of perfect competition. It is exactly the same contrast that Schumpeter (1942, 106–110) drew sixty years ago between "dynamic efficiency" that encourages the innovative process and "static efficiency" that excludes it.

Perfect competition never did exist and never could exist because even when firms are small, they do not just take the price as given but strive to make the price. All the current textbooks say as much but then they immediately go on to say that the cloud-cuckoo-land of perfect competition is the benchmark against which economists may say something significant about real-world competition in the same way that a frictionless plane in physics tells a physicist how fast a ball will travel along an actual inclined plane. But how can an idealized state of perfection be a benchmark when we are never told how to measure the gap between it and real-world competition? It is implied that all real-world competition is "approximately" like perfect competition but the degree of the approximation is never specified, even vaguely. Besides, there is a well-known Lipsey–Lancaster theorem which says that when an economy is not in a first-best optimum, say because of taxes or tariffs, there is no way of distinguishing a third-best from a second-best situation and no way of telling whether a given change takes us nearer or further away from the first-best optimum. This theorem is widely acknowledged in all the textbooks[5] and yet this has done nothing to displace the notion that perfect competition is an ideal that somehow casts light on the admittedly imperfect competition all around us.

Perfect competition is an utterly misleading concept, not least because it directs attention to what equilibrium looks like when we get to it, whereas the real problem is that of the process of converging on it. In short, competition is a disequilibrium phenomenon and yet general equilibrium *à la* Arrow and Debreu, the existence problem, the fundamental theorems of welfare economics, perfect competition, and the like, all foster concern with the end-state of competition at the expense of thinking about competition as a dynamic process.[6]

So, why do modern economists spend so much time teaching their students the model of perfect competition, while denigrating discussion of actual competition in courses on Industrial Organization as "mere description?" It is because the model of perfect competition allows one to make unambiguous comparative static predictions about prices and quantities; one may be able to say only a little, but what one says is precisely said. On the other hand, when it comes to imperfect competition, what one says covers the waterfront of business behavior but has always to be accompanied by exceptions and qualifications. A modern economist would rather say little precisely than much imprecisely, irrespective of the relative significance of what is being said, and she has learned this methodological standard sitting at the feet of Arrow and Debreu (Rosen 1997). If there is such a thing as "original sin" in economic methodology, it is the worship of the idol of the mathematical rigor more or less invented by Arrow and Debreu in 1954 and then canonized by Debreu in his *Theory of Value* five years later, probably the most arid and pointless book in the entire literature of economics.

The result of all this is that we now understand almost less about how actual markets work, than did Adam Smith or even Léon Walras. We have forgotten that markets require market-makers, that functioning markets require middlemen willing to hold inventories, that markets need to be organized, and that property rights need to be defined and enforced if markets are to get started at all.[7] We have even forgotten that markets adjust as often in terms of quantities rather than prices, as in labor markets and customer commodity markets, as Alfred Marshall knew very well but Walras overlooked. So well have we forgotten that fact that a whole branch of economics sprang up in the 1960s and 1970s to provide "microfoundations" for Keynesian macroeconomics, that is, some new explanation for the well-known fact that a decline in aggregate demand causes, not falling real wages at the same level of employment as we might expect on the basis of received Walrasian theory, but rather unemployment at the same real[8] wage.

No wonder that we have been worse than useless as a profession in advising governments in Eastern Europe to handle the transition from a command economy to a market economy (Murrell, 1991). This is the awful legacy of general equilibrium theory and the prestige accorded to analysis of end-state competition. Indeed, much of modern microeconomics might be fairly described as a type of geography that consists entirely of city-street plans without any maps of how to reach a city either from any other city or from the countryside.

3 Game theory

But, surely, this is old hat: nobody bothers much these days with general equilibrium and perfect competition? The only game in town is game theory.[9]

Game theory is made to order for modern economists: it assumes rational players seeking to maximize their own pay-offs, while taking due account of the same motivation on the part of their rivals. But game theory has turned out to be an even more seductive technique for economists than general equilibrium theory, encouraging once again the persistent tendency of modern economists to look away from the world and to engage instead in arm-chair deductive theorizing. Game theory is most powerful in dealing with one-shot cooperative games in which pay-offs can be expressed in money or any other one-dimensional variable. But economic behavior is typically a repeated noncooperative game with a complex informational structure in which outcomes are not always measurable in one-dimensional terms. It is well known that repeated games typically exhibit an infinity of equilibria and game theory itself gives no reasons why the players will prefer one equilibrium rather than another. In consequence, game theory does not provide definite predictions of behavior in repeated-game situations, that is, in the sort of situations with which economists have traditionally been concerned, such as buying and selling in highly contestable markets.

Much, if not most, game theory is prescriptive, concerned with how rational players *should* make decisions, and characteristically enough, very little experimental work has been carried out to develop a realistic description of how people actually make decisions in situations of strategic interactions (Gibbons, 1997). Like traditional economic theory, game theory has been exclusively concerned with what Herbert Simon (1976) calls "substantive" rationality and rarely with "procedural" rationality, that is, with what players do when they are perfectly informed about all the available alternatives, have unbounded calculating abilities, and have nothing to learn from experience, and not with how they decide what to do in the face of imperfect information and limited cognitive abilities to calculate. And just as general equilibrium theory solved the stability-of-equilibrium question by ruling out disequilibrium trading, game theory likewise adopted a static approach to the equilibrium outcomes of games by simply ignoring the adjustment process by which equilibrium is achieved; even sequential decision-making, which allows one player to learn what to do from the previous move of the other player, is frequently eliminated in favor of simultaneous decision-making. If anything, game theory has in recent years witnessed increasing conceptual proliferation, drawing it even further from a positive descriptive account of interactive decisions.[10] Indeed, for all its undoubted abstract intellectual appeal, game theory has fed the economist's addiction to formal modeling regardless of its practical relevance. In the field of industrial organization, which has been more systematically colonized by game theory than any other branch of economics, its principal effect has been to pour old wine into new bottles: it is difficult, nay, impossible, to think of a single novel observation that has come out of the "new" industrial organization infused by game theory that was not already part-and-parcel of the "old" industrial organization based as it was on the so-called "structure–conduct–performance" approach to business behavior.[11]

The main contribution of game theory has been rather different. It has taught us better to appreciate the infinite subtleties of so-called "rationality," reminding us that the standard economist's account of rational behavior is woefully inadequate in spelling out the implicit informational structure and learning processes on which equilibrium outcomes in markets do in fact depend This is theoretical progress, but it is not empirical progress in helping us to predict how the price system actually works.

What runs through all this is the license that Friedman's "methodology of positive economics" gave economists to make any and all unrealistic assumptions, provided only that their theories yielded verifiable implications. But even if one grants for the sake of argument that assumptions do not need to be descriptively accurate, Friedman failed to insist that they do need to be *robust*, that is, capable of being relaxed without fatal damage to the model they underpin. In consequence, the assumptions that economists typically make are reminiscent of the oldest anti-economist joke of them all: "let us assume that we have a tin-opener," says the castaway economist on a desert island. Think of the following typical assumptions: perfectly infallible, utterly omniscient, infinitely lived identical consumers; zero transaction costs; complete markets for all time-stated claims for all conceivable contingent events; no trading of any kind at disequilibrium prices; infinitely rapid velocities of prices and quantities; no radical, incalculable uncertainty in real time but only, probabilistically calculable risk in logical time; only linearly homogeneous convex production functions; no technical progress requiring embodied capital investment, etc. – all these are not just unrealistic but also singularly unrobust assumptions, and yet they figure critically in leading economic theories – remove them and hardly a single neoclassical theorem is left standing!

4 Macroeconomics, new and old

So far, we have only touched on microeconomics but, as everybody knows, if we want to study a type of economics that is intimately concerned with practical problems we should be looking at macroeconomics and not microeconomics. But in recent years even macroeconomics has fallen prey to empty formalism. Classic monetarism of the Friedmanite variety more or less died out in the 1980s, largely as a result of financial deregulation, and was superseded by the New Classical Macroeconomics with its concept of "rational expectations." This came in two different versions, which served to disseminate the new doctrine to different audiences. The weak version of rational expectations simply asserts that rational economic agents always take full advantage of profit opportunities, thus forming price expectations on the basis of all available information. This has all the appearance of a reasonable assumption but it tacitly implies continuous market-clearing, ruling out the very disequilibrium phenomena that macroeconomics was created to explain. The strong version of rational expectations, however, asserts even more controversially that the subjective expectations held by economic agents are the same as the mathematical expectations of the endogenous variables in the best probability model of the economy. What we have here is the traditional assumption of perfect information all over again, but allowing for the fact that uncertainty makes it impossible to predict each future event perfectly; all we have is perfect foresight on average, so that the mean expected error of a rationally expected forecast is always zero. With perfect stochastic foresight and competitive markets that clear continuously, even business cycles must be viewed as the unavoidable forecasting errors of rational economic agents in the face of exogenous shocks.

To say that this is an unrealistic assumption is to state the obvious. Were it so, it would follow that monetary and fiscal policies could influence real variables like output and employment only momentarily because as soon as these policies are announced, they will be incorporated into price expectations by individuals more or less instantaneously. This is the so-called "policy-ineffectiveness" hypothesis, the principal anti-Keynesian conclusion of the New Classical Macroeconomics. If expectations were indeed rational in this strong sense it would imply that the growth path of real output or employment was not correlated with *systematic* changes in the money supply, the size of budgetary deficits, the rate of interest, the exchange rate, or policy pronouncements about any of these variables, because if they were so correlated, private agents would have incorporated these correlations into their pricing forecasts, in which case they would have appeared as purely nominal adjustments to wages and prices. But the evidence that output and employment are capable of being influenced by monetary and fiscal policy, that there is a short-run trade-off between inflation and unemployment, is so overwhelming that even the leading spokesmen for the New Classical Macroeconomics, Robert Lucas and Thomas Sargent, seem to have qualified the doctrine of rational expectations in the strong version (Blaug 1992, 201–204).

The New Classical Macroeconomics has been increasingly supplanted by Real Business Cycle Theory. The notion that there is no short-run Phillips curve, that the long-run Phillips curve is vertical at "the natural rate of unemployment," which is now a standard feature of all non-Keynesian macroeconomics, suggests that business cycles can be caused only by random shocks to the economic system. Lucas and Sargent (1981) used to argue for monetary demand-side shocks, but these have now given way in Real Business Cycle Theory to the idea of supply-side shocks in the form of random changes in technology.

And indeed Real Business Cycle Theory is, like New Classical Macroeconomics, a species of the genus of equilibrium explanations of the business cycle (which would yesteryear have been considered an oxymoron): agents are relentless maximizers and form expectations rationally; markets clear continuously and even momentary disequilibria are ruled out as methodologically inadmissible; and changes in technology or new marketing practices are purely random and hence are unpredictable. Mindful of the poor empirical track record of rational expectations, Real Business Cycle theorists, such as Edward Prescott and Finn Kydland (1982), have adopted a new method for confirming their theories. Instead of providing models that are capable of being tested by standard econometric methods, they subject them to "calibration," that is, they quantify the parameters of a model on the basis of casual empiricism or a variety of unrelated econometric studies so chosen as to guarantee that the model mimics some particular feature of the historical data. The claim of Real Business Cycle theorists is that their models do indeed track the important time series fairly closely and even depict widely accepted "stylized facts" about the business cycle.

However, the hurdles that these models are expected to jump are not very high (Summers 1991; Pack 1994; Hoover 1995). It remains doubtful whether supply-side shocks are large enough – and, in particular, frequent enough–to generate the observed cyclical fluctuations of output and prices; and of course it has to be the cyclical fluctuations of actual total output. Real Business Cycle Theory has abandoned the century-old tradition of analyzing business cycles as a series of short-term output fluctuations around a smoothly growing trend level. Assuming as it does that all markets clear instantaneously, it is driven to explain the cycle not as the short-run fluctuations of a detrended time series but as fluctuations in potential output itself owing to shocks in technology. The no doubt ingenious story that Real Business Cycle theorists tell is more convincing for booms than for slumps, and indeed they have not so far provided a convincing account of why economies turn down not just occasionally but periodically. Indeed Real Business Cycle theorists remind one of what Dr. Johnson said of a dog walking on its hind legs: "It is not done well; but you are surprised to find it done at all."

Note that nothing has really changed between Lucas–Sargent and Prescott–Kydland: any unemployment we observe is still voluntary unemployment because the labor market, like all other markets, is said to be always in equilibrium. Money is "neutral"–or, alternatively expressed, there is always a long-run vertical Phillips curve, and business cycles would never occur were it not for the fact that there are unpredictable shocks of one kind or another which, for a while, surprise us until we adjust to them. In Friedman's monetarism of the 1970s, there was a negatively-sloped short-run Phillips curve, so that stabilization policies did have real effect, even though they did not last beyond two to five years (Friedman's own estimates), but by the time we reach Prescott and Kydland even this thin reed has been broken.

It is amazing how thoroughly the idea of a "natural rate of unemployment," that is, of a vertical Phillips curve, has caught on in modern macroeconomics, infecting even avowedly neo-Keynesian writers. Now, there is no denying that there is some rate of unemployment below which demand pressures on resources will cause prices to rise, so that there is something to the idea of an equilibrium rate of unemployment, a lower limit to the onset of inflation. But to draw it as a line instead of a thick band is a mistake because we have no firm idea whether it is a 3–4 percent or a 6–7 percent unemployment rate and no warrant for believing that it is a well-defined, stable level of unemployment, capable of serving as a bedrock for anti-inflationary policies. Moreover, statistical estimates of the natural rate of unemployment on both sides of the Atlantic have shown that it trails behind past rates of unemployment, rising and falling as they do; in the now fashionable language of physics, the natural rate exhibits "hysteresis"; its level depends on the path taken to reach it because the longer unemployment lasts, the greater is the proportion of the unemployed who have become unemployable (Cross 1995: chapters 2, 3). In short, the so-called natural rate of unemployment is an unstable range of rates and not a well-defined, unique single rate and it is subject to a steady, rightward drift. How did such a vaguely specified idea ever come to be regarded as an article of faith?

What is really worrying about all the recent developments in anti-Keynesian macroeconomics is not so much the unpalatable implication of policy-ineffectiveness but rather the abandonment of anything like empirical testing of macroeconomic models. The tendency now is to resort to ever-more esoteric techniques in the attempt to produce models that have no ambition other than to replicate actual time series. "Calibration" as a method of choosing between macroeconomics theories is, to put it mildly, something of a fraud because it simply cannot fail to confirm just about every model. While complaints of the inconclusiveness of econometric testing abound in the literature, the calibration methodology lacks even the discipline imposed by the older econometric methods.

Alas, matters are not much better in the Keynesian camp in which so-called "endogenous growth theory" has virtually abandoned the goal of empirical verisimilitude, preferring instead to lean and to lean heavily on the plausibility of the notion that the externalities of research and development (R&D) somehow account for the self-sustaining character of economic growth.[12]

5   What to do?

Where do we go from here? Is there any way back to a policy-relevant, problem-solving kind of economics that was the norm in the 1940s, 1950s, and perhaps the 1960s?

There may be such a way but I myself am not sanguine about reversing what has by now become a well-established professional culture that values technical facility above all else. Economics in the Western world is dominated by American economics and American economics is dominated by the 400–500 new PhDs in economics that each year seek employment in 3,000 American institutions of higher learning; the way to gain employment and to secure promotion once employed is to publish in one of the 300 or so refereed English-language journals in economics, and, preferably, in the dozen or so leading refereed journals. Whatever we may say against technique-ridden, mathematically expressed modeling of economic phenomena, the fact remains that papers written in this form are easier to produce once the formula has been learned, although the initial investment costs of acquiring the technique are high, and certainly easier to appraise and referee than those written in words and diagrams. With 300 journals publishing bi-annually or quarterly, something like 4,000–5,000 papers in economics are published every year, which are refereed by perhaps 300 academics at the top American universities, whose students will become the referees of papers in the next generation, papers which will of course look very much like the papers they are now themselves writing and publishing. In other words, we have by now created a veritable professional treadmill with a built-in momentum that feeds continually on the pressure to publish in prestigious journals in order to gain employment in prestigious institutions whose annual salaries are more or less twice those that are earned in academic "Siberia." To turn this locomotive around is to ask individuals at the beginning of their professional career to ignore the dominant fashion for economics papers and instead to write something unfashionable, like George Akerlof's "The market for 'lemons'" (a paper that was turned down three times and took four years to finally reach publication), or like Brian Arthur's "Competing technologies, increasing returns, and lock-in by historical events" (a paper that was turned down three times and was accepted only after fourteen rewrites, the entire process having taken six years) (Shepherd, 1995). Can we really believe that that is likely to happen on a scale significant enough to tip the balance?[13]

It certainly will not happen unless the older members of the profession show the way with empirically relevant research grounded in the attempt to confront outstanding policy issues. Economics is more than just a field of social engineering. There is room for the sort of economics that seeks merely to understand the economic world for its own sake. But the purely intellectual appeal of economics as a subject of scholarly fascination has always played a minor role in the history of the subject. All the great economists, without a single exception, were motivated to study economics in order to improve the world. Be that as it may, if idle curiosity were our only reason for studying economics, it is difficult to believe that governments and business firms would continue to hire economists in the numbers that they do. Policy questions are inextricably woven into the very fabric of economics and for that reason we never can avoid asking: Do we have any good reasons for thinking that economic theories are either true or false in the sense that it makes a difference for economic policy whether we act on the basis of one economic theory or another? Are some economic theories more true than others?

My answers to both of these questions is: "yes." Surprisingly enough, however, there are some economists who would deny that these are meaningful questions to ask. Perhaps the most alarming symptom of the growth of empty formalism in modern economics is the increasing appearance of "postmodernism" in the writings of economic methodologists. Postmodernism in economics takes many forms but it always begins by ridiculing the scientific pretensions of economics, by pouring cold water on the belief that there is an objective economic system "out there" against which we can measure the explanatory power of economic theories, by scoffing at the idea that economists can make accurate predictions of economic events and denying that there is any basis for choosing between competent economic theories other than on grounds of personal preference. Economists, say the postmodernists, can seek to persuade only by a variety of implicit and explicit rhetorical devices and, when all is said and done, economics as a subject is not very different from literary criticism or aesthetics or philosophy.[14] The increasing frequency with which such views are advanced by economists, not just hinted at but ever more stridently expressed, is to me one of the most alarming signs that economists may finally have abandoned all efforts at practical advice because it is easier and safer to practice economics as a scholastic pastime. "Economics for economics sake" will soon become – indeed, already is – the battle-cry. At this point, someone might observe that economics is too important a subject to be left to economists. Is that why students are increasingly choosing Business Studies and Business Management over Economics? Some observers indeed predict that departments of economics in institutions of higher education are shrinking and will continue to shrink in size as students vote with their feet and go elsewhere to learn about the practical problems of the economic order.

6   Some varieties of postmodernism

Let me pause for a moment to dig a little deeper into postmodernism. The leading figure in the postmodernist movement is Deirdre McCloskey whose *The Rhetoric of Economics* (1986) delighted some but puzzled many more.[15] Like many important books, its central message is ambiguous and it seems to change in the very course of the book. Uskali Mäki (1995) makes the telling point that McCloskey's demonstration that economics is, among other things, a form of rhetorical persuasion – which is trivially true – is entirely distinct from her Habermasian notion of truth as something arrived at by a "domination-free" discourse among professional economists obeying the moral constraints of *Sprachethik*. (Habermas 1990, 1992; Blaug 1994). McCloskey's *Sprachethik* is a Mickey Mouse version of Habermas' theory of Discourse Ethics which, whatever else we may think of it, is an idea not only distinct from, but also entirely contradictory to, McCloskey's postmodernist orientation. Habermas sets out an "ideal speech situation," which he derives from the inescapable presuppositions of rational argument; this ideal, while almost never witnessed in real discourse, nevertheless presents a standard against which we may analyze the power distortions operating within real discourse. Habermas thus offers a rational defense of truth claims in economics (or any other social science) which is totally out of keeping with McCloskey's postmodern rejection of such grounds.

Additionally, and more seriously, McCloskey has never analyzed the sources of power in the economics profession via employment, publication, leadership in professional associations, and the like, that would show the ways in which the actual discourse of economics transgresses the Habermasian ideal of domination-free discourse.[16] What has confused so many readers of McCloskey is the way she slides from rhetorical analysis of economic writings – a valuable type of analysis that she created and encouraged – to a meta-theory about how we can both identify and justify "good economics," while all the time denying that we need any meta-theory or what others call "normative methodology"; this is her rather fatuous distinction between OK methodology with a lower case m and despised Methodology with a capital M.

An equally puzzling contribution to economic methodology is Tony Lawson's *Economics and Reality* (1997), which follows Roy Bhaskar (1978, 1979) in the view that scientific "realism" necessarily implies the attempt to uncover casual mechanisms in both nature and society and not just to study correlations or Humean conjunctions of events. But however desirable it is to produce true causal explanations for scientific phenomena, (and that is after all why we reject Friedman's view that realistic assumptions do not matter), it is far from obviously true that scientific analysis does not merit the name of science unless it provides mechanisms tracing the precise manner in which cause leads to effect; think of Newton who simply ignored this requirement. Be that as it may, it is even less obvious to see what follows from "transcendental realism" for economics. Tony Lawson declares that all the limitations of neoclassical economics – its obsessive concentration on economic individualism, on omniscient and infallible rational agents, on equilibrium end-states – stem from the ontological and epistemological doctrines of "logical positivism," in particular, the deductive-nomological or covering-law model of scientific explanation, which he slates coming and going?[17] But what Bhaskar calls "transcendental" and Lawson "critical" realism is simply Popperian falsificationism in different language. If Popper had taken a real interest in social science, which he never did, he would have swallowed critical realism whole, as Lawson concedes when he admits that Popper was a realist, a fallibilist, an anti-positivist, and a demarcationist (between science and nonscience).

What we have here is a great many good ideas about the desirability of exploring deep underlying structures and mechanisms in social science, coupled with a grossly exaggerated attack on an alleged mainstream belief in "closure" and "universal laws" in economics. Lawson (1997, 288–289) denies that there are any constant-event regularities in the social sphere and hence denies that prediction is possible in a subject like economics. He agrees, however, that there are "demi-regularities" in time and space as "tendencies" or "patterns," and his own applied work on the poor growth performance of the UK economy reported in his book clearly implies the ability to predict general patterns of behavior.

His strictures against predictability in economics are entirely grounded on an unstated belief that economic theories result in exact, unconditional predictions, as if he had never heard of "the pound of *ceteris paribus*" or the gap between theories and real-world data. For him, econometrics is the black magic of testing predictions that are supposed to hold precisely (Darnell 1997). He never mentions such frequently confirmed, robust empirical regularities in economics as the law of demand, Engel's law, Okun's law, the greater-than-unity value of the income multiplier, etc. In short, his book constantly promises to deliver a totally new approach to economic methodology based on a clear rejection of the Big Bad Wolf of "positivism" and then delivers the familiar ideas of Bhaskar on the "openness" or nonergodic nature of social systems. Moreover, the assertion that the economy is an open system and hence that the "laws" of economics are at best inexact tendency laws subject to *ceteris paribus* conditions has been familiar to writers on economic methodology ever since John Stuart Mill and appears of course in John Neville Keynes' classic book on *The Scope and Method of Political Economy* (1890). In short, Lawson's characterisation of neoclassical economics and its supposed foundation in "positivism" and "deductivism" is utterly misplaced (Hands 1997).

It is the Symmetry Thesis of positivism that really raises Lawson's hackles, namely, the proposition that explanation is simply prediction written backwards, explanation coming after and prediction before an event. Now, in the strong version associated with the writings of Carl Hempel, the so-called "covering-law model of scientific explanation," the symmetry thesis is undoubtedly objectionable, implying, for example, that a prediction based on a possibly meaningless correlation is logically equivalent to an explanation. But in weaker versions, the symmetry thesis asserts quite correctly that any satisfactory explanation of a phenomenon invokes a generalization of some sort, whether statistical or historical, of which the phenomenon being explained is a particular instance.[18] It follows that a crucial test of such a satisfactory explanation is our ability to predict similar phenomena with the aid of that generalization before they have actually occurred. No wonder, then, that predictability looms large in our criteria of theory choice in science.

Attacks on predictability as a desirable feature of economic theories, and possibly a test of their verisimilitude, invariably offer "understanding" rather than "explanation" as the true goal of economic investigation, by which is meant some sort of insight or illumination of economic affairs without any ability to forecast or predict economic events even in the near future. As we have seen, Lawson is not prepared to go quite so far but others do not hesitate to do so.[19] Is it in fact possible to "understand" something unfamiliar without subsuming it, or at least relating it, to something larger that is already familiar? I think not, in which case there is some merit in the symmetry thesis. To pretend to explain in some significant sense, as Lawson does, while at the same time rejecting any notion of predictability in economics, conceding only reluctantly that perhaps there are some "demi-regularities" in economic life, is to give up the fight against postmodernists before it has even begun. It is curiously reminiscent of Hayek who also pooh-poohed economic predictions but agreed that economists could discern "patterns." But why may one declare that capitalism promotes economic growth but, at the same time, may not predict that next year's GDP in Britain will be this year's GDP plus or minus 1 percent?

7 The litmus paper test

Casting a wide net over economic methodology, it is possible to draw a sharp distinction between "scientific realism" and "postmodernism" as two philo-sophical attitudes towards methodological questions which continue to polarize economists who worry at all about the rivalry between competing theories and research programs.[20] Scientific realists ultimately validate theories in terms of a match with observational data inferred from the world-out-there. Postmo-dernists, on the other hand, argue from the social construction of knowledge and the theory-laden character of facts that appeal to empirical evidence can never settle a theoretical dispute or confirm a truth; in consequence, they would abolish methodology as a normative or even descriptive activity, leaving us with total theoretical pluralism: let a thousand flowers bloom!

Postmodernism may take a variety of forms, such as McCloskey's "rhetoric of economics," which only grants a minor role for prediction as a "good thing," or Sraffians who refuse to invoke any methodological criterion to appraise competing economic theories other than logical "consistency" (Blaug 1995; Kurz and Salvadori 1997). But in one way or the other, postmodernist arguments always amount to "anything goes." Scientific realism is likewise a broad church: it includes deductivists, inductivists, historians, institutionalists – those are just different methods, not necessarily resting on a different methodology.[21] In short, Keynes was a scientific realist, so was Kuznets, so is Friedman, so is North, so is Samuelson, which only goes to show that there is a gulf–no, a chasm–between scientific realists and postmodernists.

8 Why is predictability important?

Economic hypotheses can be judged by their logical coherence, their explana-tory power, their generality, their fecundity, and, ultimately, their ability to pre-dict. Why are economists concerned at all with predictability? Because it is the ultimate test of whether our theories are true and really capture the workings of the economic system independently of our wishes and intellectual prefer-ences. That is not to say that we should always discard hypotheses that have not yet yielded empirically falsifiable implications but simply that theories such as general equilibrium theory, which are untestable even in principle, should be regarded with deep suspicion. At the same time, economists have been unduly narrow in testing the falsifiable implications of theories in the sense that this is invariably taken to mean some statistical or econometric test. But history is just as much a test of patterns and trends in economic events as is regression analysis. Economists are loath to examine their assumptions by the use of survey techniques, by simply asking agents what they believe or what they do, because Friedman's methodology gave economists the false impression that nothing can ever be learned by such means (Hausman 1997). Perhaps the real trouble is our age-old belief, going back to Ricardo, that economics is essentially a deductive science, in which we infer economic behavior on the basis of some assumptions about motivations and some stylized facts about prevailing institutions, suppressing even the temptation to ask whether these are descriptively realistic assumptions and accurately chosen facts. It is high time economists re-examined their long-standing antipathy to induction, to fact-grubbing, to the gathering of data before and not after we sit down to theorize. There is much to be said in favor of Kaldor's insistence on starting with "stylized facts" and inductively inferring an economic model to account for these facts, whose assumptions and implications are then in turn subjected to further verification.[22]

9   Formalism again

And this brings us back to our starting point: the disease of formalism in modern economics. In a symposium on American academic culture, Bob Solow (1997) noted that "many observers in the other social sciences and in the wide, wide world perceive that economics has become formalistic, abstract, negligent of the real world. The truth is, I think, that economics has become technical, which is quite different." Yes, it *is* different but what characterizes "formalism" is that technicalities are prized as ends in themselves, so that the theories which do not lend themselves to technical treatment are set aside with the problems they address. Formalism is the worship of technique and that is what is wrong with it. Formalism usually involves the use of mathematical modeling but it is perfectly possible to indulge in formalism that employs no mathematics whatever, as witnessed by Joan Robinson's use of "verbal mathematics" in *The Economics of Imperfect Competition* (1933) and *The Accumulation of Capital* (1956). Formalism, particularly mathematical formalism, brings clarity and rigor to arguments, but such merits are almost always purchased at a price. To be dedicated to formal modeling at whatever cost is to close the door to the analysis of certain problems that so far have not lent themselves, and may never lend themselves, to rigorous treatment–as, for example, technical progress, entrepreneurship, and the long-term evolution of capitalist economies. If we are to come to grips with such problems, we may have to settle for a looser, fuzzier style of analysis than that afforded by mathematical modeling. Among the most hopeful, and I believe most fruitful, developments in economics is the growth of evolutionary economics in books like *An Evolutionary Theory of Economic Change* (1982) by Richard Nelson and Sidney Winter, *Technical Change and Economic Theory* by Giovanni Dosi *et al.* (1988), and *Exploring the Black Box* (1994) by Nathan Rosenberg.[23] The style of all these works is less mathematically rigorous, less enamored of precise results, less inclined to thought experiments employing logical deduction than we are accustomed to from reading mainstream economic literature. But they more than make up for that by their continuous reference to real-world issues and their continuous attention to empirical evidence to validate their findings.

Notes

This chapter is an extended version of my "Ugly currents in modern economics," *Policy Options*, 17 (7), 1997, 2–5. I am indebted to Roger Backhouse, David de Meza, Denis O'Brien, and Ruth Towse for helpful comments.

1. Earlier books along similar lines were Bell and Kristol (1994) and Wiles and Routh (1984).
2. One of the best is still the thirty-year-old indictment by Leontief (1971) and Morgan (1988). For a really cynical indictment, however, it is hard to beat an outsider's view, in the case of a philosopher of science: "Much of the mystery surrounding the actual development of economic theory – its shifts in formalism, its insulation from empirical assessment, its interest in proving purely abstract possibilities, its unchanged character over a period of centuries, the controversies about its cognitive status – can be comprehended and properly appreciated if we give up the notion that economics any longer has the claims or makes the claims of an empirical science of human behavior" (Rosenberg 1983, 298).
3. Strictly speaking, the rot goes back to Hicks (1939) and even Robinson (1933), but it is not my purpose here to trace the disease to its origins.
4. But as Donald Walker (1997) has shown, even Walras gradually shifted the focus of this great treatise away from the stability problem to the existence question.
5. Actually, it is acknowledged in some textbooks and simply ignored in others; Varian (1990) and Myles (1995), for example, do not even mention it.
6. I have explained all this in detail in Blaug (1997, chapter 6). The reader must forgive this blatant piece of self-advertizing as a typical example of an author attempting to increase his market share.
7. I am only echoing what has been said so much better by Robert Clower (1995a, 1995b).
8. See Howitt (1997) for the crippling influence of general equilibrium theory on the development of Keynesian economics.
9. As Ariel Rubinstein (1990, ix) has said: "Many economists describe the fifties as the era of general equilibrium, the sixties as the era of growth and the seventies as the era of economics of information. The eighties are the years in which economics has been revolutionised by game theory."

10. Even Rubinstein (1995), in a tribute to John Nash, denies that the Nash bargaining solution, the standard game-theoretic tool in modeling noncooperative interactions among agents, is a good predictor of bargaining in real markets. And he adds insult to injury by claiming that all economists employing game theory know this perfectly well.

11. A comparison between an old-style text like Scherer and Ross (1990) and a new-style text like Tirole (1988) says it all; there is nothing of substance in the latter that is not also in the former and indeed there is much less substance in the latter than in the former. For a similar judgment from the horse's mouth, see Fisher (1989).

12. As Robert Solow (1992) has trenchantly remarked: "If the goal of growth theory is the elaboration of a complete preferred model ready for formal econometric application to observed time series, as many economists seem to believe, then the new growth theory falls well short. One is struck by the proliferation of special assumptions about technology, about the nature of research activity, about the formation and use of human capital, about market structure, about family structure, and about intertemporal preferences. Most of these particular assumptions have been chosen for convenience, because they make difficult analytic problems more transparent. There is no reason to assume that they are descriptively valid, or that their implications have significant robustness against equally plausible variations in assumptions. See also Ryan and Mullineux (1997).

13. These difficulties of publication are clearly greater in the USA than in Europe, where economists value participation in local and national affairs almost as much as academic advance based on journal publications; see Frey and Eichenberger (1993).

14. See two dozen writers in *Pluralism in Economics: New Perspectives in History and Methodology*, edited by Andrea Salanti and Ernesto Screpanti (1997), and Roger Backhouse, *Truth and Progress in Economic Knowledge* (1997 chapters 3 and 4) for a hard-hitting critique of postmodernism in economics.

15. See my criticism of McCloskey in Blaug (1992, xvii–xx), which McCloskey (1994, chapter 20) answered in *Knowledge and Persuasion in Economics*.

16. For a perceptive beginning of an analysis of the power structure in the economics profession, see Tarascio (1997, 8–11)

17. See Blaug (1992, 4–10) for an explanation of all this gobbledygook.

18. For further discussion of the symmetry thesis, see Blaug (1992, 5–10).

19. In particular. Bhaskar himself, in *The Possibility of Naturalism* (1979, 57–8, 158–169). He extols "theories which are explanatory but non-predictive (such as Darwin's, Marx's or Freud's)" (1979, 207) but never addresses the question of how we know that an explanatory theory is true if prediction even of a statistical kind is ruled out.

20. I owe this distinction to Screpanti (1997, 289ff.).

21. Boylan and Gorman (1995) proclaim themselves "causal holists" and utterly reject Lawson's "critical realism," but after all the dust of philosophical labeling has settled, they clearly come down on the side of "scientific realism."

22. Kaldor (1972, 1237–1255 and 1985). This is apart from the consideration that many of the "stylized facts" that Kaldor struggled to explain in the 1950s and 1960s with

the aid of his steady-state growth theory turned out not to be facts at all (see Blaug 1998, 77–80).
23. See Hodgson (1983, 1985); Rutherford (1994); and Vromen (1995).

References

Akerlof, George (1970). The market for "lemons," quality uncertainty and the market mechanism, *Quarterly Journal of Economics,* 84, 488–500

Arrow, Kenneth J. and Gerard Debreu (1954). Competing technologies, increasing returns, and lock-in by historical events, *Economics Journal,* 99, 78–96

Backhouse, Roger (1997). *Truth and Progress in Economics Knowledge.* Cheltenham: Edward Elgar

Bell, Daniel and Irving Kristol (1994). *Crisis in Economic Theory.* New York: Basic Books

Bhaskar, Roy (1978). *A Realist Theory of Science.* Brighton: Harvester Press
  (1979). *The Possibility of Naturalism.* Brighton: Harvester Press

Blaug, Mark (1989). Nicholas Kaldor, 1908–86, in David Greenaway and John R. Presley (eds.), *Pioneers of Modern Economics in Britain.* London: Macmillan, 77–80
  (1992). *Methodology of Economics,* 2nd edn. Cambridge: Cambridge University Press, 201–204
  (1995). Afterword, in Neil De Marchi and Mark Blaug, *Appraising Economic Theories.* Cheltenham: Edward Elgar, 509
  (1997). Competition as an end-state and competition as a process, in Mark Blaug, *Not Only an Economist: Recent Essays.* Cheltenham: Edward Elgar, chapter 6

Blaug, Ricardo (1994). Habermas's treatment for relativism, *Politics,* 14(2), 51–57

Boylan, Terence A. and Peter F. O'Gorman (1995). *Beyond Rhetoric and Realism in Economics.* London: Routledge

Cassidy, John (1996). The decline of economics, *The New Yorker,* December 2, 42–49

Clower, Robert (1995a). Axiomatics in economics, *Southern Economic Journal,* 62(2), 307–319
  (1995b). Economics as an inductive science, in Robert Clower, *Economic Doctrine and Method: Selected Papers of R. W. Clower.* Cheltenham: Edward Elgar.

Coase, Ronald (1993a). The institutional structure of production, *American Economic Review,* 82, 229–234
  (1993b). The institutional structure of production, in Oliver E. Williamson and Sidney E. Winter (eds.), *The Native of the Firm: Origins, Evolution, and Development.* Oxford: Oxford University Press, 227–235

Commission on Graduate Education (1991). Report of the Commission on Graduate Education in Economics, *The Journal of Economic Literature,* 29, 1035–1087

Cross, Rodney, (ed.), (1995). *The Natural Rate of Unemployment: Reflections on 25 years of the Hypothesis.* Cambridge: Cambridge University Press, chapters 3, 5

Darnell, Adrian C. (1997). Imprecise tests and imprecise hypotheses, *Scottish Journal of Political Economy,* 44(3), 247–268

Debreu, Gerard (1959). *Theory of Value.*

Dosi, Giovanni, Chris Freeman *et al.* (1998). *Technical Change and Economic Theory.* New York: Columbia University Press

Eichner Andrew S. (ed.) (1983). *Why Economics is Not Yet a Science?* London: Macmillan, 90–125, 205–241

Fisher, Frank M. (1989). Games economists play: a noncooperative view, *Rand Journal of Economics*, 20(1), 113–124

Frey, Bruno S. and Raymond Eichenberger (1993). American and European economics and economists, *Journal of Economic Perspectives*, 7(4), 185–193

Gibbons, Richard (1997). An introduction to applicable game theory, *Journal of Economic Perspectives*, 11(1), 127–149

Habermas, Jurgen (1990). *The Philosophical Discourse of Modernity.* London: Polity Press

(1992). *Moral Consciousness and Communicative Action.* London: Polity Press

Hausman, Daniel (1997). Theory appraisal in neoclassical economics, *Journal of Economic Methodology*, 4(2), 289–296

Heilbroner, Robert and William Milberg (1996). *The Crisis of Vision in Modern Economic Thought.* Cambridge: Cambridge University Press

Hey, John (1997). The Economic Journal. Report of the Managing Editor, *Royal Economic Society Newsletter*, January, 3–5

Hicks, John (1939). *Value and Capital.* Oxford: Clarendon Press

Hodgson, Geoffrey M. (1983). *Economics and Evolution. Bringing Life Back Into Economics.* London: Polity Press

(1985). *Economics and Institutions. A Manifesto for a Modern Institutional Economics.* London: Polity Press

Hoover, Kevin D. (1995). Facts and artifacts: calibration and the empirical assessment of real-business-cycle models, *Oxford Economics Papers*, 47(1), 24–44

Howitt, Peter (1997). Expectations and uncertainty in contemporary Keynesian models, in G.C. Harcourt and P.A. Riach (eds.), *A "Second Edition" of the General Theory*, 1. London: Routledge, 239–240

Kaldor, Nicholas (1972). The irrelevence of equilibrium economics, *Economic Journal*, 82(4), 1237–1255

(1985). *Economics without Equilibrium.* Cardiff: University College Cardiff Press

Kanth, Rajani (1996). *Against Economics.* Aldershot: AshGate Publishing

Klamer, Arjo and David Colander (1987). The making of an economist, *Journal of Economic Perspectives*, 1(2), 95–111

Klamer, Arjo and David Colander (1990). *The Making of an Economist.* Boulder, CO: Westview Press

Kurz, Heinz and Neri Salvadori (1997). On critics and protective belts, in Salanti, Andrea and Evnesto Screpanti (eds.), *Pluralism in Economics: New Perspectives in History and Methodology.* Cheltenham: Edward Elgar, 232–259

Lawson, Tony (1997). *Economics and Reality*, London Routledge, 204, 288–289

Leontief, Wassily (1971). Theoretical assumptions and nonobserved facts, *American Economic Review*, 6(1), 1–7

Lipsey, Richard G. (1979). Can the market economy survive?, in Richard G. Lipsey, *Microeconomics, Growth and Political Economy: Essays by Richard G. Lipsey*, I. Cheltenham: Edward Elgar, 367–401

Lucas, Robert E., Jr. and Thomas Sargent (1981). *Rational Expectations and Econometric Practice.* Minneapolis: Minnesota Press.

McCloskey, D.N. (1986). *The Rhetoric of Economics.* Madison, WI: University of Wisconsin Press (2nd edn., 1998)

(1994). *Knowledge and Persuasion in Economics.* Cambridge: Cambridge University Press

Mäki, Uskali (1995). Diagnosing McCloskey, *The Journal of Economic Literature*, 33, 1300–1318

Malinvaud, Edmond (1997). The proper role of theory, in P.A.G. van Bergeijk *et al.* (eds.), *Economic Science and Practice.* Cheltenham, Edward Elgar, 149–165

Morgan, Thomas (1988). Theory versus empiricism in academic economics: update and comparison, *Journal of Economic Perspectives*, 2(4), 159–164

Murrell, Peter (1991). Can neoclassical economics underpin the reform of centrally planned economies?, *Journal of Economic Perspectives*, 5(4), 59–76

Myles, Gareth D. (1995). *Public Economics.* Cambridge: Cambridge University Press

Nelson, Richard R. and Sidney Winter (1982). *An Evolutionary Theory of Economic Change.* Boston: Harvard University Press

Omerod, Paul (1994). *The Death of Economics.* London: Faber.

Pack, Hal (1994). Endogenous growth theory: intellectual appeal and empirical short-comings, *Journal of Economic Perspectives*, 9(1), 55–72

Perelman, Michael (1996). *The End of Economics.* London: Routledge

Prescott, Edward and Finn E. Kydland (1982). Time-to-build and aggregate fluctuations, *Econometrica*, 50, 138–157

Robinson, Joan (1933). *The Economics of Imperfect Competition.* London: Macmillan (1956). *The Accumulation of Capital.* London: Macmillan.

Rosen, Sherwin (1997). Austrian and neoclassical economics: any gains from trade?, *Journal of Economic Perspectives*, 11(4), 139–152

Rosenberg, Alexander (1983). If economics isn't science, what is it?, *Philosophical Forum*, 14: 296–314.

Rosenberg, Nathan (1994). *Exploring the Black Box.*

Rubinstein, Ariel (1990). *Game Theory in Economics.* Cheltenham: Edward Elgar, ix (1995). John Nash: the master of economic modelling, *Scandinavian Journal of Economics,* 97(1), 9–13

Rutherford, Mark (1994). *Institutions in Economics. The Old and the New Institutionalism.* Cambridge: Cambridge University Press

Ryan, Charles and Andrew Mullineux (1997). The ups and downs of modern business cycle theory, in Brian Snowdon and Howard Vane, *Reflections on the Development of Modern Macroeconomics.* Cheltenham: Edward Elgar, 141–147

Salanti, Andrea and Ernesto Screpanti (eds.) (1997). *Pluralism in Economics: New Perspectives in History and Methodology.* Cheltenham: Edward Elgar

Scherer, F. Mark and David Ross (1990). *Industrial Market Structure and Economic Performance*, 3rd edn. Boston: Houghton Mifflin

Schumpeter, Joseph A. (1942). *Capitalism, Socialism and Democracy*, 2nd edn. New York: Harper, 106–110.

Screpanti, Ernesto (1997). Afterword: can methodological pluralism be a methodological canon?, in Andrea Salanti and Ernesto Screpanti (eds.), *Pluralism in Economics: New Perspectives in History and Methodology*. Cheltenham: Edward Elgar

Shepherd, George B. (1995). *Rejected. Leading Economists Ponder the Publication Process*. Boston: Thomas Horton & Daughters, 53–54

Simon, Herbert A. (1976). From substantive to procedural rationality, in Spiro Latsis (ed.), *Methodological Appraisal in Economics*. Cambridge: Cambridge University Press.

Solow, Robert (1992). Growth theory, in David Greenaway *et al.* (eds.), *Companion to Contemporary Economic Thought*. London: Routledge, 393–415

(1997). How did economics get that way and what way did it get?, *Daedalus*, 126, 39–58

Summers, Lawrence H. (1991). The scientific illusion in empirical macroeconomics, *Scandinavian Journal of Economics*, 93(2), 129–148

Tarascio, Vincent (1997). The problem of knowledge in economics, *Southern Economic Journal*, 64(1), 8–11

Tirole, Jan (1988). *The Theory of Industrial Organization*. Boston: MIT Press

Varian, Hal R. (1990). *Intermediate Microeconomics. A Modern Approach*, 2nd edn. New York: W.W. Norton

Vromen, Jack (1995). *Economic Evolution. An Enquiry into the Foundations of the (New) Institutional Economics*. London: Routledge

Wade Hands, D. (1997). Empirical realism as meta-method: Tony Lawson and neoclassical economics, *Ekonomia*, 1(2), 39–53

Walker, Donald (1997). *Advances in General Equilibrium Theory*. Cheltenham: Edward Elgar

Wiles, Peter and Guy Routh (1984). *Economics in Disarray*. Oxford: Basil Blackwell

3   Modern economics and its critics

Partha Dasgupta

1   Prologue

Most economists I know have little time for the philosophy of economics as an intellectual discipline. They have even less patience with economic methodology. They prefer instead to *do* economics. If they are involved in serious methodological discussion at all, it is during the process of conducting economics research or preparing their findings for publication. They do so in the latter stage, for example, and they do so often unashamedly, when commenting on the weaknesses of previous work before saying why they feel their own work is superior.

There is much to be said for this habit. Far and away the most effective criticisms of current-practice economics that I have read have come from those who themselves have been engaged in research in economics, rather than in its philosophy or, more narrowly, in its methodology. Indeed, I know of no contemporary practicing economist whose investigations have been aided by the writings of professional methodologists.

Why has this been so? One reason may be that people who do economics usually know more about the strengths and weaknesses of current-practice economics than those who have neither acquired nor sifted data, nor experimented with alternative theoretical constructions so as to judge which construction is likely to improve upon that which has been explored and which is unlikely to do so. It would have been of no moment, for example, to tell those econometricians in the 1950s who developed the linear-expenditure system for studying consumer behavior in the UK that it is a restrictive system: they already knew it, *but* nevertheless had good reasons for adopting it.

This said, I think there is a wider reason, having probably to do with the fact that economic philosophers and methodologists find it difficult to keep abreast of the professional literature in economics. For example, it is a commonplace criticism of modern economics voiced by those who are uncomfortable with it that the subject is becoming increasingly mathematical, indeed, that the gap between economic models and "reality" is ever-increasing. My own experience has been quite otherwise. When I was a graduate student in the mid-1960s, economics appeared far more compartmentalized into the "theory" and "applied" categories than it is today. The cutting edge of theory then consisted of problems of a seemingly esoteric and transparently mathematical kind.[1] In saying this I don't imply criticism. Those investigations yielded technical tools. Training in the use of such tools enabled young economists to work on problems of the "applied–theoretic" kind the analysis of which dominate leading economics journals today.

If my reading of the shift in economics research over the past quarter-century or so is even approximately correct, it should be a puzzle that modern economics has recently come under attack – often virulent attack – from both without and within the profession for its lack of contact with "reality."[2] External attack on current-practice economics is not new; it goes back at least to the first half of the nineteenth century, when romantics bemoaned the "dismal science." So far as I know, though, it is internal attack that is new. Moreover, the internal attacks I allude to are not of a sort reflected in such professional disputes as, for example, the one that dominated macroeconomics during the 1980s over the worth of Real Business Cycle theories, or the famous nineteenth-century controversy between David Ricardo and Thomas Malthus on the Corn Laws. In a professional dispute protagonists speak a common language and share something like an understanding of what constitutes evidence and an argument. Differences frequently occur among experts because the evidence is often at best translucent: several interpretations are simultaneously possible. Such disputes are the stuff of any productive research community and economics is no exception. If the disputes are on occasion shrill, it is because they involve policy prescriptions and personal egos. However, I know of no evidence which suggests that disputes among modern economists are more pronounced than they are among experts in such other overarching disciplines as biology, history, and physics.[3]

The internal attacks I will be concerned with in this chapter are something else. They appear to be part of a lineage that earlier consisted of commentaries and presidential addresses by elderly economists disaffected with the direction in which economics research had been moving since the end of the Second World War.[4] The lineage's current manifestation, however, often operates at an Olympian height of generality, it usually works round what modern economists *say* in their "literary" moments, rather than what they actually *do* in their technical work, it frequently advocates the need for a "paradigm shift," and it is almost always so scholarly as to lack focus. To an unreconstructed practicing economist like myself, reading such attacks proves to be puzzling and frustrating; indeed, on occasion it feels rather like grasping at air.

My fellow economists choose simply to ignore these writings. Understandably, they think they have better things to do. Some have told me I waste my time worrying about such attacks. But worry I do, at least in part because of a possibility that some of the critiques may indeed prove helpful in our work. So it has seemed to me that the critiques ought to be met, by someone who is engaged in research in modern economics and so could be expected to know something of it.

But there is a wider, social reason for my worrying about the critics. Criticism accumulates if it is not answered, or if it is generally not understood that it has been answered. Cumulative criticism can erode the confidence the lay public should have that such a large enterprise as modern, and largely academic, economics does have in place internal checks and balances, incentives for constructive work, and the many other instruments and devices that make for a progressive republic of social science. We economists not only conduct research, we also teach the subject and produce the next generation of economists and a fraction of policy-makers and shapers of opinion of the future. A good deal of the teaching and research that is undertaken in economics, at least in Europe and in the poor countries of the world, is supported by the taxed public. If, as I believe is the case, economics (especially microeconomics) has for quite some while been enjoying a supremely productive phase, during which any number of social phenomena that earlier made no obvious economic sense have come within its orbit, the public should know about it. The matter is made urgent by the fact that critics of modern economics enjoy a far wider readership than does the modern economist. They appear regularly in literary magazines and are, superficially at least, an easy read. Moreover, their writings are polemical and offer the occasion for controversy. It is also not uncommon for them to assume the role of a maverick, battling against a reactionary establishment. All this makes them particularly attractive to the literary editor.

Some time ago I was asked by a literary magazine to review a pair of books by Professor Robert Heilbroner, a distinguished historian of economic ideas and a critic of the character of modern economics.[5] Given Heilbroner's formidable scholastic reputation, I tried hard to understand his approach to economics research. It transpired that I tried so hard that I was slower to read the two books that had been sent to me than he was at writing two further books that were subsequently sent to me.[6] Fortunately, there is unity in Professor Heilbroner's intellectual explorations. So his four books offered me an opportunity to understand one major strand in the current criticism of modern economics. As I understand it now, this strand deplores the abandonment by modern economists of what is in effect an amalgam of the intellectual agenda of classical political economists and that of John Maynard Keynes.

I felt I wanted to write not so much a review as a methodological essay, one that would weave together in a narrative form not only why "political economy" in the late eighteenth-to-mid-nineteenth-century sense holds no attractions for the modern economist, but would also give the reader an idea of how very much farther economics has progressed in recent years than its critics realize. The Heilbroner works offer an excellent opportunity to do so because at least two of the books I will be discussing here are not critiques at all; they involve quite different intellectual explorations.

But of course, I wanted also to respond to the specific criticisms Heilbroner makes of modern economics. The way I have done so is to use examples Heilbroner relies upon to give expression to his frustration as a springboard for my own illustrations. Needless to say, many of the examples I have chosen for this purpose are from those fields of study with which I am most familiar. For both these reasons, there is a selection bias. As this was unavoidable, I offer no apology for it.

The essay I consequently wrote was too long to be a review. But shortening it significantly would have compromised the intellectual unity in Heilbroner's critique. For some time the essay circulated among colleagues and I had no plans for publishing it. So I am particularly grateful to Uskali Mäki for asking me to submit it for the present collection. The chapter should be seen as a response to the works of a leading critic within the profession. In a sequel I hope to respond to critics without. Some of the latter whom I have already read take quite a different stand from the one adopted by Professor Heilbroner. A few deplore the mathematical treatment of human concerns, while others relish the prospect of a "paradigm shift" without worrying if it would involve more, or less, mathematical material. I am discovering that critics of modern economics come with differing agenda. They don't share a common dislike for modern economics; rather, what they share in common is dislike for it.

2   Economics and its history

Not so long ago, economics was taught in tandem with the history of economic ideas. So far as I am able to judge, even creative economists were versed in the canon. For example, at the University of Dhaka in the late 1930s, my father, Amiya Dasgupta, lectured on both advanced economic theory and the history of economic thought. In later life he often told me he wouldn't have known how to proceed on one front without keeping a look-out on the other. In this he had been influenced by his teacher, Lionel Robbins, whose legendary undergraduate lectures and Faculty seminar at the London School of Economics displayed a similar mix. Robbins in turn had been a student of Edwin Cannan, whose teaching had the same flavor, or so I am told. Nicholas Kaldor's lectures at Cambridge on value, distribution, and growth, which I attended as a student in the mid-1960s, made more than a passing reference to the great nineteenth-century economist, David Ricardo. Although people more knowledgeable than I maintain that Kaldor's Ricardo was more Kaldor than Ricardo, the point remains that Kaldor at least *tried* to link his thoughts to those of a past Master.

Things are different today. You can emerge from your graduate studies in economics without having read any of the classics, or indeed, without having anything other than a vague notion of what the great thinkers of the past had written. The modern economist doesn't even try to legitimize her inquiry by linking it to questions addressed in the canon; she typically begins her article by referring to something in the literature a few months old. She reads Ricardo no more than the contemporary physicist reads James Clerk Maxwell. What today's economics student gets of the classics are those bits that have survived the textbook treatment, dressed in modern garb. The history of economic ideas has not died; it has simply metamorphosed into a specialized field. It is taught, but it is not compulsory for students, at least not in the major economics departments. And just as most working economists today know little of the ideas that have shaped their subject, your average historian of economic thought understands little of what is currently going on in economics, and why. The separation is as complete as can be.

It may seem obvious that this is an altogether bad state of affairs; and yet, on reflection, it is not clear that it is so. To be sure, the practicing economist has lost something valuable by the separation of economic analysis from its history, but the loss, it seems to me, is one of culture, not fecundity. Maybe the research economist would have greater self-knowledge if she were versed in the history of her own discipline. But she would also likely be more self-conscious, and this could prove inhibiting. Moreover, as time is scarce, it is even possible that today's economics student would be better equipped to study live problems if she were to read a good graduate text on, say, ecology, than *Das Kapital*. In order to do creative work, there is a further advantage in not being knowledgeable about the intellectual concerns and struggles of bygone eras: there would be a lower risk that the past was setting the present's research agenda.

Almost fifty years ago, in a charming book, *The Worldly Philosophers* (1953), Robert Heilbroner offered an account of economics to both students and the lay public by inviting them to view the development of the subject in terms of the lives, times, and ideas of great economic thinkers. Heilbroner's classic reads as the work of a scholarly patrician, a rare quality in so technocratic a group as modern economists. The book also displays the author's love for the subject's past Masters and his admiration for what it is capable of achieving when practiced at its loftiest scales. Now he has produced *Teachings from the Worldly Philosophy* (1996) which contains passages from the writings of the Masters (the line stretches from the Bible and Aristotle to Keynes and Joseph Schumpeter) on specific themes. These are accompanied by Heilbroner's commentaries, designed to help the reader to understand the motivations of the Masters and to get her to view the links that form a connection between intellectual struggles across time.

As one would expect from *The Worldly Philosophers*, this is a work of erudition. Admittedly, it is frustrating to be given only tiny fragments of the writings of authors who often wrote and wrote and wrote, but it will prove useful to students if read as a companion to the earlier book. It may even encourage them to read a few of the Masters in the original. I have never had the pleasure of meeting Professor Heilbroner, who is the Norman Thomas Professor of Economics, Emeritus, at the New School of Social Research in New York City, but having read him extensively in preparation for this chapter, I am convinced he communes daily with the authors of the canon. In fact, I would go further: I think he speaks to Adam Smith in the morning, Karl Marx at noon, John Maynard Keynes in the evening, and so on. The trouble is, he has little time left over to study modern economics. This poses a number of problems for each of his offerings under discussion here. In *Teachings from the Worldly Philosophy*, however, there is an immediate problem facing the reader: the scribe often leaves the Masters' musings hanging in the air, having offered no clue as to their current status.

Take, as an example, the long struggle (literally, across centuries, as Heilbroner tells it) economists faced in trying to determine the *exchange value* of a commodity, such as a table. Here is Marx's famous solution (quoted in 1996, 164): "Along with the useful qualities of the products themselves, we put out of sight both the useful character of the various kinds of labor embodied in them, and the concrete forms of that labor; there is nothing left but what is common to them all; all are reduced to one and the same sort of labor, human labor in the abstract."

The language is sufficiently opaque for it to have required several generations of scholars to decipher the construct which embodies this thought. Today we are able to offer a precise formulation of this part of Marx's schemata and, if required, also expose its empirical irrelevance; for modern economic analysis has shown that Marx's account is not coherent in the world we know.[7] But reading Heilbroner, the unwary reader would not know this. She would think either that the problem Marx wrestled with is alive and kicking (i.e. his claim is still in need of confirmation) or that Marx was right in being confident he had the correct answer to the question he had posed.[8] Admittedly, this is merely an omission on Heilbroner's part, and perhaps I shouldn't make a thing of it. Nevertheless, it is a symptom of the pitfalls facing someone who studies the history of economic thought in the manner in which Heilbroner writes it.

As it happens, they are likely to face further pitfalls. Part of my intention in this chapter is to explore them.

3   The character of modern economics

Economics, as a distinct body of inquiry, emerged from moral philosophy, but it is quite a different species. If, to the moral philosopher, Aristotle is alive, it is because he asked questions that continue to be in need of response. Moreover, the tools at the disposal of the modern moral philosopher are not so different from those that Aristotle wielded. What he regarded as an argument is, often enough, not far removed from what the moral philosopher today regards as an argument. That is why the subject can be, and most often is, taught in the form of a running dialogue with past Masters.

Economics is not like that. In a justly famous discourse on economics, Robbins identified it as the science that studies human behavior as a relationship between ends and scarce means which have alternative uses.[9] Now, even although this identifies the terrain of economics, it does not tell us where we should be within it, or how we should study it. Robbins' definition gives us no more clue to what an economist should be investigating than a definition which says that physics is an inquiry into the laws that govern the physical world would help a physicist to identify what he should be investigating. Economics cannot be identified by the questions it entertains, because the questions themselves change with changing circumstances.[10] The institutions of our own era are substantially different from those prevailing at the time *The Wealth of Nations* (1776) was published. That people use the same term, *capitalism*, to refer to the economic systems in England of both 1776 and 1976 doesn't mean it is analytically illuminating to do so. The physicist, Steven Weinberg, once remarked that when you have "seen" one electron, you have seen them all. In contrast, the objects of study in economics are not immutable, in Weinberg's sense. When you have observed one transaction, you have not observed them all. More tellingly, when you have met one human being, you have by no means met them all.

It is a recognition of the commonality of the human experience, on the one hand, and the separateness of every human being and the particularity of the circumstances she faces, on the other, that gives economics its special flavor and is a reason why it is an awesomely difficult subject. Each generation of economists accommodates these opposing pulls, at least, to a certain extent, in the light of the questions to which it seeks answers. Even the way a question is framed often reveals the kind of accommodation being reached. This is not relativism. In the absence of firm guidance from either psychology or sociology, the hapless economist is forced to regard the accommodation, initially, as a matter of choice, and to evaluate it repeatedly on the basis of empirical evidence on the implications of the theory. If modern economics possesses a distinctive *character*, it is that it treats human beings with respect (a matter to which I will return). This it does by trying to illuminate the various pathways through which millions of decisions made by individual human beings can give rise to emergent features of communities and societies. Since individual decisions are, in turn, influenced by these emergent features (e.g. rate of inflation, productivity gains, level of national income, prices, cultural values, and social norms), there is mutual feedback over time. If the period being studied is short, one can simplify by taking some of the emergent features (e.g. cultural values and norms) as given, and thereby, not subject them to analysis. But if the period is long, we are led to study dynamic processes with mutual feedback between millions of micro decisions and the emergent (macro) features. This character of modern economics is not, of course, new; but it has never been espoused with such abandon as it is today and so, when the modern economist says she seeks a *microfoundation* for some observation or the other, it is not an admission on her part, it is an assertion.

This motivation has meant that a good deal of economics is conducted on a piecemeal, small-scale basis. A typical article may seek to explain why there are exclusionary contracts between purchasers and incumbent firms in some industries and not in others, or it may ask if richer people spend a greater proportion of their income on environmental amenities; it may try to discover why there are strikes, or why workers are paid on a piece rate in some lines of work in some parts of the world and not in others, or why some industries are vertically integrated while others are not, or whether welfare payments in cash are a more effective form of transfer than those in kind; it may try to determine if personal saving and corporate investment are responsive to interest rates, or if a minimum wage legislation would reduce employment in a particular industry, or whether mother's education is a determinant of fertility in rural regions of poor countries, and, if so, why; and so forth. These questions are hard enough, and so, most economists would shift uncomfortably in their chairs if asked to pronounce on the laws of motion of capitalism, or to speculate on the future of the multinational firm. It is not so much that grand themes have disappeared (this too is something I will come to later), it is that "small," sharp questions dominate economics journals today.

Why? One reason is that this enterprise has proved to be immensely more illuminating than the search for answers to what appear to be grand questions, but are in fact badly posed questions, or questions to which currently no useful answer can be given, or there is no way of judging if answers to them are true or false. Nevertheless, to someone steeped in the canon, such a research agenda could well appear small-time, possibly irrelevant, perhaps not worth bothering about. While something of this attitude pervades all of Professor Heilbroner's writings under review, it is displayed most vividly in two of them, *Visions of the Future: The Distant Past, Yesterday, Today, Tomorrow* (1995) and *21st Century Capitalism* (1993).

4   The nature of economic life: past and present

The books address giant themes, concerned as they are with the nature of economic life in the past and present, and its prospects for the future. In *Visions of the Future*, both the brevity and the canvas beggar the imagination: in precisely

124 pages, we are taken through 150,000 years of the human enterprise. Heilbroner's *Distant Past* is a stretch that began 150,000 years ago and ended at the beginning of the eighteenth century, during which, he says, nothing much happened: "the tools and techniques of production remained the same from one generation to the next . . . economic life, insofar as it was distinguishable from social life in general, was a force for stasis, not for change" (1995, 8). In contrast, hope and progress were the features of *Yesterday*, a 250-year period that ended sometime in the second half of the twentieth century. It was a period when (1995, 11), "the future . . . enters the human consciousness as a great beckoning prospect . . . [it] denotes an era in which we look to the future with confidence, because men and women believe that forces will be working there for their betterment, both as individuals and as a collectivity." *Today*, in contrast, "is marked by a new degree of pessimism" (1995, 15), where "science, economics, mass political movements. . . appear as potentially or even actively malign, as well as benign; both as threatening and supportive" (1995, 13). In short (1995, 69): "Resignation sums up the Distant Past's vision of the future; hopefulness was that of Yesterday; and apprehension is the dominant mood of Today."

Well, I know very little about the *Distant Past* (although I am reliably informed that during that stretch of time, a period characterized by "stasis," animals got domesticated, agricultural societies emerged, cities were established, writing was constructed, and Athens invented democracy), but the contrast Heilbroner draws between *Yesterday* and *Today*, even when confined to the Occident, does not ring true to me. In *The Rhetoric of Reaction* (1991), Albert Hirschman showed that for each of the great social revolutions that have taken place in Western Europe during the past three centuries and more (that of civil liberties in the eighteenth century, political liberties in the nineteenth, and socio-economic liberties in the twentieth), there were doubters, who not only doubted, but wielded three separate counterarguments, based on *perversity* ("your proposal, if implemented, will bring forth a response from society that yields the exact opposite of what you intend"), *futility* ("society will react to nullify the movement you are espousing, so why espouse it?") and *jeopardy* ("your proposal is good, but you must appreciate that implementing it would ruin that other social good you value highly"). Now these critics were not a random assortment of society's malcontents; they included such thinkers as Edmund Burke, Alexis de Tocqueville, Thomas Carlyle, John Ruskin, and Vilfredo Pareto. And they were deeply worried about the changes taking place round them. Nor is the "anti-scientific" element a feature unique to Heilbroner's *Today*. William Morris, like Carlyle and Ruskin, reacted against the industrial revolution and the age of mechanization, but added to it "the Romantic prejudice that a mechanical civilization had been created by a mechanical science, and that science was attempting to substitute for art."[11]

I cannot imagine how anyone could see wisdom in trying to carve three epochs out of a 150,000-year stretch, the shortest of which, a mere forty-to-fifty-year spell, being one to which they themselves belong. Moreover, Heilbroner offers no more than a few pages of assertions in support of his thesis. Thus, in providing evidence that apprehension is the dominant mood of *Today*, we are given not much more than a sentence (pp. 69–70) on "the totally unforeseen outburst of bloodthirsty violence in what used to be called Yugoslavia, . . . the descent into desperation of Soviet society, following the dissolution of its empire; the maelstrom of Central Africa; the rise of skinheads in Germany and neo-fascist movement in Italy; and not least the breakdown of civil society at home, both within and, to a lesser extent, outside the boundaries of the inner city." After this, as evidence of *Today*'s loss of confidence in science, the reader would duly expect references to the Chernobyl disaster and the late Paul Feyerabend's fatuous characterization of scientific activity, to wit, *anything goes*.[12] She will not be disappointed: they appear on pp. 73 and 76, respectively.

5   Are we especially apprehensive today?

Any stretch of time, and I mean *any* stretch of time, could be identified as a period when apprehension was the prevailing mood if you were to point your finger only at disasters and the hand-wringing of intellectuals. I know of no evidence that Heilbroner's anxiety is shared, for example, by the rising middle classes in Asia, or by the bulk of the voting public in Western Europe. To be sure, there are experts who argue that we *should* be apprehensive today; for example, about the adverse links between environmental stress and large-scale poverty in the South, and about the ecological damage that is associated with the unprecedented levels of consumption of material goods in the Occident and the East.[13] But they lament that their message on, say, global warming is *not* getting across, that people in democratic societies are *not* apprehensive enough to force their governments to tackle the problems in a coordinated manner; they have not concluded that the reason not much is being done is that we are paralyzed through despondency about the possibilities of collective action. Work by economists, such as Scott Barrett, Carlo Carraro, Michael Hoel, Karl-Göran Mäler, and Domenico Siniscalco, on the theory and practice of international negotiations on the global commons, appears to support the view that failure to achieve collective action has not been due to pessimism. Barrett, for example, notes that, while little has been achieved in the case of carbon emissions or biodiversity protection, international negotiations over the protection of the ozone layer have been remarkably successful (nearly all countries have cooperated in creating a regime in which the emission of chlorofluorocarbons will soon be reduced to nil). From this and other evidence he infers that the costs of reducing both carbon emissions and biodiversity destruction are, even today, *perceived* to be much greater than the benefits, especially when note is taken of the side-payments nations would have to make among one another and the changes in the institution of property rights that would be required if any such agreement were to be implemented.[14]

Then there is evidence of a different kind that *Today* is not marked by especial despondency about the value of political action. A remarkable development over the past twenty-five years or so has been the rise of local non-government organizations (NGOs), especially in poor countries. A great many have on their agenda the poorest of the poor, especially the women, children, and the old among them. Worldwide, NGOs today number over 20,000. Moreover, their ability, reach, and importance are such that, in order to be effective, international organizations increasingly act through them, and national governments are wary of ignoring them.[15] The past quarter-century has also been the period when women, in the Occident at least, acted upon and achieved success in realizing a number of measures designed to improve their life-chances. These happenings do not add up to Professor Heilbroner's *Today*.

6 Visions of tomorrow

What of *Tomorrow*? On this, *Visions of the Future* overlaps with *21st Century Capitalism*. In other respects, though, the two books are different, in that the latter is a discourse on the character of economic institutions under capitalism. The evolution of capitalist order in the West has been the subject of a large number of studies over the years, and it would be astonishing if anything really new could be said on it. Heilbroner does not astonish, but his narrative reflects his expertise and is interesting.[16] Economics, as a distinct body of inquiry, arose at about the time the Industrial Revolution began; so, the history of economic thought is intertwined with an important segment of the history of capitalism. Heilbroner exploits this fact by turning to past Masters of economics. He does not offer much quantitative data in support of the picture he wants to portray of capitalism; he relies in the main on what past Masters said of the institution. So while it may seem that Heilbroner is taking a historical view of economic life, he is not actually doing that: he is approaching economic history through the history of economic thought. This gives the reader a feel for how capitalism at a past date appeared to a Master writing at that date, but not much else. In other respects, though, the fare Heilbroner offers is standard: the central role of market signals (e.g. prices) in directing private production outlays and investment plans is noted; the (to me, questionable) notion of immanent change through the drive for capital, with the accompanying "feeling of self-propulsion along a rising gradient that constitutes the core idea of progress" (1995, 42), is stressed; the periodic tendencies under capitalism toward deficiencies in aggregate demand for goods and services are recounted; and it is followed by a discourse on the politics of capitalism, in particular, on the symbiotic relationship between Business and Government, reflected in the changing agenda of the private and public sectors of an economy.

Like those of the past Masters he surveys (1995, 121–129), Heilbroner's long-term prognosis on capitalism is gloomy. For he writes (1995, 130), "capitalism's uniqueness in history lies in its continuously self-generated change, but it is this very dynamism that is the system's chief enemy." He then adds to the past Masters' considerable list of problems inherent in a capitalist order the threat of ecological disaster; for he stresses that "the threat . . . is rooted in the inability of the market mechanism to resolve the global problem of pollution." At this point *21st Century Capitalism* merges with *Visions of the Future*. Heilbroner claims (1993, 140) that the problems of capitalism lie with the workings of the private sector, not of the public; and concludes that the prospects of twenty-first-century capitalist societies will depend on the success with which they can marshall and apply the forces of government to deal with such problems.

7   Societal ills and market failure: are they the same?

Coming as it does as the main conclusion of two books on the grandest of themes, this could appear bland to readers. But they should know it is also deeply misleading. It is one thing to say that an unaided market mechanism cannot be relied upon to ensure a sustainable pattern of use of, say, environmental services; it is another thing to say that the sole culprit behind a misuse of the environmental resource-base is the market mechanism. The first is a finding in modern economics;[17] but the second has been demonstrated, again by contemporary economists, to be false: different kinds of environmental degradation are traceable to different forms of institutional failure, they are not all due to market failure. For example, Hans Binswanger[18] has shown that, in Brazil, the exemption from taxation of virtually all agricultural income (allied to the fact that logging is regarded as proof of land occupancy) provided strong incentives to the rich to acquire forest lands and to then deforest them. This is not market failure, it is government failure. Binswanger has also argued that the subsidy the government has implicitly paid to the private sector has been so large that a reduction in deforestation is in *Brazil's* interests, not merely in the interest of the rest of the world. This has implications for international negotiations. The current consensus appears to be that, as a country, Brazil has much to lose from reducing the rate of deforestation she has been engaged in. If this were true, there would be a case for the rest of the world to subsidize her, as compensation for losses she would sustain if she were to restrain herself. But, as Binswanger's account suggests, it is not at all clear that the consensus is correct.

Then there are environmental problems whose cause can be traced to the fact that such micro institutions as the household can be dysfunctional. In rural communities of poor countries, for example, men typically have the bulk of the political voice. We should then expect public investment in, say, environmental regeneration to be guided by male preferences, not female needs. On matters of afforestation in the drylands, for instance, we should expect women to favor planting for fuelwood and men for fruit trees, because it is the women and children who collect fuelwood, while men control cash income (and fruit can be sold in the market). This explains why, even as the sources of fuelwood continue to recede, fruit trees are often planted. This too is not a case of market failure.[19]

That political instability (at the extreme, civil war) is a visible cause of environmental degradation is obvious. What may not be so obvious is that it is a hidden cause as well. As political instability creates uncertainty in property rights, people are reluctant to make the investments that are necessary for the protection and improvement of the environmental resource base: the expected returns are low. In a study comprising 120 countries, Robert Deacon has offered statistical evidence of a positive link between political instability and forest depletion.[20] This isn't evidence of market failure either.

8 Beyond the market–government dichotomy

The narrow, market–government dichotomy of society has little to commend it, but orthodox discussions of economic life cling to it. Someone wedded to the dichotomy would, understandably, want to jump into the arms of the state whenever market failure were observed, and Professor Heilbroner is not alone here. But people all over the world have explored a wide variety of resource-allocation mechanisms: society is usually cleverer than scholars of society. When they have needed to, and have been able to, people have developed what are often criss-crossing institutions, such as extended-family and kinship networks; civic, commercial, and religious associations; charities; production units; and various layers of what is known as government. Each serves functions the others are not so good at serving. They differ not only in terms of the emotional bonds that connect members, but also in regard to the information channels that serve them, the kinds of agreements that bind them, and the investment outlays and severence costs that help sustain them. Their elucidation, in particular our increased understanding of their strengths and weaknesses, has been the most compelling achievement of economics over the past twenty-five years or so.[21]

Related to the orthodox, market–government dichotomy is a rhetoric I have found curious. While discussing the symbiotic relationship between the private and public sectors under capitalism, Professor Heilbroner writes in *Visions of the Future* (1995, 78), that "business rushes to the support of government more from patriotism and possibly also profit, than in defense of political principles.

Perhaps one can sum it up by saying that business stands behind government in emergencies and government stands behind business between emergencies." Similarly, in his discussion of future scenarios in *21st Century Capitalism*, he refers (1993, 135) to, "the possibility that capitalism may attempt to assure its required expansion by using public investment to provide whatever transformational impetus is lacking in the private sector."

What is curious is the dehumanized viewpoint reflected here. Business, capitalism, and government are stripped of the people who comprise them. Reading passages such as these, one would not know that firms are owned and controlled by people; nor that, in representative democracies, all arms of government are manned by people who serve as agents of citizens; nor that someone can simultaneously be a citizen, a worker, and a shareholder, with potentially conflicting interests and motivations. To be sure, the control shareholders and citizens are able to exercise is often vastly limited. Not only do managements possess and acquire relevant information shareholders do not and cannot (resource-allocation failures owing to this are sometimes, somewhat inaccurately, called "adverse selection" among potential managements), they are also capable of doing things shareholders cannot observe (this is sometimes, again a little inaccurately, called "moral hazard" facing shareholders). Moreover, shareholders typically hold different beliefs; so their motivations differ. Even their assessment of the relative desirability of alternative investment policies would be expected to differ. But they can buy and sell, and this gives each shareholder some leeway. In a not dissimilar manner citizens, in a "principal–agent" relationship with politicians and civil servants, also face an agency problem. The character of liberal democracies is shaped by it. In the typical scenario, political competition among contending parties and performance-related compensation schemes for civil servants ease the agency problem facing citizens, but even this isn't an easy matter to prove.[22]

I said earlier that modern economics treats people with respect;[23] it does not regard them as mere dupes and foils of Business and Government. It sees people as having aspirations and goals that are, in part, influenced by the prevailing culture, a matter to which I will return below. But it is *particularly* concerned with the constraints people face in their ability both to be and to do, and it unravels the various pathways by which such constraints are shaped. Typically, they are shaped by the access people have to resources (material goods, skills, *and* information), but, and this is the point, the access itself is affected by the choices made. A major achievement of modern economics has been the elucidation of the many routes by which reasoned (and honorable) choices on the part of each person in society, be it a *capitalist society or otherwise*, can result in failure to achieve an efficient, a just, or even a decent outcome. The achievement is real because the pathways that have been identified are often subtle, difficult to detect, and hard to understand. Prior intuition is often of little help. That is why mathematical modeling has proved to be indispensible. The achievement is also deep, because it does not rely on postulating predatory governments, or thieving aristocracies, or grasping landlords. This is not to deny their existence, but you don't need an intellectual apparatus to conclude that a defenseless person will be robbed if there is an armed robber bent on robbing her.

9 Economics and the ethical life

It is a character of present-day sensibility pretty much throughout the world that we arrive at our economics from our politics, our politics from our political philosophy, and our political philosophy from our conception of the ethical, or indeed religious, life. An example of this directional mode is provided by John Rawls' great work, *A Theory of Justice* (1972), where the author says something about the kind of economic life that best sits within a just society (chapter 5, section 42) only *after* having arrived at the principles of justice. In a similar vein, there is a passage in *21st Century Capitalism* (1993, 131–134) where Professor Heilbroner inquires into the moral basis of capitalism. As always, he goes to past Masters for guidance and discovers that they have found little to no basis for it. But the passage contains no mention of a crucial matter, that of the kind of *incentives* people have to accumulate and create within various socio-economic environments. Heilbroner instead talks elsewhere of the unseemliness of impersonal market transactions and the corrupting influence of advertisement, which are common complaints of the aristocratic temperament.[24] But you can entertain personal aspirations and have needs without being greedy or self-centered. It is entirely possible for someone to be concerned with their own self, while at the same time to abide by norms of behavior pertaining to production and exchange, even when the risks of being caught violating the norms are negligible; it is even possible for such a person to be charitable toward others. Being self-regarding in the private sphere is not the same as being immoral, nor is it the same as being amoral. When someone is in search of the best buy in a market, it is not necessarily their intention to chisel anyone. Nor is the notion of a fair price alien to the self-regarding household. Internalized social norms of behavior work by making people feel good about abiding by them. But to ignore the existence of the self when discussing the moral basis of a social order and, thereby, to neglect matters of incentives, is to create social theories out of thin air. An ethical theory, or for that matter a moral theory, that is not grounded on deep facts is unlikely to be illuminating. For this reason, the reverse mode of inquiry into the nature of ethical life – *from* economics, through politics, via political philosophy – is equally necessary.[25] Ultimately, we would want to iterate between the findings of the two routes to arrive at an understanding of the intersection of the possible and the desirable. Unhappily, we are as yet far from such an understanding.

10   Critiques of modern economics

None of this receives any notice in *The Crisis of Vision in Modern Economic Thought*, a book Heilbroner has co-authored with his colleague, William Milberg. As the title suggests, this is a different sort of work. It is an assault on what the authors have been able to take from modern economics. They express moral outrage at its failings, they charge practicing economists of having disconnected themselves from reality, and they tell us what we must do if we are to improve our performance. Of course, they don't show us how to do it with a demonstration of their own: they preach, they don't practice.

By *vision*, the authors mean (1995, 4) "the political hopes and fears, social stereotypes, and value judgments – all unarticulated . . . – that infuse all social thought, not through their illegal entry into an otherwise pristine realm, but as psychological, perhaps existential, necessities."

The tone is confrontational from the outset (1995, 5): "Our . . . purpose is . . . polemical and political. It is to lay bare what we believe to be the disastrous consequences of the failure of the economics profession . . . to bear in mind the inescapable presence of vision in defining the tasks that economic inquiry arrogates to itself."

Strong words, these. I will now provide an account of the Heilbroner–Milberg line of attack. I want then to explain why it is not at all fruitful.[26]

Heilbroner and Milberg have in their sight (chapter 1) the whole of modern economics. But the bulk of the book (chapters 3–6, 25–96) is actually a case-study, in that it offers an account of the way *macroeconomics* has evolved since the publication, in 1936, of John Maynard Keynes' *The General Theory of Employment, Interest and Money*.

Macroeconomics is concerned with the study of economies described in aggregate terms. Typical variables whose interrelationships are under investigation in macroeconomics are the level of employment, national output, the general price level, government deficit, the "money" supply, the rate of inflation, government debt, the trade balance, and so forth. One reason macroeconomics looms large in public consciousness whenever economics is mentioned is that economic journalists love writing about it. Many of my noneconomist friends think macroeconomics *is* economics, and are surprised when I tell them it is not so. Macroeconomics is among the most problematic of fields within economics, because it is very, very hard. Lord only knows why you should expect to be able to get things "right" if you have to describe an entire economy in terms of nine or ten variables.[27] But then, Lord only knows why you should expect to say very much of practical moment if you were to work with models comprising thousands of commodities and millions of households. So macroeconomic reasoning is essential. Moreover, many of the tools at the disposal of government (e.g. interest rates and public debt) are macroeconomic, in the sense that they have economywide repercussions, and there is a need to know the effect of changes in their magnitudes on such aggregate economic indicators as the level of employment, gross output, and so forth.

In the authors' opinion, macroeconomics went off the rails laid down by Keynes almost immediately after the publication of his book, but has been in an especially degenerate shape since the end of the Keynesian consensus, which prevailed over a period that began just after the Second World War and ended some time in the early 1970s, a period now known for a different, though I believe related, reason as the "golden age of capitalism." Hence their anger.[28]

It is often thought that Keynes invented public works. This isn't true. Scandinavian economists had already arrived at the idea that modern, capitalist economies could be lifted out of severe depressions by means of judicious government expenditure. German economists in the mid-1930s not only had the same thought; they even put the thought into considerable practice. The importance of Keynes' book lay elsewhere. In it he tried to provide the economic *theory* that would explain the need for active monetary policy and public expenditure as ways of maintaining full employment of labor in each period of time. As is now well known, he did this by focusing attention on the determinants of the overall demand for goods and services in modern market economies, a major innovation in economic analysis.

Keynes is widely admired for his clarity. In fact, his *General Theory* is obscure. But the obscurity is so well hidden by the charm and confidence of the prose that readers are beguiled into thinking it is all very, very clear. That it is not even very clear is reflected in the fact that more than sixty years after the publication of his classic, his disciples still rage over what they regard as continued misinterpretations of Keynes by others. When I say "disciples," I mean *Disciples*, for deification of Keynes began even before his book was published. It was initiated among a group at the University of Cambridge; it spread outward after the Second World War, and it has continued in various universities throughout the world. Needless to say, this has not helped the development of macroeconomics.

I am sorry to have to report that Heilbroner and Milberg write like disciples. They say, for example, (1995, 44–45) that, "by the early post-World War years ... Keynes' 'general' theory had become accepted by economists ... although at the expense of a considerable weakening of its originality and power ... the disruptive, uncertainty-centered model of the *General Theory* was converted into a pastiche of ideas, not so much blended as permitted to co-exist, with their mutual contradictions and inconsistencies allowed to go unresolved. The result was termed 'bastard keynesianism.'" At no point do the authors entertain the possibility that the *General Theory*, great work that it is, was itself constructed out of a pastiche of ideas, based in part on ad hoc assumptions, and that subsequent work on Keynesian macroeconomics by many whom Heilbroner and Milberg criticize (e.g. the construction of the "neo-classical synthesis" by, among others, John Hicks, James Meade, Paul Samuelson and, later, Franco Modigliani and James Tobin) was an attempt to make sense of it.

11   Why are microfoundations necessary?

No macroeconomist of any substance, *including* Keynes, has ever thought that you could construct a sensible macro model of an economy without building on behavior at the micro level, that is, without basing the model on an account of behavior at the level of the householder, voter, shareholder, manager, bureaucrat, and so forth. But because the aggregation that is required for arriving at macroeconomic variables form microbehavior is gigantic, attempts at aggregation have often been avoided. It was, thus, not uncommon in the immediate post-1945 period for macroeconomic models to be based on behavioral rules characterizing representative types of agents (e.g. households, firms, and government) that were not founded on such matters as the motivations of the various actors and the constraints under which they make choices. In short, early macro models were often without what by current standards would be deemed as an adequate microfoundation.

At a practical level, does it matter that a macro model lacks an adequate microfoundation? After all, if the model works well, why worry that it lacks foundation?

There are four reasons why one must worry. First, it is difficult to judge if a macro model works well (e.g. if it provides good forecasts). Even the many ingenious tests that have been devised by econometricians cannot clinch matters. Microfoundations provide a needed discipline in the design of macro models; they serve as an anchor. The second, related, reason is that there may be several macro models that interpret the macro facts, such as they are, equally well. Microfoundations could enable us to choose among them. The third reason is purely intellectual. Even if we have constructed a sound macro model by some holistic leap of the imagination, we would still want to know what accounts for its soundness. The fourth reason is prudence: since circumstances will undoubtedly change, a macro model which currently works well will almost certainly not continue to work well. In other words, macro relationships should be expected to undergo changes over time. Good microfoundations would enable us to know how to adapt the model to changing conditions.

The need for adequate microfoundations in macroeconomic models was increasingly felt and expressed in the late 1960s by a new generation of mathematically trained economists. For example, when I was a student, it was an open scandal that there was no convincing model of involuntary unemployment, the central matter of concern in Keynes' classic. This is not to say that we concluded involuntary unemployment could not occur. Many of my generation were persuaded by Keynes' insights, but felt his was the beginning of a research program, not its end. In the event, the problem area appeared to us to be too hard. As most of us had no insights to offer then, we worked on other problems.

Heilbroner and Milberg express outrage at the usurpation of macroeconomics during the 1970s by those who built economywide models on a microfoundation that excluded involuntary unemployment *by assumption* and avoided even mentioning the short run, which is the span of concern in a good deal of government deliberation.[29] Many others were puzzled at the time, some even appalled, but moral outrage is no substitute for persuasive counterarguments; and the fact is, there still was no convincing set of models that yielded persistent involuntary unemployment, not to mention the new phenomenon of "stagflation" (i.e. high unemployment combined with inflation), as a possible outcome. By the late 1970s, though, a new direction in macroeconomic research began to take shape in the form of small-scale, piecemeal inquiries into separate markets, such as those for labor, credit, savings, and skills. I believe it is precisely *because* the initiators of this line of work chose to be modest in their goal that they were successful in building not unconvincing models that yielded macroeconomic resource-allocation failures – for example, involuntary unemployment, and the more difficult phenomenon of stagflation. The embarrassment now is not that we do not have good models of involuntary unemployment; rather, it is that we have too many contenders. So there is a long way to go.[30] Heilbroner and Milberg (1995, 88–91) are contemptuous of even these achievements and say the problem with them is that they do not capture Keynes' ideas, a remark that, again, reflects scholasticism and not much else.

This is not the place to raise technical matters, but I cannot resist one. Heilbroner and Milberg write:

perhaps the decisive identifying aspect of the school is its insistence that the proper scope of macroeconomic discussion is limited to the supply side . . . demand factors are considered of secondary importance. Such a view leads to a fundamental abandonment of Keynes's insight that a monetary economy, even with perfectly functioning markets, will be prone to unemployment due to insufficient effective demand . . . Having attributed involuntary unemployment to coordination failures and market imperfections rather than the failure of aggregate demand, many New Keynesian economists are silent on questions of macropolicy. (1995, 90)

This passage is wrong on several counts, an immediate one being that "coordination failure" can itself be the reason for a "failure of aggregate demand."[31] In any event, what was distinctive of new-Classical macroeconomics (see n. 29) was not its desire for microfoundations, but the particular microfoundations that were chosen by its practitioners. The key to correcting their Panglossian view of the world is to model alternative microfoundations, and test the macro models built on those foundations, seeking less conventional data (especially "natural experiments") on which to do the testing. This has been under way for some time now.[32]

12   Choice vs. propensities

What Heilbroner and Milberg want is a return to the old ways of doing macro-economics, which they see as relying on *propensities* as the basis of human behavior. They think this was a virtue, not a tactical necessity. They want to see a shift in the character of economic analysis from the one I sketched of modern economics at the beginning of this chapter to one where "considerations of norm-driven mass behavior are placed at the center of a specifically capitalist order" (1995, 33–34). They also insist (1995, 8) that, "the recognition of the inextricably social roots of all behavior leads to the view that macrofoundations must precede microbehavior, not the other way around, as modern economic thought perceives the issue."

I should say at once that modern economists often enough incorporate social norms (i.e. rules of behavior that are subscribed to by all) as raw data for arriving at an account of human behavior. For example, in the most famous article ever written on descriptive economic growth, the author postulated that aggregate savings are a constant proportion of national income, but provided no explanation for it.[33] But this was a tactical move on the author's part, not a matter of principle: the author had other things in mind in that article than savings behavior. The difference between research *tactic* and *principle* is all-important here. One problem with regarding social norms invariably as raw data is that it does not allow us to ask what purposes norms serve, nor how they are enforced; nor does it allow us to inquire why norms change when they do change. Moreover, in the absence of microfoundations, one can easily have debased arguments over whether a certain pattern of behavior is a norm at all. Similarly, it is an easy enough matter to model herd behavior among consumers and in stock markets by *postulating* herd behavior (e.g. that people like, or feel safe, imitating one another). But this will not tell us why there is herd behavior in some activities, under certain circumstances, and not in others. That is why the modern economist isn't satisfied until there is something like a microfoundation for social norms and herd behavior.[34]

On a closely related matter, echoing the narrative in *21st Century Capitalism*, Heilbroner and Milberg identify economics with the study of *modern* eco*nomies*. They say (1995, 5, emphasis in the original), "what prevents economics from claiming for itself a genuinely universal character is that the vision by which we 'see' and 'understand' capitalism is not, and cannot be the vision by which we would see and understand tribal, imperial, feudal, or communitarian societies, *if we were ourselves members of those societies."*

It is not easy to know what to make of this. To me it reads like a modern version of the colonial conceit that Orientals are inscrutable. Nor is it dissimilar to the conceit's seemingly progressive manifestation of recent years, that people in the East display a different (but equally valid, of course!) form of "rationality" than those in the West.

One may ask if there is any evidence of such fundamental differences. Indeed, one may ask in which ways the Oriental, or for that matter the African, is so inscrutable. Pioneering empirical work by Peter Bauer and Theodore Schultz established many years ago that traders and farmers in Africa and Asia respond to changes in prices and technological opportunities in much the same way as their counterparts do in the Occident.[35] You do not have to live in a capitalist society to want to improve your own lot and that of your nearest and dearest. Nor is it a response specially tailored for people in capitalist societies to mourn the loss of one's children. Nor, indeed, is there any evidence that the peasant farmer in traditional societies is not averse to the risk of being obliterated through bad harvest; nor that households there do not wish to smooth their consumption over the annual cycle. Even the Law of the Excluded Middle appears to be easily understood by the Oriental; and I know no African who doesn't appeal to it when counting change. As Jack Goody has shown, one can go further. Our societies are obviously not all the same, but as they were "fired in the same crucible," their differences must be seen as diverging from a common base. He shows, moreover, that these differences are rarely if ever of the deep-seated kind that would prevent "modernization", or even its onset.[36]

In an early passage in *21st Century Capitalism*, Heilbroner quotes from the anthropologist Elizabeth Marshall Thomas' account of the way a kill is shared among the !Kung people of the Kalahari desert. It is observed that, while the hunter keeps the largest portion, the remainder of the kill is allocated in a precise manner among the group. Moreover, there is no fuss made over the allocation – no quarrels, no resentment: the allocation is supported by *tradition*. Heilbroner seems to think this community is not within the purview of economics, in the sense that one does not need economic analysis to understand the way the Bush people operate. He says (1993, 24), "Once we know about their culture, their politics, and their technology, nothing remains to be explained with regard to their 'economy.'"

But it isn't an unreasonable demand to wish to *understand* the Bush people's culture and politics, not simply know them. Thus, to the modern economist the allocation rule described by Thomas would, in broad terms, appear to be an obvious one to follow if people want to pool risks, so as to reduce individual risks, in a world where meat does not keep and incentives are required in order to motivate individual members to *make* a kill. I have not read Thomas' account, so I don't know if she asked what would have happened if Gai, the hunter, had refused to share the kill in the manner specified by tradition. Heilbroner doesn't tell us, but it is an important matter. It could be, for example, that the hunter would be shunned, or be awarded a very small portion on the occasion of the next kill, or whatever. Recent developments in the theory of games have taught us that, among people engaged in repeated interchanges, rules of punishment for deviant behavior, when judiciously chosen, enable norms of behavior to be *self-enforcing*; that is, if everyone else were to follow the norm, it would be in each person's interest to follow the norm. When such punishment schemes are put in place (and they have to be so designed that they are *credible*), no external agency is required for sustaining cooperation among members of a group.[37]

This sort of argument has been put to use in a variety of contexts. Avner Greif, for example, has shown how the Maghribi traders during the eleventh century in Fustat and across the Mediterranean acted as a collective to impose sanctions on agents who violated their commercial codes.[38] It has also been put to successful use in explaining the way local common property resources, such as river water, grazing lands, swidden fallows, and local forests, have been collectively managed in rural societies in contemporary poor countries. Empirical studies have confirmed that resource users in many instances cooperate, on occasion through not undemocratic means, so as to ensure that the resource base is not eroded. Attempts have also been made by social scientists to explain observed asymmetries in the distribution of benefits and burdens of cooperation in terms of underlying differences in the circumstances of the various parties. For example, in her study of collectively managed irrigation systems in Nepal, Elinor Ostrom has explained observed differences in benefits and burdens among users (e.g. who gets how much water from the canal system and who is responsible for which maintenance task) in terms of such facts as that some farmers are headenders, while others are tailenders. In an earlier work, Ostrom also tried to explain why cooperation failed to get off ground where it did not get established.[39]

There are a number of curious implications of modern game theory that too have been useful in interpreting evidence. In a summary of her research findings on local irrigation in Nepal, Ostrom notes that systems that had been improved by the construction of permanent headworks were in worse repair, delivered substantially less water to the tailend than to the headend of the systems, and had lower agricultural productivity than the temporary, stone-trees-and-mud headworks that had been constructed and managed by the farmers themselves.[40]

Ostrom has an explanation for this. She suggests that, unless it is accompanied by countermeasures, the construction of permanent headworks alters the relative bargaining positions of the headenders and tailenders, resulting in so reduced a flow of benefits to the latter group that they have little incentive to help repair and maintain the headworks, something the headenders on their own cannot do. Headenders gain from the permanent structures, but the tailenders lose disproportionately. She also notes that traditional farm-managed systems sustained greater equality in the allocation of water than modern systems managed by such external agencies as the government and foreign donors.[41]

13 Theory and empirics in modern economics

It is the fate of some disciplines to begin as a fit subject for educated gentlemen to advert upon, and to become technical, to the displeasure of educated gentlemen. At the root of it all, I believe what really galls Heilbroner and Milberg are the increased technical requirements demanded by contemporary economists before they are persuaded by an argument. But the authors do not want to say it in so many words. So they say instead (1995, 3): "The thrust of our criticism [of modern economics] . . . becomes explicit in the first of the attributes that we have ascribed to economics up to the post-Keynesian period – namely, its continuously visible concern with the connection between theory and 'reality.' By way of contrast, the mark of modern-day economics is its extraordinary indifference to this problem."

In this article I have offered evidence that this claim is quite incorrect. But in order to conduct a statistical test of the claim, I consulted five years (1991–1995) of the *American Economic Review*, the flagship journal of the American Economic Association. This journal reflects establishment economics in a manner no other journal does today. I classified articles into three categories: (1) pure theory, (2) applied theory (by which I mean a piece of theoretical analysis that tries to explain some observed fact, or which analyses the implications of particular types of policies), and (3) experimental and / or empirical economics. Here is what I discovered: Of the 281 articles published in the journal during 1991–1995 (in order to save time, I excluded "short articles and notes"), 25 were in category (1), 100 in (2), and 156 in (3). In other words, more than 90 percent of the articles were about the "real world," in the Heilbroner–Milberg sense of the word.[42] To be sure, there are journals that specialize in the purest of pure theory; but then there are journals which publish only empirical articles. I don't know what one is to infer from this.

Of course this is not to say that the allocation of research effort in economics is "optimal" (whatever that might mean); and *of course* much that is routinely published is of little to no worth (I have published more than my fair share myself). Given that research is risky business, a good part of this is inevitable. But there is another part, which has to do with the fact that many of us not infrequently address problems that are internally generated by the prevailing literature and which serve to answer puzzles and curiosities, but not much else. This adds to the path-dependence of the process of economic inquiry. Needless to say, there can also be self-indulgence in the choice of research problems, where the published material displays no more than the product of a finger exercise on what many others would find a boring question. But I don't know why one should think that this kind of slack is unique to economics, nor how it could be removed without stifling creativity. More to the point, there is no evidence that the prevalence of *mathematics* in contemporary economics plays a role in such slack as that which exists. One has only to look at, say, pre-Second World War editions of the then most prominent economics journal in the English-speaking world, *The Economic Journal*, to confirm this. Nor do I know how one can influence other people's research interests other than by producing fertile research of one's own. In the late 1970s, I used to complain regularly about the lack of interest my professional colleagues showed toward the links I felt must surely exist between rural poverty in poor countries and the use of the local environmental resource base. I even wrote a book on the subject so as to create interest among development and environmental economists.[43] I failed then, presumably because I was unable to demonstrate to others that it was an intellectually productive field. In the event, research in that field did not become active until nearly a decade later.

14   Quantification and the social sciences

It is simply no good moaning unless you can offer something that can be used as a springboard for others.[44] Despite what Heilbroner and Milberg think of the profession, there is much constructive criticism that economists make of one another's works: indeed, every creative piece of work is an implicit criticism of the existing literature. That a problem area is *important* has never been a clinching argument for rushing to work on it. Wisely, I think, contemporary economists study an important problem only when they think there is a chance that it will yield fruit. If I were to give an example of this from a field of research with which I am very familiar, it would be the study of those economic processes that lead to inequality and to poverty traps. Surprising though it may seem, even a decade ago there was little of any theoretical depth in the economics literature on inequality in contemporary societies. This was not because economists did not regard this to be an important problem area (ways of measuring inequality and poverty had been under scrutiny by economists during the previous fifteen years or so[45]), but because there were no promising analytical leads on the matter. Today we not only understand why certain classes of people can be caught in poverty traps even when an economy experiences a general rise in prosperity (i.e. why the fruits of economic growth do not necessarily trickle down to the poorest in society), we also understand why and how extreme patterns of inequality in the distribution of assets can act as a drag on aggregate economic performance. Our theories and empirical findings show that even though the pathways by which these phenomena can occur are different across countries and across "stages" of economic development, they share a number of common analytical features.[46]

What was only very recently the purest of academic research, expressed in technical language, has now seeped through sufficiently to make it appear almost as a commonplace observation. Today international agencies write about it as if it should be "conventional wisdom."[47] However, such rapid acceptance of contemporary research findings has its own dangers. The qualifications that are inevitably underlined in academic discoveries tend to get blurred by the time they reach and excite policy-makers. I cite this example also to show that the incentives are in place for economists to chase promising avenues of research. As is well known, God created graduate students so as to keep tenured Faculty honest and hardworking. If you have a promising idea, you can be almost sure that some economist, somewhere, will run with it; and if you make a mistake, you can be absolutely sure that some economist, somewhere, will pounce on it.

Economics is a quantitative subject. When the Chancellor of the Exchequer asks his expert advisers to tell him of the fiscal advantages and disadvantages of an increase in the tax on petrol, he does not want a philosophical discourse, nor a lecture on what Marx would have thought about the matter. He wants to know how much revenue he would be able to raise, what effects its imposition would have on other sectors of the economy, what it would mean to the lives of different categories of people, and, if the Minister of Environment is within earshot, he will also ask if it would reduce carbon emissions. So mathematical modeling is essential and is here to stay. But mathematical modeling of volition is, inevitably, a repugnant exercise, because it seems to demean the human experience. Certainly, when I lecture to first-year undergraduates on the theory of consumer choice, I feel the economist's "consumer" is not the sort of person I would invite home to dinner. But in order to make progress, we have to simplify in suitable ways. In many applications, individual choice, as modeled by the economist, is a grotesque caricature of ourselves. Those who find mathematical modeling unsatisfactory think they would avoid making such compromises if they were to go the literary route. So they take refuge in such aphorisms as that "it is better to be vaguely right than precisely wrong."[48] What this misses, however, is that you won't even know if you are vaguely right if you operate within a framework in which you cannot be precisely wrong; there is no way to controvert a vague statement.

If a discipline tries to do everything, it will succeed in doing nothing well. If it tries to be all things to all people, it will be of little use to anyone. If it is to illuminate, it must have boundaries. To be sure, innovative work sometimes involves extensions of the boundaries, when the discipline's techniques illuminate problems in another discipline. But such explorations are like reconnaissance exercises: you try to see what lies beyond, but just for size; if it looks as though the probe will work, you try some more. Modern economists have demonstrated the power of their discipline by crossing into law, political science, anthropology, demography, ecosystem ecology, and behavioral ecology, often on the basis of a narrow viewpoint of human motivation. What I have tried to explain in this chapter is that it is possible to look *outward* from the narrow viewpoint to catch a glimpse of the larger enterprise called living. The techniques of economics (yes, mathematical techniques) have been borrowed by people in a number of other fields.[49] People who sneer at what they see as the narrowness of modern economics often also complain of its imperialistic tendencies; but you cannot have it both ways.

Economics does not encompass the whole of the social and moral sciences. So it is a dangerous mistake to expect from it everything one desires to learn of the social world. But if you want to reach a measure of understanding of the limits to what people can realistically achieve in their search for a social order that makes life more than just liveable, then you simply can't afford to ignore economics' modern version.

Notes

I have benefitted greatly from the comments I received on an earlier draft from Kenneth Arrow, Avinash Dixit, Frank Hahn, Geoffrey Harcourt, Ira Katznelson, Wolf Lepenies, Assar Lindbeck, Karl-Göran Mäler, James Mirrlees, Paul Seabright, Gavin Wright, Stefano Zamagni and, most especially, Robert Solow.

1. For example, even among economic theorists who were not mathematicians, there was much interest in the existence of optimum programs in infinite-horizon economic models, and in the kind of fixed-point argument that would be required for establishing that a particular economic system possesses a general equilibrium.
2. See, for example, Cassidy (1996, 50–64) and Heilbroner and Milberg (1995). Some of the remarks that follow have been prompted also by the second and third of Professor Stephen Toulmin's 1998 Tanner Lectures at Cambridge, entitled "Economics: from theodicy to chaos" and "Situated understanding," respectively.
3. The often acrimonious debate that took place among leading physicists in the USA on the worth of the superconducting super-collider provides a good example.
4. For a critical review of one such commentary, see Hahn (1973).
5. Heilbroner (1993, 1995).
6. Heilbroner and Milberg (1995) and Heilbroner (1996).
7. By this I mean that the assumptions under which Marx's construct holds are violated in our world, and that this is a deep fact, not an incidental one. For Marx's claim to be true, we need to assume, among other things, that each and every commodity has a competitive market, that joint production of a certain kind (e.g. mutton and wool) is not possible, that there is a single nonproduced good (labor), and that the economy is stationary (i.e. history has ended). In saying we "need to assume" these, I do not mean the assumptions are necessary, but that they are tight, in that, dropping any renders Marx's claim invalid. A simple proof, following the original proofs offered

by Nicholas Georgescu-Roegen and Paul Samuelson, is provided in Koopmans (1957). To the best of my knowledge, the most general statement is in Mirrlees (1969).

A common criticism I have heard Marxian scholars make is that the model economy studied in the articles referred to above does not capture what Marx had in mind. But I know of no attempt by them to provide a formal account of what Marx meant *and thereby* check if the account finds empirical support.

8. Some ecologists in recent years have sought to establish an account of the value of commodities in terms of the energy that is embodied in their production. Any such account is incoherent in the world we know, and for the same reasons.

9. Robbins (1932, 15).

10. This reading of economics is demonstrated in Dasgupta (1985), where the author views every "epoch" in terms of an interpretation of the problems that were perceived to be central in *that* epoch. Dasgupta's book also assesses the achievements and shortcomings of the answers that were given to these problems.

11. Williams (1971, 154). As Williams shows, Morris was not alone in harboring such anxieties.

12. Feyerabend (1978).

13. Here I am referring to such thinkers as Bert Bolin, Paul Ehrlich, Murray Gell-Mann, John Holdren, Henry Kendall, Harold Mooney, David Tilman, and Edward O. Wilson. See, for example, Bolin (1989); Wilson (1992); Gell-Mann (1994); and Ehrlich and Ehrlich (1996). For a collection of expert essays on the nature of ecosystems, see Daily (1997).

14. Barrett (1990, 1996).

15. See, for example, Serageldin (1993) and Fumo (1996).

16. *21st Century Capitalism* was selected by Fortune Book Club and was included in the *New York Times'* list of one of the notable books of the year.

17. See, for example, Meade (1973); Mäler (1974); Baumol and Oates (1975); and Dasgupta and Heal (1979).

18. Binswanger (1991).

19. These issues are discussed more fully in Dasgupta (1993) and in my Keynes Lecture to the British Academy (Dasgupta 1996a), an expanded version of which is Dasgupta (1996b).

20. Deacon (1994).

21. This has not come about in one swoop, but like most advances, by accretion. The literature is gigantic. It is also often technical, because many of the issues *are* technical. American colleagues, fast as they are with new labels, refer to it, alternatively, as "the new institutional economics," "the economics of information," "transaction-costs economics," and "the new political economy." When they christen aspects of it merely as "agency theory" and "the theory of contracts," one feels let down.

22. For book-length accounts of such agency problems, see Arrow (1974); Dasgupta (1993); Stiglitz (1994); Hart (1995); Dixit (1996).

23. Here I am using Professor Heilbroner's rhetorical device of anthropomorphizing an abstraction.

24. Possible parallels between our exposure to smiling faces extolling the pleasures of automobiles and shampoos and that of the subjection to political propaganda of

citizens of the former Soviet Union about the glories of coal and tractor production have been drawn by the sociologist, Michael Schudson. Heilbroner finds the parallel compelling. He says (1990, 111) their "effect is much the same. As the public voice of the private sector, advertising is the propaganda of the market system, just as propaganda is the advertising of the centralized one." There is a difference, though: citizens of the Soviet Union could not vote propagandists out of office in the way citizens of the USA can refuse to buy goods from advertizers. Heilbroner provides no evidence that this difference does not matter.

25. I have explored this route briefly in Dasgupta (1982a) and, more fully, in Dasgupta (1993).

26. Hardly a season passes when a book-length attack on modern economics is not published. From this one can only conclude that such books sell. I know of no other discipline whose practitioners are castigated as frequently as those of modern economics. Most often, such books are written by people who are not known for any original contribution to the subject. I have no explanation for the phenomenon. Heilbroner and Milberg modestly list (1995, 128) nine other books over the previous nine years that have expressed "very deep dissatisfaction with the condition of contemporary theory." I can assure readers that they would discover many more if they were to look in libraries.

27. Modern macro models are more disaggregated, numerical models containing 20–30 commodities being quite routine these days.

28. The period in question has been so christened because, during it rates of growth of productivity and gross national product in Western Europe and the USA attained figures well in excess of their historical trends.

Heilbroner and Milberg may not agree that the bulk of their book is a case-study. They sometimes write as though they think macroeconomics is the whole of economics (1995, 9): "Our study focuses on the development of modern economic thought, using that phrase to refer to changes in economic theory since the decline of the Keynesian doctrine that exercised a seemingly uncontestable hegemony in the post-World War II era."

29. Inevitably these economists were given a label in the USA. They are called "new-Classical" economists.

30. For major syntheses of what, no doubt, my American colleagues are now calling "the new macroeconomics" (to supplant an earlier term, "New Keynesian economics"), see Edmond Malinvaud (1984, 1994); Lindbeck and Snower (1988); Layard, Nickell, and Jackman (1991); Stiglitz (1992); Phelps (1994); and Hahn and Solow (1995).

I have focused on the theoretical problems that were detected in macroeconomics by a generation of economists. For a fuller account of the evolution of macroeconomics in the post-1945 period, see Krugman (1994). Krugman did not stress the points I have made here, because his motivation was different: he wanted to explore the various pathways by which findings in academic research are transmitted, often in a distorted form, to interested parties. His is an account of the intellectual shortcomings of those who act as "middlemen" in the process of transmission from research papers to policy decisions.

31. On other counts see, for example, Stiglitz (1992) and Hahn and Solow (1995).
32. See the references in n. 30, and the works cited there.
33. Solow (1956).
34. Interesting work on herd behavior includes Banerjee (1992); Birchandani, Hirschleifer, and Welch (1992); and Bernheim (1994).
35. Bauer (1954); Schultz (1964).
36. Goody (1996). Goody is concerned only with Eurasian societies. But I have reasons to believe he would not stop with them.
37. See Fudenberg and Maskin (1986). To be sure, we also internalize social norms, such as that of paying our dues, keeping agreements, returning a favor; and higher-order norms, as for example frowning on people who break social norms, and so forth. By internalizing such norms as keeping agreements, a person makes the springs of his actions contain the norm. The person therefore feels shame or guilt in violating a norm, and this prevents him from doing so, or, at the very least, it puts a break on his violating it unless other considerations are found by him to be overriding. In short, his upbringing ensures that he has a disposition to obey the norm. When he does violate it, neither guilt nor shame is typically absent, but the act will have been rationalized by him. A general disposition to abide by agreements, to be truthful, to trust one another, and to act with justice is an essential lubricant of societies. Communities where the disposition is pervasive save enormously on transaction costs. There lies its instrumental value. In the world as we know it, such a disposition is present in varying degrees. When we refrain from breaking the law, it isn't always because of a fear of being caught. On the other hand, if relative to the gravity of the misdemeanor the private benefit from malfeasance were high, some transgressions could be expected to take place. Punishment assumes its role as a deterrence because of the latter fact.
38. Greif (1993). See also Greif, Milgrom, and Weingast (1994), where the authors offer an account of the rise of merchant guilds in late medieval Europe. These guilds afforded protection to members against unjustified seizure of their property by city-states. Guilds decided if and when a trade embargo was warranted against the city.
    A somewhat reverse set of actions also occurred in medieval Europe, where transgressions by a party were sometimes met by the rest of society imposing sanctions on the entire kinship of the party, or on the guild to which the transgressor belonged. The norm provided collectives with a natural incentive to monitor their own members' behavior.
39. Ostrom (1990, 1996).
40. Ostrom (1996).
41. For other, fine uses of the theory of games to explain the many ways in which the local commons have been managed in traditional societies, see Baland and Platteau (1996) and Seabright (1997).
42. I should add that I was most generous to Heilbroner and Milberg in my choice of criterion for inclusion in (1). For example, in my list, (1) includes two Nobel Lectures, both on foundational work: one was the basis of much of "the new institutional economics," the other was the forerunner of "the economics of information."

43. Dasgupta (1982b).
44. Here is an example of the sort of sentiment Heilbroner and Milberg think could influence economics research (1995, 122): "As with earlier classical situations, today's vision must incorporate the socioeconomic essence of the historical setting in its choice of the fundamental agents who will set into motion the economic drama itself." No doubt, but try doing something with this instruction.
45. See Kolm (1969); Atkinson (1970); Sen (1973).
46. See, for example, Dasgupta and Ray (1986, 1987); Braverman and Stiglitz (1989); Benabou (1994); Durlauf (1994); Persson and Tabellini (1994); Dasgupta (1977, 1995). For cross-country evidence that is suggestive of the existence of certain types of positive links between an absence of extreme income inequality and economic growth, see Deininger and Squire (1997).
47. See, for example, UNDP 1996.
48. The aphorism appears in Shove (1942) and is attributed to one Wildon Carr.
49. For example, they are now routine in behavioral ecology. See Krebs and Davies (1991, 1993).

References

Arrow, Kenneth (1974). *The Limits of Organization*. New York: W.W. Norton

Atkinson, Anthony B. (1970). On the measurement of inequality, *Journal of Economic Theory*, 2

Baland, Jean-Marie and Jean-Philippe Platteau (1996). *Halting Degradation of Natural Resources: Is There a Role for Rural Communities?* Oxford: Clarendon Press

Banerjee, Abhijit (1992). A simple model of herd behaviour, *Quarterly Journal of Economics*, 107

Barrett, Scott (1990). The problem of global environmental protection, *Oxford Review of Economic Policy*, 6

    (1996). Comments on the 1995 Keynes Lecture, *Proceedings of the British Academy: 1995 Lectures and Memoirs*. London: British Academy

Bauer, Peter (1954). *West African Trade*. Cambridge: Cambridge University Press

Baumol, William and Wallace Oates (1975). *The Theory of Environmental Policy*. Englewood Cliffs, NJ: Prentice-Hall

Benabou, Roland (1994). Human capital, inequality and growth: a local perspective, *European Economic Review*, 38

Bernheim, Douglas (1994). A theory of conformity, *Journal of Political Economy*, 102

Binswanger, Hans (1991). Brazilian policies that encourage deforestation in the Amazon, *World Development*, 19

Birchandani, Sushil, David Hirschleifer, and Ivo Welch (1992). A theory of fads, fashion, custom, and cultural change as informational cascades, *Journal of Political Economy*, 100

Bolin, Bert (1989). Changing climate, in Laurie Friday and Ronald Laskey (eds.), *The Fragile Environment*. Cambridge: Cambridge University Press

Braverman, Avishay and Joseph Stiglitz (1989). Credit rationing, tenancy, productivity, and the dynamics of inequality, in Pranab Bardhan (ed.), *The Economic Theory of Agrarian Institutions*. Oxford: Oxford University Press

Cassidy, John (1996). The decline of economics, *New Yorker*, December 2, 42–49

Daily, Gretchen C. (ed.) (1997). *Nature's Services: Societal Dependence on National Ecosystems.* Washington, DC: Island Press

Dasgupta, Amiya (1985). *Epochs of Economic Theory.* Oxford: Basil Blackwell

Dasgupta, Partha (1977). Nutritional status, the capacity for work and poverty traps, *Journal of Econometrics*, 77

   (1982a). Utilitarianism, information and rights, in Amartya Sen and Bernard Williams (eds.), *Utilitarianism and Beyond.* Cambridge: Cambridge University Press

   (1982b). *The Control of Resources.* Cambridge, MA: Harvard University Press

   (1993). *An Inquiry into Well-Being and Destitution.* Oxford: Clarendon Press

   (1995). The population problem: theory and evidence, *Journal of Economic Literature*, 33

   (1996a). The economics of the environment, *Proceedings of the British Academy: 1995 Lectures and Memoirs.* London: British Academy

   (1996b) The economics of the environment, *Environment and Development Economics*, 1

Dasgupta, Partha and Geoffrey Heal (1979). *Economic Theory and Exhaustible Resources.* Cambridge: Cambridge University Press

Dasgupta, Partha and Debraj Ray (1986). Inequality as a determinant of malnutrition and unemployment, 1: theory, *Economic Journal*, 96

   (1987). Inequality as a determinant of malnutrition and unemployment, 2: policy, *Economic Journal*, 97

Deacon, Robert (1994). Deforestation and the rule of law in a cross section of countries, *Land Economics*, 70

Deininger, K. and Lynn Squire (1997). Economic growth and income inequality: re-examining the links, *Finance and Development*, 34

Dixit, Avinash (1996). *The Making of Economic Policy: A Transaction-Cost Politics Perspective.* Cambridge, MA: MIT Press

Durlauf, Steven (1994). Spillovers, stratification and inequality, *European Economic Review*, 38

Ehrlich, Paul R. and Anne H. Ehrlich (1996). *Betrayal of Science and Reason: How Anti-Environmental Rhetoric Threatens Our Future.* Washington, DC: Island Press

Feyerabend, Paul (1978). *Against Method: Outline of an Anarchistic Theory of Knowledge.* London: Verso

Fudenberg, Drew and Eric Maskin (1986), The Folk Theorem in repeated games with discounting and incomplete information, *Econometrica*, 54

Fumo, Claudia (1996). The *World Bank's Partnership with Nongovernmental Organizations.* Washington, DC: World Bank

Gell-Mann, Murray (1994). *The Quark and the Jaguar.* New York: W.H. Freeman

Goody, Jack (1996). *The East in the West.* Cambridge: Cambridge University Press

Greif, Avner (1993). Contract enforceability and economic institutions in early trade: the Maghribi traders' coalition, *American Economic Review*, 83

Greif, Avner, Paul Milgrom, and Barry Weingast (1994). Co-ordination, commitment, and enforcement: the case of the merchant guild, *Journal of Political Economy*, 102

Hahn, Frank (1973). The winter of our discontent, *Economica*, 40

Hahn, Frank and Robert Solow (1995). *A Critical Essay on Modern Macroeconomic Theory*. Cambridge, MA: MIT Press
Hart, Oliver (1995). *Firms, Contracts and Financial Structure*. Oxford: Clarendon Press
Heilbroner, Robert (1993). *21st Century Capitalism*, New York: W.W. Norton
  (1995). *Visions of the Future: The Distant Past, Yesterday, Today, Tomorrow*. New York: Oxford University Press
  (1996). *Teachings from the Worldly Philosophy*. New York: W.W. Norton
Heilbroner, Robert and William Milberg (1995). *The Crisis of Vision in Modern Economic Thought*. Cambridge: Cambridge University Press
Hirschmann, Albert (1991). *The Rhetoric of Reason*. Cambridge, MA: Harvard University Press
Keynes, John Maynard (1936). *The General Theory of Employment, Interest and Money*. London: Macmillan.
Kolm, S.-C. (1969). The optimal production of social justice, in J. Margolis and H. Guitton (eds.), *Public Economics*. London: Macmillan
Koopmans, Tjalling (1957). The price system and the allocation of resources, in Tjalling Koopmans, *Three Essays on the State of Economic Science*. New York: McGraw-Hill
Krebs, J.R. and N.B. Davies (eds.) (1991). *Behavioural Ecology: An Evolutionary Approach*. Oxford: Basil Blackwell
  (1993). *An Introduction to Behavioural Ecology*, 3rd edn. Oxford: Basil Blackwell
Krugman, Paul (1994). *Peddling Prosperity: Economic Sense and Nonsense in the Age of Diminished Expectations*. New York: W.W. Norton
Layard, Richard, Stephen Nickell, and Richard Jackman (1991). *Unemployment: Macroeconomic Performance and the Labour Market*. Oxford: Oxford University Press
Lindbeck, Assar and Dennis Snower (1988). *The Insider–Outsider Theory of Employment and Unemployment*. Cambridge, MA: MIT Press
Mäler, Karl-Göran (1974). *Environmental Economics: A Theoretical Enquiry*. Baltimore: Johns Hopkins University Press
Malinvaud, Edmond (1984). *Mass Unemployment*. Oxford: Basil Blackwell
  (1994). *Diagnosing Unemployment*. Cambridge: Cambridge University Press
Meade, James (1973). *The Theory of Externalities*. Geneva: Institute Universitaire de Hautes Etudes Internationales
Mirlees, James (1969). The dynamic non-substitution theorem, *Review of Economic Studies*, 36
Ostrom, Elinor (1990). *Governing the Commons: The Evolution of Institutions for Collective Action*. Cambridge: Cambridge University Press
  (1996). Incentives, rules of the game, and development, *Proceedings of the Annual World Bank Conference on Development Economics, 1995* (Supplement to the *World Bank Economic Review* and the *World Bank Research Observer*)
Persson, Torsten and Guido Tabellini (1994). Is inequality harmful for growth?, *American Economic Review*, 84
Phelps, Edmund (1994). *Structural Slumps*. Cambridge, MA: Harvard University Press
Rawls, John (1972). *A Theory of Justice*. Oxford: Clarendon Press

Robbins, Lionel (1932). *An Essay on the Nature and Significance of Economic Science*. London, Allen & Unwin

Schultz, Theodore W. (1964). *Transforming Traditional Agriculture*. New Haven, CT.: Yale University Press

Seabright, Paul (1997). Is cooperation habit-forming?, in Partha Dasgupta and Karl-Göran Mäler (eds.), *The Environment and Emerging Development Issues*. Oxford: Clarendon Press

Sen, Amartya (1973). *On Economic Inequality*. Oxford: Oxford University Press

Searageldin, Ismail (1993). *Development Partners: Aid and Cooperation in the 1990s*. Stockholm: Swedish International Development Authority

Shove, Gerald (1942). The place of Marshall's *Principles* in the development of economic theory, *Economic Journal*, 52

Solow, Robert (1956). A contribution to the theory of economic growth, *Quarterly Journal of Economics*, 70

Stiglitz, Joseph (1992). Capital markets and economic fluctuation in capitalist economies, *European Economic Review* (Supplement)

(1994). *Whither Socialism?* Cambridge, MA: MIT Press

United Nations Development Program (UNDP) (1996). *Human Development Report*. New York: Oxford University Press

Williams, Raymond (1971) *Culture and Society 1780–1950*: Harmondsworth: Penguin

Wilson, Edward O. (1992). *The Diversity of Life*. New York: W.W. Norton

4   Some nonreasons for nonrealism about economics

Uskali Mäki

1 Introduction

Many participants in the debate over the current state and recent developments of economics make claims that are unrefined, simplistic, often exaggerated. This is understandable: the stakes are high, the issues trigger emotional responses, and few participants are motivated or equipped to seek more nuanced analyses. To assert, or to deny, that economics as a scientific discipline or a particular part of it (such as a model) is about reality – or refers to reality, represents it, is true about it, or is truthlike about it – is to make a very complex and highly ambiguous claim.[1] The disputants often make claims that have parallels in the philosophical controversy between scientific realists and their opponents, or at any rate those claims can be partly analyzed in terms of some of the arguments presented in this philosophical controversy. The question addressed here is whether realism about economics is a viable position. The argument proceeds by way of refuting a number of arguments against realism about economics. I suggest a genuine controversy over the factuality of any *particular* strand or piece of economics requires realism as a *general* interpretation of economics – or at any rate requires debunking the anti-realist arguments discussed below.

"The issue of realism" as most economists would recognize it, is not exactly the issue of realism as philosophers recognize it. "The issue of realism" in economics is about *realisticness as a property of theories*, while (part of) the issue of realism in philosophy is about *realism as a theory of theories*. But some parts of the issue of realisticness (such as those related to reference and truth) in economics can be translated into aspects of the issue of realism as a theory of theories. Thus there is also an issue of realism (with no quotation marks) in economics. It is this issue of realism that has to be settled as a prerequisite for critical assessments of important forms of realisticness of economic theories.[2]

90

2 Approaches

Much of the recent philosophy and methodology of economics has followed a "top-down" approach in the study of its subject matter. On this approach, one adopts a favored philosophical account of science, imposes its descriptive categories and prescriptive rules upon this or that bit of economics or economics as a whole. Inquiry in this mode is a matter of applying a ready-made philosophical theory to the special case of economics. More often than not, the outcome of the exercise is the conclusion that economics appears to be in more or less bad shape as it does not meet the presumed criteria of good science. Some claims recently made about the connection between realism – perhaps defined by a Popper or a Bhaskar – and economics are of this sort.

My own approach has been somewhat different. The philosophical literature on realism is vast, and the study of it in the course of more than the last quarter of a century has not revealed to me any single version of realist philosophy that would fit with economics without major modifications. I have therefore become sensitive to the peculiar characteristics of economics and selective about my philosophical sources. In regard to the philosophical resources, I have learned to appreciate a critical and creative attitude: I believe those resources have to be adjusted and tailored so as to do justice to the specificities of the target of study, economics. The other side of the strategy is an empirical attitude: our philosophical account of economics should be informed about the actual theories, methods, and meta-theories that practicing economists hold. "Bottom-up approach" may be an approximately accurate label for some of my work, but taken together, it may be more accurate to view the totality of my research on the topic as a manifestation of a dialectical approach where philosophical concepts are adjusted and created in the light of empirical information concerning the actualities of economics.

One key question is whether economics and realism fit with one another. It is obvious that there are many concrete versions of realism with which the fit is poor or nonexistent. It is often informative to make such negative discoveries. It is important, though, to look for versions of realism that fit better. These versions may be very abstract – as will be the case later on in this chapter – or more specific and concrete.

How does one argue about the connection between economics and realism? My own work seems to have followed two separate approaches to this. The first is to look at the actual theories, methods, and meta-theoretical views held by practicing economists, and to see whether there are plausible interpretations and reconstructions that would be consistent with versions of realism.[3] If there is a discovery that could be reported in a tentative manner, it is a general one: there is more realism in economics than easily meets the eye (even Milton Friedman emerges as a realist at the end!). Using an old realist distinction, I might say that the *appearance* is that a lot of economics is nonrealist, whereas in *reality* there is much more realism there.

The second approach to arguing about the economics–realism connection is to argue against arguments that have been put forth for a nonrealist view of economics. Some of my work has had this character. There are popular arguments, held either by economists themselves or meta-theoretical commentators of economics, which suggest that this or that feature of economics or human cognition in general prohibits a realist view of economics. The range of the premises behind these arguments, depicting such features, is broad.[4] My counterarguments have the form, "Even if P, realism about economics is not thereby discredited" where "P" designates such a premise which is believed to entail nonrealism. The present brief chapter summarizes and refines my earlier suggestions following this second approach. Before listing some of the nonreasons for nonrealism, we need a general idea of what realism is.

3 Definitions

"Realism about economics" and "Realism in economics" are ambiguous notions. We may say that "realism about economics" is a view (attitude or theory) to be held at a meta-level by people such as philosophers of economics on weekdays and economists on Sundays; and that "realism in economics" is an attitude held by practicing economists *qua* practitioners, during office hours, explicitly or implicitly. Both of these share at least the following theses:

> [R1] Entity X might exist
> [R2] Theory T might be true

Here, [R1] is a formulation of an ontological realism where "X" stands for an entity (thing, complex of properties, structure, process) purportedly referred to by an economic theory or its constituents. [R2] is a formulation of a semantic realism where "T" stands for an economic theory or model. Some necessary specifications will be given in a moment.

Doubts about realism are then based on two kinds of more specific doubts:

> [~R1] Given the kind of thing that X is, it cannot possibly exist
> [~R2] Given the kind of thing that T is, it cannot possibly be true

Note that while [~R1] and [~R2] define quite strong forms of anti-realism, [R1] and [R2] characterize only moderate forms of realism. Stronger kinds of ontological and semantic realism have the form,

> [R3] Entity X exists
> [R4] Theory T is true

while weaker kinds of nonrealism deny these two claims:

[∼R3] Entity X does not exist (even though it might)
[∼R4] Theory T is not true (even though it might)

From this it is obvious that an advocate of [∼R3] subscribes to [R1], while an advocate of [∼R4] subscribes to [R2], thus these weaker nonrealisms imply weak ontological and semantic realisms.

For these formulations to serve as definition sketches of varieties of realism and nonrealism, further qualifications are needed (see Niiniluoto 1999; Mäki 2001). One concept in need of specification is that of existence. The standard specification, in terms of mind-independence, will not do in our case, as it would destroy any hope of realism about economics at the outset: after all, economics is about mind-dependent entities. "Exists inquiry-independently" is a more promising candidate, so is "exists independently of particular representations of it." Realisms about truth of theories include two items in need of specification. One is "theory": the idea of theories – or models – being true is problematic given that theories often are rather complex systems with obviously false elements in them. The other is "truth." The traditional realist concept of truth is one based on some idea of a truth-bearer (sentence, statement, utterance) corresponding to a truth-maker (fact, state of the world, causal connection), but one may try to be an ontological realist without this conception.[5] Truth is one of the many senses of realisticness and should be disentangled from others, such as observationality, concreteness, empirical confirmation, plausibility, and policy relevance. These other forms of realisticness do not have a direct conceptual connection to realism, while truth as correspondence does, or may be taken to.[6]

The reader may notice that the concepts of realism outlined above are very abstract and that more concrete versions are needed to understand the characteristic features of economics. I fully agree. The justification for using the above concepts in this context is simple. The arguments we will next identify and then attack are arguments against such abstract ideas about realism, and they are arguments that have been popular in the debates over economics. If these abstract notions of realism were to be defeated, this would undermine any of the more concrete versions. If we can salvage the abstract forms, the controversy can be moved to more concrete levels. Furthermore, as will be seen, even these abstract notions of realism will help us comment on some peculiarities of economics.

The main focus here will be on the first pair of realisms and nonrealisms ([R1] . . . [∼R2]). I believe this is where any examination of realism about this or that thing has to begin, starting with [R1]. Questions about the second pair ([R3] . . . [∼R4]) can be raised subsequently. It should be clear that the arguments relevant for settling the issue concerning the first pair are often of a different kind than those relevant for settling the issue concerning the second pair.

4 Reasoning

My argument here for realism about economics proceeds through arguments against anti-realisms based on a number of different premises. The premises are phrased in terms of the generic "economic theory" and "economic entities" – this leaves open the precise extension of the expressions, that is, whether the claim is supposed to be true of all economic theories and entities or just a selection of them. In responding to the arguments based on the following premises, I will not ascribe them to any particular writers. I take all of them to be easily recognizable, even though evidently different in popularity.

(1) Economic theory postulates unobservables
(2) Economic theory simplifies and includes false assumptions
(3) Economic theory does not refer to anything that would fit its description
(4) Economics is policy-ineffective
(5) The economy is economics-dependent
(6) Accepted theories and statements of fact are results of rhetorical persuasion
(7) Economic entities are mind-dependent.

These claims – the list is far from comprehensive – are supposed by nonrealists to have nonrealist implications. A successful rebuttal of these arguments suggests the minimum claim that these arguments do not give sufficient reasons for nonrealism about economics. At least some general versions of realism should be defensible in the context of economics, such as [R1] and [R2]. It should be possible to defend them while granting the premises above. The rebuttal takes on the form of "even if ..." arguments. These arguments say, "even if (1) is true, economics might be factual"; "even if (2) is true, economics might be factual"; and so on, where "might be factual" means either [R1] or [R2] or both.

This strategy attempts to hit two targets: a certain class of defenses of economics and another class of critiques of economic theory. In regard to the first target, it aims to demolish some of the popular excuses that economists and others have been prone to offer whenever a given economic theory or the whole discipline of economics has been challenged regarding its factuality. In particular, (2) is part of a popular excuse in the hands of economists: since all theories are false anyway, there is nothing especially blameworthy about economic theories that are known to involve false elements. (6) is perhaps becoming more popular as a defensive instrument, too. It can easily be adopted as part of a globalizing argument in the vein of (2): since all established theories are socially constructed, such as outcomes of rhetorical persuasion – and therefore not factual – there is nothing specifically blameworthy about economic theories.

In regard to the second target, my arguments also serve to undermine some of the popular criticisms of current economics, such as those based on complaining about the unrealisticness of the assumptions of a given theory, and pointing out the rhetoricality of the arguments offered for mainstream economics. Abstract arguments of this sort are not only powerless, they are also unsound.

(1) Economic theory postulates unobservables

Economic theory appears to talk about entities such as preferences and expectations as well as other unobservables and unmeasurables (or hard-to-measurables). One may then suggest that the presence of such elements in economic theories precludes a genuinely realist view of such theories. Another premise behind the conclusion is the presumption that being real implies being observable.

One obvious way of challenging the argument is to question the second premise: being real by no means implies being observable. The fact of the matter is quite different: much or most of (the most significant features of) the world is unobservable. Therefore it is not surprising that natural sciences postulate unobservables and that this does not exclude realism about them. On the contrary, this is regarded as a significant feature of theories in natural sciences: thanks to employing theoretical concepts that are taken to refer to unobservables – which may be real – theories are such powerful aids in explanation, prediction, and control of phenomena (see, for example, Tuomela 1973).

Another angle of attack is to question the first premise by pointing out the ambiguity of "unobservable" and then suggesting that there is an important sense of this expression on which much of, most of, or all of, economics does not postulate unobservables. The sense of "is unobservable" behind such a claim is not "is inaccessible by sense perception" (like photons and quarks) but rather something like "radically departs from the ordinary commonsense furniture of the world." Given this stipulation, preferences and expectations are not unobservables but rather observables – or "commonsensibles" as I have suggested (Mäki 1998b). Economic theory talks about the commonsense furniture of the human world: costs and benefits, tastes and choices, firms and households, money and the market. Of course, such commonsensibles, or observables in a broad sense, are represented in economic theory rather differently from the way they are represented in the ordinary commonsense conception of the world. This gives rise to further arguments that are best treated separately (see (2) and (3) below).

(2) Economic theory simplifies and includes false assumptions

The argument using (2) as a premise can be made stronger by suggesting that all theories are by nature false. The implication is that there is nothing special about economic theory in this regard, thus no reason to worry on these grounds. This argument is rather popular among economists. In response to this argument, I have written at some length in my earlier work (but more needs to be done), and I will just summarize the main intuitions here. What is at stake is (*R*2) rather than (*R*1). Two questions arise:

(a) Could a theory involving falsehood possibly serve the pursuit of truth?

(b) Could a theory involving falsehood possibly be true?

The conventional answer to the first question is to say that the false assumptions of a theory will be gradually relaxed and replaced by true assumptions, thus turning the initial simplified account into a closer approximation of the complex reality. When so employed by the method of "decreasing abstraction" or "increasing approximation," falsehood serves the pursuit of truth. One problem with this response is that in economics the process is usually not taken very far beyond the first step of many very false assumptions. The modified versions of theory always continue to involve a number of false assumptions that are not relaxed. The second question thus arises.

There are several possible answers to question (b); I have elsewhere considered two of them. Both require an ontology that helps us understand the work an assumption is supposed to do in a theory. One answer is based on the idea that some assumptions that appear to be false can be paraphrased so as to turn them into true claims. For example, as Musgrave (1981) has shown, the assumption that factor F is absent may be false, but when paraphrased as the assumption that F has only a negligibly small impact on the phenomenon under study, it may be true (for refinements of Musgrave's argument, see Mäki 2000).

The other answer to question (b) is based on the idea that theories with false assumptions may be able to give nothing-but-true accounts of limited aspects of the relevant domain without giving the-whole-truth of it. A theory or model will violate the-whole-truth, while its false assumptions will violate nothing-but-the-truth. The intuition is that a falsehood is not only harmless but also useful provided it helps us slice the world into pieces so as to facilitate focusing on, or isolating whatever deserves such focused attention according to whatever happens to be our favored ontology. An isolative theory should truthfully highlight a limited set of real dependencies in the social world. Note that so put this idea is ontologically almost fully neutral. Perhaps the only ontology that would imply its denial is one which views the universe as a giant organism, all parts of which are tied together by unbreakable internal relations. No theory of only a part of such a universe could be true; the true theory has to embrace the whole universe. The rejection of such a radically wholistic ontology does not, of course, imply that just any theoretical isolation is fine for truth-seeking. Any particular theoretical isolation must meet specific ontological constraints of less radical kinds.

(3) Economic theory fails to refer to anything real that would fit its description

Here the route to fictionhood is more direct than in (2), but it uses (2) as a premise. The point in (3) is that economic theory does not even get off the ground, so to speak. It does not get off the ground in the sense that it cannot be taken even to refer to anything that exists. And because it does not hook up with the world by referring to entities in the world, the issue of whether the theory is true or false does not relevantly arise at all. So economic theory is about fictions at most, if it is *about* anything at all.

One premise behind this reasoning is the so-called description theory of reference (it is "behind" it in the strong sense of being hidden or implicit). Description theories of reference suggest that the reference of a term is determined by the descriptions associated with the term, and whenever the descriptions do not fit with anything in the world, the term fails to refer. Accordingly, "ideal gas" fails to refer since nothing in the world satisfies the associated idealizing assumptions. Likewise, the term "firm" in the context of the theory of perfect competition fails to refer to anything real, because there is nothing in the world that would possess the properties attributed to firms by the highly idealizing assumptions of the theory. Theories including such nonreferential expressions are about fictional entities at most, and therefore the issue of factual truth does not arise at all: in order to be true (or false) about X a theory must refer to X. The conclusion of the argument is that realism in the form of [R1] and [R2] cannot be maintained.

Again, a realist holding [R1] and [R2] may accept premise (3) without accepting the nonrealist conclusion. We may easily grant that there are no firms in the world with all the properties of a perfectly competitive firm, and yet hold that the theory of perfect competition may be used to refer to real business firms. This is because of what I have called *the multifunctionality of language*: the simple idea that language can be used to serve a number of different purposes. Keith Donnellan's (1966) distinction between the referential and attributive uses of definite descriptions is an example that can be invoked here. The idea is that we can use an expression for referring to something even if the associated description (given by a set of assumptions, for example) is wrong – deliberately or mistakenly. Thus, false assumptions do not preclude successful reference. On the other hand, in using a set of assumptions attributively, assertions are made about the properties of an entity. Since false assumptions attribute properties that the entity does not possess, they fail in the attributive task – even if they may succeed in the referential task. The falsehood of assumptions does not undermine reference – even though it undermines their truth. (For more details, see Mäki 1999.) And even though it undermines the truth of the assumptions, it does not necessarily undermine the truth of the theory – this is the point of the response to argument (2) above.

(4) Economics is policy-ineffective

Suppose one believes that economics has not been able to indicate the kind of uncontroversial technological success with which we usually credit physical sciences. Suppose further that one also believes that the best or the only sound argument for scientific realism is the argument from technological success – the "no-miracle argument" (see Boyd 1981). According to this argument, scientific realism – in this case the thesis that a given scientific theory factually refers and is at least approximately true – is the best explanation of the technologically successful implications of the theory. One then suggests that this argument is not available in the case of economics: it has not indicated the kind of uncontroversial technological success that we ascribe to physics. The conclusion is that since nothing better or nothing else can be used to support realism in the case of economics, we had better do without realism about economics.

Again, we do not have to (even if we may want to) question the first premise of this argument – that is, (4) – in order to challenge the argument. All we need to do is to question the second premise, that is, the no-miracle argument. And we do not have to question the no-miracle argument globally (even if we may do that, too), for it is sufficient to question it in the local case of economics. To do this, we may adopt the argument held by economists in the tradition of John Eliot Cairnes (1875) and Lionel Robbins (1935) to the effect that economics is different from physics in that economists have a more direct access to the fundamental entities of the economy they deal with. Therefore the sort of roundabout reasoning that we find in the no-miracle argument is not needed to substantiate our belief in the referential and veristic capacities of economic theories.

Economists who share the key tenets of the Cairnes–Robbins tradition might consider radically twisting the no-miracle argument. One may hold the view that economics is bound to be relatively weak in predictive power since its theories always at most capture a limited subset of all the factors that shape the phenomena: the uncontrollable complexity of economic systems and their surroundings makes the consistently accurate prediction of phenomena difficult if not impossible and thereby undermines technological success of the sort physical sciences are reported to exhibit. Now this is a statement of matters of fact – a kind of statement that to make it one needs a realist outlook to start with. From such a realist point of view one may then reverse the role of miracles: rather than saying that the technological success of science would be a miracle if scientific realism were not true, one might now say that *it would be a miracle if economics were technologically successful comparable to physics*, given our factual beliefs about the economy and economics – beliefs that are themselves premised upon scientific realism. On the latter reasoning, scientific realism serves as one of the premises, and the lack of technological success serves as a conclusion – while in the standard no-miracle argument, technological success is one of the premises and scientific realism is the conclusion. I should perhaps add that it is not until the very idea of technological success is qualified properly that this argument can be seriously considered.

More has to be said about argument (4). It can be resisted more directly. The proponents of the no-miracle argument typically fail to notice that the argument infers from technological success to *actual referential and veristic success*, thus implying something stronger than was included in realism according to our initial definitions [R1] and [R2] – namely the stronger theses [R3] and [R4]). The weaker definitions required only that economic theories may be true and that economic entities may exist. This means that one can be a realist about economics in the weaker senses (i) without using the no-miracle argument and (ii) without sharing the Cairnes–Robbins type of confidence in the referential and veristic successes already achieved by economics.

(5) The economy is economics-dependent

Saying that the economy is economics-dependent may mean at least two different things, depending on whether dependence is supposed to be conceptual or causal. In both cases, we may also say that economics contributes to the (social) construction of the economy. The argument from *conceptual construction* is a version of the old idealist doctrine according to which the world is essentially dependent on our thoughts of it – e.g. the world is a creation of our thinking. Thus, the economy is dependent on the economists' ways of conceptually representing it. There cannot be any gulf between the world and the economists' representations, since economists make worlds by means of conceptual representations, in particular by way of building models. Accordingly, representing amounts to world-making rather than world-uncovering. There is no distinction to be drawn between the world of a model and the real world: to create the former is to create the latter. Realism does not easily accommodate this idea without strong qualifications. There are many specific versions of this reasoning, such as the one discussed as argument (6) below.

The argument from *causal construction* is a popular claim and has sometimes been used against realism about social sciences. The implementation of a plan based on a theory is an exemplification of this idea: the world is shaped after the model of the theory. The phenomena of so-called self-fulfilling and self-defeating prophecies are also often cited in this context.

The first clarificatory point to make is this. It is certainly not the case that *theories* causally produce their objects in society, even though the idea is often formulated in this fashion. Unfortunately, the very phrasing of one of the major ideas is misleading here: it is as if the prophecies themselves fulfill or defeat themselves. At most, if the argument is to make any sense, it has to be phrased so as to state that *people* having the contents of those theories as the contents of their beliefs may act so as to causally help produce social realities and changes in them.

We have to make a distinction between two statements: (i) People inspired by theory *T* or the prediction it entails engage in action that produces or reproduces a social fact – and they act in that way *because* they are inspired by *T* or the prediction. *T* is made true – or, in other words, the object of *T* is made real – by people acting on *T*. (ii) The act of representing the social world by *T* creates a social fact – not only does it (re)conceptualize our view of the world, but also (re)constitutes the structure of the world. *T* is made true – or, in other words, the object of *T* is made real – by people expressing or holding *T*.

Statement (i) is completely compatible with realism, whereas (ii) is not. Realism accommodates causal construction, but rejects the above form of conceptual construction.

(6) Economic theory is a result of rhetorical persuasion

The perception of economics as rhetorical held by many observers after McCloskey's "The rhetoric of economics" (1983) has led some of them to a nonrealist image of economics. I can imagine the reasoning behind this argument might proceed like this. First there is the observation that rhetorical persuasion plays a major role in determining which theories economists accept and which they reject. One may then presume that both the truth and falsehood of economic theories, and the existence and nonexistence of the entities the theories appear to be about are closely – perhaps conceptually – linked to the acceptances and rejections of theories. One is then led to conclude that whatever helps determine acceptances and rejections also helps determine truth and existence and the lack thereof.

Those who are persuaded by an argument with (6) as a premise and nonrealism as a conclusion may be motivated by the obvious inadequacy of an alternative naive view which nobody holds, namely that the acceptances and rejections of theories are somehow determined by truth and falsehood which are determined by reality. And because in fact (*sic*!) acceptances and rejections are rather determined by us and our social interactions, so are truth-values and reality itself. As I see it, the problem with both the nonrealist argument from rhetoric and this naive "realist" alternative which may have motivated it, is one and the same: the link between (acceptance and rejection of) theory and reality is made too close on *a priori* grounds.

My response to the nonrealist argument from rhetoric loosens up the link between theory and reality and grants premise (6): yes, of course theories and their acceptance and rejection and modification and what have you may involve rhetoric. But this should not be taken to imply that existence and truth involve rhetoric. (Two qualifications may be needed here to block unnecessary misunderstandings: the existence of the economy does involve rhetorical persuasion on the part of economic agents, and claims to truth are often rhetorical acts.)

Just like in the case of argument (3) from the description theory of reference, I have invoked the idea of multifunctionality of language in dealing with argument (6). In the present case, the idea is the simple one that one and the same sentence or set of sentences may serve rhetorical and representational functions, even at the same time. Using a piece of language rhetorically does not exclude its (simultaneous) use for making possibly true claims about reality. Whatever persuades economists may be true – or false. Persuasion does not make it so.

(7) Economic entities are mind-dependent

We then come to the idea that since economic entities are dependent on the human mind for their existence, this undermines ontological realism. Now it is clear that no realist should deny the mind-dependence of the entities in the economic domain. Some such entities are mental entities, such as preferences and expectations. Some others are causally dependent on mental entities, such as the phenomena and institutions that are among the unintended consequences of human action. We may even consider going as far as granting that some economic entities are conceptually dependent on the mental even though they are not mental themselves.

Realism about mind-dependent entities constitutes a vast and complex issue, and there is no possibility of going into it here. I will instead adopt a very simple line. First of all, any notion of ontological realism supposedly capable of accommodating the subject matter of the social sciences must be defined in terms other than mind-independent existence. Unfortunately, most philosophical writing on realism does define realism exactly in those unhappy terms. Secondly, the relevant question for the issue of realism about economics is whether economic entities are dependent on the minds of economists *qua* economists, granting that economic entities are dependent on the minds of economic actors. One may then point out that the presumed dependence may be conceptual or causal as in the case of (5) above. One can then suggest that it is an empirical matter whether there is such a causal dependence or not. One may further suggest that even though economists *qua* economists (in the role of policy advisors, propagandists, teachers, etc.) may occasionally have some impact on what happens in the economy, the existence of the major economic entities (such as the institutions of money and credit, market and firm) is not dependent on the minds of economists *qua* economists. And one may then say that, after all, all this is almost irrelevant: whatever the degree of such dependence, the reasoning presented above in the context of (5) would apply here, too.

5 Conclusion

Realism about economics may be resisted and should be resisted – if for no other reason, at least in order to urge further refinements of realism about economics. But it should not be resisted for wrong reasons. I have listed some arguments against realism that I believe are not sound. That some of these arguments tend to be somewhat popular confirms what I said in the beginning: there is more realism in economics than easily meets the eye.

If what I have said in the foregoing sounds too complacent or uncritical about current economics, I can add one final remark. I have defended the applicability of rather weak concepts of realism – [R1] and [R2]. I have said nothing or little about whether the stronger forms [R3] and [R4] apply to concrete cases in actual economics. This strategy is deliberate, and the grounds are twofold: first, the issue concerning [R1] and [R2] has to be settled before trying to settle the issue concerning [R3] and [R4]; second, the arguments relevant for settling the two issues are not the same – other kinds of arguments would be needed to tackle the issue of [R3] and [R4]. Economics has to survive the arguments against [R1] and [R2] in order even to confront the arguments against [R3] and [R4]. Ultimately, one wants to critically examine particular economic theories for their truth and particular postulated entities for their existence. Such an examination will not get off the ground if economics as a discipline does not yield to a realist interpretation in the sense of [R1] and [R2]. In this modest but indispensable way, the present chapter has outlined a groundwork exercise.

My fear is that giving up [R1] and [R2] would result in the worst kind of complacency. The resolution of the ultimate issue of whether economics is in touch with facts or whether it is a game of just playing with fictions would be biased towards the latter alternative.

Notes

1. In chapter 3 in this volume, Partha Dasgupta reports the discovery that 90 percent of the articles published in the *American Economic Review* during 1991–1995 were about the "real world" (Dasgupta's quotes). Such articles, according to his definitions, are either "applied theory" (by which he means "a piece of theoretical analysis that tries to explain some observed fact, or which analyses the implications of particular types of policies"), or "experimental and/or empirical economics." In statements like this, notions such as being "about the real world" require a lot of clarification in order for those statements to be assessable.
2. Among the several forms of realisticness attributable to economic models and their assumptions are referentiality, truth, comprehensiveness, observationality, plausibility, and policy relevance.
3. In this spirit, I have written on economic theories and methods in general (e.g. Mäki 2000), Friedman's views (e.g. Mäki 1992a), transaction cost economics, in particular Coase's and Williamson's contributions (e.g. Mäki 1998a), and Austrian economics,

in particular Menger's views, as well as theories of money and the market process (e.g. Mäki 1992b, 1997).

4. The premises of these arguments range from the recognition of the violation of the truth by good theories (e.g. Mäki 1998b, 2000); the observation maintained by sociologists of scientific knowledge that aspects of science and perhaps its objects are socially shaped (e.g. Mäki 1993a); to the special case of suggesting that science has a rhetorical character (e.g. Mäki 1993b); and others.

5. The notion of truth – and the notion of the advisability of pursuing the truth – is often regarded as an essential ingredient of scientific realism. However, a realist notion should not be conflated with pragmatist notions of truth, such as the idea in Mark Blaug's chapter 2 in this volume, according to which "economic theories are either true or false in the sense that it makes a difference for economic policy whether we act on the basis of one economic theory or another" (45).

6. In his chapter 2, Mark Blaug contrasts scientific realism and postmodernism as the major alternative methodological outlooks in current economics: realists are concerned with empirical testing and truth, while for the postmodernists anything goes. In clarification, one should point out that while most scientific realists regard empirical testing as a necessary ingredient of science, the notion of empirical testing – or the doctrine of methodological empiricism – is not an ingredient in *the concept* of scientific realism itself.

References

Boyd, Richard (1981). Scientific realism and naturalistic epistemology, *PSA 1980*, 2, eds. Peter Asquith and Ronald Giere. East Lansing: Philosophy of Science Association

Cairnes, John Eliot (1875). *The Character and Logical Method of Political Economy*. London: Macmillan

Donnellan, Keith S. (1966). Reference and definite descriptions, *Philosophical Review* 75, 281–304

McCloskey, D.N. (1983). The rhetoric of economics, *Journal of Economic Literature*, 31, 434–461

Mäki, Uskali (1992a). Friedman and realism, *Research in the History of Economic Thought and Methodology*, 10, 171–195

(1992b). The market as an isolated causal process: a metaphysical ground for realism, in Bruce Caldwell and Stephan Boehm (eds.), *Austrian Economics: Tensions and New Developments*. Dordrecht: Kluwer, 35–59

(1993a). Social theories of science and the fate of institutionalism in economics, in Uskali Mäki, Bo Gustafsson, and Christian Knudsen (eds.), *Rationality, Institutions and Economic Methodology*. London: Routledge, 76–109

(1993b). Two philosophies of the rhetoric of economics, in Willie Henderson, Tony Dudley-Evans, and Roger Backhouse (eds.), *Economics and Language*. London: Routledge, 23–50

(1997). Universals and the *Methodenstreit*: a reexamination of Carl Menger's conception of economics as an exact science, *Studies in History and Philosophy of Science*, 28, 475–495

(1998a). Is Coase a realist?, *Philosophy of the Social Sciences*, 28, 5–31

(1998b). Aspects of realism about economics, *Theoria*, 13, 301–319

(1999). Representation repressed. Two kinds of semantic scepticism in economics, in Roberto Scazzieri, Rema Rossini Favretti, and Giorgio Sandri (eds.), *Incommensurability and Translation: Kuhnian Perspectives on Scientific Communication and Theory Change*. Cheltenham: Edward Elgar, 307–321

(2000). Kinds of assumptions and their truth: shaking an untwisted F-twist, *Kyklos*, 53, 317–336

(2001). Realisms and their opponents, in Neil J. Smelser and Paul B. Baltes (eds.), *International Encyclopedia of the Social and Behavioral Sciences,* 19. Amsterdam: Elsevier, 12815–12821

Musgrave, Alan (1981). "Unreal assumptions" in economic theory: the F-twist untwisted, *Kyklos,* 34, 377–387

Niiniluoto, Ilkka (1999). *Critical Scientific Realism*. Oxford: Clarendon Press

Robbins, Lionel (1935). *An Essay on the Nature and Significance of Economics*. London: Macmillan

Tuomela, Raimo (1973). *Theoretical Concepts*. Berlin: Springer Verlag

Part III
Economic models and economic reality

5 Credible worlds: the status of theoretical models in economics

Robert Sugden

I write this chapter not as a methodologist or as a philosopher of social science – neither of which I can make any claim to be – but as a theoretical economist. I have spent a considerable part of my life building economic models, and examining the models that other economists have built. I believe that I am making reasonably good use of my talents in an attempt to understand the social world. I have no fellow-feeling with those economic theorists who, off the record at seminars and conferences, admit that they are only playing a game with other theorists. If their models are not intended seriously, I want to say (and do say when I feel sufficiently combative), why do they expect me to spend my time listening to their expositions? Count me out of the game. At the back of my mind, however, there is a trace of self-doubt. Do the sort of models that I try to build really help us to understand the world? Or am I too just playing a game, without being self-critical enough to admit it?

My starting point is that model-building in economics has serious intent only if it is ultimately directed towards telling us something about the real world. In using the expression "the real world" – as I shall throughout the chapter – I immediately reveal myself as an economic theorist. This expression is standardly used by economic theorists to mark the distinction between the world inside a model and the "real" world outside it. Theory becomes just a game when theorists work entirely in the world of models. As an analogy, we might think of chess, which was once a model of warfare, but has become a game – a self-contained world with no reference to anything outside itself.

My strategy is to focus on two models – George Akerlof's "market for lemons," and Thomas Schelling's "checkerboard city" – which exemplify the kind of model-building to which I aspire. Of course, these are not typical examples of economic models: they represent theory at its best. Nevertheless, at least at first sight, these models have many of the vices that critics attribute to theoretical economics: they are abstract and unrealistic, and they lead to no clearly testable hypotheses. It would be easy to caricature them as examples – perhaps unusually imaginative and, from a mathematical point of view, unusually informal examples – of the games that economic theorists play. Thus, they provide suitable case studies for an attempted defense of model-building in economics.

I believe that each of these models tells us something important and true about the real world. My object is to discover just what these models do tell us about the world, and how they do it.

1   Akerlof and the market for "lemons"

Akerlof's 1970 paper "The market for 'lemons'" is one of the best-known papers in theoretical economics. It is generally seen as having introduced to economics the concept of *asymmetric information*, and in doing so, sparking off what is now a whole branch of economics: the economics of information. It is a theoretical paper that almost all economists, however untheoretical they might be, would now recognize as important. It is also a paper that just about every economic theorist would love to have written. Because there is no dispute about its value, Akerlof's paper is particularly suitable for my purposes. Everyone can see that this is a major contribution to economics.[1] The puzzle is to say exactly what the contribution is. Is Akerlof telling us anything about the real world, and if so, what?

It is worth looking closely at the structure of the paper. Here is the opening paragraph:

This paper relates quality and uncertainty. The existence of goods of many grades poses interesting and important problems for the theory of markets. On the one hand, the interaction of quality differences and uncertainty may explain important institutions of the labor market. On the other hand, this paper presents a struggling attempt to give structure to the statement: "Business in underdeveloped countries is difficult"; in particular, a structure is given for determining the economic costs of dishonesty. Additional applications of the theory include comments on the structure of money markets, on the notion of "insurability," on the liquidity of durables, and on brand-name goods. (1970, 488)

Clearly, Akerlof is claiming that his paper has something to say about an astonishingly wide range of phenomena in the real world. The paper, we are promised, is going to tell us something about the institutions of the labor market, about business in underdeveloped countries, about insurability, and so on. But what kind of thing is it going to tell us? On this point, Akerlof is rather coy. In the case of the labor market, he seems to be promising to *explain* some features of the real world. (Or is he? See later.) But in the case of business in underdeveloped countries, he is only going to *give structure to [a] statement* that is often made about the real world. Here, the implication seems to be that Akerlof's model will somehow reformulate an empirical proposition which is generally believed to be true (but might actually be false). In the other cases, we are promised *comments* which are to be understood as applications of the theory he is to present.

Akerlof then says that, although his theory has these very general applications, he will focus on the market for used cars: "The automobile market is used as a finger exercise to illustrate and develop these thoughts. It should be emphasized that this market is chosen for its concreteness and ease in understanding rather than for its importance or realism" (1970, 489).

On first reading, it is tempting to interpret "the automobile market" as the market in which real people buy and sell real cars, and to think that Akerlof is going to present some kind of case-study. One can see why he might focus on one particular market which is easy to understand, even if that market is not very important on the scale of the economy as a whole. But then what does Akerlof mean when he says that this market is not *realistic*? The object of a case-study may be unrepresentative, but it cannot be unrealistic. To make sense of this passage, I think, we have to recognize that it marks a transition between the real world and the world of models. Akerlof *is* using the real automobile market as an example. But what he is going to present is not an empirical case study; it is a *model* of the automobile market. Although it is the real market which may be unimportant, it is the model which may be unrealistic.

Akerlof moves straight on to the central section of his paper, section II, entitled "The Model with Automobiles as an Example." The transition from reality to model is made again at the very beginning of this section:

The example of used cars captures the essence of the problem. From time to time one hears either mention of or surprise at the large price difference between new cars and those which have just left the showroom. The usual lunch table justification for this phenomenon is the pure joy of owning a "new" car. We offer a different explanation. Suppose (for the sake of clarity rather than realism) that there are just four kinds of cars. There are new cars and used cars. There are good cars and bad cars. (1970, 489)

The first four sentences are about an observed property of the real world: there is a large price difference between new cars and almost-new ones. Akerlof suggests that, at least from the viewpoint of the lunch table, this observation is difficult to explain. If we assume that Akerlof takes lunch with other economists, the implication is that *economics* cannot easily explain it; the "pure joy" hypothesis sounds like an ad hoc stratagem to rescue conventional price theory. So far, then, the mode of argument might be Popperian: there is a received theory which makes certain predictions about market prices; observations of the used-car market are contrary to those predictions; therefore, a new theory is needed.[2]

But from the word "Suppose" in the passage above, we move out of the real world, and into the world of the model. Akerlof sets up an imaginary world which makes no pretence to be realistic. In this world, there are two groups of traders, "type one" and "type two." All traders of a given type are alike. There are n cars, which differ only in "quality." Quality is measured in money units, and is uniformly distributed over some range. Each group of traders maximizes an aggregate utility function. For group one, utility is the sum of the qualities of the cars it owns and the monetary value of its consumption of other goods. For group two, the utility function is the same, except that quality is multiplied by $3/2$. Thus, for any given quality of car, the monetary value of a car to type one traders is less than its monetary value to type two traders. All cars are initially owned by type one traders. The quality of cars has a uniform distribution. The quality of each car is known only to its owner, but the average quality of all traded cars is known to everyone.

Akerlof admits that these assumptions are not realistic: they are not even close approximations to properties of the real used-car market. He justifies them as simplifications which allow him to focus on those features of the real market that he wishes to analyze. For example, he defends his assumptions about utility (which implicitly impose risk neutrality) against what he takes to be the more realistic alternative assumption of risk aversion by saying that he does not want to get "needlessly mired in algebraic complication": "The use of linear utility allows a focus on the effects of asymmetry of information; with a concave utility function we would have to deal with the usual risk-variance effects of uncertainty and the special effects we have to deal with here" (1970, 490–491).

Akerlof investigates what happens in his model world. The main conclusion is simple and startling. He shows that if cars are to be traded at all, there must be a single market price p. Then:

> However, with any price p, average quality is $p/2$ and therefore at no price will any trade take place at all: in spite of the fact that *at any given price* [between certain limits] there are traders of type one who are willing to sell their automobiles at a price which traders of type two are willing to pay. (1970, 491)

Finally, Akerlof shows what would happen in the same market if information were symmetric – that is, if neither buyers nor sellers knew the quality of individual cars, but both knew the probability distribution of quality. In this case, there is a market-clearing equilibrium price, and trade takes place, just as the standard theory of markets would lead us to expect. Akerlof ends section II at this point, so let us take stock.

What we have been shown is that in a highly unrealistic model of the used-car market, no trade takes place – even though each car is worth less to its owner than it would be to a potential buyer. We have also been given some reason to think that, in generating this result, the crucial property of the model world is that *sellers know more than buyers*. Notice that, taken literally, Akerlof's result is too strong to fit with the phenomenon he originally promised to explain – the price difference between new and used cars.[3] Presumably, then, Akerlof sees his model as describing in extreme form the workings of some *tendency* which exists in the real used-car market, by virtue of the asymmetry of information which (he claims) is a property of that market. This tendency is a used-car version of Gresham's Law: bad cars drive out good. In the real used-car market, according to Akerlof, this tendency has the effect of reducing the average quality of cars traded, but not eliminating trade altogether; the low quality of traded cars then explains their low price.

Remarkably, Akerlof says nothing more about the *real* market in used cars. In the whole paper, the only empirical statement about the used-car market is the one I have quoted, about lunch table conversation. Akerlof presents no evidence to support his claim that there is a large price difference between new and almost-new cars. This is perhaps understandable, since he clearly assumes that this price difference is generally known. More surprisingly, he presents no evidence that the owners of nearly-new cars know significantly more about their quality than do potential buyers. And although later in the paper he talks about market institutions which can overcome the problem of asymmetric information, he does not offer any argument, theoretical or empirical, to counter the hypothesis that such institutions exist in the used-car market. But if they do, Akerlof's explanation of price differences is undermined.

However, Akerlof has quite a lot to say about *other* real markets in section III of the paper, "Examples and Applications." In four subsections, entitled "Insurance," "The Employment of Minorities," "The Costs of Dishonesty," and "Credit Markets in Underdeveloped Countries," Akerlof presents what are effectively brief case-studies. We are told that adverse selection in the insurance market is "strictly analogous to our automobiles case" (1970, 493), that "the Lemons Principle . . . casts light on the employment of minorities" (1970, 494), that "the Lemons model can be used to make some comments on the costs of dishonesty" (1970, 495), and that "credit markets in underdeveloped countries often strongly reflect the Lemons Principle" (1970, 497). These discussions are in the style that economists call "casual empiricism." They are suggestive, just as the used-car case is, but they cannot be regarded as any kind of *test* of a hypothesis. In fact, there *is* no hypothesis. Akerlof never defines the "Lemons Principle"; all we can safely infer is that this term refers to the model of the used-car market. Ultimately, then, the claims of section III amount to this: in these four cases, we see markets that are in some way like the model.

The final part of the paper (apart from a very short conclusion) is section IV, "Countervailing Institutions." This is a brief discussion, again in the mode of casual empiricism, of some real-world institutions which counteract the problem of asymmetric information. The examples looked at are guarantees, brand names, hotel and restaurant chains, and certification in the labor market (such as the certification of doctors and barbers). The latter example seems to be what Akerlof was referring to in his introduction, when he claimed that his approach might "explain important institutions of the labor market." Here, the claim seems to be that there are markets which *would* be like the model of the used-car market, were it not for some special institutional feature; therefore, the model explains those features.

From a Popperian perspective, sections III and IV have all the hallmarks of "pseudo-science." Akerlof has not proposed any hypothesis in a form that could be tested against observation. All he has presented is an empirically ill-defined "Lemons Principle." In section III, he has assembled a fairly random assortment of evidence which appears to confirm that principle. In section IV, he argues that the real world often is *not* like the model, but this is to be seen not as refutation but as additional confirmation. What kind of scientific reasoning is this?

2   Schelling's "checkerboard" model of racial sorting

My other example of a theoretical model in economics is not quite as famous as the market for lemons, but it is a personal favorite of mine.[4] It also deserves to be recognized as one of the earliest uses of what is now a well-established theoretical method: evolutionary game theory with localized interactions in a spatial structure. This is the chapter "Sorting and mixing: race and sex" in Schelling's book *Micromotives and Macrobehavior* (1978).

The book as a whole is concerned with one of the classic themes of economics: the unintended social consequences of uncoordinated individual actions. Using a wide range of novel and surprising examples, Schelling sets out to show that spontaneous human interaction typically generates unintended patterns at the social level; in some cases these patterns are desirable, but in many cases they are not.

Schelling opens this chapter with an extended and informal discussion of segregation by color and by sex in various social settings. His concern is with patterns of segregation that arise out of the voluntary choices of individuals. One important case of such self-segregation, he suggests, is the housing market of American cities. Blacks and whites[5] tend to live in separate areas; the boundaries of these areas change over time, but the segregation remains. Schelling suggests that it is unlikely that almost all Americans desire to live in such sharply segregated areas. He asks us to consider the possibility that the sharp segregation we observe at the social level is an unintended consequence of individual actions which are motivated only by a preference for not living in an area in which people of the other color form an overwhelming majority. In the context of tables in a cafeteria for a baseball training camp, Schelling puts his hypothesis like this:

Players can ignore, accept, or even prefer mixed tables but become uncomfortable or self-conscious, or think that others are uncomfortable or self-conscious, when the mixture is lopsided. Joining a table with blacks and whites is a casual thing, but being the seventh at a table with six players of the opposite color imposes a threshold of self-consciousness that spoils the easy atmosphere and can lead to complete and sustained separation. (1978, 144)

Having discussed a number of cases of self-segregation, both by color and by sex, and in each case having floated the hypothesis that sharp segregation is an unintended consequence of much milder preferences, Schelling presents a "self-forming neighborhood model." He begins disarmingly:

Some vivid dynamics can be generated by any reader with a half-hour to spare, a roll of pennies and a roll of dimes, a tabletop, a large sheet of paper, a spirit of scientific enquiry, or, failing that spirit, a fondness for games. (1978, 147)

We are instructed to mark out an 8×8 grid of squares. The dimes and pennies "represent the members of two homogeneous groups – men and women, blacks and whites, French-speaking and English-speaking, officers and enlisted men, students and faculty, surfers and swimmers, the well dressed and the poorly dressed, or any other dichotomy that is exhaustive and recognizable" (1978, 147). We then distribute coins over the squares of the grid. Each square must either be allocated one coin or left empty (it is important to leave some empty spaces). Next, we postulate a condition which determines whether a coin is "content" with its neighborhood. For example, we might specify that a coin is content provided that at least one-third of its neighbors (that is, coins on horizontally, vertically or diagonally adjacent squares) are of the same type as itself. Then we look for coins which are not content. Whenever we find such a coin, we move it to the nearest empty square at which it *is* content (even if, in so doing, we make other coins discontented). This continues until there are no discontented coins. Schelling suggests that we try this with different initial distributions of coins and different rules. What we will find, he says, is a very strong tendency for the emergence of sharply segregated distributions of coins, even when the condition for contentedness is quite weak. I have followed Schelling's instructions (with the help of a computer program rather than paper and coins), and I can confirm that he is right. Clearly, Schelling expects that after we have watched the workings of this model, we will find his earlier arguments about real-world segregation more convincing.

The general strategy of Schelling's chapter is remarkably similar to that of Akerlof's paper. Each author is claiming that some regularity R (bad products driving out good, persistent racial segregation with moving geographical boundaries) can be found in economic or social phenomena. Each is also claiming that R can be explained by some set of causal factors F (sellers being better-informed than buyers, a common preference not to be heavily outnumbered by neighbors not of one's own type). Implicitly, each is making three claims: that R occurs (or often occurs), that F operates (or often operates), and that

F causes R (or tends to cause it). Neither presents any of these claims as a testable hypothesis, but each offers informal evidence from selected case studies which seems to support the first two claims. Each uses a formal model in support of the claim about causation. In each case, the formal model is a very simple, fully described and self-contained world. The supposedly causal factors F are built into the specification of the model. In the model world, R is found in an extreme form. This is supposed to make more credible the claim that in the real world, F causes R. But just how is that claim made more credible?

3   Conceptual exploration

Before going on, we need to consider an alternative reading of Akerlof and Schelling, in which their models are not intended to support any claims about the real world.[6] As Daniel Hausman (1992, 221) has pointed out, theoretical work in economics is often concerned with "conceptual exploration" rather than "empirical theorizing." Conceptual exploration investigates the *internal* properties of models, without considering the relationship between the world of the model and the real world.

Such work can be seen as valuable, even by someone who insists that the *ultimate* purpose of model-building is to tell us something about the real world. For example, it can be valuable because it finds simpler formulations of existing theories, or discovers useful theorems within those theories. (Consider Paul Samuelson's, 1947, demonstration that most of conventional demand theory can be deduced from a few simple axioms about consistent choice.) Or it can be valuable because it discovers previously unsuspected inconsistencies in received theories. (For example, Kenneth Arrow's impossibility theorem, 1951/1963, can be interpreted as a demonstration of the incoherence of Bergson-Samuelson welfare economics.[7]) There are also instances in which the development of a theory intended for one application has generated results which have later proved to be useful in completely different domains. (Think how much has grown out of John von Neumann and Oskar Morgenstern's exploration of strategies for playing poker.) Thus, to characterize Akerlof's and Schelling's models as conceptual exploration need not be to denigrate them.

So let us consider what we would learn from these models if we interpreted them as conceptual exploration and nothing else. Take Akerlof first. Akerlof's contribution, it might be said, is to show that some implications of the standard behavioral assumptions of economic theory are highly sensitive to the particular simplifying assumptions that are made about knowledge.[8] More specifically, the usual results about Pareto-efficient, market-clearing equilibrium trade can be radically altered if, instead of assuming that buyers and sellers are equally well-informed, we allow some degree of asymmetry of information. The message of Akerlof's paper, then, is that some commonly invoked theoretical propositions about markets are not as robust as was previously thought. Thus, conclusions derived from models which assume symmetric information should be treated with caution, and new theories need to be developed which take account of the effects of asymmetric information. On this reading, the discussion of used cars is no more than a "story" attached to a formal model, useful in aiding exposition and comprehension, but which can be dispensed with if necessary.[9] The paper is not about used cars: it is about the theory of markets.

What about Schelling? We might say that Schelling is presenting a critique of a commonly held view that segregation must be the product either of deliberate public policy or of strongly segregationist preferences. The checkerboard model is a counterexample to these claims: it shows that segregation *could* arise without either of those factors being present. On this reading, Schelling is making an important contribution to debates about segregation in the real world, but the contribution is conceptual: he is pointing to an error in an existing theory. In terms of the symbols I introduced in section 2, Schelling is not asserting: "R occurs, F operates, and F causes R." All he is asserting is: "R could occur, F could operate, and it could be the case that F caused R."

It must be said that there is at least some textual evidence that both Akerlof and Schelling are tempted by this kind of interpretation of their models. As I have already suggested, Akerlof often seems to be taking care *not* to draw inferences about the real world from his model. For example, although he does claim to be offering an explanation of price differences in the real car market, his other references to "explanation" are more nuanced. Notice that in the opening paragraph he does not claim that *his model* explains important institutions of the labor market: what *may* (not does) explain them is "the interaction of quality differences and uncertainty." The final sentence of the paper uses a similar formulation: "the difficulty of distinguishing good quality from bad . . . may indeed explain many economic institutions" (1970, 500). On one reading of "may" in these passages, Akerlof is engaged only in conceptual exploration: he is considering what sorts of theories are possible, but not whether or not these theories actually explain the phenomena of the real world. However, I shall suggest that a more natural reading is that Akerlof is trying to say something like this: I believe that economists will be able to use the ideas in this paper to construct theories which *do* explain important economic institutions.

Schelling is more explicit about his method, and what it can tell us:

What can we conclude from an exercise like this? We may at least be able to disprove a few notions that are themselves based on reasoning no more complicated than the checkerboard. Propositions beginning with "It stands to reason that . . . " can sometimes be discredited by exceedingly simple demonstrations that, though perhaps true, they do not exactly "stand to reason." We can at least persuade ourselves that certain mechanisms could work, and that observable aggregate phenomena could be compatible with types of "molecular movement" that do not closely resemble the aggregate outcomes that they determine. (1978, 152)

Schelling does not elaborate on what notions he *has* disproved. Possibly what he has in mind is the notion that either deliberate policy or the existence of strongly segregationist preferences is a necessary condition for the kind of racial segregation that is observed in American cities. His claim, then, is that he has discredited this notion by means of a counterexample.

Whatever we make of these passages, neither work, considered as a whole, can satisfactorily be read as conceptual exploration and nothing else. The most obvious objection to this kind of interpretation is that Akerlof and Schelling both devote such a lot of space to the discussion of real-world phenomena. Granted that Akerlof's treatment of the used-car market has some of the hallmarks of a theorist's "story," what is the point of all the "examples and applications" in his section III, or of the discussion of "countervailing institutions" in section IV, if not to tell us something about how the world really is? This material may be casual empiricism, but it is empiricism none the less. It is not just a way of helping us to understand the internal logic of the model. Similarly, Schelling's discussion of the baseball training camp is clearly intended as a description of the real world. Its purpose, surely, is to persuade us of the credibility of the hypothesis that real people – it is hinted, people like us – have mildly segregationist preferences. If all we were being offered was a counterexample to a general theoretical claim, such material would be redundant.

Clearly, neither Akerlof nor Schelling wants to claim that his work is a completed theory. The suggestion seems to be that these are preliminary sketches of theories. The models that are presented are perhaps supposed to stand in the sort of relation to a completed theory that a "concept car" does to a new production model, or that the clothes in a *haute couture* fashion show do to the latest designs in a fashion shop. That is, these models are suggestions about how to set about explaining some phenomenon in the real world. To put this another way, they are sketches of processes which, according to their creators, *might* explain phenomena we can observe in the real world. But the sense of "might explain" here is not just the kind of logical possibility that could be discovered by conceptual exploration. (The latter sense could be paraphrased as: "In principle, it is possible that processes with this particular formal structure could explain regularities with that particular formal structure.") The theorist is declaring his confidence that his approach is likely to work *as an explanation*, even if he does not claim so to have explained anything so far.

If Akerlof's and Schelling's disclaimers were to be read as saying "This work is conceptual exploration and nothing else," they would surely be disingenuous. We are being offered potential explanations of real-world phenomena. We are being encouraged to take these potential explanations seriously – perhaps even

to do some of the work necessary to turn these sketches of theories into production models. If we are to do this, it is not enough that we have confidence in the
technical feasibility of an internally consistent theory. Of course, having that
confidence is important, and we can get it by conceptual exploration of formal
models. But what we need in addition is some confidence that the production
model is likely to do the job for which it has been designed – that it is likely to
explain real-world phenomena. In other words, we need to see a sketch of an
actual explanation, not just of a logically coherent formal structure. We should
expect Akerlof's and Schelling's models to provide explanations, however tentative and imperfect, of regularities in the real world. I shall proceed on the
assumption that these models are intended to function as such explanations.

4   Instrumentalism

This brings us back to the problem: how do unrealistic economic models explain
real-world phenomena?

Many economists are attracted by the instrumentalist position that a theory
should be judged only on its predictive power within the particular domain in
which it is intended to be used. According to one version of instrumentalism,
the "assumptions" of a theory, properly understood, are no more than a compact notation for summarizing the theory's predictions; thus, the question of
whether assumptions are realistic or unrealistic does not arise. An alternative
form of instrumentalism, perhaps more appropriate for economics, accepts that
the assumptions of a theory *refer to* things in the real world, but maintains that it
does not matter whether those assumptions are true or false. On either account,
the assumptions of a theory *function* only as a representation of the theory's
predictions.

Instrumentalist arguments are often used in defense of the neoclassical theory of price determination which assumes utility-maximizing consumers, profit-
maximizing firms, and the instantaneous adjustment of prices to market-clearing
levels. In the instrumentalist interpretation, the object of the neoclassical theory is to predict changes in the prices and total quantities traded of different
goods as a result of exogenous changes (such as changes in technology or
taxes). On this view, aggregated economic statistics play the same role in economics as the movements of the heavenly bodies through the sky did in early
astronomy:[10] they are the only phenomena we want to predict, and the only (or
only acceptable) data.[11] The neoclassical theory is just a compact description
of a set of predictions. To ask whether its assumptions are realistic is either to
make a category mistake (because assumptions do not refer to anything that has
real existence) or to miss the point (because, although assumptions refer to real
things, the truth or falsity of those references has no bearing on the value of the
theory).

But is it possible to understand Akerlof's and Schelling's models instrumentally? These models are certainly similar to the neoclassical model of markets in their use of highly simplified assumptions which, if taken literally, are highly unrealistic. But if these models are intended to be read instrumentally, we should expect to find them being used to generate unambiguous predictions about the real world. Further, there should be a clear distinction between assumptions (which either have no truth values at all, or are allowed to be false) and predictions (which are asserted to be true).

In fact, neither Akerlof nor Schelling proposes any explicit and testable hypothesis about the real world. Nor does either theorist maintain an instrumentalist distinction between assumptions and predictions. Akerlof's case studies seem to be intended as much to persuade us of the credibility of his assumptions about asymmetric information as to persuade us that the volume of trade is suboptimal. As I have already said, Schelling's discussion of the baseball camp seems to be intended to persuade us of the credibility of his assumptions about preferences. On the most natural readings, I suggest, Akerlof and Schelling think they are telling us about forces or tendencies which connect *real* causes (asymmetric information, mildly segregationist preferences) to *real* effects (suboptimal volumes of trade, sharp segregation). Akerlof's and Schelling's unrealistic models are supposed to give support to these claims about real tendencies. Whatever method this is, it is not instrumentalism: it is some form of realism.

5   Metaphor and caricature

Allan Gibbard and Hal Varian (1978) offer an interpretation of economic models which emphasizes explanation rather than prediction. They characterize a model as the conjunction of two elements: an uninterpreted formal system, within which logical deductions can be made, and a "story" which gives some kind of interpretation of that formal system. With Schelling's checkerboard model apparently in mind, they describe a form of modeling in which the fit of the model to the real world is *casual*:

> The goal of casual application is to explain aspects of the world that can be noticed or conjectured without explicit techniques of measurement. In some cases, an aspect of the world (such as price dispersal, housing segregation, and the like) is noticed, and certain aspects of the micro-situation are thought perhaps to explain it; a model is then constructed to provide the explanation. In other cases, an aspect of the micro-world is noticed, and a model is used to investigate the kinds of effects such a factor could be expected to have. (1978, 672)

This seems a fair description of what both Akerlof and Schelling are doing. But Gibbard and Varian have disappointingly little to say about *how* a casual model explains an aspect of the real world, or how it allows us to investigate the likely effects of real-world factors on real-world phenomena.

Gibbard and Varian recognize – indeed, they welcome – the fact that casual models are unrealistic; but their defense of this lack of realism is itself rather casual:

> When economic models are used in this way to explain casually observable features of the world, it is important that one be able to grasp the explanation. Simplicity, then, will be a highly desirable feature of such models. Complications to get as close as possible a fit to reality will be undesirable if they make the model less possible to grasp. Such complications may, moreover, be unnecessary, since the aspects of the world the model is used to explain are not precisely measured. (1978, 672)

The suggestion here seems to be that the purpose of a model is to *communicate* an idea to an audience; simplicity is a virtue because it makes communication easier. But this puts the cart before the horse. What has to be communicated is not just an idea: it is a claim about how things really are, along with reasons for accepting that claim as true. Simplicity in communication has a point only if there is something to be communicated. While granting that Akerlof's and Schelling's models are easy to grasp, we may still ask what exactly we have grasped. How do these models come to be explanations? And explanations of what?

One possible answer is given by Deirdre McCloskey (1983, 502–507), who argues that models are *metaphors*. According to McCloskey, the modeler's claim is simply that the real world is *like* the model in some significant respect (1983, 502). In evaluating a model, we should ask the same questions as we would when evaluating a metaphor: "Is it illuminating, is it satisfying, is it apt?" (1983, 506). The claim "models are metaphors" must, I think, be understood as a metaphor in itself. As a metaphor, it is certainly satisfying and apt; but, in relation to our examination of Akerlof's and Schelling's models, just how illuminating is it?

Clearly, Akerlof and Schelling *are* claiming that the real world is like their models in some significant respects. What is at issue is what exactly these claims amount to, and how (if at all) they can be justified. Translating into McCloskey's language, what is at issue is how illuminating and how apt Akerlof's and Schelling's metaphors are. But this translation of the question does not take us any nearer to an answer.

Gibbard and Varian (1978) perhaps come closer to an understanding of the status of models like Akerlof's and Schelling's when they suggest that models are *caricatures*. The concept of caricature is tighter than that of metaphor, since the ingredients of a caricature must be taken from the corresponding reality. (Compare cartoons. John Bull, the fat, beef-eating yeoman farmer, was originally a caricature of a characteristic Englishman. Although no longer a valid caricature, he is still recognizable as a symbol of, or metaphor for, Englishness.) According to Gibbard and Varian, the assumptions of a model may be chosen "not to approximate reality, but to exaggerate or isolate some feature of reality" (1978, 673). The aim is "to distort reality in a way that illuminates certain aspects of that reality" (1978, 676).

The idea that models are caricatures suggests that models may be able to explain the real world because their assumptions describe certain features of that world, albeit in isolated or exaggerated form. Gibbard and Varian do not pursue this idea very far, but it is taken up in different ways by Hausman (1992, 123–151) and by Uskali Mäki (1992, 1994), whose work will now be discussed.

6   Economics as an inexact deductive science, and the method of isolation

I have suggested that Akerlof and Schelling are each pointing to some *tendency* in the real world, which each claims to explain by means of a model. One way of trying to make sense of the idea of "tendencies" is by means of what Hausman calls "implicit *ceteris paribus* clauses." The underlying idea is that the phenomena of the real world are the product of the interaction of many different causal factors. A tendency (some writers prefer the term "capacity") is to be understood as the workings of some small subset of these factors.

In order to describe a tendency, we must somehow isolate the relevant subset of factors from the rest. Thus, the description is expressed in counterfactual terms, such as "in the absence of all other causal factors, L" or "if all other causal factors are held constant, L" where L is some law-like proposition about the world. Hausman argues that in economics, *ceteris paribus* clauses are usually both implicit and vague. He uses the term *inexact generalization* for generalizations that are qualified by implicit *ceteris paribus* clauses.

Hausman argues that economics arrives at its generalizations by what he calls the *inexact deductive method*. He summarizes this method as the following four-step schema:

1. *Formulate* credible (*ceteris paribus*) and pragmatically convenient generalizations concerning the operation of relevant causal variables.
2. *Deduce* from these generalizations, and statements of initial conditions, simplifications, etc. predictions concerning relevant phenomena.
3. *Test* the predictions.
4. If the predictions are correct, then regard the whole amalgam as confirmed. If the predictions are not correct, then *compare* alternative accounts of the failure on the basis of explanatory success, empirical progress, and pragmatic usefulness. (1992, 222)

For Hausman, this schema is "both justifiable and consistent with existing theoretical practice in economics, insofar as that practice aims to appraise theories empirically" (1992, 221).[12] By following this schema, economists can arrive at inexact generalizations about the world which they are entitled to regard as confirmed. The schema is an adaptation of John Stuart Mill's (1843, book 6, chapters 1–4) account of the "logic of the moral sciences." (The most significant amendment is that, in Hausman's schema, the premises from which deductions are made are merely "credible generalizations" which may be called into question if the predictions derived from them prove false. In contrast, Mill seems to have thought that the inexact predictions of economics could be deduced from *proven* "laws of mind.")

Mäki's account of how economic theories explain reality has many similarities with Hausman's. Like Hausman, Mäki argues that theoretical assumptions should be read as claims about what is true in the real world. But where Hausman talks of *inexact* propositions, Mäki talks of *isolations*. Economics, according to Mäki, uses "*the method of isolation*, whereby a set of elements is theoretically removed from the influence of other elements in a given situation" (1992, 318, emphasis in the original). On this account, a theory represents just some of the factors which are at work in the real world; the potential influence of other factors is "sealed off" (1992, 321). Such sealing-off makes a theory unrealistic; but the theory may still claim to describe *an aspect of* reality.

As Mäki (1992, 325) notices, there is a parallel between his concept of theoretical isolation and the idea of *experimental isolation*. Laboratory experiments investigate particular elements of the world by isolating them; the mechanisms by which other elements are sealed off are experimental *controls*. The laboratory environment is thereby made unrealistic, in the sense that it is "cleaner" than the world outside; but this unrealisticness is an essential feature of the experimental method. On this analogy, models are *thought experiments*.[13] But if a thought experiment is to tell us anything about the real world (rather than merely about the structure of our own thoughts), our reasoning must in some way replicate the workings of the world. For example, think how a structural engineer might use a theoretical model to test the strength of a new design. This kind of modeling is possible because the theory which describes the general properties of the relevant class of structures is already known, even though its implications for the new structure are not. Provided the predictions of the general theory are true, the engineer's thought experiment replicates a physical experiment that could have been carried out.

On this interpretation, then, a model explains reality by virtue of the truth of the assumptions that it makes about the causal factors it has isolated. The isolations themselves may be unrealistic; in a literal sense, the assumptions which represent these isolations may be (and typically are) false. But the assumptions which represent the workings of the isolated causal factors need to be true. So, I suggest, the implications of the method of isolation for theoretical modeling are broadly similar to the first two steps of Hausman's schema. That is, the modeler has to formulate credible generalizations concerning the operation of the factors that have been isolated, and then use deductive reasoning to work out what effects these factors will have in particular controlled environments.

So is this what Akerlof and Schelling are doing? Even though neither author explicitly proposes a testable hypothesis, we might perhaps interpret them as implicitly proposing *ceteris paribus* hypotheses. (Later, I shall suggest what these hypotheses might be.) But if Akerlof's and Schelling's models are to be understood as instances of the inexact deductive method, each model must be interpreted as the deductive machinery which generates the relevant hypothesis. For such an interpretation to be possible, we must be able to identify the simplifying assumptions of the model with the *ceteris paribus* or noninterference clauses of the hypothesis. That is, if the hypothesis takes the form "X is the case, provided there is no interference of types $i_1, \ldots, i_n$," then the model must deduce X from the conjunction of two sets of assumptions. The first set contains "credible and pragmatically convenient generalizations" – preferably ones which have been used successfully in previous applications of the inexact deductive method. The second set of assumptions – which Mäki would call "isolations" – postulate the nonexistence of $i_1, \ldots, i_n$.

Take Akerlof's model. Can its assumptions be understood in this way? *Some* certainly can. For example, Akerlof implicitly assumes that each trader maximizes expected utility. Correctly or incorrectly, most economists regard expected utility maximization as a well-grounded generalization about human behavior; there are (it is thought) occasional exceptions, but these can safely be handled by implicit noninterference clauses. Similarly, Akerlof assumes that if an equilibrium price exists in a market, that price will come about, and the market will clear. This, too, is a generalization that most economists regard as well-grounded. There is a standing presumption in economics that, if an empirical statement is deduced from standard assumptions such as expected utility maximization and market-clearing, then that statement is reliable: the theorist does not have to justify those assumptions anew in every publication.

As an example of the other type of assumption, notice that Akerlof's model excludes all of the "countervailing institutions" which he discusses in his section IV. Presumably, if Akerlof is proposing an empirical hypothesis, it must be something like the following: "If sellers know more than buyers about the quality of a good, and if there are no countervailing institutions, then the average quality of those goods that are traded is lower than that of goods in general." The absence of countervailing institutions is a noninterference clause in the hypothesis, and therefore also a legitimate property of the model from which the hypothesis is deduced.

The difficulty for a Hausman-like or Mäki-like interpretation is that Akerlof's and Schelling's models both include many assumptions which *neither* are well-founded generalizations *nor* correspond with *ceteris paribus* or noninterference clauses in an empirical hypothesis. Akerlof assumes that there are only two types of trader, that all traders are risk neutral, that all cars are alike except for a one-dimensional index of quality, and so on. Schelling assumes that all individuals are identical except for color, that they live in the squares of a rectangular grid, and so on again. These are certainly not well-founded empirical generalizations. So can they be read as *ceteris paribus* clauses?

If we are to interpret these assumptions as *ceteris paribus* clauses, there must be corresponding restrictive clauses in the hypotheses that are deduced from the models. That is, we must interpret Akerlof and Schelling as proposing counterfactual empirical hypotheses about what would be observed, *were those assumptions true*. But if we pursue the logic of this approach, we end up removing all empirical content from the implications of the models – and thereby defeating the supposed objective of the inexact deductive method. Take the case of Schelling's model. Suppose we read Schelling as claiming that *if* people lived in checkerboard cities, and *if* people came in just two colors, and *if* each person was content provided that at least a third of her neighbors were the same color as her, and *if* . . . . , and *if* . . . . (going on to list all the properties of the model), *then* cities would be racially segregated. That is not an empirical claim at all: it is a theorem.

Perhaps the best way to fit Akerlof's and Schelling's models into Hausman's schema is to interpret their troublesome assumptions as the "simplifications etc." referred to in step 2 of that schema. But this just shunts the problem on, since we may then ask why it is legitimate to introduce such simplifications into a *deductive* argument. The conclusions of a deductive argument cannot be any stronger than its premises. Thus, any hypothesis that is generated by a deductive method must have implicit qualifying clauses corresponding with the assumptions that are used as premises. And this does not seem to be true of Akerlof's and Schelling's hypotheses.

To understand what Akerlof and Schelling are doing, we have to realize that results that they derive deductively within their models are not the same as the hypotheses that they want us to entertain. Consider exactly what Akerlof and Schelling are able to show by means of their models. Akerlof shows us that under certain specific conditions (there are just two types of trader, all cars are identical except for quality, sellers' valuations of cars of given quality are 2/3 those of buyers, etc.), no trade takes place. Among these conditions is a particular assumption about asymmetric information: sellers know the quality of their cars, but buyers don't. Akerlof also shows that if the only change that is made to this set of conditions is to assume symmetric information instead of asymmetric, then trade *does* take place. Thus, Akerlof has proved a *ceteris paribus* result, but only for a *particular* array of other conditions. This result might be roughly translated as the following statement: If all other variables are held constant at the particular values assumed in the model, then an increase in the degree of asymmetry of information reduces the volume of trade.

What about Schelling? Schelling shows – or, strictly speaking, he invites us to show ourselves – that under certain specific conditions (people come in just two colors, each person is located on a checkerboard, etc.) individuals' independent choices of location generate segregated neighborhoods. Among these conditions is a particular assumption about individuals' preferences concerning the color composition of their neighborhoods: people prefer not to live where more than some proportion p of their neighbors are of the other color. Schelling invites us to try out different values of p. We find that segregated neighborhoods eventually evolve, whatever value of p we use, provided it is less than 1. If $p = 1$, that is, if people are completely indifferent about the colors of their neighbors, then segregated neighborhoods will not evolve. (Schelling does not spell out this latter result, but a moment's thought about the model is enough to derive it.) Thus, we have established a *ceteris paribus* result analogous with Akerlof's: we have discovered the effects of changes in the value of p, when all other variables are held constant at the particular values specified by the model.

To put this more abstractly, let x be some variable whose value we are trying to explain, and let $(v_1, \ldots, v_n)$ be an array of variables which might have some influence on x. What Akerlof and Schelling each succeed in establishing by deductive reasoning is the truth of a proposition of the form: If the values of $v_2, \ldots, v_n$ are held constant *at the specific values* $v_2^*, \ldots, v_n^*$, then the relationship between v_1 and x is ... The values $v_2^*, \ldots, v_n^*$ are those built into the relevant model. Taken at face value, this proposition tells us nothing about the relationship between v_1 and x in the actual world. It tells us only about that relationship in a counterfactual world.

But Akerlof and Schelling want us to conclude that certain much more general propositions are, if not definitely true, at least credible. When Akerlof talks about the "lemons" principle, he has in mind some broad generalization, perhaps something like the following: For *all* markets, if all other features are held constant, an increase in the degree of asymmetry of information reduces the volume of trade. Similarly, what Schelling has in mind is some generalization like the following: For *all* multi-ethnic cities, if people prefer not to live in neighborhoods where the vast majority of their neighbors are of another ethnic group, strongly segregated neighborhoods will evolve. In my more abstract notation, the generalizations that Akerlof and Schelling have in mind have the form: If the values of $v_2, \ldots, v_n$ are held constant *at any given values*, then the relationship between v_1 and x is ...

If these generalizations are to be interpreted as hypotheses, the models are supposed to give us reasons for thinking that they are true. If the generalizations are to be interpreted as observed regularities, the models are supposed to explain why they are true. But deductive reasoning cannot fill the gap between the specific propositions that can be shown to be true in the model world (that is, propositions that are true if $v_2, \ldots, v_n$ are held constant at the values

$v_2^*, \ldots, v_n^*$) and the general propositions that we are being invited to entertain (that is, those that are true if $v_2, \ldots, v_n$ are held constant at *any* values). The difficulty is that these general hypotheses cannot be derived from the models by deductive reasoning. Somehow, a transition has to be made from a *particular* hypothesis, which has been shown to be true in the model world, to a *general* hypothesis, which we can expect to be true in the real world too.

7   Inductive inference

So how can this transition be made? As before, let R stand for a regularity (bad products driving out good, persistent racial segregation with moving geographical boundaries) which may or may not occur in the real world. Let F stand for a set of causal factors (sellers being better-informed than buyers, a common preference not to be heavily outnumbered by neighbors not of one's own type) which may or may not operate in the real world. Akerlof and Schelling seem to be reasoning something like this:

> *Schema 1: Explanation*
>
> *E*1 In the model world, R is caused by F
> *E*2 F operates in the real world
> *E*3 R occurs in the real world
> *Therefore, there is reason to believe*:
> *E*4 In the real world, R is caused by F

Alternatively, if we read Akerlof and Schelling as implicitly proposing empirical hypotheses, we might represent their reasoning as:

> *Schema 2: Prediction*
>
> *P*1 In the model world, R is caused by F
> *P*2 F operates in the real world
> *Therefore, there is reason to believe*:
> *P*3 R occurs in the real world

A third possible reading of Akerlof and Schelling involves *abductive* reasoning (inferring causes from effects):[14]

> *Schema 3: Abduction*
>
> *A*1 In the model world, R is caused by F
> *A*2 R occurs in the real world
> *Therefore, there is reason to believe*:
> *A*3 F operates in the real world

In each of these three reasoning schemata, the "Therefore" requires an inductive leap. By "induction" I mean any mode of reasoning which takes us from specific propositions to more general ones (compare the similar definition given by Mill 1843, book 3, chapter 1, 186). Here, the specific proposition is that R is caused by F *in the case of the model*. In order to justify each of the "Therefores," we must be justified in inferring that R is caused by F more generally. *If* there is a general causal link running from F to R, then when we observe F and R together in some particular case (the case of the real world), we have some reason to think that the particular R is caused by the particular F (explanation). Similarly, when we observe F in a particular case, we have some reason to expect to find R too (prediction). And when we observe R in a particular case, we have some reason to expect to find F too (abduction). It seems, then, that Akerlof's and Schelling's method is not purely deductive: it depends on induction as well as on deduction. But how might these inductions be justified?

8   Justifying induction: separability

One possible answer is to appeal to a very general hypothesis about causation invoked by Mill (1843, book 3, chapter 6, 242–247). Mill defines phenomena as *mechanical* if the overall effect of all causal factors can be represented as an addition of those separate factors, on the analogy of the vector addition of forces in Newtonian physics. Given this hypothesis of the *composition of causes*, we are entitled to move from the *ceteris paribus* propositions which have been shown to be true in a model to more general *ceteris paribus* propositions which apply to the real world too.[15] But what entitles us to use that hypothesis itself?

In some cases, it may be legitimate to treat that hypothesis as a proven scientific law – as in the paradigm case of the composition of forces in physics. Then the reasoning schemata I have been considering would not be inductive at all; they would be purely deductive, with the proven law as an additional premise. Mill seems to have taken it to be an *a priori* truth that "In social phenomena the Composition of Causes is the universal law" (1843, book 6, chapter 7, 573). However, the argument Mill gives in support of this claim is quite inadequate. He simply asserts that "Human beings in society have no properties but those which are derived from, and may be resolved into, the laws of the nature of individual man." But even if we grant this assertion, all we have established is that social facts are separable into facts about individuals. We have not established the separability *of causal factors*. Thus, for example, the fact that society is an aggregate of individuals does not allow us to deduce that if an increase in the price of some good in one set of circumstances causes a decrease in consumption, then the same cause will produce the same effect in other circumstances.

Hausman (1992, p. 138) offers a defense for Mill's method in economics. He claims that Mill's supposition that economic phenomena are mechanical is "implicit in most applications of economic models," and then says: "Its only justification is success." In other words, this supposition is an inductive inference from the general experience of economic modeling.

But this argument seems to beg the question. For the sake of the argument, let us grant that economic modeling has often been successful – successful, that is, in relation to Hausman's criterion of generating correct predictions about the real world. Even so, the explanation of its success may be that economists are careful not to rely on models unless they have some independent grounds for believing that the *particular* phenomena they are trying to explain are mechanical – or, more generally, unless they have some independent grounds for making particular inductive inferences from the world of the model to the real world. Given the *prima facie* implausibility of the assumption that all economic phenomena are mechanical, it would be surprising to find that this assumption was the main foundation for inductive inferences from theoretical models. We should look for other foundations.

9 Justifying induction: robustness

One way in which inductions might be justified is by showing that the results derived from a model are *robust* to changes in the specification of that model. Gibbard and Varian (1978, 675) appeal to the robustness criterion when they suggest that, in order for caricature-like models to help us to understand reality, "the conclusions [should be] robust under changes in the caricature." Hausman (1992, 149) makes a somewhat similar appeal when he considers the conditions under which it is legitimate to use simplifications – that is, propositions that are not true of the real world – in the second stage of his schema of the inexact deductive method. He proposes a set of conditions which he glosses as "reasonable criteria for judging whether the falsity in simplifications is irrelevant to the conclusions one derives with their help."

One significant feature of this approach is that simplifications need not be isolations. Take Schelling's checkerboard city. The simplicity of the checkerboard city lies in the way that its pattern repeats itself: if we ignore the edges of the board, every location is identical with every other. (More sophisticated mathematicians would draw the checkerboard on a torus, so that there were no edges at all; this would give us a city located on a doughnut-shaped planet.) This property makes the analysis of the model much easier than it otherwise would be. But it does not seem right to say that the checkerboard *isolates* some aspect of real cities by sealing off various other factors which operate in reality: just what do we have to seal off to make a real city – say, Norwich – become like a checkerboard? Notice that, in order to arrive at the checkerboard plan, it is not enough just to suppose that all locations are identical with one another (that is, to use a "generic" concept of location): we need to use a *particular form* of generic location. So, I suggest, it is more natural to say that the checkerboard plan is something that Schelling has *constructed* for himself. If we think that Schelling's results are sufficiently robust to changes in the checkerboard assumption, that assumption may be justified, even though it is not an isolation.[16]

Robustness arguments work by giving reasons for believing that a result that has been derived in one specific model would also be derived from a wide class of models, or from some very general model which included the original model as a special case. Economic theorists tend to like general models, and much effort is put into generalizing results. By experience, theorists pick up a feel for the kinds of results that can be generalized and the kinds that cannot be. The main way of making this distinction, I think, is to examine the links between the assumptions of a model and its results, and to try to find out which assumptions are (as theorists say) "doing the work." If a model has already been presented in a somewhat general way, it is often useful to strip it down to its simplest form, and then to see which assumptions are most closely associated with the derivation of the relevant result.[17]

In both Akerlof's and Schelling's models, there are good reasons to think that most of the simplifying assumptions are orthogonal to the dimension on which the model "works": these are simplifying assumptions which could be changed or generalized without affecting the qualitative results. In many cases, Akerlof argues exactly this. Recall, for example, his discussion of risk neutrality. Akerlof could have assumed risk aversion instead, which would have made the model much less easy to work with; but there does not seem to be any way in which the major qualitative conclusions are being driven by the assumption of risk neutrality. Similarly, in the case of Schelling's model, the checkerboard layout seems to have nothing particular to do with the tendency for segregation. Schelling is confident enough to invite the reader to try different shapes of boards, and might easily have suggested different tessellations (such as triangles or hexagons).

Notice how this mode of reasoning remains in the world of models – which may help to explain why theorists feel comfortable with it. It makes inductive inferences from one or a small number of models to *models* in general. For example: having experimented with Schelling's checkerboard model with various parameter values, I have found that the regularity described by Schelling persistently occurs. Having read Schelling and having thought about these results, I think I have some feel for why this regularity occurs; but I cannot give any proof that it *must* occur (or even that it must occur with high probability). My confidence that I would find similar results were I to use different parameter values is an inductive inference. I also feel confident (although not quite as confident as in the previous case) that I would find similar results if I used triangles or hexagons instead of squares. This is an inductive inference too.

Obviously, however, it cannot be enough to stay in the world of models. If the theorist is to make claims about the real world, there has to be some link between those two worlds. For example, it is not enough to be convinced that what Schelling has shown us to be true of checkerboard cities is also true of other *model* cities: we have to be convinced that it is true of *real* cities. We have to think something like the following: If what Schelling has shown us is true of checkerboard cities, then it will probably tend to be true of cities in general. What makes that inductive inference credible?

10 Justifying induction: credible worlds

Inductive reasoning works by finding some regularity R in some specific collection of observations $x_1, \ldots, x_n$, and then inferring that the same regularity will probably be found throughout a general set of phenomena S, which contains not only $x_1, \ldots, x_n$ but also other elements which have not yet been observed. For example, $x_1, \ldots, x_n$ might be the n different versions of Schelling's checkerboard city that I have so far experimented with, R might be the emergence of segregation in model cities, and S might be the set of all checkerboard cities. Having found R in the n particular cities, I infer that this is a property of checkerboard cities in general.

Unavoidably, inductive reasoning depends on prior concepts of similarity: we have to be able to interpret S as the definition of some *relevant* or *salient* respect in which $x_1, \ldots, x_n$ are similar. Many of the philosophical puzzles surrounding induction stem from the difficulty of justifying any criterion of similarity.[18] Obviously, I am not going to solve these deep puzzles towards the end of a paper about models in economics.[19] For my purposes, what is important is this: if we are to make inductive inferences from the world of a model to the real world, we must recognize some significant similarity between those two worlds.

If we interpret Akerlof and Schelling as using schema 1 or schema 2 (see section 6), it might be said that this similarity is simply the set of causal factors F: what the two worlds have in common is that those factors are present in both. To put this another way, the real world is equivalent to an immensely complicated model: it is the limiting case of the process of replacing the simplifying assumptions of the original model with increasing realistic specifications. If (as I argued in section 9) we can legitimately make inductive inferences from a simple model to slightly more complex variants, then we must also have *some* warrant for making inferences to much more complex variants, and hence also to the real world. Nevertheless, the enormous difference in complexity between the real world and any model we can hope to analyze suggests that we ought to be very cautious about making inferences from the latter to the former.

So what might increase our confidence in such inferences? I want to suggest that we can have more confidence in them, the greater the extent to which we can understand the relevant model as a description of how the world *could be*.

Let me explain. Inductive inferences are most commonly used to take us from one part of the real world to another. For example, suppose we observe racial segregation in the housing markets of Baltimore, Philadelphia, New York, Detroit, Toledo, Buffalo, and Pittsburgh. Then we might make the inductive inference that segregation is a characteristic of large industrial cities in the northeastern USA, and so form the expectation that there will be segregation in say, Cleveland. Presumably, the thought behind this inference is that the forces at work in the Cleveland housing market, whatever these may be, are likely to be broadly similar to those at work in other large industrial cities in the northeastern USA. Thus, a property that is true for those cities in general is likely to be true for Cleveland in particular. One way of describing this inference is to say that each of the housing markets of Baltimore, Philadelphia, New York, etc. constitutes a *model* of the forces at work in large industrial northeastern US cities. These, of course, are *natural* models, as contrasted with *theoretical* models created in the minds of social scientists. But if we can make inductive inferences from natural models, why not from theoretical ones? Is the geography of Cleveland any more like the geography of Baltimore or Philadelphia than it is like the geography of Schelling's checkerboard city?[20]

What Schelling has done is to construct a set of *imaginary* cities, whose workings we can easily understand. In these cities, racial segregation evolves only if people have preferences about the racial mix of their neighbors, but strong segregation evolves even if those preferences are quite mild. In these imaginary cities, we also find that the spatial boundaries between the races tend to move over time, while segregation is preserved. We are invited to make the inductive inference that similar causal processes apply in real multi-ethnic cities. We now look at such cities. Here too we find strong spatial segregation between ethnic groups, and here too we find that the boundaries between groups move over time. Since the same effects are found in both real and imaginary cities, it is at least credible to suppose that the same causes are responsible. Thus, we have been given some reason to think that segregation in real cities is caused by preferences for segregation, and that the extent of segregation is invariant to changes in the strength of those preferences.

Compare Akerlof. Akerlof has constructed two variants of an imaginary used-car market. In one variant, buyers and sellers have the same imperfect information about the quality of cars, and trade takes place quite normally. In the other variant, sellers know more than buyers, and no trade takes place at all. When we think about how these markets work, it becomes credible to suppose that many variant imaginary markets can be constructed, and that these share the common feature that, *ceteris paribus*, the volume of trade falls as information becomes less symmetric. We are invited to make the inductive inference that similar causal processes apply in real markets, with similar effects. Thus in real markets too, *ceteris paribus*, the volume of trade is positively related to the symmetry of information.

We gain confidence in such inductive inferences, I suggest, by being able to see the relevant models as instances of some category, some of whose instances actually exist in the real world. Thus, we see Schelling's checkerboard cities *as possible cities*, alongside real cities like New York and Philadelphia. We see Akerlof's used-car market *as a possible market*, alongside real markets such as the real market for used cars in a particular city, or the market for a particular type of insurance. We recognize the significance of the similarity between model cities and real cities, or between model markets and real markets, by accepting that the model world *could be* real – that it describes a state of affairs that is credible, given what we know (or think we know) about the general laws governing events in the real world.

On this view, the model is not so much an abstraction from reality as a *parallel reality*. The model world is not constructed by starting with the real world and stripping out complicating factors: although the model world is *simpler* than the real world, the one is not a *simplification* of the other. The model is realistic in the same sense that a novel can be called realistic. In a realistic novel, the characters and locations are imaginary, but the author has to convince us that they are *credible* – that there could be people and places like those in the novel. As events occur in the novel, we should have the illusion that these are natural outcomes of the way the characters think and behave, and of the way the world works. We judge the author to have failed if we find a person acting out of character, or if we find an anachronism in an historical novel: these are things that *couldn't* have happened. But we do not demand that the events of the novel *did* happen, or even that they are simplified representations of what really happened.

Akerlof in particular puts a lot of effort into making his model credible in this sense. The world of his model is much more uniform and regular than the real world, but Akerlof clearly wants us to think that there *could* be a used-car market which was like his model. The "cars" and "traders" of his model are not just primitives in a formal deductive system. They are, I suggest, cars which are *like* real cars, and traders which are *like* real traders, inhabiting a world which Akerlof has imagined, but which is sufficiently close to the real world that we can imagine its being real. Recall the sentence in which Akerlof seems to slip between talking about the real used-car market and talking about his model: the fact that such slippage is possible may be an indication that Akerlof has come to think of his model as if it were real.

At first sight, Schelling seems rather less concerned to make us believe in his model world as a possible reality. Instead of following Akerlof's strategy of basing his model on one typical case, Schelling almost always refers to the two types of actor in his model as "dimes" and "pennies." But this is perhaps dictated by Schelling's strategy of asking the reader to perform the actions in the model: he has to say "now move that dime" rather than "that dime now moves." Possibly, too, it reflects an embarrassment about dealing directly with the issue of racial prejudice. But when Schelling describes the laws of motion of these coins, it is clear that we are expected to think of them as people. For example, one of his suggestions is that "we can postulate that every dime wants at least half its neighbors to be dimes, every penny wants a third of its neighbors to be pennies, and any dime or penny whose immediate neighborhood does not meet these conditions gets up and moves" (1978, 147–148). Or again, officially referring to a dime or penny in a world of dimes and pennies: "He is content or discontent with his neighborhood according to the colors of the occupants of those eight surrounding squares" (1978, 148). Even allowing for the fact that the use of "he" and "color" rather than "it" and "type of coin" are probably slips, it is surely obvious that Schelling wants us to think of the dimes and pennies as people of two groups who have some embarrassment about being together. Similarly, we are expected to think of the checkerboard as a city (or some other social space, such as a dining room). Further, we are encouraged to think of these people's attitudes to one another as credible and understandable – even forgivable (recall the passage about mixed tables in the cafeteria, which precedes the checkerboard model). What Schelling has constructed is a model city, inhabited by people who are *like* real people.

11   Conclusion

I have referred several times to a puzzling common feature of the two papers. Both authors seem to want to make empirical claims about properties of the real world, and to want to argue that these claims are supported by their models. But on closer inspection of the texts, it is difficult to find any explicit connection being made between the models and the real world. Although both authors discuss real-world phenomena, neither seems prepared to endorse any specific inference from his model, still less to propose an explicit hypothesis which could be tested.

I suggest that the explanation of this puzzle is that Akerlof and Schelling are engaged in a kind of theorizing whose usefulness depends on inductive inferences from the world of models to the real world. Everyone makes inductive inferences, but no one has really succeeded in justifying them. Thus, it should not be surprising if economists leave gaps in their explicit reasoning at those places where inductive inferences are required, and rely on their readers using their own intuitions to cross those gaps. Nor should it be surprising if economists use rhetorical devices which tend to hide these gaps from view.

Nevertheless, the gap between model and real world has to be bridged. If a model is genuinely to tell us something, however limited, about the real world, it cannot just be a description of a self-contained imaginary world. The difficulty is that theoretical models in economics often *are* descriptions of self-contained and imaginary worlds. These worlds have not been formed merely by abstracting key features from the real world; in important respects, they have been *constructed* by their authors.

The suggestion of this chapter is that the gap between model world and real world can be filled by inductive inference. On this account, models are not internally consistent sets of uninterpreted theorems; but neither are they simplified or abstracted or exaggerated descriptions of the real world. They describe credible counterfactual worlds. This credibility gives us some warrant for making inductive inferences from model to real world.

Notes

A previous version of this chapter was prepared for the conference "Fact or Fiction? Perspectives on Realism and Economics" at the Erasmus University of Rotterdam, November 14–15, 1997. The chapter has been much improved as a result of the discussion at that conference. I particularly thank Nancy Cartwright, Stephan Hartmann, Daniel Hausman, Maarten Janssen, Uskali Mäki, Mary Morgan, and Chris Starmer for advice. I did most of the work on the chapter while visiting the Centre for Applied Ethics at the University of British Columbia, for whose hospitality I am grateful.

1. But it was not immediately recognized as a major contribution: it was turned down three times before being accepted for publication. Mark Blaug (1997) uses this fact to suggest that Akerlof's paper is the exception which proves the rule – the rule being that modern economics is becoming "an intellectual game played for its own sake and not for its practical consequences," creating models which are "scandalously unrepresentative of any recognizable economic system" (1997, 2–4, see also chapter 2 in this volume). However, he does not explain why Akerlof is to be acquitted of this charge.

2. An alternative reading is possible. Akerlof never claims outright that the "pure joy" explanation is false, or that his own explanation is correct – only that it is "different." So could it be that he does not want to make any such claims? In section 3, I consider – and reject – the suggestion that Akerlof is not claiming to explain any features of the real world.

3. Akerlof deals with this problem to some degree by sketching a model with four discrete types of cars. (This sketch is contained in the passage beginning "Suppose . . . ") In the four-types model, there is a market in bad used cars but not in good ones. However, this model is not developed in any detail; it serves as a kind of appetizer for the main model, in which no trade takes place at all.

4. As a result of presenting this paper, I have discovered that Schelling's model is much more widely known and admired than I had imagined. It has not had the obvious influence on economics that Akerlof's paper has, but it clearly appeals to methodologically inclined economists.

5. In passing, I must record my puzzlement at the two-way classification of "colors" or "races" which seems to be a social fact in America, despite the continuity of the actual spectra of skin color, hair type, and other supposed racial markers. The convention, I take it, is that anyone of mixed African and European parentage, whatever that mix, is black unless he or she can "pass" as pure European.

6. When I have presented this paper, I have been surprised at how many economists are inclined towards this interpretation.

7. Arrow (1951/1963, 4–5) hints at this interpretation when, as part of the introduction to his presentation of the theorem, he says that welfare economists need to check that the value judgments they invoke are mutually compatible. He goes on: "Bergson considers it possible to establish an ordering of social states which is based on the indifference maps of individuals, and Samuelson has agreed." Arrow's form of social choice theory investigates whether this is indeed possible.

8. This interpretation of Akerlof's model was suggested to me by Daniel Hausman. Hausman also suggested the "counterexample" interpretation of Schelling's model, discussed in the next paragraph.

9. Here I am using "story" in the sense which Deidre McCloskey (1983, 505) correctly identifies as standard usage among economic theorists: "an extended example of the economic reasoning underlying the mathematics [of a theory], often a simplified version of the situation in the real world that the mathematics is meant to characterize." Allan Gibbard and Hal Varian (1978) use "story" in a similar way (see section 5). Mary Morgan (1997) has a quite different concept of a story. For Morgan, models are inert mechanisms which need to be "cranked" by some external event in order to set them in motion; a story is a description of that event and of how its impact is transmitted through the model. Morgan's approach conflates two distinctions – static/dynamic and model/story – which I prefer to keep separate.

10. Early astronomy provides a classic example of the conflict between instrumentalism and realism. The only available observations were of the movements of points and areas of light across the sky. Highly accurate predictions of these movements could be made by using theories based on apparently fantastic and (at the time) completely unverifiable assumptions about how the workings of the universe might look, viewed from outside. With hindsight, we know that some of these fantastic assumptions proved to be true (which supports realism), while others proved false (which supports instrumentalism).

11. The idea that there might be some value in predicting the consumption decisions of individual consumers would perhaps not occur to an economist in the 1950s, when there were no practicable means to collect or to analyze individual-level data. Developments in retailing and in information technology are now opening up the possibility of making profitable use of predictions about the decisions of individual consumers.

12. Hausman adds the qualification that "a great deal of theoretical work in economics is concerned with conceptual exploration, not with empirical theorizing" (1992, 221). In section 3, I considered and rejected the suggestion that Akerlof's and Schelling's models could be interpreted as conceptual explanation.

13. The parallel between models and experiments is explored in detail by Francesco Guala (1999).

14. This interpretation was suggested to me by Maarten Janssen.
15. Nancy Cartwright (1998) explores the role of this kind of reasoning in Mill's scientific method.
16. There is an analogy in experimental method. Think of how experimental biologists use fruit flies to test and refine hypotheses about biological evolution. The hypotheses in which the biologists are interested are intended to apply to many other species – sometimes, for example, to humans. Fruit flies are used because they are easy to keep in the laboratory and breed very quickly. But fruit flies are not simplified versions of humans, arrived at by isolating certain key features. Rather, the biologists' claim is that certain fundamental evolutionary mechanisms are *common to* humans and fruit flies.
17. Akerlof and Schelling are perhaps atypical in that they are satisfied to present simple, imaginative models, leaving it to the technicians of economic theory to produce the generalizations. In contrast, most theorists feel compelled to present their models in the most general form they can. If I am right about the importance of stripping down a model in order to judge how generalizable it is, it is at least arguable that Akerlof's and Schelling's way of presenting models is the more informative.
18. The "grue" problem discovered by Nelson Goodman (1954) is particularly significant – and intractable.
19. For what it is worth, I am inclined to agree with David Hume's (1740, book 1, part 3, 69–179) original diagnosis: that induction is grounded in associations of ideas that the human mind finds natural. If that diagnosis is correct, the concepts of similarity which underpin inductive reasoning may be capable of being *explained* in psychological terms, but not of being *justified* as rational.
20. Notice that one implication of thinking in this way is that regularities *within the real world* (here, across cities which in many respects are very different from one another) can give us grounds for greater confidence in inductive inferences from a model to the real world. The fact that racial segregation is common to so many different cities suggests that its causes are not to be found in any of those dimensions on which they can be differentiated.

References

Akerlof, George A. (1970). The market for "lemons": quality uncertainty and the market mechanism, *Quarterly Journal of Economics*, 84, 488–500

Arrow, Kenneth J. (1951/1963). *Social Choice and Individual Values*, 2nd edn. New Haven, CT: Yale University Press

Blaug, Mark (1997). Ugly currents in modern economics, paper presented at the conference "Fact or Fiction? Perspectives on Realism and Economics," Erasmus University of Rotterdam, November 14–15; see chapter 2 in this volume

Cartwright, Nancy (1998). Capacities, in John Davis (ed.), *The Handbook of Economic Methodology*. Cheltenham: Edward Elgar

Gibbard, Allan and Hal Varian (1978). Economic models, *Journal of Philosophy*, 75, 664–677

Goodman, Nelson (1954). *Fact, Fiction, and Forecast*. Cambridge, MA: Harvard University Press

Guala, Francesco (1999). Economics and the laboratory, PhD thesis, London School of
    Economics and Political Science
Hausman, Daniel M. (1992). *The Inexact and Separate Science of Economics.*
    Cambridge: Cambridge University Press
Hume, David (1740/1978). *A Treatise of Human Nature.* (Oxford: Clarendon Press,
    page references to 1978 edn.)
McCloskey, D.N. (1983). The rhetoric of economics, *Journal of Economic Literature*,
    21, 481–517
Mäki, Uskali (1992). On the method of isolation in economics, *Poznań Studies in the
    Philosophy of Science and the Humanities*, 26, 316–351
    (1994). Isolation, idealization and truth in economics, *Poznań Studies in the
    Philosophy of Science and the Humanities*, 38, 147–168
Mill, John Stuart (1843/1967). *A System of Logic* (London: Longmans, page references
    to 1967 edn.)
Morgan, Mary S. (1997). Models, stories and the economic world, paper presented at the
    conference "Fact or Fiction? Perspectives on Realism and Economics," Erasmus
    University of Rotterdam, November 14–15; see chapter 8 in this volume
Samuelson Paul (1947). *Foundations of Economic Analysis.* Cambridge, MA: Harvard
    University Press
Schelling, Thomas C. (1978). *Micromotives and Macrobehavior.* New York: Norton

6 The limits of causal order, from economics to physics

Nancy Cartwright

1 Introduction

The topic that I will focus on here is not that of realism in science – i.e. how accurately can the sciences, including economics, represent the world – but rather the question of the range of science – how much of the world it can represent. The idea of a science unified and complete has been advocated throughout the history of thought, but the sciences have steadfastly resisted this kind of regimentation. They remain distinct and confined, and they continue to cover only very small patches of the world we live in. We may dream that the sciences will some day cover everything, but, I shall argue, that is not likely to be a dream that is even "in principle" achievable. The very ways we do our sciences when they are most successfully done confine them within limited domains. This is true, I believe, from the social sciences through the natural sciences and especially for fields like economics and physics that have embraced mathematics as their principal form for representation.

When I talk of "science" here I am assuming the positivist idea of exact science: science as a body of explicit knowledge, systematically organized, from which precise and unambiguous claims can be rigorously derived. It is my underlying view that it is this quite reasonable demand that scientific claims be precise and unambiguous that imposes limits on how far the sciences can stretch, for not much of the world lends itself to this kind of description. Basically the world as it comes, unengineered by us, is for the most part both messy and arbitrary and not the sort of thing about which the kind of knowledge we call scientific is possible.

I shall discuss three cases to illustrate:

1. The use of broad-scale nonexperimental statistics for causal modeling across the social sciences
2. An economic exercise from the work of one of my colleagues at the London School of Economics (LSE)
3. Quantum theory, and in particular the quantum theory of superconductivity.

The role of models is key to my arguments. In all three cases, our scientific treatments require a model to represent the world, and the demands on these models constrain the extent of our treatments.

2 Social statistics

We use non-experimental statistics throughout the behavioural sciences as a tool for causal inference.[1] Methodologies for doing so were explicitly developed by Sewall Wright in his work on path analysis; by the founders of econometrics and their immediate descendants in the early days of the Cowles Commission; and more recently at UCLA and at Carnegie Mellon, where groups working with Judea Pearl[2] and with Clark Glymour[3] have produced the most powerful and philosophically well-grounded techniques available, using directed acyclic graphs (DAGS).

Consider two examples, one from me and one from Judea Pearl. Pearl's example is shown in figure 6.1, mine in figure 6.2. Both examples deal with a number of measurable quantities that are represented as random variables and over which a probability measure P is defined. The graphs represent generic-level causal relations among the quantities. We assume that these two kinds of relations among the variables – probabilities on the one hand and causal connections on the other – are not independent, but that they constrain each other. Pearl and Glymour propose some general minimal constraints that they assume will always hold between the two. From that they have developed powerful techniques for inferring information about one or the other from partial information on the two of them.

Where do these two sets of relations come from? What gives rise to the causal laws and the probabilities represented here? For many empiricists this question will not make sense: causal laws and probabilistic – or, in the limiting case, deterministic – relations are fundamental to nature. What happens, happens on account of them; they do not hold on account of anything else. I do not know anything about the growth of either eel worms or oats, nor about chemical fumigants and the possible interactions among the three that are depicted by Pearl. So I cannot postulate where his graph comes from. But I can tell you where mine comes from.

It comes from the machine in figure 6.3, designed by Towfic Shomar. The machine gives rise to the causal relations and regularities depicted in the associated graph. The machine pictured in figure 6.3 has fixed components with known capacities arranged in a stable configuration. It is the fixed arrangement among the parts that ensures both that the causal relations among the vertices of the consequent graph are as they are and that it makes sense to write down a probability measure over them.

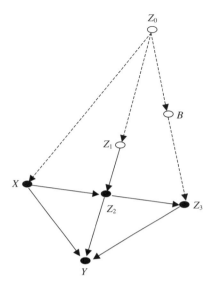

X:	fumigants
Y:	yields
B:	the population of birds and other predators
Z_0:	last year's eelworm population
Z_1:	eelworm population before treatment
Z_2:	eelworm population after treatment
Z_3:	eelworm population at the end of the season

Figure 6.1   A causal diagram representing the effects of fumigants, X, on yields, Y
Source: Pearl (1995).

I call machines like this "nomological machines." I have been spending a great deal of time lately looking at our law claims in various sciences, especially in economics and in physics, at how we use them and at the kinds of evidence we can offer to support them. One of my conclusions from this work is that we always need a nomological machine to get laws – any laws, causal or otherwise. Sometimes God supplies the arrangements, as in the planetary systems, but very often we must supply them ourselves, in courtrooms and churches, institutions and factories. Where they do not exist, there is no sense in trying to pick out event-types and asking about their nomological relations, whether these nomological relations are causal laws or probabilities. That would be like asking: "Given we drop six balls in a bucket, what is the probability that a second bucket ten feet away will rise by six inches?" That question makes no

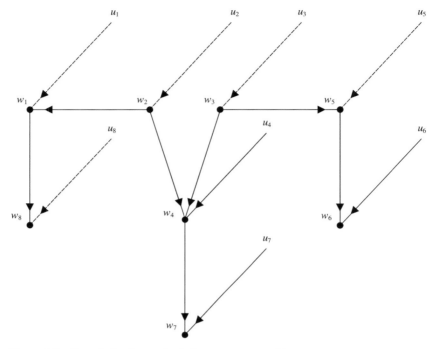

Figure 6.2   Generic-level causal relations among quantities

sense unless we have in mind some background machine to which the buckets are bolted.

In *The Logic of Statistical Inference*, Ian Hacking[4] defends the close connection between chance set-ups and probabilities. This is a connection that I want to endorse. A chance set-up may occur naturally or it may be artificially constructed, either deliberately or by accident. In any case probabilities are generated by chance set-ups, and their characterization necessarily refers back to the chance set-up that gives rise to them. We can make sense of the probability of drawing two red balls in a row from an urn of a certain composition with replacement. But we cannot make sense of the probability of 6 percent inflation in the UK next year without an implicit reference to a specific social and institutional structure that will serve as the chance set-up that generates this probability.

The originators of social statistics followed this pattern, and I think rightly so. When they talked about the "iron law of probability" that dictated a fixed number of suicides in Paris every year or a certain rising rate of crime, this was not conceived as an association laid down by natural law as they (though not I) conceived the association between force and acceleration. Rather they thought of it as an association generated by particular social and economic structures

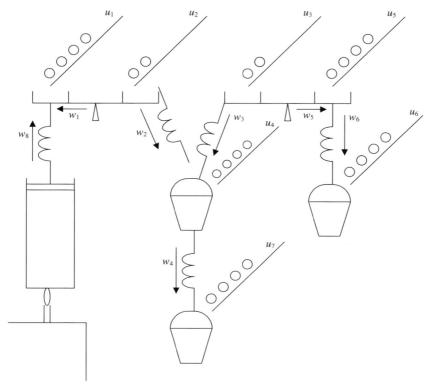

Figure 6.3 Machine showing fixed components with known capacities arranged in a stable configuration
Sources: Design, Towfic Shomar; recreation George Zouros.

and susceptible to change by change in these structures. The same, I claim, is true of all our laws, whether we take them to be iron – the typical attitude towards the laws of physics – or of a more flexible material, as in biology, economics or psychology. I repeat the lesson to be learned from Ian Hacking: probabilities make sense only relative to the chance set-up that generates them, and that is equally true whether the chance set-up is a radioactive nucleus or a socio-economic machine.

With reference to the behavioral sciences, we can summarize my point this way: sets of probability and causal laws like those depicted in figures 6.1 and 6.2 cannot be free-standing. Rather they need a socio-economic machine to generate them. The view of course makes sense only if the kind of knowledge that we need to understand the operation of a socio-economic machine is not itself more knowledge of "deeper" probabilistic and causal laws. And that is just the claim I argue: the knowledge we need here is knowledge not of laws but of *capacities*. And I claim that in fact much of the knowledge we have in exact science is just that – although, out of mistaken empiricist loyalties, we often try to reconstruct this knowledge as knowledge of laws. In the simplest case these capacities can be thought of as probabilistic propensities. Patricia Cheng, a psychologist from UCLA, argues that in judging what causal relations hold given some information about associations, people "interpret their observations of covariations as manifestations of the operation of unobservable causal powers, with the tacit goal of estimating the magnitude of those powers."[5] What Patricia Cheng says people do in ordinary life is very close to what I see done in our most advanced sciences.

Rather than take you through a philosophical discussion of causal powers, I would like to illustrate one case of where these philosophical matters make a real difference. The hero of the case is Amartya Sen. The case involves Sri Lanka, a very poor country which for years had an active state entitlement system providing health care, education and food vouchers. Sri Lanka also came out high on usual measures for standard of welfare among developing countries despite being in the low-income group. This gives rise to an obvious question: was Sri Lanka's social expenditure a significant cause of the high standard of welfare in its population?

Here is how some social scientists want to study this. They ask: is high social expenditure in general a cause of a high standard of welfare in developing countries? And to answer that they write down an equation like this:

$$H_{it} = a_t + bY_{it} + dE_{it} + I_i + u_{it}$$

where a_t is a time-specific but country-invariant effect assumed to reflect technological advances; Y_{it} is *per capita* income; E_{it} is social welfare expenditure; d is the marginal impact of social expenditure on living standards; I_i is a country-specific and time-invariant "fixed effect"; and u_{it} is a random error term. They then try to use social statistics to estimate d. If d is positive and large, the answer is "yes"; otherwise, "no."

Now what strikes me is that this methodology is crazy. That is because what this equation represents is a "free-standing association": there is no good reason to think there is a chance set-up that generates it. One can of course use statistics as what the word originally meant – a *summary* of some data. In so far as there is data about the relevant quantities in a number of countries, one can write it out in lists or can summarize it in statistics. And we can do that whether or not there is any probability over the quantities. That is irrelevant to the issue of whether there is a probability or not.

To suppose that there really is some fixed probability relation between welfare expenditure and welfare like that in the equation we need a lot of good

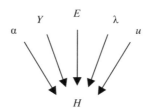

α: technological advances

Y: *per capita* income

E: social welfare expenditure

λ: country-specific "fixed effect"

u: "error"

H: living standard

Figure 6.4   Anand–Kanbur causal model for standard of living
Source: Anand and Kanbur (1995).

arguments. These arguments must be at both the phenomenological level – the frequencies pass strong tests for stability – and at the theoretical level – we have got some understanding of what kind of shared socio-economic structure is at work to generate them.

The equation I have written down comes from work by Anand and Kanbur[6] criticizing Amartya Sen for estimating the wrong equation, for estimating an equation in the level of the quantities rather than in their first differences. But this is odd since Sen does neither. Rather than the single graph pictured in figure 6.4, which expresses a hypothesis Anand and Kanbur criticize about the causal relations that hold among the designated quantities across all developing countries, Sen's hypotheses dictate different graphs for different countries (pictured in figure 6.5a and 6.5b). And he does it this way exactly for the reasons I say. Each of the countries studied has a different socio-economic structure constituting a different socio-economic machine that will generate different causal relations true in that country and concomitantly different probability measures appropriate for the quantities appearing in these relations.

Look just at how Sen talks about South Korea and Taiwan on the one hand versus Sri Lanka on the other.[7] In Taiwan and South Korea the immediate level of causation for poverty removal on Sen's account is employment expansion with growing demand for labor, and in this case export expansion was the immediate cause of the growing demand for labor. But, considering South Korea, "the fact that export expansion provided a very good vehicle for such explanation . . . has to be viewed in the perspective of the total economic picture." Sen tells us "*behind* (emphasis mine) the immediate explanation" stand lots of other factors, like rapid capital accumulation, availability of a labor force suited by education to modern manufacture, and "overwhelming control of the organized banking sector" by the government. When these kinds of factors are arranged appropriately they constitute a kind of socio-economic machine in which causal links between export expansion and poverty removal can arise.

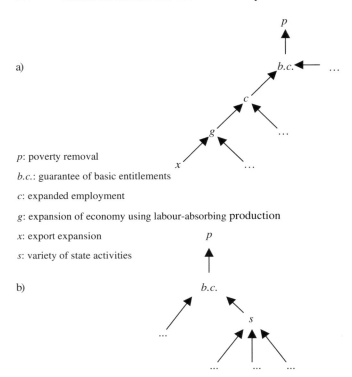

a)

p: poverty removal

b.c.: guarantee of basic entitlements

c: expanded employment

g: expansion of economy using labour-absorbing production

x: export expansion

s: variety of state activities

b)

Figure 6.5   Sen's causal structures for (a) South Korea and Taiwan, (b) Sri Lanka
Source: Design, Sang Wook Yi.

3   An economics example

The paper I will look at for an example from economics is entitled "Loss of
Skill during Unemployment and the Persistence of Unemployment Shocks" by
Christopher Pissarides (1992).[8] The idea investigated in the paper is that loss
of skill during unemployment leads to less job creation by employers, which
leads to continuing unemployment. The method is to produce a model in which
f_t = the probability of a worker getting a job at period t:

(i) depends on the probability of getting a job at the previous period f_{t-1}
   (i.e. shows persistence) if there is skill loss during unemployment; and

(ii) does not depend on f_{t-1} if not.

The model supposes that there is such a probability and puts a number of
constraints on it in order to derive a further constraint on its dynamics:

(i) $\partial f_t / \partial f_{t-1} > 0$, given skill loss

(ii) $\partial f_t / \partial f_{t-1} = 0$, given no loss of skill.

The point for us is to notice how finely tuned the details of the model plus the constraints on the probability must be in order to fix even a well-defined constraint on the dynamics of f_t, let alone to fix f_t itself.

The model is for two overlapping generations each in the job market for two periods only: at the end of each period every worker is, at least for the moment, unemployed. "Short-term unemployed" refers to "young" workers just entering the job market at a given time with skills acquired through training plus those employed, and thus practicing their skills, in the previous period; "long-term unemployed" refers to those from the older generation who were not employed in the previous period. The probability f_t of a worker getting a job in the between-period search depends critically on the matching technology χ, the number of times a job and worker meet and are matched so that a hire would take place if the job and the worker were both available. By assumption, χ at t is a determinate function of the number of jobs available at t (J_t) and the number of workers available at t ($2L$). Wages in the model are determined by a static Nash bargain. The central features of the first model are listed in table 6.1. Variations on the basic model that relax the assumptions that all workers search in the same way and thus have the same probability for a job match are developed in later sections of the paper.

The trick in the derivation is to get f_t to be a determinate function (via χ) of a product of f_t and f_{t-1}. χ is a function of J_t and L. In this model the product form in χ is achieved by getting J_t, which is determined by profits to be earned from offering a job, to depend on the product of f_t and f_{t-1}. This comes about because J_t depends on the probability of a job being filled by a short- (or long-) term worker. This in turn is equal to the probability of a worker being short- (or long-) term unemployed – into which f_{t-1} enters – times the probability of a short- or long-term worker getting a job, which is indifferently f_t for both.

The derivation of persistence or nonpersistence in the rest of the models in the paper also depends on the fact that the relevant probability analogous to f_t in model 1 is a function of the product of $f_t f_{t-1}$.

What lesson do we wish to draw from looking at Pissarides search model? Turn again to table 6.1. It takes a lot of assumptions to define this model and, as we have seen, the exact arrangement matters if consequences are to be fixed about whether there is persistence in the dynamics of unemployment probability or not. Those arrangements are clearly not enough to fix the exact nature of the persistence, let alone the full probability itself. In Pissarides' model 1, where job openings are endogenous, the dependence of jobs on workers' histories must be engineered just so, so that J_t will be a function of the product $f_t f_{t-1}$. In the next model, where the product could not possibly enter through J_t, the facts about how workers search must be aligned just right to get the product into the search function S_t. And so forth.

Table 6.1   *Assumptions of Pissarides' model 1 (1992)*

1	Discrete time
2	Two overlapping generations
	a. Each of fixed size, L
	b. Each generation is in the job market exactly two periods
3	Each job lasts one period only and must be refilled at the beginning of every period
4	The number of jobs, J_t, available at beginning of period t is endogenous
5	Workers in each of their two life periods are either employed or unemployed
6	a. Output for young workers and old, previously employed workers $= 2$
	b. Output for old, previously unemployed workers $= 2y, 0 < y < 1$
	($y < 1$ represents skill loss during unemployment)
7	Unemployed workers have 0 output, no utility, no income
	(This is relevant to calculating wages and profits)
8	In each period all workers and some jobs are available for matching
9	Each job must be matched at the beginning of a period to be filled in that period
10	In each period workers and jobs meet at most one partner
11	The number of matches between a job and a worker is designated by χ, where
	a. χ is at least twice differentiable
	b. The first derivatives of χ are positive, the second negative
	c. χ is homogeneous of degree 1
	d. $\chi(0, 2L) = \chi(J_t, 0) = 0$
	e. $\chi(J_t, 2L) = \max(J_t, 2L)$
12	There is a probability that a worker meets a job at the beginning of t, designated by f_t
	a. f_t does not depend on what a worker does nor on whether the worker is employed or unemployed
	b. f_t is a function only of J_t and L
13	There is a probability that a job meets a worker at the beginning of period t
	a. This probability is independent of what jobs do
	b. This probability is a function only of J_t and L
14	The cost of opening a job and securing the output as described in 6 is equal to $1/k$ (whether the job is filled or not)
15	Wages are determined by a Nash bargain
16	Workers and employers maximize expected utility

My claim is that it takes hyperfine-tuning like this to get a precise probabilistic claim. As with the previous case probabilities are associated with very special kinds of models before they are linked to the world. What I have pointed to – the need for a very finely honed model in order to derive any results – is not special to this case but is characteristic of economic theory. I think we can understand why.

The basic ideas I want to appeal to were formulated by Carl Menger in his attack on historical economics.[9] Menger argued that economics could be a proper science and by "proper science" he meant one that uses precise concepts that have exact deductive relations among them. The paradigm is "$f = ma$." In mechanics we do get this exact relation, but the relation we get involves an abstract concept "force," whose relation to the world is always mediated via some more concrete concepts. These more concrete concepts are not geared to describe every arbitrary situation but are rather very specific in their form.

The forms are given by familiar models, e.g. two compact masses separated by distance r, a linear harmonic oscillator, or a charge moving in a uniform magnetic field. Thus the concept "force" is limited in its application to situations that can be represented by these highly specialized models. This is just what Menger said we should expect from economics: we can have concepts with exact deductive relations among them but those concepts will not be ones that represent features that are regularly found immediately in what he called "full empirical reality." This does not mean they never really occur, but if they do it would generally be in circumstances with special structures.

Now much of the theorizing we do in economics right now goes exactly the opposite direction to that recommended by Menger. It uses, not abstract or theoretical or newly invented concepts – like "force", or "energy", or "electromagnetic field" – concepts partially defined by their deductive relations to other concepts, but rather, as Uskali Mäki teaches us,[10] very mundane concepts that are unmediated in their attachment to full empirical reality.

We study, for instance, the capacity of skill loss during unemployment to produce persistence in employment shocks, or whether the limited enforceability of debt contracts will lead to inefficiencies, or whether when food shortages produce famines the effect is generally mediated by failures of food entitlement arrangements. Nevertheless we want our treatments to be rigorous and our conclusions to follow deductively. And the way to get deductivity when it cannot come out of the relations of the concepts is to put enough of the right kind of structure into the model.

That is the trick of building one of these economic models: you have to figure out some circumstances that are constrained in just the right way that results of interest can be derived deductively. The other part of the trick is to pick circumstances that are in some way transparent: they let you see what you think is important about the relations of the concepts themselves.

This makes for a kind of dilemma: on the one hand nothing follows from the concepts themselves without embedding them in a structure, and only special structures will yield any deductive consequences at all. But on the other, we do not want the circumstances really to matter. That is one of the chief reasons why economics theory is concerned with the robustness of the "lessons" to be learned or understanding gained across models. But that is not what I want to focus on.

My point is that theories in physics and economics get into similar situations but via opposite strategies. In both cases we can derive consequences rigorously only in highly stylized models. But in the case of physics that is because we are working with abstract concepts that have considerable deductive power but whose application is limited by the range of the theory's models that provide more concrete forms for the abstract terms employed in the theory. In economics, by contrast, the concepts have a wide range of application but we can get deductive results only by locating them in special models.

4   The case of superconductivity

We are invited to believe in the truth of our favourite explanatory theories because of their precision and their empirical successes.[11] The Bardeen–Cooper–Schrieffer (BCS) account of superconductivity must be a paradigmatic case.[12] We build real operating finely tuned superconducting devices using the Ginsburg–Landau equations. And (with appropriate corrections) the Ginsburg–Landau equations can be derived from quantum mechanics or quantum field theory using the BCS model. So every time a SQUID (Superconducting Quantum Interference Device) detects a magnetic fluctuation, we have reason to believe in quantum theory.

But the Hamiltonian used in the quantum equations of motion, like the classical force function, is abstract: we apply it to a situation only when that situation is deemed to satisfy certain other more concrete descriptions. These are the descriptions provided by what are called the "interpretive" models of quantum mechanics. Albert Messiah's text *Quantum Mechanics*[13] provides four basic interpretive models: the central potential, scattering, the Coulomb interaction, and the harmonic oscillator, to which we should add the kinetic energy – which is taken for granted in his text.

Philosophers like Carl G. Hempel and Ernst Nagel taught us to divide the principles of a theory into two kinds: internal principles, which give the relations between the abstract theoretical quantities, and bridge principles, which "interpret" the theoretical concepts in more concrete terms. The quantum bridge principles give the corresponding Hamiltonians for each of the concrete interpretive models available in quantum mechanics.

The point I want to stress is this: Hamiltonians are assigned by bridge principles in any proper theoretical treatment; and in particular this is how they are assigned in *just those derivations that we take to be the best cases where predictive success argues for the truth of quantum theory*. When there is no bridge principle that licenses the application of a Hamiltonian to the situation in question, its introduction is ad hoc and the power of the derived prediction to confirm the theory is much reduced. For the cases that give us really good reasons to believe in the truth of quantum theory, we need Hamiltonians that are assigned in a principled way; and for quantum mechanics as it is practiced that means ones that are licensed by principles of the theory – by bridge principles.

When we think about the range and limits of quantum theory there is something to be noticed. Bridge principles are just like internal principles in one respect: there are just a handful of them. And that is in keeping with the point of abstract theory as it is described by empiricists and rationalists alike. We aim to cover as wide a range as we can with as few principles as possible. But the fewer the bridge principles, the fewer the concrete models we have available to model the world. Since the theory can be applied only when its concrete "interpretive" models fit, the range of the theory will be severely restricted, even though the predictions within that range may be enormously precise and impressively accurate.

So far I have mentioned four basic bridge principles from Messiah. We may expect more to be added as we move from fundamental quantum theory to more specific theories for specific topics. The BCS account of superconductivity that I mentioned is a good example. I chose this example to study because it was one I knew something about from my work on SQUIDs at Stanford and from our research project on modeling at LSE. It turns out to be a startling confirmation of my point. The fundamental Hamiltonian of the BCS paper uses only the basic models I have already described plus just one that is new: the kinetic energy of moving particles, the harmonic oscillator, the Coulomb interaction, scattering between electrons with states of well-defined momentum, and then in addition the "Bloch" Hamiltonian for particles in a periodic potential. And this last even is not entirely new since it is closely related to the central potential, which is already among the basic models. Superconductivity is a quantum phenomenon precisely because superconducting materials (at least low temperature, "type-I" materials) can be represented by the special models that quantum theory supplies.

How much of the world altogether can be represented by these models is an open question. Not much, as the world presents itself, looks on the face of it like harmonic oscillators and Coulomb interactions between separated chunks of charge. Superconductivity is a case where a highly successful representation can be constructed from just the models quantum theory has to offer. My point is that with each new case it is an empirical question whether these models, or models from some other theory, or no models from any theory at all will fit. Quantum theory will apply to phenomena that these models can represent, and nothing in the theory, nor anything else we know about the structure of matter, tells us whether they can be forced to fit in a new case where they do not at first appearance do so.

5   Conclusion

So, how far does the causal order we represent in our exact sciences stretch? Consider physics with its highly abstract concepts. In so far as we are concerned with theories that are warranted by their empirical successes, the bridge principles of the theory will provide us with an explicit characterization of its scope. The theory applies exactly as far as its interpretive models can stretch. Sticking to Messiah's catalogue of bridge principles as an example, that means that quantum theory extends to all and only those situations that can be represented as composed of central potentials, scattering events, Coulomb interactions and harmonic oscillators.

The kind of economic theory of which we saw an example works in the reverse way. Economics uses very concrete concepts, like the level of employment or length of time between jobs, which do not have very strong deductive relations built into them, even given the handful of principles we may be willing to accept from economic theory. So a lot of very particular kinds of constraints need to be supplied by a model before any exact conclusions can be derived.

From my first case we learn that, where we want to postulate a determinate set of causal relations or a probability measure over a set of quantities of interest, there must be a socio-economic structure to generate them. We can understand many of our typical models in political economics as blueprints for these structures.

In all cases, where we can expect causal order depends on where we can fit our models. And by the nature of how models do – and should – get constructed in exact science, the kinds of models available are not very flexible. They fit readily onto only very special bits of the world around us. It seems to be in the nature of how we do exact science that what it can cover is very limited in scope.

Notes

Research for this chapter was supported by the project "Modelling in Physics and Economics" at the Centre for Philosophy of Natural and Social Science at the London School of Economics. Special thanks to Towfic Shomar, Wook Yi and George Zouros for help.
1. For a more detailed discussion of issues raised in this section, see Cartwright (1996, 1997).
2. Pearl (2000).
3. Spirtes, Glymour, and Scheines (1993).
4. Hacking (1965).
5. Cheng (1997).
6. Anand and Kanbur (1995).
7. Sen (1988).
8. For a more detailed discussion of issues raised in this section, see Cartwright (1996, 1999).

9. Menger (1883).
10. See Mäki (1996), 427–447.
11. For a more detailed discussion of issues raised in this section, see Cartwright (1996, 1999).
12. Bardeen, Cooper, and Schreiffer (1957).
13. Messiah (1961).

References

Anand, Sudhir and S.M. Ravi Kanbur (1995). Public policy and basic needs provision: intervention and achievement in Sri Lanka, in Jean Drèze, Amartya Sen and Athar Hussain (eds.), *The Political Economy of Hunger: Selected Essays*. Oxford: Clarendon Press

Bardeen, J., L.N. Cooper, and J.R. Schrieffer (1957). Theory of superconductivity, *Phys. Rev. U.*, 108, 1175

Cartwright, Nancy (1996). What is a causal structure?, in Vaughan R. McKim and Stephen P. Turner (eds.), *Causality in Crisis? Statistical Methods and the Search for Causal Knowledge in the Social Science*. Notre Dame: University of Notre Dame Press

(1997). Where do laws of nature come from?, *Dialectica*, 51(1), 65–78

(1999). *The Dappled World: A Study of the Boundaries of Science*. Cambridge: Cambridge University Press

Cheng, P.W. (1997). From covariation to causation: a causal power theory, *Psychological Review*, 104, 367–405, at 369

Hacking, Ian (1965). *The Logic of Statistical Inference*. Cambridge: Cambridge University Press

Mäki, Uskali (1996). Scientific realism and some peculiarities of economics, in Robert S. Cohen, Resto Hilpinen and Qui Renzong (eds.), *Realism and Anti-Realism in the Philosophy of Science*, Boston Studies in the philosophy of Science, 169. Dordrecht: Kluwer.

Menger, C. (1883). *Untersuchungen bei die Methode der Sozialwissenschaft, und der politischen Ekonomie insbesondere*. Leipzig: Duncker & Humblot; trans. as *Problems of Economics and Sociology*. Urbana: University of Illinois Press, 1963

Messiah, A. (1961). *Quantum Mechanics*. Amsterdam: North-Holland

Pearl, J. (1995). Causal diagrams for experimental research, *Biometrica*, 82, 670

(2000) *Causality*. Cambridge: Cambridge University Press

Sen, Amartya (1998). Sri Lanka's Achievements: how and when, in T.N. Srinivasan and P.K. Bardhan (eds.), *Rural Poverty in South East Asia*. New York: Columbia University Press

Spirtes, P., C. Glymour, and R. Scheines (1993) *Causation, Prediction, and Search*. New York: Springer-Verlag

7 Econometrics and reality

Kevin D. Hoover

1 Econometrics and reality

Is econometrics possible? The question reminds me of an argument between two divines at an ecumenical conference. BAPTIST MINISTER: "I don't believe in infant baptism." ROMAN CATHOLIC ARCHBISHOP: "Not only do I believe in infant baptism, I have seen it done." Every applied economist has seen it done; yet Tony Lawson in his book, *Economics and Reality* (1997), assures us that, splash the econometric holy water as you may, economic heaven will not be a whit closer. The metaphor is perfectly apt; for Lawson's reason for dismissing econometrics is metaphysical: transcendental realism provides an accurate ontology of the economic world; econometrics is necessarily incompatible with transcendental realism. Nancy Cartwright, who is also a realist, appears more favorably disposed to econometrics. After all, in her *Nature's Capacities and Their Measurement* (1989), she stokes the self-esteem of economists by suggesting that quantum physicists might learn a thing or two about handling probabilities from econometricians (see also chapter 6 in this volume). Beneath a cheery exterior, her views are in fact stunningly pessimistic: the conditions in which econometric methods can succeed are strict; they may be met in the land of quantum physics, but never in their country of origin. Against both Lawson and Cartwright, I maintain that econometrics and realism are compatible and, indeed, that realism helps us better to understand the role and successes of econometrics.

2 Realism

According to Uskali Mäki (1996) *ontological realism* is the doctrine that entities beyond the realm of the commonsense exist externally (i.e. independently of any individual human mind) and objectively (i.e. unconstituted by our representations of them). Scientific realism is opposed to Humean empiricism (or as Lawson, following Bhaskar, terms it "empirical realism"). Empiricism

152

maintains that reality consists of "objects of experience constituting atomistic events" (Lawson 1997, 19). For Hume, one billiard ball strikes another, and the other moves. There is no more to the story than what our own minds supply. Lawson (1997, part I) adopts the transcendental realism of Roy Bhaskar (1975). Bhaskar (1975, chapter 1) proposes a stratified ontology of mechanisms, events, and experiences. Experiences are people's direct (subjective) perceptions of events. Events are the realizations of mechanisms. And mechanisms are the underlying, not directly accessible structures whose complex interactions determine which events are actually realized. It is the reality of such mechanisms, of their powers, dispositions, capacities, efficacy, and necessary connections, that Humean empiricism denies (or, at least, denies us the knowledge of).

Bhaskar offers a transcendental argument in favor of the reality of the stratum of mechanism and, hence, terms his metaphysics *transcendental realism*. Cartwright (1994, 279), like Bhaskar, develops a similar argument based on Kant's classic "puzzling" form. Let X be features of the world we are loth to deny; let Φ be an "abstruse philosophical position." The argument then runs: without Φ, X would be inconceivable; hence Φ. Both Bhaskar and Cartwright use Kant's transcendental argument to move from the accepted success of experimental sciences to the reality of a realm of powers, capacities, dispositions, or mechanisms. Cartwright, in fact, goes somewhat further, including in her X "the possibility of planning, prediction, manipulation, control and policy setting."

Transcendental realism gets started with the observation that regularities of the sort contemplated by Hume are relatively hard to find and must be created experimentally, and experiments are manipulations that presuppose that the things manipulated act in reliable ways. For Bhaskar, experiments are about making things happen in regular relationships that they do not normally show in the world. This requires intervention and manipulation. To show that a feather and a stone fall from the same height in the same time, to exemplify Newton's law of gravity, requires experimental control – removing the air from the space through which they fall. For such an experimental procedure to make sense the feather and the stone must have the disposition to fall according to a similar rule, but quite different dispositions to react to air resistance; the scientist must be able to reliably remove the air from the chamber in which they fall (i.e. some machine must be disposed to act as a vacuum pump and to respond to his initiation); and so forth. A world of dispositions or powers is presupposed, a world in which such dispositions and powers mix in varying ways, an *open* world in which a scientist may intervene to create *closure* to isolate and separate enduring capacities or dispositions that are not normally distinct Humean empirical regularities. Some closures may be spontaneous (the solar system, for example, which runs according to nearly Humean regularity without controls). Most closures are the product of experimental intervention.

The necessity of closure for the appearance of regularity is nearly tautological in Bhaskar's account: closed systems are defined as "systems in which constant conjunctions occur" (Bhaskar 1975, 33; cf. Lawson 1997, 19).

Although Bhaskar in *The Possibility of Naturalism* (1979) goes out of his way to defend the view that essentially the same analysis that he applies to physical sciences can also be applied to social sciences, Lawson denies that an analogous transcendental argument can be applied directly to "mainstream" economics. The argument cannot get started, Lawson (1997, 56) believes, because the social sciences do not have the demonstrated success needed as a premise of the transcendental argument. With respect to "mainstream" economics, Lawson regards the lack of success simply to be a fact. But that fact is partly explained by the nature of social sciences generally. It is not usually possible to create experimental closures of social situations. There are practical difficulties: society is too complex and heterogeneous; there are legal and ethical barriers. And there is human agency: planets, atoms, and rocks do not make choices; people do. Lawson's strategy is not to start with the practice of economics, as Bhaskar started with the practice of natural sciences, but to use the insights of Bhaskar's ontology as the basis for a methodological reform of economics. Transcendental realism is transcribed into a new mode: *critical realism*. Whereas for physical sciences, their success was an explanatory premise, for social sciences – particularly for economics – its failures are the explanandum.

3   What's wrong with econometrics

Tony Lawson: the search for covering laws and the failure of closure

Lawson characterizes "mainstream" economics as engaged in a search for covering laws – universal regularities that connect observable events. "[E]conometricians concern themselves with attempting to determine constant event conjunctions . . . of a probabilistic sort" (Lawson 1997, 69). Econometrics is an example of *regularity stochasticism*:

> for every (measurable) economic event or state of affairs y there exists a set of conditions or events, etc., $x_1, x_2, \ldots x_n$ say, such that y and $x_1, x_2, \ldots x_n$ are regularly conjoined under some (set of) "well-behaved" probabilistic formulation(s). In other words, *stochastic closures* are everywhere assumed to hold; for any (measurable) economic event y a stable and recoverable relationship between a set of conditions $x_1, x_2, \ldots x_n$ and the average or expected value of y (conditional upon $x_1, x_2, \ldots x_n$) or some such, is postulated. (Lawson 1997, 76, emphasis in the original)

The axioms and assumptions of economic theory are similarly regarded as claims about constant conjunctions. Theoretical explanation in economic theory is based on deductions from covering laws, "constant conjunctions of the form 'whenever event x then event y,'" and initial or boundary conditions

(Lawson 1997, 91). The theorist subscribes to a "degenerate" form of regularity stochasticism – *regularity determinism* (Lawson 1997, 98).

Lawson's argument against econometrics starts with the claim that there are no laws in economics (Lawson 1997, 70). The Lucas critique provides an explanation of this fact from within economics itself.[1] Lucas (1976) argued that large-scale econometric models, and more generally, empirically estimated aggregate relationships, are likely to be unstable because they reflect the decisions made by economic agents in particular policy environments and those policy environments change. For example, the expectations-augmented Phillips curve, which relates the unemployment rate to rate inflation, would not remain stable if there were a change in monetary policy. Agents would integrate their knowledge of how policy was conducted into their expectations of future policy outcomes (e.g. knowledge of the central bank's money supply rule into knowledge of the future path of the money supply), changing the phenomenal relationship of unemployment to inflation with each shift in policy regime. Lawson (1997, 71–75) regards the Lucas critique as sound as far as it goes. But he stigmatizes responses such as Sargent's program of providing microfoundationally based econometrics as unable to succeed because the Lucas critique is merely a symptom of a larger failure of macroeconomic systems to achieve intrinsic or extrinsic closure.

In physical sciences, regularity stochasticism fails when there is insufficient shielding to isolate a system from conflating causes. In macroeconomics, regularity stochasticism fails for at least two additional reasons. First, a microfoundational approach such as Sargent's fails because the technical conditions needed for aggregation of individual behavior to well-ordered relations among aggregates are not met (Lawson 1997, 80–91). Second, an econometric model can fulfill the conditions of regularity stochasticism only if it can limit the range of agent's behavior in definite conditions to "only one outcome or 'exit' " (Lawson 1997, 79). But this is a misrepresentation of the intrinsic openness of economic systems in which agents can genuinely choose and in which, therefore, their behavior cannot be governed by a predictive law.

Lawson's argument against econometrics stands or falls with his characterization of the discipline as principally concerned with establishing covering laws. To establish this Lawson quotes on behalf of economic theory from Frank Hahn (e.g. 1997, 18) and on behalf of econometricians from David Hendry (1997, 301). Setting aside the (fairly serious) issue of whether these economists – eminent as they are – are actually representative of their subdisciplines, we nevertheless should heed D.H. Lawrence's dictum to trust the tale, not the teller. When we examine the practice of economists, Lawson's characterization of the discipline as searching for covering laws seems misconceived.

The concerns that animated Lucas (1976) are old. He acknowledges some precursors, such as Tinbergen, and overlooks others, such as Haavelmo, but makes no claims for originality. Reading the early contributions to econometrics collected in Hendry and Morgan (1995) one cannot but be struck with the clearness with which early econometricians understood the difficulties of isolating particular causal relationships from the dense webs of economic influences and of accounting for the ever-changing institutions and background conditions. It is inconceivable that one could believe these econometricians to be, or that they could have believed themselves to be, in search of covering laws, if by that one means invariant event regularities that remain constant over time and against all changing background conditions. Yes, they sought robust regularities, but they expected neither the precision nor the freedom from context and contingency that is implied in Lawson's covering-law characterization.

Nor has this changed recently. Sargent (e.g. Hansen and Sargent 1980) seeks to resolve the Lucas critique by actually modeling the processes of expectation formation (in Lawson's language, to achieve closure). The intent (whether it is successful is another question) is to model rock-bottom tastes and technology, the so-called "deep parameters," utility functions (representing people's preferences), budget constraints, and production functions (representing engineering relations). I have argued elsewhere (Hoover 1988, 1992) that this program is not likely to succeed. But the point now is just that these components do not look like covering laws. A utility function is not an empirical relationship at the level of events. It is more like a power or capacity; it is a description of the disposition of an agent to act, provided that a situation is constructed around him (that is the role of the budget constraint) that permits him to realize his disposition. Lucas (1987) and Kydland and Prescott (1991, 1996) are skeptical of Sargent's program. They prefer to construct theoretical models that are "calibrated" to yield empirical content, yet are not estimated econometrically (see Hoover 1995a and Hartley, Hoover, and Salyer, 1997, 1998). But this is an in-house dispute with Sargent over realisticness (to use Mäki's term) or idealization or deducibility. The conception of models as being built up out of components that are not covering laws but more like powers or capacities is shared by all the disputants. Seen this way, Lucas and company are much closer to transcendental realism than to positivism.[2]

Nancy Cartwright: the difficulty of constructing closures

Cartwright is more sympathetic to "mainstream" economics, though her ontology is similar to Lawson's and Bhaskar's. Cartwright (1983) maintains that the "laws of physics lie" in the sense that they are never instantiated without substantial human interference in the form of experimental controls and substantial interpretive license. More recently, Cartwright (1994, 1995, undated[3]) has refined her objection to laws: it is not so much that they lie, but that they are properties of highly particular organizations of things and are known to be true only within the limited domains in which we have instantiated them.

Cartwright stigmatizes the claims that laws are universal as "fundamentalist" and describes her own views as "local realism" (Cartwright 1994). This distinguishes her somewhat from Lawson (1997, 23) who believes that the actions of mechanisms are not subject to *ceteris paribus* conditions, but are universal, even though rarely observed acting in isolation.[4]

Like Bhaskar and Lawson, Cartwright believes that to observe a law directly is possible only in contrived circumstances – e.g. in experiments shielded from outside interferences. In such "set-ups," what empirical regularities result depends upon the interactions of the capacities of the components. A law of physics such as $F = ma$ really describes such a capacity. It operates for all forces (F), masses (m), and accelerations (a) so long as those terms can be meaningfully applied. It interacts with other such capacities and is not guaranteed to hold outside its local domain.

Cartwright (undated) calls the set-ups, the "highly structured arrangements" that generate reliable empirical regularities, *nomological machines*. The solar system (an example also favored by Bhaskar and Lawson) is an unusual naturally occurring nomological machine. A more typical example is a particular harmonic oscillator: say, a spring and a weight. A model, in Cartwright's account, is a blueprint for a nomological machine. It tells us how to construct them out of parts with the necessary capacities. To provide a model is at once to establish or to widen the domain for the underlying capacity and to provide a recipe for producing an empirical regularity. The capacities of a harmonic oscillator are described by a formula:

$$A\frac{d^2z}{dt^2} + Bz = 0$$

Models connect this formula to physical set-ups. Both the spring and weight and a coil and capacitor can be configured into analogous oscillators of different physical forms but conforming to the formula. In the one case, A, B, and z are interpreted as mass, distance, and force constant; and, in the other, as inductance, (inverse) capacitance, and charge.[5] "[O]nce you call something a harmonic oscillator, then mechanics [or electronics, we might add] can get a grip on it." (Cartwright undated).

The central message of *Nature's Capacities and Their Measurement* (Cartwright 1989) was that structural econometrics in the Cowles Commission tradition, the estimation of identified systems of causally interpretable equations, was possible only with strong (singular) causal assumptions. Though she did not use this terminology then, the central claim can be put in other words: to measure causal probabilities in an econometric system, the nomological machine must be completely articulated. Cartwright's interest in econometrics in *Nature's Capacities* was instrumental. She looked to it for a logical or methodological lesson for quantum physics. For that purpose it did not matter whether econometrics was actually successful in its own domain.

Cartwright (undated) illustrates the kind of specific causal knowledge needed "to get causes from probabilities" with a schematic design (a "blueprint") for a machine that delivers a particular set of stochastic regularities, in this case ones in which a true cause lowers the conditional probability of the effect. The details of the machine, originally designed by Towfic Shomar, are not important, except to note that they are quite specific and as straightforwardly instantiated as the recipe for *Pfeffernüsse* in *The Joy of Cooking*. Instead of pepper, molasses, flour and butter, Shamor uses chambers, a source of alpha particles, a proton, and magnetic fields. To understand or to explain the probabilistic behavior of the proton in Shamor's machine is, according to Cartwright, to be able to model the nomological machine and to measure the relevant probabilities. This synthetic understanding is not, however, all that there is to understanding. The probabilistic behavior of Shamor's machine is driven by a radioactive source with well-behaved probabilities of emission of alpha particles. My understanding is that, while quantum mechanics provides some further synthetic explanation analogous to that provided by Shamor's machine, we need not go too far down before we reach Hume's rock bottom in which we cannot say why, but merely that, a regularity occurs. This too is knowledge.

The story of Shamor's machine reinforces the theme begun in *Nature's Capacities*: regular probabilistic behavior is a property that is assured only in tightly controlled set-ups. Only if one were to repeat Shamor's set-up with considerable precision could one expect Shamor's probabilistitic relations to recur. Haavelmo's (1944) well-known example of the regular relationship between throttle-setting and the speed of a car is similar. The relationship can be reproduced only with the same make of car in very similar circumstances (air temperature, humidity, road surface, and so forth). Cartwright (undated) provides an example of a nomological machine in economics in the guise of Pissarides' (1992) model of the persistence of unemployment. We shall consider Pissarides' model presently. In the meantime the important point is that Cartwright shows that, to pin down probabilities for observables in the model, things "must be engineered just so." She proceeds (undated, table 3) to list sixteen particular assumptions needed to make Pissarides's model deliver its results.

Despite offering the example of a nomological machine in economics, Cartwright's pessimism about econometrics is implicit in the example. The assumptions of the Pissarides' model are too particular and too implausible to be fulfilled, so that, while econometrics seems possible in principle, it is hard to imagine how it could possibly succeed practically. Once the image of nomological machines is firmly rooted, it is hard to imagine them in the economy, and yet harder to imagine that two economies might possess nomological machines of the same make and model. In a public lecture, Cartwright was able to illicit gales of laughter from the audience (largely of philosophers) simply by describing (with hardly a raised eyebrow and certainly no smirk) economists trying to determine the effect of educational expenditure on living standards in Sri Lanka by treating Sri Lanka and other countries as draws from a stable regular association common to them all.[6] If there are nomological machines in economics, *that* surely is not one.

Anand and Kanbur (1995, 321) consider a number of related studies. Each can be understood in relationship to a common model in which for some measure of living standard, H_{it}, for country i and time t:

$$H_{it} = \alpha_t + \beta Y_{it} + \delta E_{it} + \lambda_i + u_{it}''$$

where Y_{it} is *per capita* income; E_{it} is social welfare expenditure; α_t is a time-specific but country-invariant effect assumed to reflect technological advances (e.g. disease eradication techniques); λ_i is a country-specific and time-invariant "fixed effect"; δ is the marginal impact of social expenditure on living standards; and u_{it}'' is a random error term.

The object of these studies is to measure δ or, at least, to better understand the relationship between E and H. I am too ignorant of this literature to pass any judgment upon it in economic or econometric terms. The important point here is that it is characteristic of large areas of empirical economics; so, if Cartwright can dismiss these studies on the basis of a prior understanding of the requirements of local realism, that is a pessimistic conclusion indeed.

4 The possibility of econometrics

The second transcendental argument

Cartwright's pessimistic conclusion is not, I think, an implication of her realism; it is hardly compatible with it. Cartwright argues for the realism of mechanisms and their component capacities from the essential role they play in making the practice of experimentation possible. While Cartwright correctly stresses the stringent conditions often necessary to establish stable regularities in an experimental context, perhaps too much of her focus is on the mechanisms that those regularities instantiate. Bhaskar's and Lawson's (1997, 25) argument for a world of structured, intransitive objects emphasizes the same point. Yet Cartwright draws a second conclusion from the success of experimentation. Experiments must be structured and shielded. To engineer and construct them, we must be able to control and manipulate things and environments. In so doing, we rely on prior knowledge, some of which is no doubt theoretically warranted and precise, but much of which comprises imprecise facts of whose domain we have only limited knowledge. The transcendental argument is straightforward: "If I do not know these things, what do I know and how can I come to know anything?" (Cartwright 1994, 280).

Bhaskar and Lawson conclude that the world must be "open" if experiments are to make sense. The second transcendental argument establishes that there also must be a useful number of reliable and manipulable pre-theoretical regularities if scientists are to be able to create closures in an open world. Lawson (1997, 27, emphasis in the original) writes: "outside of astronomy at least, most of the constant-event conjunctions which are held to be significant in science, in fact occur *only* under the restricted conditions of experimental control." That could be true only if "constant conjunction" means exceptionless conjunction on a universal domain. True, the path of a falling leaf (Lawson's example) or of a $1,000 bill blowing through St. Stephen's Square (Neurath's example cited by Cartwright, 1994, 283) is hard to predict. Still, though we know exceptions, the general rule "if I drop it, it falls" is reliable and essential to our making our way through the world. A coin dropped from an upper story window exemplifies that regularity, while the coin that returns to one's hand after being cast over the cliff at Blowing Rock, North Carolina is the exception that proves the rule. We adapt our expectations for the coin to the altered circumstances fairly easily. Nor is it just a matter of some regularities being overwhelmed with exceptions, while others have fewer. Some regularities might be perfectly exceptionless but imprecise. An iron ball dropped from Carfax tower will land in Oxford city center; a balsa wood glider in Oxfordshire; a helium balloon on Earth.

Openness is relative. Uncontrolled, nonexperimental situations, not just in astronomy, may be closed enough to deliver regularities of varying degrees of precision and reliability. Conversely, no experiment is perfectly immune to outside influences. Closure too is relative. And, in large measure, closure is secured using regularities readily to hand in the world as instruments.

The success of economics

There are social regularities as well. These are not all the result of laws or institutional restrictions or conventions, although people are seldom found outside such contexts. That I can predict the route my daughter will take home from school, even though there are many possible routes, accurately enough to meet her mid-way, even though we had no prior coordination, is based on a social (or at least human) regularity. It does not call her agency into question; she genuinely chooses her own route home. Making our way in the world requires us to exploit many social regularities: traffic is heavy from 4 to 6 p.m.; a store manager will tolerate verbal aggression up to a point; a punk on the streets will tolerate much less verbal aggression; money will purchase goods; people will understand me when I talk. These examples are "micro" (except perhaps the traffic example). Yet, reliable social regularities may also be "macro" or at least aggregate: electricity usage in California is higher in January and August than in April or October; the crime rate is higher when the proportion of men 16–24 years old to the whole population is higher. Again, the reliability of such regularities is no threat to agency. I must decide when to turn my air conditioner on;

I have a choice. Pacific Gas and Electric Company would have a difficult time modeling my individual choice in a precise way, yet it may be able to predict its aggregate load rather accurately.

Lawson overstates the failures of econometrics – or at least of empirical economics. As in physical sciences, what are in practice referred to as "laws" are a hodge-podge of summary statements of differing epistemological status. Some are axioms, some analytical truths, some heuristic rules; but some are also empirical generalizations. Although one can posit models in which they are deductive consequences, the law of demand, Engel's law, Okun's law, Gresham's law are, first and foremost, robust empirical generalizations. They are like the regularity of the balsa wood glider thrown from Carfax Tower landing in Oxfordshire: robust because imprecise. Lawson (1997, 70 and n. 3, 301) cites the well-documented inaccuracies of economic forecasts. But econometrically based forecasts, however inaccurate, are better than noneconometric forecasts. And, what is more, there is a difference between a relationship holding in different times, the sense of robustness that is analogous to constant conjunction, and a relationship being useful to connect the present to the future, as in an unconditional forecast. The theory of efficient markets predicts (in the sense of asserting the robust relationship to hold in different times and places) that the price of publicly traded shares is unpredictable (in the sense of tomorrow's value being foreseeable today). Robust, but imprecise, relationships are routinely made more locally precise. This is what Pacific Gas and Electric does when it estimates electricity demand on the basis of temperature, time of day, price, and other variables. The relationships are well known qualitatively, but its business decisions require more quantitatively precise information. They do not regard it as a threat to those decisions if the precise relationship they estimate for California in 1998 is not the same as for California in 1958 or for Holland in 1998. Academic economists too easily forget that business and government employs large numbers of their peers in part because of the practical and monetary value that they correctly assign to their quantitative conclusions (also see Hoover 1995b).

Lawson (1997, esp. chapter 14) recognizes the existence of "demi-regularities," precisely the sort of local, temporally specific regularities that I have illustrated in the preceding examples. But the existence of demi-regularities sits uneasily with the uncompromising rejection of econometrics in the earlier parts of his book. Similarly, Lawson (1997, 69) says that he does not question the use of means, growth rates, or other summary statistics which are legitimate where feasible. A substantial part of my argument below is that much of econometrics is in fact more sophisticated versions of these "legitimate" activities and investigation into the conditions of their "feasibility." One strategy open to Lawson would be to define econometrics as the search for constant conjunctions so that it necessarily fails if there are no such constant conjunctions; but this would do little justice to the reality of econometrics as it is practiced.

The role of experiments

If Lawson exaggerates the failures of empirical economics, Cartwright exaggerates the centrality of experiments. Cartwright takes an engineer's view: the problem is how to construct nomological machines or experiments. Her focus is on a certain sort of knowledge. Other sorts of knowledge should not be neglected. There are observational sciences as well as experimental or analytical sciences. The balance between observation and analysis corresponds roughly to the ease of experimentation. There is a growing field of experimental economics; nevertheless, economics is more like meteorology, vulcanology, or epidemiology than it is like physics or chemistry. The problem in these sciences is less how to *construct* nomological machines than how to infer what nomological machines in fact operate (i.e. what the principles of their operation (their capacities) are) on the basis of feasible observations.

The difference is illustrated by an exercise set to some college electronics classes. One learns the natures or powers of electronic components by learning Ohm's law, Kirchoff's law, and so forth, and by learning the ways in which particular resistors, capacitors, transistors, and other components exemplify these natures or powers (that is, one learns their capacities). This knowledge permits the student to construct radios, oscillators, and other nomological machines. In the exercise, the situation is flipped around. A particular circuit is embedded in epoxy, so that only its various termini are exposed. Using measuring instruments, the student must infer the structure of the internal circuit. The student is aided by the fact that she has a pretty good idea of the menu of capacities: she knows Ohm's law and how particular resistors might embody it. It would be a harder case, if she had to both infer the structure and characterize the capacities simultaneously.

Economics presents us with this harder case. To be sure, John Stuart Mill and Austrian economists generally have argued that economics is a compositive discipline in which components with well-understood capacities are combined (see Hausman 1992). One might see the elements of neoclassical heuristics, such as utility functions and budget constraints, as the analogues of resistors and capacitors. Unfortunately, their capacities are generic, unlike the capacity of, say, U^{235} to emit alpha particles, suitable only for rough sketches of nomological machines – not for blueprints.

5   An illustrative case

Pissarides' machine

Econometrics is possible and compatible with realism because the argument for realism implies the existence of robust regularities. Econometrics aims to characterize those regularities. It seems to be an impossible discipline only when we either think of it as aiming to quantify covering laws or to characterize directly the performance of nomological machines. The issues can be illustrated with Cartwright's (undated; also chapter 6 in this volume) example of a nomological machine in economics: Pissarides' (1992) model of the persistence of unemployment.

Cartwright (undated) makes the same point about Pissarides' model as she does about Shamor's proton machine: "it takes hyperfine-tuning...to get a probability." In the case of Shamor's machine, this hyperfine-tuning took the form of choosing a radioactive source with just the right rate of emission of alpha particles, an electric field of just the right strength, and so forth. In the case of Pissarides' model, the hyper-fine tuning takes the form of assuming that people are identical, live exactly two periods, are equal in number in each generation, engage in Nash wage bargains with their employers, have matching probabilities that can be described according to rather precise formulae, and so forth. It is striking that, while Shamor's machine could be built according to his blueprint, I would not know where to begin to build a real-world version of Pissarides' machine. Shamor's design is a recipe for *Pfeffernüsse*; Pissarides' is a recipe using salt with spherical crystals, unsweet sugar, and the spice of the fairy bush. I can build Pissarides' machine, but only as a computer simulation, not in an actual economy. The probabilities of Shamor's machine are rooted in the fact that the radioactive source really does emit alpha particles randomly with known probability; the probabilities of Pissarides' machine are deductions from axiomatic assumptions about the probabilities of job match. If the economy were the way that Pissarides describes it, then these deduced probabilities would be observed. But it is not really that way.

The point is not that Pissarides' model is wrong or useless, but merely that it stands in a different relationship to the world than Shamor's model. It is, perhaps, a toy, bearing the same relationship to the economy as a model airplane does to a Boeing 747. Toys have their uses – even scientifically. In the movie of *Planet of the Apes*, the intelligent apes deride the astronauts' claim to have flown to their planet, on the grounds that flight is impossible. A paper airplane, quickly folded and flown the length of the room, provides an eloquent refutation. At best, Pissarides' model is an idealization. As such it raises subtle questions about the relationship of idealizations to real-world data that interest not only methodologists and philosophers, but, implicitly, serious, practically minded economists as well. The contrasting reactions to the Lucas critique of Sargent, on the one hand, and Lucas, Kydland, and Prescott, on the other (section 3 above; cf. Hoover 1994a, 1995a) illustrate the issue in a genuine economic context.

It is instructive to examine Pissarides' (1992, section V) own discussion of the empirical implications of his model. He considers an empirical model of two equations:[7]

$$v = F(\phi, w, s, d) \tag{31}$$

and

$$q = G(v, s, c, \sigma),\tag{32}$$

where v is the measure of vacant jobs, ϕ and w "are the usual variables that influence the demand for labor in frictionless models" (1992, 1387), s is the number of job seekers, d is the duration structure of unemployment, q is the probability of a match between a job seeker and a job opening, c is the intensity of search, and σ is a measure of mismatch or sectoral shifts.

How do these equations map onto Pissarides' theoretical model? Equation (31) is supposed to correspond to (7) in the theoretical model:

$$J_t = Lk[1 + y + (1 - y)q_{t-1}]q_t,\tag{7}$$

where J is the number of jobs, L is the number of workers in each generations, k is the inverse of the cost of opening a job for one period, y is a productivity parameter, q is the probability of a match between a job seeker and a job opening, and subscripts indicate the relevant time. Roughly, v in (31) corresponds to J (7). ϕ and w are parameters in the theoretical model ($\phi = 2$ and $w = 1$) and so do not show up explicitly. d is a summary measure reflecting the time-dependence induced by the interaction of the two matching probabilities at different dates, q_{t-1} and q_t.

Equation (32) is supposed to correspond to (8) (1992, 1377):

$$q_t = \min\{x(J_t/2L, 1), 1\},\tag{8}$$

where $x(.,.)$ is a twice-differentiable function with positive first-order and negative second-order derviatives, homogeneous of degree 1 and satisfying

$$x(0, 2L) = x(J_t, 0) = 0\tag{2}$$

and

$$x(J_t, 2L) \leq \max\{J_t, 2L\}.\tag{3}$$

Again, v in (32) corresponds to J in (8) and s to L. c "is implicit in"

$$S_t = q_t\left[1 + y + q_{t-1}^2(1 - y)\right]L.\tag{19}$$

"[S]ectoral shifts [σ] were ignored in the theoretical discussion."

The point of recounting these details of Pissarides' model is to show just how rough the correspondence is between his theoretical model, with its painstaking details needed to achieve closure and to deliver probabilities, and the schematic empirical model of (31) and (32). The variables are vaguely defined and not perfectly analogous. What data do they represent? The functional forms are left general. To estimate (31) and (32), these forms would have to be made concrete, most likely linear or log-linear, though, in any case, they could not be direct transcriptions of (7) and (8), since they include variables omitted in the theoretical model. At best, Pissarides' model is suggestive of the qualitative relationships one might look for in the data. Unlike Shamor's proton machine, the hyper-fine details of Pissarides' model do virtually no work in helping us to create a chance set-up. They are not the elements of the blueprints for a nomological machine.

If we admit that Pissarides' model is not a blueprint of a nomological machine, does that mean that the idea of a nomological machine can do no work in econometrics? Not at all. Another feature omitted from (31) and (32) are the error terms always tacked onto econometrically estimated equations to reflect factors of which we are ignorant or have ignored. Let's add them:

$$v = F(\phi, w, s, d) + \varepsilon \tag{31'}$$
$$q = G(v, s, c, \sigma) + \omega. \tag{32'}$$

It is a necessary, though not sufficient, condition for the econometric model connecting two variables to have accurately recapitulated the probabilistic relationship generated by the underlying mechanism that the error terms, ε and ω, be random and uncorrelated with each other. If, say, we choose particular functional forms for (31') and (32') and the errors are not random, then we know that the estimated equations do not belong to the class of possible recapitulations. Econometricians worry about specification, appealing to entirely statistical criteria, precisely because they worry about a mismatch between what they estimate and what the *unknown mechanism* must have generated. The nomological machine is a regulatory ideal. We do not necessarily need a blueprint, though we do need to understand the implication of a machine being there in reality.

Pissarides (1992, 1390) particularly concerns himself with the possibility – suggested not by his theoretical model, but by general considerations – that d in (31') might be a function of q in (32'). The two equations would then be simultaneous, the error terms correlated; and the estimate of the marginal effect of d on v, which is his primary interest, would be biased. He considers the problem of finding instruments that would permit him to obtain unbiased estimates. The criterion on which he judges most instruments to be unsuitable is statistical – the fact that they are not correlated with d and/or are correlated with v. Such instruments are the genuine equivalents of shielding in experiments. Their utility is found not with respect to the probability structure that Pissarides' assumptions guarantee for his theoretical model, but with respect to the probability structure of the error terms, which are not mentioned in his model at all. The important probabilities are not the ones that find their source in the analogue to Shamor's source of alpha radiation, but ones that reflect the fact the estimated system is carved out of a more complex system. The idea of the nomological machine has a heuristic role even when we lack a recipe.

The theoretical model is not a blueprint; it is interpretive; and in economics there is usually a gap in precision between the interpretation (often only qualitative) and the estimated regularity. This is not a necessity. It is not that a nomological machine could not exist, though Pissarides' model is not a blueprint for one. Fortunately, the possibility and usefulness of econometrics does not depend on it being one.

A bit of old-fashioned and primitive econometrics

Pissarides (1992, 1390) mentions that an implication of his analysis is that a plot of the unemployment and the vacancy rate should make counterclockwise loops over the business cycle, the overall relationship (the Beveridge Curve) between them being inverse. Furthermore, he states that such loops are observed. I did not know that. Is it true? A little investigation into this question will provide a concrete example that may illustrate some of the points about econometrics and realism that I have made more abstractly already.

Vacancy data is better for the UK than the USA, but having easiest access to US data I plotted a measure of help-wanted advertizements in newspapers against the unemployment rate for the USA quarterly from 1951 (earliest available data) through 1986, retaining ten years of observations for checking stability.[8] Figure 7.1 presents the scatterplot with a regression line. The data seem to indicate the relationship is not inverse as expected but direct. These data certainly do not look like data from a well-defined chance set-up. In figure 7.2, I connect the data points in chronological sequence. They are not random. They show two patterns: loops, indicative of serial correlation; and a drift up and to the right, indicative of nonstationarity. Figure 7.3 plots the two time series against the business cycle. Vacancies reach a high and unemployment a low near the peak of each business cycle. The extreme points drift higher with each cycle.[9] Figure 7.4 plots data transformed by subtracting the value at the previous cyclical peak from each series eliminating the drift. Figure 7.5 is the scatterplot of this data with a fitted regression line, which is now clearly inverse. The data is clearly still serially correlated, though the loops are now difficult to see since they are all centered on the regression line. Is it stable? Figure 7.6 plots the data from 1951 to 1996. A formal test of stability rejects the constancy of the regression coefficients. Nevertheless, comparision of figures 7.5 and 7.6 suggest that, as a coarse, economic regularity, the relationship is robust. The regression slopes are not very different and there is no dramatic change in the scatter of the points. Elimination of the trends from the two series and their positive long-run associations clearly reveals an inverse relationship, but does not eliminate the serial correlation – the loops remain. Figure 7.7 plots a representative loop, from the 1981–1990 business cycle (peak to peak) in which the counterclockwise pattern is evident. The relationship appears to be stable.

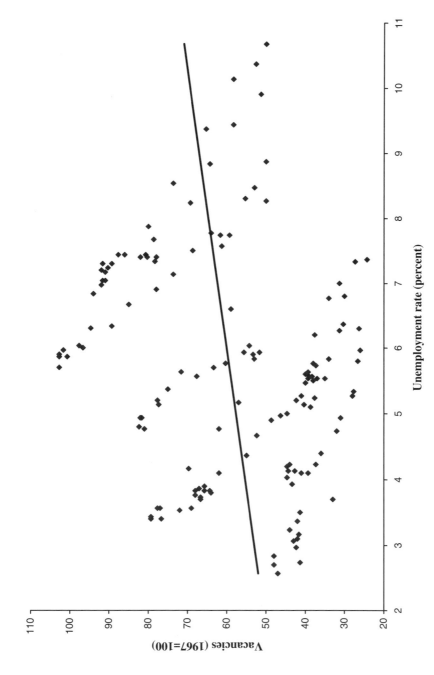

Figure 7.1 Vacancies and unemployment, 1951–1986

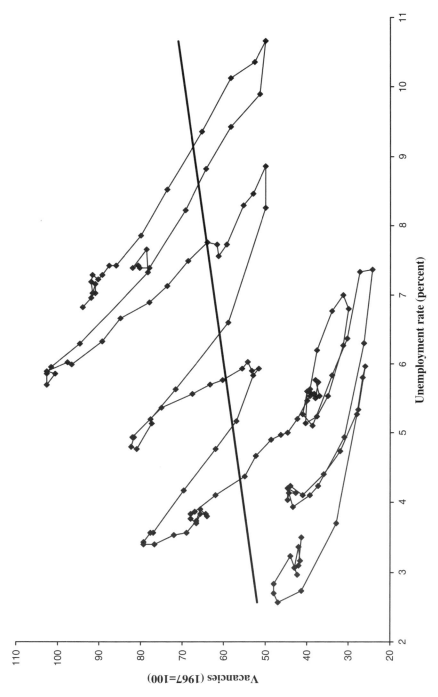

Figure 7.2 Vacancies and unemployment, 1951–1996

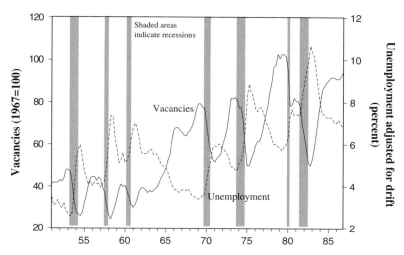

Figure 7.3   Vacancies, unemployment, and the business cycle, 1951–1986

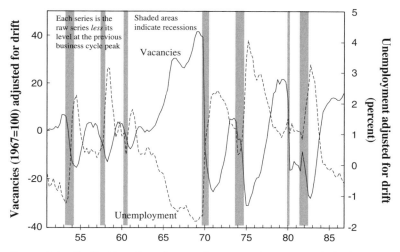

Figure 7.4   Cyclically adjusted vacancies, unemployment, and the business cycle, 1951–1986

This exercise is econometrics of a very primitive sort. It actually exemplifies pretty well the sort of econometrics that was done in the period before electronic computers (see Morgan 1989; Hendry and Morgan 1995; Klein 1997). It differs in detail, not in spirit, from the econometrics discussed in Pissarides' article and much of the econometrics currently practiced. It illustrates a number of points with respect to this chapter.

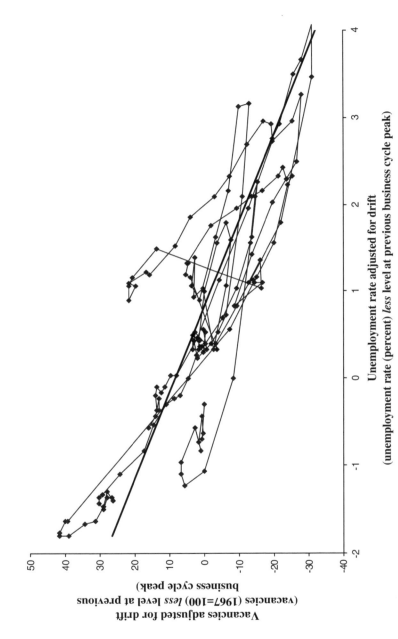

Figure 7.5 Cyclically adjusted vacancies and unemployment, 1951–1986

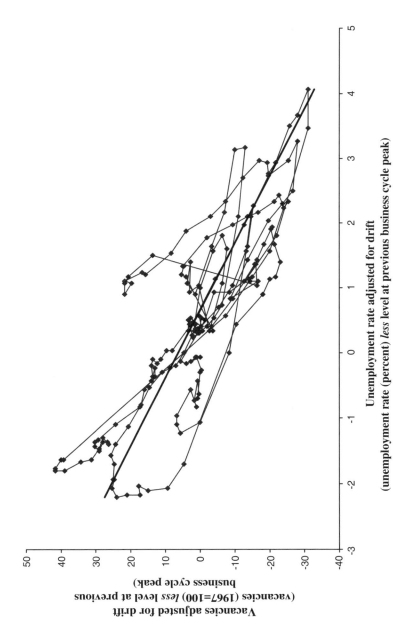

Vacancies adjusted for drift
(vacancies (1967=100) *less* level at previous
business cycle peak)

Unemployment rate adjusted for drift
(unemployment rate (percent) *less* level at previous business cycle peak)

Figure 7.6 Cyclically adjusted vacancies and unemployment, 1951–1996

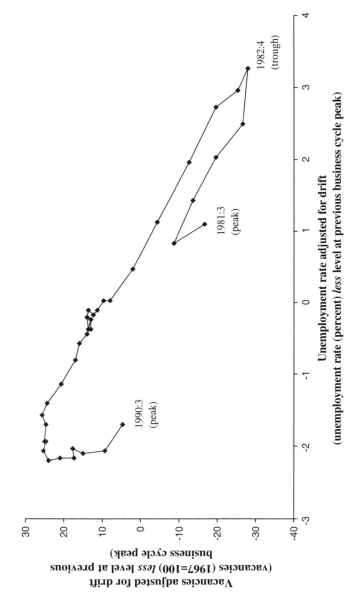

Figure 7.7 Cyclically adjusted vacancies and unemployment over the business cycle, 1981:3 (peak) to 1990:0 (trough)

We have uncovered three robust facts: (1) unemployment and vacancies trend together in the long run; (2) they are inversely related for any business cycle; (3) their relationship is nonlinear (the loops). These facts are robust, but they are imprecise. It is clear from comparing figure 7.1 and figure 7.6 that Lawson and Cartwright are perfectly right to conclude that what we observe are complex products of deeper interactions. The superficial conjunctions of data, if they show any pattern at all, may be profoundly misleading. To discover what the enduring relationships are requires interventions or, at least, accounting for conflating factors, as we did in controlling for the trend in going from figure 7.2 to figure 7.5. The control here was of a rather unspecific kind, unlike the hyper-fine assumptions of the nomological machine. We set aside the trend movements without shedding any light on what factors govern the trend. We were governed by an economic intuition that economic relations are more likely to be stable within a business cycle than from one cycle to another. There were no guarantees. It worked; but it might not have.

We have not found a covering law or directly exhibited the capacity of a nomological machine. On general economic grounds, it is more likely that the relationship between unemployment and vacancies is the result of a common cause than that one causes the other directly.[10] Yet, it may nevertheless be useful to know this noncausal correlation. It is probably not a bad guide to newspaper managers of the demand for advertizements conditional on forecasts of the unemployment rate.

Despite the ambitions and rhetoric of the Cowles Commission, econometrics is rarely about the measurement of completely articulated causal systems. It is about observation (cf. Hoover 1994b). As such, there is no conflict with realism. What is observed is the consequence of the underlying (Lawson's intransitive) reality. Observations invite explanation. Even if a fact, such as the relationship of unemployment to vacancies, were to vanish (say, for the reasons highlighted in the Lucas critique), its having been so now stands in need of explanation.

6   To end optimistically

I am more optimistic about the prospects for econometrics than either Lawson or Cartwright. I cannot agree with Lawson that realism implies the impossibility of econometrics. Econometrics is not about measuring covering laws. It is about observing unobvious regularities. The existence of such regularities, at least locally, is a requirement of realism.

Nor can I agree with the message implicit in Cartwright's work that the conditions under which econometrics could succeed are too demanding to be met. The goal of econonometrics is not to serve as a nomological machine nor as its blueprint, but to discover facts that are generated by unobservable nomological machines, facts that theoretical models explain by providing rough drawings, if not blueprints. The situation is like the British code-breakers during the Second World War. There were intercepted messages (data); patterns were discovered in the messages (econometrics); a design was formulated for a machine that could generate such patterns, starting first with a general conceptualizations (an idealized theoretical model) and ending with a working model (a goal which for many practical and, perhaps, metaphysical reasons may be beyond economics).

The robustness of econometric facts is an argument for the existence of nomological machines, but the tools for discovering those facts do not presuppose (fully articulated) knowledge of the construction of those machines. The existence of robust facts is always contingent. Consider the attempts described in Anand and Kanbur (1995) to determine the effect of social expenditure on economic welfare in Sri Lanka. There may be good economic reasons to doubt that this can be measured accurately by situating Sri Lanka in a cross-country study that presupposes that each country in the study is the outcome of a common process. Anand and Kanbur implicitly reason that, if there is enough commonality of structure between the countries in the study (if the data are examples of the successful operation of a nomological machine), then the data will have certain econometrically observable features. When that proves not to be the case, they conclude that the cross-sectional investigation is fruitless and move on to a time-series study of Sri Lanka alone. Realistic metaphysics could not have told us *a priori* that they were right to do so.

Notes

This chapter was prepared for the conference "Fact or Fiction? Perspectives on Realism and Economics" at the Erasmus University of Rotterdam, November 14–15, 1997. It owes its existence to the conjunction of several events. It is largely a reaction to the work of Tony Lawson and Nancy Cartwright, which I have followed with great interest for many years. The immediate stimulus was the publication of Lawson's *Economics and Reality* (1997) and the two lectures, "Where do laws of nature come from?" and "The rule of physics/the rule of economics: empire or alliance?," delivered by Cartwright on April 10, 1997 in the University of California, Davis. I had for some time believed that Lawson was wrong to see econometrics and critical realism as incompatible. When I made this point to Jochen Runde at the Vancouver meetings of the History of Economics Society in 1996, he urged me write my thoughts down on the grounds that "Tony likes a good argument." I thank him for his encouragement, as well as for comments on an earlier draft. And I thank Uskali Mäki for having early on stimulated my thinking about realism and, more practically, for providing the venue and the deadline that ensured that this chapter would be written.

1. The acclaim of the Lucas critique among economists overshadows the fact that there is relatively little empirical support for its importance, which undercuts Lawson's thesis; see Ericsson and Irons (1995).
2. Lawson's central evidence for the claim that economic theory subscribes to the covering-law model is found in two quotations from Hahn (Lawson 1997, 92).

These are a weak reed. One contrasts the "complex, institution and history dependent 'facts' of the econometrician" with deeper regularities. The other claims that the axioms of theory are not arbitrary but widely agreed characterizations with empirical content. The first quotation could easily be read as consistent with transcendental realism, and the second falls far short of endorsing a covering-law account. Rosenberg (1992, 24–25) argues that economics has been less affected by positivism than any other social science. Hausman (1992) offers a non-positivist interpretation of microeconomic theory.

3. Cartwright's contribution to this volume (chapter 6) summarizes many of the key points of the cited papers.
4. The sense in which Lawson asserts the universality of the mechanisms is not spatial or temporal. Even laws of physics, he argues (Lawson 1997, 223–224) may not be constant over time or in different parts of the universe. And they do not act where there is no occasion for them to act: sugar is not soluble in water, where there is no sugar and no water. Yet, where they do act, they act fully and consistently. Our inability to see them simply instantiated arises from the interference of countervailing mechanisms. Cartwright, on the other hand, argues that the consistency and completeness of lawlike action is more than we do, or can, know.
5. See, for example, Halliday and Resnick (1962, 855–856) which spells out the formal analogy in detail.
6. The lecture "Where do laws of nature come from?" was given in the Philosophy Department of the University of California, Davis, and is published under the same title (see Cartwright 1997).
7. Equations numbers are reproduced from the original.
8. Data for vacancies are "Index of Help-wanted advertizing in newspapers (1967 = 100)," series LHEL; for unemployment, "unemployment rate, total civilian labor force," series LHUR. Both series are from the *DRI Basic Economics: Macroeconomic Database* (New York: McGraw-Hill, September 1996 edn.).
9. Formally, neither series can reject the hypothesis of a unit root on standard tests.
10. Unlike the equations that usually represent them, regressions are directed. In a causal context, one would treat the independent variables as causes of the dependent variable. If I am right, that unemployment and vacancies are correlated because of a common cause, then there is no reason to prefer the regression of vacancies on unemployment, which is the regression line in the diagrams to one of unemployment on vacancies. The former minimizes the variance of the error measured as deviations between the regression line and observed vacancies; the latter as deviations between the regression line and observed unemployment. The fitted curves have different slopes, although they are qualitatively similar.

References

Anand, Sudhir and S.M. Ravi Kanbur (1995). Public policy and basic needs provision: intervention and achievement in Sri Lanka, in Jean Drèze, Amartya Sen, and Athar Hussain (eds.), *The Political Economy of Hunger: Selected Essays*. Oxford: Clarendon Press

Bhaskar, Roy (1975). *A Realist Theory of Science*. Leeds: Leeds Books

(1979). *The Possibility of Naturalism A Philosophical Critique of the Contemporary Human Sciences*. Atlantic Highlands, NJ: Humanities Press

Cartwright, Nancy (1983). *How the Laws of Physics Lie*. Oxford: Clarendon Press

(1989). *Nature's Capacities and Their Measurement*. Oxford: Clarendon Press

(1994). Fundamentalism vs. the patchwork of laws, *Proceedings of the Aristotelian Society*, 93, 279–292

(1997). Where do laws of nature come from?, *Dialectica*, 51(1), 65–78

(undated). Models: the blueprints for laws, typescript

Ericsson, Neil and John Irons (1995). The Lucas critique in practice: theory without measurement, in Kevin D. Hoover (ed.), *Macroeconometrics: Developments, Tensions, and Prospects*. Dordrecht: Kluwer, 263–312

Haavelmo, Trgyve (1944). The probability approach in econometrics, *Econometrica*, 12 (Supplement), July

Halliday, David and Robert Resnick (1962). *Physics for Students of Science and Engineering*, combined edn. (part I, first edn., part II, second edn.). New York: Wiley

Hansen, Lars-Peter and Thomas J. Sargent (1980). Formulating and estimating dynamic linear rational expectations models, *Journal of Economic Dynamics and Control*, 2(1), 7–46

Hartley, James E., Kevin D. Hoover, and Kevin D. Salyer (1997). The limits of business cycle research: assessing the Real Business Cycle model, *Oxford Review of Economic Policy*, 13(3), 34–54

Hartley, James E., Kevin D. Hoover, and Kevin D. Salyer (eds.) (1998). *Real Business Cycles: A Reader*. London: Routledge

Hausman, D.M. (1992). *The Inexact and Separate Science of Economics*. Cambridge: Cambridge University Press

Hendry, David F. and Mary Morgan (eds.) (1995). *The Foundations of Econometric Analysis*. Cambridge: Cambridge University Press

Hoover, Kevin D. (1988). *The New Classical Macroeconomics: A Sceptical Inquiry*. Oxford: Blackwell.

(1992). The rational expectations revolution: an assessment, *Cato Journal*, 12(1), 81–96

(1994a). Six queries about idealization in an empirical context, *Poznán Studies in the Philosophy of the Sciences and the Humanities*, 38, 43–53

(1994b). Econometrics as observation: the Lucas critique and the nature of econometric inference, *Journal of Economic Methodology*, 1(1), 65–80

(1995a). Facts and artifacts: calibration and the empirical assessment of Real-Business-Cycle models, *Oxford Economic Papers*, 47(1), 24–44

(1995b). Why does methodology matter for economics?, *Economic Journal*, 105(430), 715–734

Klein, Judy L. (1997). *Statistical Visions in Time: A History of Time Series Analysis, 1662–1938*. Cambridge: Cambridge University Press

Kydland, Finn E. and Edward C. Prescott (1991). The econometrics of the general equilibrium approach to business cycles, *Scandinavian Journal of Economics*, 93(2), 161–78

(1996). The computational experiment: an econometric tool, *Journal of Economic Perspectives*, 10(1), 69–86

Lawson, Tony (1997). *Economics and Reality*. London: Routledge

Lucas, Robert E., Jr. (1976). Econometric policy evaluation: a critique, in Karl Brunner and Allan H. Meltzer (eds.), *The Phillips Curve and Labor Markets*. Carnegie–Rochester Conference Series on Public Policy, 1. Amsterdam: North-Holland

Lucas, Robert E., Jr. (1987). *Models of Business Cycles*. Oxford: Blackwell

Mäki, Uskali (1996). Scientific realism and some peculiarities of economics, in R.S. Cohen, R. Hilpinen, and Qiu Renzong (eds.), *Realism and Anti-Realism in the Philosophy of Science*. Dordrecht: Kluwer, 427–447

Morgan, Mary (1989). *The History of Econometric Analysis*. Cambridge: Cambridge University Press

Pissarides, Christopher A. (1992). Loss of skills during unemployment and the persistence of employment shocks, *Quarterly Journal of Economics*, 106(4), 1371–1392

Rosenberg, A. (1992). *Economics: Mathematical Politics or Science of Diminishing Returns?* Chicago and London: Chicago University Press

8   Models, stories, and the economic world

Mary S. Morgan

It is conventional among philosophers of science to think of models in their relation to theory, and thus to concentrate on the model–theory relationship. Here I want to concentrate on the relation of models to the world. In this chapter I claim that the way models help us to describe and to understand the economic world we live in is by telling stories about the world. That story may be a story about the real world (past, present or future), or it may be a story about the hypothetical world portrayed in the model: the relationship of the story to the model structure is the same. Modeling involves a style of scientific thinking in which the argument is structured by the model, but in which the application is achieved via a narrative prompted by an external fact, an imagined event or question to be answered. Economists use their economic models to explain or to understand the facts of the world by telling stories about how those facts might have arisen. The stories are neither "merely heuristic" nor "just rhetoric" but an essential part of the way models are labeled and used.

1   The story so far

There are two accounts in which stories figure prominently in the method-ological literature on models in economics. First, chronologically, we have the account by Gibbard and Varian (1978). They claim, in one of the few philo-sophical accounts of models in economics, that stories are an integral part of the way models work. Their account is relevant for my purposes because they set out to deal with the models of economic theorists (not econometricians), and concentrate on 'descriptive' models which 'attempt to describe, *in some sense,* economic reality' (1978, 665, emphasis in the original) rather than on "ideal" models. They liken such descriptive models to realistic drawings which help us to gain greater understanding of the thing depicted. On their definition:

A model . . . is a *story* with a specified *structure*. The *structure* is given by the logical and mathematical form of a set of postulates, the *assumptions* of the model. The structure forms an uninterpreted system, ... Although the term 'model' is often applied to a structure alone, we shall use it in another sense. In economists' use of models, there is always an element of interpretation: the models always tells a story. (1978, 666, emphasis in the original)

This sounds very promising until we read on and find that the interpretation necessary for an applied economic model is rather narrow. It consists of telling us what the symbols in the model refer to in the world (firms, consumers, and the like):

If we think of the structure as containing uninterpreted predicates, quantifiers, and the like, we can think of the story as telling what kind of extension each predicate has and what kind of domain each quantifier has. The story may be vague ... the structure itself must be specified with the precision needed for mathematical reasoning. (1978, 666–667)

It is not clear what "the story may be vague" means, nor that the interpretation necessarily involves a connected sequence of events which could be described as story telling. Gibbard and Varian also make the more conventional point that they derive theorems from the postulates and this tells us things about the structure that we did not know before, but there is no mention of stories in this context either.

Remarkably, then, having introduced the story motif, they more or less ignore it. Two other elements of their argument can be brought together to suggest how we might proceed to make their account into one in which stories do matter.

One element is their claim that "all economic models ... pose[s] a question of the form 'What would happen if such and such were the case?' in such a way that it can be answered deductively" (1978, 668). This characterization makes models into some kind of counterfactual. They are counterfactuals in that they begin, as they say, with assumptions which are known to be unrealistic – counter to the facts. A prominent usage of counterfactuals in economics has been in economic history where they work by taking the known/agreed facts, assuming that they did not hold, and exploring the implications in an empirical way – spinning out alternative possible facts or false histories (as in the classic example of Fogel and the railroads, Fogel 1964). In this kind of counterfactual, the exercise is empirical. In the Gibbard and Varian case, the exercise starts from assumptions which we take to be true (when we know they are not) and "deductions" not "facts" follow from assumptions. Thus the question posed can only be answered deductively. But this does not necessarily require any stories, for deductions do not necessarily have a narrative structure. And if the models provide only deductive answers to the question, and the assumptions are thought to be unrealistic, how then do models relate to the world?

The relevant part of Gibbard and Varian's paper which might answer this question comes in their discussion of "The fit of models to the world."

Remember that they are concerned with the application of theoretical models, not empirical models, and here they suggest that one of the ways that economists apply models to situations is "casually":

> The goal of casual application is to explain aspects of the world that can be noticed without explicit techniques of measurement. In some cases, an aspect of the world (such as price dispersal, housing segregation, and the like) is noticed, and certain aspects of the micro-situation are thought perhaps to explain it; a model is then constructed to provide the explanation. In other cases, an aspect of the micro-world is noticed, and a model is used to investigate the kinds of effects such a factor could be expected to have. (1978, 672)

So their applied models relate to casually observed facts about the economy and the function of the model is to provide an explanation for that casually observed fact. But how?

According to Gibbard and Varian, then, models pose a question in such a way that it can be answered deductively and are used to explain our casual observations about the world. We might assume that the model question "What would happen if . . . ?" can be answered only by a story. But why should this be so? We might be tempted to read into their account of how models explain that they do this by telling a story about the observed phenomena. But why should models explain in this way? I agree with Gibbard and Varian when they say you need stories, but it is not yet clear why their account of modeling requires stories or exactly what they mean when they say that a model is a "story with a specified structure." The gaps in the Gibbard and Varian account are that they do not explain how the story is told from the model: they do not deal with the relationship of the story to the structure, nor how such stories might be deductive.

The second account of why we need stories in economics is by Deirdre McCloskey. In her original account of stories (1990a, 1990b) (there are one or two wrinkles which creep in later), models are metaphors, and stories are something entirely different. Metaphors and stories provide two different ways of understanding things, two ways of answering the question "Why?":

> When a biologist is asked to explain why the moulting glands of a crab are located just as they are he has two possibilities. Either he can call on a model – a metaphor – of rationality inside the crab, explaining that locating them just *there* will maximise the efficiency of the glands in operation; or he can tell a story, of how crabs with badly located glands will fail to survive. If he is lucky with the modelling he will discover a mathematical model with analytical solutions. If he is lucky with the storytelling he will discover a true history of some maladapted variety of crabs, showing that it is dying out. Metaphors and stories, models and histories, are the two ways of answering "why." (1990a, 61, emphasis in the original)

McCloskey goes on to suggest that metaphorical and narrative explanations answer each other. In other words, the unsatisfactory elements of the answer provided by the first mode prompts an explanation in the second mode. "A story answers a model. Likewise a model answers a story. The modes can, of course, mix" (1990a, 61), but it is not clear how, rather they seem to follow each other in sequence, each answering the holes in the other's account. She also suggests that metaphors and stories each play a critical (criticizing?) role v. the other (1990b, vii). It is not entirely clear to me how this works. It might mean they should provide balance for each other, or perhaps that they should work against each other, or in separate spheres?

Later in her accounts, metaphors and stories come to feature as two of the four necessary elements of "good" economics, along with facts and logic (see particularly 1994, 62), though the separateness of metaphors and stories remain the norm for economics. There are two ways in which she sees them occasionally combining. The two may come together in the form of allegory and though the allegory is a form which meets with approval, it is an unusual form to find in economics: "Any rich account of a real economy is going to be allegorical, requiring its stories and metaphors to coexist. The point is that they coexist uneasily." Do they coexist uneasily because they answer "why" questions in different format? Yes, for in an allegory "in which both must function, they can contradict each other," (1990b, 94). Allegories, in which they combine, are a good thing to find in economics, but it is not clear why they are better than the two separate elements, nor indeed how they can ever combine in an explanatory framework to answer the question "Why?" given that they provide different types of explanation.

Stories also come together with models in counterfactuals, and here the co-existence is more clearly recognized as being necessarily part of the mode of argument. But, McCloskey argues, the inherent contradictions between the two elements persist. The vaguer the model the better the story can fit into the historical world, while the more exact the model, the more absurd the history becomes. Counterfactuals are about impossible historical worlds, but they are not purely fantasy constructions since they begin with the factual world and face limitations in the "counter" claims made. They might in the end expect us unduly to suspend our disbelief, but always they have some point at which they remained glued to the world.

There is also one particular form of a model – the differential equation – for which McCloskey recognizes a "similarity between the most technical scientific reasoning and the most humanistic literary reasoning" (1991, 25). But in this account, the form is characterized as a "mixed" one, standing between "the pure . . . metaphor and pure . . . story" (1991, 22). This is to argue for a special case in which the story is "thematized" and the metaphor "dynamized" whereas, as I argue below, it is in the *use* of models (i.e. metaphors) that one typically tells stories, and that story telling is generic to the use of models, not dependent on whether the model structure is static or dynamic.

Some might think that since the rhetoric approach is largely concerned with how economists argue and persuade, it doesn't necessarily connect with the facts of the economy. But we would be mistaken in thinking these are absent in McCloskey's account. Metaphors and stories play different roles but both connect, as we have seen, with economists' explanations of the world. Metaphors are static and forward-looking, stories are historical and time-based. The stories in McCloskey's account are of economies at specific times and places; mostly, she takes stories as histories which means that they are typically about actual economies, not about imaginary economies in which benevolent dictators might rule over perfectly rational, far-sighted individuals. The examples of metaphors (models) that McCloskey gives us often involve hypothetical economies with clearly imagined, but not necessarily idealized, properties. Sometimes they are about worlds which we might easily live in, a world in which taxes are changed, pension plans are made, etc. In other words, the examples of models in McCloskey's account are often like the examples of applied economic models discussed by Gibbard and Varian, relying on ad hoc or casual observations.

It is probably evident from this discussion that, while I am sympathetic to both the Gibbard and Varian and the McCloskey accounts in certain respects, neither of them provides an account which explains why stories are important for models or tells us exactly how they relate. I claim that an economic model can not be accurately characterized as either a metaphor or a structure, for both labels fail to fully describe models and prevent us from fully understanding how models function. Rather our ability to relate our models to the world and use models to understand the world depends upon narrative devices as well as upon structures or metaphors. Model usage requires both structures (or metaphors) and stories – they are complementary and they relate in a particular way. These claims and my characterization of model usage require me to explore two aspects of modeling. First, in what particular way are stories an integral part of modeling? That is: How do stories relate to the mathematics of a model? Second: How do stories figure in relating our models to the world?

2   Why models need stories

Defining models either as metaphors or as structures is equally incomplete and for the same reason. Economists' use of models involves not just a metaphor or a structure but nor are models just stories. In practical terms, models and stories go hand in hand. I agree with Gibbard and Varian when they say that a model is "a story with a specified structure," but the story is not wholly given by the structure. The structure constrains and shapes the stories that can be told with a model, but the structure itself, like the metaphor in McCloskey's account, cannot do the work expected of a model on its own. Using a model necessarily involves both.

To portray models as passive objects in economics misses the point of modeling. As Margie Morrison and I have argued elsewhere, scientific models help us to learn things mainly by being used (see Morrison and Morgan 1999). A similar point is made in the DDI (denote, demonstrate, interpret) account of how models function by Hughes (1997). His account is very general, and is compatible with my discussions here. But even in the DDI account, there is something missing. As Hughes argues: "To be predictive, a science must provide representations that have a dynamic of this kind [provided by mathematics] built into them. That is one reason why mathematical models are the norm in physics. Their internal dynamic is supplied – at least in part – by the deductive resources of the mathematics they employ" (1997, 332). Hughes' account is general: the deductive resources of the model need not be mathematical – the model could be a material one. Nor need a mathematical model have any particular form, it could be geometric (Hughes' example) and it might, but need not, involve a dynamic form (McCloskey's special case). Models of all sorts involve resources which allow for manipulation: this is what Hughes calls the "internal dynamic" of the model.

But what supplies the other part of the dynamic, and how does the demonstration begin? My answer to the Hughes' conundrum is that models have to be "questioned" to make use of their "internal dynamic," and answering the question using the "deductive resources" of the model typically involves storytelling.[1] How does the story start? The story is suggested by a question, or by an ad hoc observation which needs accounting for, or by a supposed change to some term in the model, or by the modification of an assumption. This "question" begins the work done by the model: some term or element in the model is set or altered to represent this arrangement, possibly there is a sequence of changes, and finally there is a new outcome.

This process of putting the model to work to answer a question amounts to the "demonstration" in Hughes' account and to the "successful application" of the model in Gibbard and Varian's account. Structures or metaphors need questions and stories because it is only in this combination that models can be active participants in the production of knowledge. Story telling occurs because it is only by using structures to answer questions that models help us to find out things we did not know or understand before, such as: "What happens if . . . ?" or "How does it happen that . . . ?" Gibbard and Varian are right, then, that we use the model to answer questions, but the "model" itself does not pose the question as Gibbard and Varian suggest. We choose and pose the questions, and use the mathematics or other resources of the metaphor or structure to help us answer them. Our questions are the "external dynamic" which enables us to make use of the 'internal dynamic' of the structure noted by Hughes.

The simplest example of a model in economics and one which can be interpreted in both the McCloskey mode and Gibbard and Varian mode is the supply and demand curve model. This commonest of economic models is a representation, in two-dimensional space, on which economists draw one downward-sloping curve which they label "Demand" and one upward-sloping curve which they label "Supply." The model crosses the micro–macro divide, for sometimes this is presented as a market-level analysis and the model represents the outcome of the behavior of firms and consumers. Othertimes we find it as a macro-level model, depicting the total or aggregate supply and demand curves for the economy. This model can easily be interpreted as a "structure" in the Gibbard and Varian sense (though there might be many arguments about exactly how it is derived from a set of postulates or theoretical assumptions) while the model has been interpreted as a metaphor by Klamer and Leonard (1993).

So what happens next in this classroom example? Typically, the intersection point is noted as the point at which demand for the good is equal to its supply. Maybe this is also an equilibrium point. "Solving" the model for its market-clearing point, the point of intersection is the first step, but all such a first step does is check out that certain properties (thought desirable by economists) hold in the model. The model is then ready for its real use which is to provide the answers to a number of typical questions: What happens if, at a given price, the amount supplied is greater than that demanded? What happens if there is a sudden increase in demand? What happens if consumers' incomes increase? What happens if there is technical change in the production of the good? Each question may also be motivated by reference to some ad hoc observation about the economic world, or some hypothetical situation which can easily be imagined to be real.

For example, let us take the question "What happens if consumers' incomes increase?" Recall that consumers' incomes were not even on the original diagram. But they were one of the hidden *ceteris paribus* assumptions, which can now be taken out of the pound (see Hausman 1990). If incomes increase, it is conventional to show this by shifting the demand curve to the right on the diagram: there is increased demand at all prices, and this results in an initial rise in price and quantity to the new intersection point. The question creates a change in something inside the model, which creates a new outcome. But the sequence of changes may not end here, indeed in both the Smithian verbal description and the Marshallian account there may be a reaction by the supplying industry to the higher market price, so that in the longer run, supply increases and the supply curve is also depicted as shifting to the right. What is the new outcome? Well that depends on the relevant shifts and the exact slope of the curves. But the story told will also depend on whether the economist thinks they are in a Walrasian or Marshallian world, that is, by convention, whether it is quantities or prices which adjust to changes. To provide an answer to such questions in this genre of models typically requires some change or movement up or down the curves (from the starting intersection point) and/or shifting of the curves in the space (see Morgan, 2002 for further discussion of this case).

Economists might argue that this well-used method of comparative statics is merely the comparison of static solution points, and does not involve any kind of a narrative.[2] But their protestations tend not to accord with their practice. Economists typically do fill in the gaps in such a way when using this model. They do so because using the model involves answering questions, and the structure cannot demonstrate these answers by sheer deductive logic or unadulterated mathematics without the prompt given by the question which sets off the changes. The question gives us the starting point; and there may be many possible ones using the constraints of the structure. Each time one of these questions is asked, the economist gives an account which begins with the situation proposed in the question and is taken to be a question about the world defined by the economic model. The elements in the model have to be mentally or physically shifted around on the diagram, or the algebra has to be manipulated and solved through, to suggest an answer or demonstrate outcomes. This is not just because economic models are "paper tools" (see Klein 1999), such manipulation may be equally the case with material models (think, for example, of some of the early planetary motion models). Nor is it because our example uses the method of comparative statics. Even with models where the system solves itself (so to speak), as in certain kinds of dynamic mathematical models or the hydraulic Phillips machine (see Morgan and Boumans 1998), each time the scientist asks a question, the model has to be properly calibrated and set going to answer the relevant question. Models may require more or less manipulation to provide demonstrations, but they don't manipulate (or solve) themselves, nor will they do so in the absence of an external dynamic.

What are the characteristics of the way these questions and answers work that allows me to characterize them as narratives? First, typically these sequence of changes, prompted to answer the question, have the structure of a narrative. The question proposes an event which changes something in the model which suggests that something else happens (and maybe another round of changes result) and then we arrive at a final outcome (different from the starting point) or a new "solution" point. Secondly, the elements in the interpretation are related, with implied, rather than overt, causal connections. Thirdly, whenever we ask and answer these questions, we tend to bring in the interpretative level and discuss the changes in the elements in terms of the things in the world we have represented in our model.

These first two characteristics relate directly to certain peculiarities of narrative modes of reasoning which seem particular apt for our discussion of story telling in connection with economic models, apt in as much as they fit the prejudices and the tensions we may experience, as economists, in working with models. Narratives are ambiguous about causality and necessity in a way which is entirely natural to most economists, who prefer to avoid making direct causal claims: 'narrative does not demonstrate the necessity of events

but makes them intelligible by unfolding the story which connects their significance' (Mink 1970, 545, summarizing Gallie on historical narrative). Narratives
involve chronological sequences, but at the same time are often ambiguous
about whether elements in the story are connected by logical or time relations,
and again this suits economists' preference: 'the mainspring of narrative is precisely the confusion of consecutive and consequence, what comes *after* being
read in narrative as what is *caused by*' (Barthes 1982, 265–266, emphasis in
the original). The tension for economists is that economic models of the type
discussed here, models used in theorizing, should seem to be governed solely
by deductive or theoretical modes of arguing, yet when we make use of them
we make use of another logic – the logic of narrative.[3] When we look at the
practices of economists, particularly in seminars rather than in written papers,
we see how this tension, which stems from the fact that modeling involves both
deductive and narrative modes of argument, may sometimes be resolved. I will
return to this point, and the place of interpretation, in the final section of this
chapter.

   In this section, I have argued that using a model means using it to answer
questions and this involves telling stories. Thus the identity of the model is not
only given by the structure (or the metaphor), but also the questions we can ask
and the stories we can tell with it. These in turn are constrained and shaped by
the structure (or metaphor): we can only ask questions and tell stories about
terms and relations that are represented in the structure, and only within the
range allowed by the mathematics or materials of the structure. Nevertheless,
the structure does not determine the questions, and it is only by asking questions
and telling stories that we explore and demonstrate the full range of features and
outcomes compatible with the structure (i.e. stories which are consistent with,
and use the resources of, the "dynamic" of the model, to use Hughes' term). So,
Gibbard and Varian are right when they say that modeling involves questions,
structures, and stories. I have shown how these three elements fit together:
it is the question we choose or the prompting real or imagined event in the
economy (the external dynamic) which sets off our story with the structure, and
the story is deductive because it uses the logic of the mathematics or materials
(the internal dynamic) of the model to answer the question. In terms of the
McCloskey account, we have neither a separation, nor uneasy coexistence of
model and story – each answering "Why?" questions in different ways, but
instead a compatible interdependence of the two, metaphors and stories, both
answering the question "What happens if . . . ?"

   This section relied upon a classroom or textbook example, and its explanation
was somewhat labored. Dan Hausman (1990) considers a series of good examples of modeling using the demand–supply diagram. His discussions support
my claims, in the sense that he makes his points about how economists explain
by describing a set of their narrative sequences as they use the model – a point

to which I return later. Let me now turn to professional-level economics for a more sophisticated case.

3 Modeling Keynes' *General Theory*

In a period when the majority of the economics profession did not indulge in economic modeling, the immediate reactions to the publication of Keynes' *General Theory* are somewhat startling. Though modeling was not a standard method, and not all such attempts were self-described as "models," Darity and Young (1995) have rightly referred to the various algebraic and geometric constructions built to try to understand and make sense of the *General Theory* as "models purporting to represent Keynes's message." Their survey of these models (translated into common format, and with modern modeling terminology) discusses eight papers, reviews, or responses which appeared in print in the period 1936–1938. The purpose of these model-building attempts was to try and capture the essence of the Keynesian theory, and, in some cases, to provide a representation of it which would allow comparison with other systems, particularly the classical theory. The most famous of these attempts was the one by Hicks which gave us the IS/LM diagram. I prefer to concentrate on the one by Meade, as it exhibits the more typical characteristics of model-building (both good and bad) and model usage in economics. His work can be more easily characterized in terms of the Gibbard and Varian account of a model as a structure than in the McCloskey account of a model as a metaphor.[4]

The stated object of Meade's paper (1937), evident in his title, was

to construct a simple model of the economic system discussed in Mr. Keynes' *General Theory* . . . in order to illustrate:
  (i) the conditions necessary for equilibrium;
 (ii) the conditions necessary for stability of equilibrium; and
(iii) the effect on employment of changes in certain variables. (1937, 98)

The order of Meade's paper is as follows. First, we find seven assumptions about specific elements in the economy (1937, 98) and these are followed (1937, 99) by a list of the eight conditions under which an economy meeting the seven initial assumptions will be in equilibrium. These verbal conditions "construct" eight "relationships" which are mirrored in the mathematical model given in his appendix 1.[5] So far there are no stories: there is a structure, and it has been built to satisfy certain requirements: that the volume of employment can be determined in the short-run equilibrium.[6] But where did that requirement come from? It did not come from the structure of the model, but rather from Meade's interpretation of the main contribution of Keynes' book and an understanding of the main policy question of the day.

Meade's paper continues in stereotypical modeling form (for economics) by considering next the stability of the equilibrium:

The system is in short-period equilibrium when these eight relationships are satisfied. But is this equilibrium stable? Suppose that the money wage-rate and the proportion of income saved remain constant, but that there is an accidental increase in total expenditure on commodities (1937, 100)

We can note two things about the argument. First of all its form: suppose something changes, other things being held constant, what will be the effects? The treatment is verbal: Meade's argument involves a narrative sequence of connected events traced through the various relationships in the model. It ends with the particular equilibrium condition that comes out of the tracing process (also demonstrated formally in the appendix with the mathematical model). He then repeats the same type of narrative argument with various different banking policies. Each exploration depends on its own story using the model. What he is doing is working out the equilibrium conditions for stability, given various different events taken from the world which might occur with such a system.[7]

The main point of the modeling is yet to come. The really good stories about events which might happen in the world of the 1930s occur in part III of his article. We have already noticed that the demand for labor is a critical criteria for Meade. As before, his working of the model is verbal, tracing through effects of changing one thing in the model while holding others constant to see what effect such changes have on all the intervening elements as well as on the "short-period demand for labour." He works through four cases to see the effect on employment of a reduction in interest rates, an increase in money supply, a reduction in money wage rates, and a reduction in the proportion of income saved. Once again we have the same method, basically the method of comparative statics but involving a complex eight-equation system made up of equations involving differential terms. Once again, causality is implied in the order in which the tracing process is followed, and the interpretation also allows consideration of whether the links that occur are plausible ones. In all cases Meade's tracing process provides the narrative to accompany the resources of the mathematical model (under assumptions of stable equilibrium worked out in the previous section). The narrative begins with the starting point and the question, and depends on the order that the model structure is solved to reach outcomes: of course the narrative does not alter these mathematical resources, it uses them.

We can see that in using his model, Meade required both a structure (the eight equations) and to tell stories. The stories were shaped by the mathematics of the structure and constrained by it, but not fully determined by it. The way the question was asked, the objects of interest, what else was held constant and what allowed to vary, and the order of solution: all these affected the way any particular story was told. The decision what to change and the description of what happened was told in terms of an economic story in which the effect on the demand for labor (the point of the 1930s problems) was assessed in its own terms but also for various other impacts. The stories enabled him to tell not just the outcomes, but also something of the processes by which the results were arrived at, and the side-effects involved. As Barthes wrote (in a different context): "meaning is not 'at the end' of the narrative, it runs across it" (1982, 259). Typically the questions Meade answered were not "Why?" questions, but, given the model, "What happens if?," and "How does it happen?" questions, questions which require attention not only to final outcomes but to the *intervening path* to them.

But why were so many questions and stories necessary to Meade? Understanding the possibilities of any structure, how it can be used and applied, means gaining knowledge of its flexibility (and limitations) to tell a range of stories. Since this relative flexibility is indeed an important characteristic of models, it provides support for my stronger claim, namely that we cannot fully identify a model just by its mathematical structure, even with an interpretation of its terms. We need also to know what kind of stories it can be used to tell. For further discussion of this point, I turn to two other model building examples of the time, one of Samuelson's earliest papers (1939) and, briefly, the paper by Hicks (1937) which introduced the famous IS/LM model.

Samuelson (1939) used model simulations on Hansen's model of a Keynesian-type system to explore the nature of the multiplier and accelerator in conjunction in answering the question: "What happens if government expenditure increases?" He first used arithmetical simulations taking both into account using a verbal discussion (without even giving the reader the mathematical structure). Starting with an investment of government spending, he traced out sequences of quantitative outcomes over time. These outcomes varied according to the values chosen for the parameters in the two relations. That is, the structure did not alter, but the simulations showed that the stories which attended them altered as the parameter values altered. Some of these simulations showed little change in national income over the time period, some produced explosive cycles in national output and some produced exponential increases in output as a result of a very small increase in government expenditure. As Samuelson noted:

By this time the investigator is inclined to feel somewhat disorganized. A variety of qualitatively different results emerge in a seemingly capricious manner from minor changes in hypotheses. Worse than this, how can we be sure that for still different selected values of our coefficients new and stronger types of behaviour will not emerge? Is it not even possible that if Table 2 [the simulation results] were extended to cover more periods, new types of behaviour might result for these selected coefficients? (1939, 76)

Fortunately, these questions can be given a definite negative answer. Arithmetical methods cannot do so since we cannot try all possible values of the coefficients nor compute the endless terms in each sequence. Nevertheless, comparatively simple algebraic analysis can be applied which will yield all possible qualitative types of behaviour and enable us to unify our results. (1939, 76)

But such analytical methods could not be done in abstract, they required an algebraic model which he duly provided. Using this, he solved for the different roots of the equation system (a two-period difference equation, nonlinear in parameters but not variables) to show the effects of different combinations of the parameters on the behavior of national income in terms of periodicity, damping factors, and effectiveness of pump-priming funds.

Samuelson claimed that the generality (meaning the full range) of these new stories compared to previous analyses was useful:

Contrary to the impression commonly held, mathematical methods properly employed, far from making economic theory more abstract, actually serve as a powerful liberating device enabling the entertainment and analysis of ever more realistic and complicated hypotheses. (1939, 78)

By the use of analytical solution methods, he was able to take account of joint variation in both multiplier and accelerator parameters and to map how these varied together over the full range. He was also able to show how some rather bizarre results came from what seemed to be simple and plausible assumptions about policy options.

Here we have examples of story telling, not in conjunction with comparative static methods of analysis, but in conjunction with simulation methods and with analytical solution methods. Yet, as before, both methods of model usage involved some kind of story telling. The simulation, like the comparative statics, required some initial external input (the question about government expenditure) to get the system working, and thereafter each story developed with the simulation over time. The algebraic solution allowed Samuelson to classify these various stories according to a certain criterion, namely the qualitative behavior of national income in relation to the original stimulus. Both methods, whether they dealt with hypothetical numbers or general characteristics, told stories about the behavior of the national income according to the variation in behavioral parameters of the model. The specific details of these different stories were not known in advance, but came from the way the model was calibrated and simulated to answer questions about the model economy. There was only one model structure being used, constructed to combine the multiplier and accelerator relations, one question being asked – and then it was used to tell various different stories according to varying values in the relations.

The Hicks (1937) example is rather well-known among economists for introducing the celebrated IS/LM model of the Keynesian system, which Hicks called at the time a "little apparatus." Though I would hesitate to depict Hicks' reasoning in this article as providing a paradigmatic example of modeling, it is nevertheless the case that he constructed the model in order to compare the stories that could be told, within the same graphic structure, about both the Keynesian and the classical system of theory. By the 1970s, it became even more widely used, but knowing that an IS/LM structure is being used did not determine what kind of a macroeconomic story was being told.

A much more general case of this nature can be given by the example of the Edgeworth–Bowley box diagram. This box has been used for the last hundred years to tell stories about consumers in exchange situations, about firms and production decisions, about countries and trade policy, about welfare questions and so forth (see the survey paper by Humphrey 1996). The structure remains the same, the interpretation of the elements differs, and the stories that are told alter. Knowing that a piece of economics uses an Edgeworth–Bowley box diagram does not even enable you to predict the domain of the economic story it will be used to tell.

4 How models connect to the world

How do models connect to the world? The kind of reflective, but nonanalytical, accounts that economists occasionally give of their own practice recognize that story telling is somehow involved in this. For example, Krugman, in autobiographical mode, noted that "The models I wrote down that winter and spring were incomplete, if one demanded of them that they specify exactly who produced what. And yet they told meaningful stories" (Krugman 1993, 26).

McCloskey made the following observation on the rhetorical practice of economists:

Economists, especially theorists, are for ever spinning "parables" or telling "stories." The word "story" has in fact come to have a technical meaning in economics, though usually spoken in seminars rather than written in papers. It means an extended example of the reasoning underlying the mathematics, often a simplified version of the situation in the real world that the mathematics is meant to characterize. . . . Here the story is the modifier, the mathematics the subject. (McCloskey 1983, 505)

This observation suggests two *simultaneous* roles for stories: they are an "extended example of the reasoning underlying the mathematics," and *at the same time* a "simplified version of the situation in the real world that the mathematics is meant to characterize." I like McCloskey's rather loose description[8] because it points to the way stories relate the mathematics to the world and comes very close to what I have been arguing above about the relation between the story and the mathematics.

McCloskey and Hughes are both right that there are two links between models and the world. First we characterize something about the world in our mathematics. Then we use that mathematical characterization to answer questions relevant to the world and in doing so we tell stories which link back to the world. (McCloskey portrays these two links as happening together; Hughes sees the latter link as two separate steps of demonstration and interpretation.) The first link is about how models are built. This in turn involves deeper questions about the nature of representation or denotation used (see Morrison and Morgan 1999, Hughes 1997). How models are built also brings in the major, but well-known, problem of the realism of assumptions. Certainly one way in which models might connect to the world is via their assumptions: if the assumptions on which they are constructed are realistic to the world, we might find them useful tools to learn about the world. Economists recognize that most economic models are not built on realistic assumptions. And, although it makes sense to ask if the assumptions of a model are realistic to the world, it doesn't seem sensible to dwell on this as the *sole* aspect of realistic correspondence. As Gibbard and Varian characterize the practice of economists, "successful application" means using the model to produce outcomes which connect with the world (and are not dependent upon the realism of the assumptions). We might interpret this as the stereotyped instrumentalist position – worry about the predictions, forget about the assumptions. But this would be a misinterpretation of Gibbard and Varian. Let me set aside the onerous problems of representation and the realism of assumptions, and concentrate on the second link, on how stories link our mathematics to the world.

Telling stories about the world is one way of explaining the world to ourselves. Gibbard and Varian suppose that economists apply models to the world in a rather casual way to explain facts about the world (but without being able to say exactly where stories fitted in to this application). McCloskey supposed, in her more formal analysis of the rhetoric of economics, that stories were one way of answering questions and providing explanations about the world (though remember in her account, this was different from explaining using metaphors (models)). This conjunction of "stories" and "explanations" in discussions of model usage can also be found in Hausman's (1990) account. Because he wants to demonstrate how the demand and supply diagram is used to answer questions about events which have happened in the world by using such simple models, he puts the model to work. As soon as he does this, he cannot avoid story telling with the model. The ability of such model usage to explain something about the world in such cases is recognized by Hausman as follows: "But the simple supply and demand explanation surely captures *the heart of the story*" (1990, 169, emphasis added). Mäki, in support of this statement, continues: "'The heart of the story' may be taken as akin to a potentially true account of the isolated essence or the primary determinants and their causal mechanisms involved in the process. 'The actual story,' on the other hand, is a more comprehensive account which encompasses many secondary factors as well" (Mäki 1992, 344). It is important to note that in Hausman's statement, it is the simple supply and demand *explanation* which captures the heart of the story, not that the simple supply and demand *diagram*. The diagram on its own with interpretative labels explains nothing (or at least very little). As I have argued already, it must be questioned and put to work, it must be used to explore the (causal) mechanisms through a series of narratives in order to offer any explanations.[9]

Explanations are often characterized as answers to the question "Why?" Our cases of model usage suggest a wider version of the question, something like "What happens if . . . ," and in which explanation and story telling go together in the answering process. In portraying stories as answers to questions and in linking this to explanation, we are pointing to the use of narrative explanation in economics: that is, we use narrative as a cognitive tool, a tool by which we explain something or come to understand something about the world. Apart from the rhetoric accounts of McCloskey, there seems to have been little reflection within the methodology of economics about this cognitive role of narrative and its explanatory power, in contrast to the discussions in philosophy of history or literature. In the philosophy of history, narratives are sometimes taken to provide a "causal–genetic" account while others portray them as entailing some loose version of the D–N covering law mode of explanation or as an alternative type of rational action explanation.[10] In the philosophy of literature, perhaps the most salient discussion of the cognitive role of stories in comparison with other modes of explanation is by Mink:

> narrative is a primary cognitive instrument – an instrument rivalled, in fact, only by theory and by metaphor as irreducible ways of making the flux of experience comprehensible. Narrative form as it is exhibited in both history and fiction is particularly important as a rival to theoretical explanation or understanding. (Mink 1978, 131)

Mink's determination to present these modes of explanation as mutually exclusive might seem to make my account of model usage problematic, both because I presented metaphors and stories as complementary and because I suggested that models in science might use both deductive and narrative reasoning (as discussed in section 2). But just because we can recognize these differences between cognitive tools does not mean that they can not be used in complementary ways.

One way to understand this complementarity is to remember that models relate to the world in two ways. In *building* the model, we try to represent the situation in the world in such a way that we incorporate our general theoretical claims or hypotheses about the world.[11] Cartwright's (1983) simulacrum account of models in physics suggests that getting a good model consists of choosing the right theoretical equation to fit the prepared description of the phenomenon, so that "To explain a phenomenon is to find a model that fits it into

the basic framework of a theory" (Cartwright 1983, 152). In this relationship of model to theories and laws, finding or constructing such a model seems
to give us access to a scientific explanation for the phenomenon. But models
also relate to the world via their interpretations, where I have argued we tell
stories in answering questions and in doing so we make points about concrete
cases (specific or typical, but not necessarily real) which have, or which might
have, occurred in the world. That is, when we *use* economic models, we do
so to relate the general (theoretical or lawlike) claims back to the specifics of
the world. But what kind of explanation does story telling give of that specific
case? And how is it different from scientific explanation? Further attention to
the force of narrative explanation is needed to understand the cognitive role of
model-based story telling.

In asking how we come to comprehend a set of objects, Mink contrasts the
theoretical mode of natural science with the configurational mode of history. In
the scientific mode, we understand how objects are related by all being instances
of the same thing (with its covering law view of explanation, which he suggests
is "powerful but thin"). In the configurational mode of history (the one relevant
for the concept of a story) we comprehend objects as "elements in a single and
concrete complex of relations" not by constructing a theory about the elements
or events, nor by relating them to a concept, but by showing "how it [the object]
belongs to a particular configuration of events like a part to a jigsaw puzzle"
(Mink 1970, 551).

Although Mink paints these as alternatives in terms of comprehension and
cognitive domain, once again they may well prove complementary in practice.
A very nice example is given by van Fraassen (1988, 136–137) in which he asks
why a certain tower must be so high that it casts a shadow at a particular spot.
The length of the shadow is explained by the laws of physics: the scientific
explanation; but in explaining the height of the tower he reverts to narrative
explanation giving us a choice of stories about why the tower was built just so
high. The latter explanations are case-specific, and would hold nowhere else,
while the former are general and are supposed to hold everywhere. The two
explanations, scientific and narrative, are clearly complementary.

The same seems to hold in using economic models. To the extent that we
make use of general theoretical claims we have embodied in the structure of
the model, then we make use of theoretical (scientific) explanation, but when
we use the model to discuss specific cases, we also rely on the complementary
explanatory power of narrative. Thus, to go back to the simple example, the
theoretical explanation says that when price is high, demand is low because it
is a case of the law of demand. A powerful, but thin, explanation, because it
uses the power of the law, but explains nothing of the detail. In telling stories
with the model, we use it to explain the specifics of why coffee prices are
high in 1976 (to take Hausman's example). In Meade's case, the structure of

the model incorporates a version of the Keynesian theory, but when he uses the model to create narratives, he is describing specific cases (relevant for the 1930s experience) which might occur to understand how they would work out in the model economy. It is because of the dual nature of a model's relationship with the world that in using models we can call on the explanatory power of more than one mode of argument: the theoretical and narrative forms.

Models are mixed instruments. In model-based story telling, the relationships between the elements of the models are covered by the economic theories and incorporate the logic of whatever mathematics they are expressed in. But where to start the tale, which questions are interesting and relevant, and even the order of solving the model is somewhat open – the user has to make sensible choices in order to tell meaningful stories, stories which are plausible and interesting about the world. In economic model usage, the logic of story telling has to be combined with the logic of the theory and the mathematics, but it is the narrative which connects with the specifics of the world and in which the configurational mode of explanation and cognition dominates.

It is probably because of this potential double nature of models that we have difficulty characterizing their usage:- namely that in the model–theory relationship, the model is an exemplar for a general claim (see Cartwright 1993), so in applying the model, the scientific explanation form is called upon, but in the model–world relationship, the model is applied to the specific case and this is associated with the narrative form of explanation. The configurational (narrative) mode may be used in close conjunction with the theoretical mode as for example in the way the supply and demand curve model is used (see the examples in Hausman). This is in contrast with the van Fraassen (1988) example, where the two modes are more clearly separate but complementary to each other. It is no wonder that a certain confusion results when the narrative and scientific modes seem to point in different directions, as with Samuelson's 'capricious' narratives resulting from apparently plausible scientific explanations.[12]

There is, however, more to be said about the cognitive nature of narrative explanation. Economists' unwillingness to recognize the role of narratives except in informal conversation and informal writings may be because narrative is often misunderstood when viewed from the scientist's viewpoint; it seems only to answer "and then what happened" questions and gives no understanding beyond that. But as philosophers of the humanities know, narratives offer more than chronicles, narratives always give something more than a listing of the order of events, they provide some kind of an account of the relationship of events. Narrative helps us to understand the world, in part as Mink suggests, because narrative sits between theory and the world in terms of a generalizing device:

On the one hand, there are all the occurrences of the world – at least all that we may directly experience or inferentially know about – in their concrete particularity. On the other is an ideally theoretical understanding of those occurrences that would treat each as nothing other than a replicable instance of a systematically interconnected set of generalizations. But between these extremes, narrative is the form in which we make comprehensible the many successful interrelationships that are comprised by a career. (Mink 1978, 132)

So the characteristic kind of understanding that comes from narrative is the phenomenon of grasping things together at this intervening level between complete and exhaustive detail and complete generalization. This is not just a question of grasping a typical temporal sequence, or of seeing how parts relate to each other or to the whole (though both these may be involved), but that in narrative we gain the possibility of grasping the whole rather than the parts: "That grasping together a complex sequence of inference is possible is attested to by mathematicians, who commonly are able to see a demonstration as a whole rather than as merely a sequence of rule-governed transformations" (Mink 1970, 548). Bruna Ingrao (1998), in a paper on the role of novels, claims something similar: that what novels teach us about is complexity – a complexity involving both the essential and the details, as well as the importance of time, chance and necessity in events.[13]

It seems that what is being said here is that stories allow you to grasp a certain degree of complexity in the whole, whereas the common argument about models in economics is that they are required because the detailed real world is too complex to understand and so we need to simplify it. These points are not necessarily inconsistent. In constructing models, one of the processes involved is that of *simplification*. The hypothetical world constructed in our models is simpler (we imagine) than the real world. This creates the difficulty that when we have built the model, satisfied ourselves about the model, we still do so only in terms of that simplified world in the model. But though simplification is part of the construction, the suggestion we might take from the literature on narrative as a cognitive instrument is that in using the model to tell stories about the world, we are able to grasp not only the model as a whole, but we are also in some way trying to regrasp the complexity of the real whole world and the typical elements in it. Samuelson's model of the world was very simple, but by telling stories with the model, he was able to picture the full range of outcomes compatible with the structure. Meade's model was more complex, but he too used the narratives to explore the full range of behavior compatible with his structure. This ability to take hold again of the complex world relies upon our explorations with the model. These explorations, answering questions and telling stories, are the means by which we explore the limits and full behavioral characteristics of the model we have built, in which we learn all the possible processes and outcomes compatible with the structure – and, indeed, which questions it can answer and which not. Thus, in considering how we learn things by using models in economics, I would reverse the claims made by Haydon White for history. White (1975) wrote that "We understand the specific story being told about the facts when we identify the generic story-type of which the particular story is an instantiation" (1975, 58). This suggests that we only understand the model when we understand the more general theory it embodies. I think, on the contrary, we fully understand our model only when we have identified all the specific stories that it can encompass or tell about the world.

5 Conclusion

In the context of a complex world, models are an accepted way of representing the economic world in a simpler way so that we can think about its features. By asking questions and then manipulating models, we are able to tell ourselves stories about the hypothetical world portrayed in the model. But these stories also help us to explain the real world, for it is these stories, an integral part of modeling, rather than the typically unrealistic assumptions from economic theory, which make the stronger connections to the real world. We expect these stories to be related to our questions about the world, our typical experience of the world, and to the kinds of events we find in our world. We don't expect them to be exactly true to any particular events of the world. If they were, they would not be stories. But nevertheless, they connect by the questions that prompt the story, by the fact that the events they portray correlate to events in the world, and by the congruence of outcomes. It is by telling stories about the economy that we most effectively connect our models to the facts of the world.

Notes

This chapter was written at Nuffield College, Oxford, during my period in residence as the Norman Chester Senior Research Fellow, Fall 1997, for presentation at the conference "Fact or Fiction: Perspectives on Realism and Economics," at the Erasmus University of Rotterdam, November 14–15, 1997. It circulated in revised form as a University of Amsterdam working paper in 1999 and appeared in the *Journal of Economic Methodology* in 2001 (vol 8:3, pp. 361–384): I thank the publishers, Routledge, and editors of that journal for permission to reprint it in this volume. I thank the Warden, Fellows and Students at Nuffield for their hospitality and many discussions of the role of models and my NAKE students (classes of 1997 and 1999) for pertinent questions when I taught the topic. I have benefited from discussion by participants at the Rotterdam conference, as well as at subsequent seminars at Nuffield College, Oxford, at Groningen, at the WRR (Dutch Scientific Council for Government Policy in The Hague), and at the HES meeting in Montreal. I thank particularly Ben Gales, Roger Backhouse, Margie Morrison, Harro Maas, and Nancy Cartwright for comments.

1. I should distinguish here the role and importance of stories *in model construction* compared with *in model usage*. A very nicely observed case, of the role of the story in the *construction* of the "MIT bag model" of quark confinement, is reported by Stephan Hartmann (1999).
2. This issue was raised by the Rotterdam conference audience and is answered in this paragraph, and discussed further in section 4 of the chapter in terms of the forms of explanation involved in model usage.
3. Indeed, if one views narrative from the viewpoint of science, 'narrative would be a systematic application of the logical fallacy' (Barthes 1982, 266) This may be why economists find it difficult to give a convincing account of the role of models, for economists want models to work in the mode of scientific reasoning, even while they work in part with a narrative reasoning. To some extent the problem is a shared one: some scholars of narrative in the literary genre insist on the chronology of narrative, others on the logical relations involved.
4. I have given an extensive account of the use of analogical, or metaphorical models elsewhere (see Morgan 1999) in which my claims about the relation of narrative to metaphorical elements are easily demonstrated. Irving Fisher's mechanical balance model for the equation of exchange had to be manipulated to demonstrate old stories about the quantity theory and to tell new stories about the processes of adjustment. His hydraulic model of the monetary system was used to tell stories about how Gresham's Law worked as well as to demonstrate the possibility of bimetallism.
5. This is an article from 1937, so it is perhaps not surprising that both in stating the assumptions, and in describing the conditions for the simple economy to be in equilibrium, the verbal form is used and he gives the mathematical model only in the appendix.
6. A feature of modeling, nonspecific to this type of macro, or comparative static, modeling, is that solutions must meet certain conditions, so that we often find a rather uninteresting first usage of the model (checking that such conditions hold) before the model is used to answer more interesting questions.
7. Somewhat disarmingly (and perhaps not a feature of later modeling) he concludes this section: "It is of course possible that in the real world the system is unstable' (1937, 102) but he continues with the assumption of stability (i.e. that the conditions do hold) because of the difficulty of analyzing the impact on volume of employment in his next section without such an assumption.
8. Similarly with Mäki (1992) who suggests that 'A *model* provides a more or less rigorous and skeletal representation of the relations within an isolated field, while a *story* attached to the model is a looser and thicker commentary', (1992, 330, emphasis in the original). I find both statements somewhat "loose" in the same kind of way as the account by Gibbard and Varian. McCloskey's account, though highly suggestive, implies that the mathematics and the situation it is taken to represent both have a narrative form, without being able to tell us why this is so. Mäki does not explain how a "thicker" story relates to and is attached to a skeletal representation.
9. A parallel example is the way that chemical formulae were first used with short narrative devices to explain the details of how chemical reactions actually took place: see Klein (1999).

10. The classic comparison is found in Hempel (1962) Special attention to narrative explanation is found in Ankersmit (particularly his summary paper of 1986 and his 1988); Dray (1989); Roth (1988, 1989); and the essays in Ankersmit and Kellner (1995).

11. Hausman (1992) and Giere (1988) suggest that models are sets of statements and a theory is a hypothesis that the model applies to the world This suggests that theoretical claims are relevant only in model usage. This does not seem to be quite how economists use the term "models," in the sense that certain theoretical claims or resources are built into the model though that is not all that is in the model (see Boumans 1999) – and to this extent economists' practice may be more compatible with Cartwright's (1983) definition for physics than with those of Hausman for economics.

12. The second confusion which sometimes follows from the conflation of the science and narrative mode is the tendency to treat the narrative form like a hypothesis in science (Mink 1978, 145), but a narrative cannot be confirmed or disconfirmed, it can be plausible or implausible, satisfying or not, meaningful or not, insightful or not. This probably relates to the misunderstandings which arise in discussions about "testing" mathematical economic models, and reinforces the stance taken by Hausman (1992) that one can test only theories not models.

13. Ingrao indicates the possibility of rethinking our economic models in terms of the form, character, and actions characteristic of events in novels.

References

Ankersmit, Frank R. (1986). The dilemma of contemporary Anglo-Saxon philosophy of history, *History and Theory*, 25: 1–27

(1988). Historical representation, *History and Theory*, 27(3), 205–228

Ankersmit, Frank R. and Hans Kellner, (1995). *A New Philosophy of History*. London: Reaktion Books

Barthes, Roland (1982). Introduction to the structural analysis of narratives, in S. Sontag (ed.), *A Roland Barthes Reader*. London: Vintage, 251–295

Boumans, Marcel (1999). Built-in justification, in Mary S. Morgan and Margaret Morrison (eds.), *Models as Mediators*. Cambridge: Cambridge University Press, 66–96

Cartwright, Nancy (1983). *How the Laws of Physics Lie*. Oxford: Clarendon Press

(1993). How we relate theory to observation, in P. Horwich (ed.), *World Changes. Thomas Kuhn and the Nature of Science*. Cambridge, Mass: MIT Press, 259–273

Darity, William and Warren Young (1995). IS-LM: an inquest, *History of Political Economy*, 27, 1–41

Dray, William H. (1989). *On History and Philosophers of History*. Leiden: E.J. Brill

Fogel, Robert (1964). *Railroads and American Economic Growth*. Baltimore: Johns Hopkins University Press

van Fraassen, Bas (1988). The pragmatic theory of explanation, in J.C. Pitt, *Theories of Explanation*. Oxford: Oxford University Press, 136–155

Gibbard, Allan and Hal R. Varian (1978). Economic models, *The Journal of Philosophy*, 75(11), 664–677

Giere, Ronald N. (1988). *Explaining Science: A Cognitive Approach.* Chicago: University of Chicago Press

Hartmann, Stephen (1999). Models and stories in hadron physics, in Mary S. Morgan and Margaret Morrison (eds.), *Models as Mediators.* Cambridge: Cambridge University Press, 326–346

Hausman, Daniel M. (1990). Supply and demand explanations and their *ceteris paribus* clauses, *Review of Political Economy* 2(2), 168–187

(1992). *The Inexact and Separate Science of Economics.* Cambridge: Cambridge University Press

Hempel, Carl G. (1962). Explanations in science and in history, in R.G. Colodny (ed.), *Frontiers of Science and Philosophy.* London: Allen & Unwin, and Pittsburgh: University of Pittsburgh Press, 54–79

Hicks, John R. (1937). Mr. Keynes and the "Classics"; a suggested interpretation, *Econometrica*, 5: 147–159

Hughes, R.I.G. (1997). Models and representation, *Philosophy of Science*, 64, S325–336

Humphrey, Thomas M. (1996). The early history of the box diagram, *Federal Reserve Board of Richmond Economic Quarterly*, 82(1), 37–75

Ingrao, Bruna (1998). Economic life in 19th century novels. What economists might learn from literature, ECHE conference paper, April

Klamer, Arjo and Thomas C. Leonard (1993). So what's an economic metaphor? in P. Mirowski (ed.), *Natural Images in Economics.* New York: Cambridge University Press, 20–51

Klein, Ursula (1999). Paper tools and techniques of modeling in classical chemistry, in Mary S. Morgan and Margaret Morrison (eds.), *Models as Mediators.* Cambridge: Cambridge University Press, 146–167

Krugman, Paul (1993). How I work, *The American Economist*, 37(2), 25–31

McCloskey, Deirdre N. (1983). The rhetoric of economics, *Journal of Economic Literature*, 21, 481–517

(1990a). Storytelling in economics, in D. Lavoie (ed.), *Economics and Hermeneutics.* London: Routledge, 61–75

(1990b). *If You're So Smart*, Chicago: University of Chicago Press

(1991). History, differential equations, and the problem of narration, *History and Theory*, 30(1), 21–36

(1994). *Knowledge and Persuasion in Economics.* New York: Cambridge University Press

Mäki, Uskali (1992). On the method of isolation in economics, in Craig Dilworth (ed.), *Intelligibility in Science, Poznán Studies in the Philosophy of the Sciences and Humanities*, 26. Amsterdam and Atlanta, GA: Rodopi, 319–354

Meade, James E. (1937). A simplified model of Mr. Keynes' system, *Review of Economic Studies* 4(2), 98–107

Mink, Louis O. (1970). History and fiction as modes of comprehension, *New Literary History*, 1, 541–558

(1978). Narrative form as a cognitive instrument, in R.H. Canary and H. Kozicki (eds.), *The Writing of History.* Madison, University of Wisconsin Press, 129–149

Morgan, Mary S. (1999). Learning from models, in Mary S. Morgan and Margaret Morrison (eds.), *Models as Mediators*. Cambridge: Cambridge University Press, 347–388

(2002). Model experiments and models in experiments, in Lorenzo Magnani and Nancy J. Nercessian (eds.), *Model-Based Reasoning: Science, Technology, Values*. New York: Kluwer Academic/Plenum

Morgan, Mary S. and M. Boumans (1998). The secrets hidden by two-dimensionality: modeling the economy as a hydraulic system, University of Amsterdam Research Memorandum, in S. de Chadarevian and N. Hopwood (eds.) (2002), *Displaying the Third Dimension: Models in the Sciences, Technology and Medicine*. Stanford: Stanford University Press

Morgan, Mary S. and Margaret Morrison (eds.) (1999). *Models as Mediators*. Cambridge: Cambridge University Press

Morrison, Margaret and Mary S. Morgan (1999). Models as mediating instruments, in Mary S. Morgan and Margaret Morrison (eds.), *Models as Mediators*. Cambridge: Cambridge University Press, 10–37

Roth, Paul A. (1988). Narrative explanations: the case of history, *History and Theory*, 27, 1–13

(1989). How narratives explain, *Social Research*, 56(2), 449–478

Samuelson, Paul A. (1939). Interactions between the multiplier analysis and the principle of acceleration, *Review of Economics and Statistics*, 21, 75–78

White, Hayden (1975). Historicism, history and the figurative imagination, *History and Theory*, 14(4), 48–67

9 Economic models and reality: the role of informal scientific methods

Roger E. Backhouse

This bleak alternative between the rationalism of a machine and the irrationalism of blind guessing does not hold for live mathematics [or real economics].

(Lakatos 1977, 4)

1 Models and mechanisms

The most important question in economic methodology concerns the relationship between economic models and reality. How can economic models based on unrealistic and even false assumptions provide an explanation of real-world economic phenomena? A good starting point is Cartwright's (2002) idea that models are believed to say something about the world because they are intended to describe causal processes or mechanisms operating in the world. In economics, such mechanisms are typically sequences of actions and changes in the constraints facing agents (changes in prices and incomes). They link an initial stimulus to some outcome. Thus the multiplier links a rise in government expenditure (ΔG) to a rise in income greater than ΔG, the mechanism involving a series of steps in which rises in income cause consumers to spend more and rises in spending generate rises in income. Creating a theoretical model involves finding a set of simplifying assumptions such that it is possible to demonstrate, to generally accepted standards of rigor, that the outcome will follow from the initial conditions. The model shows that the mechanism is coherent – that it *could* operate, if only under some ideal set of conditions.

Cartwright is correct to observe that deriving theoretical results normally requires 'a very finely honed model' (2002, 146). Honing models so that they produce clear results is what occupies economic theorists most of the time, for models which are discovered to have logical defects are generally not considered publishable. Given this, how can economists believe that the model tells them anything about reality? The answer, as Hoover (2002) points out, is that after constructing a theoretical model, the economist then constructs a *new* model – an empirical model – in which the mechanism she has isolated in the theoretical model is combined with other mechanisms in such a way as to produce a testable hypothesis. The problem Cartwright sees with this is that, while there is a clear "nomological machine" underlying the theoretical model, there is no such machine underlying the empirical model. Because of this, there is no reason for believing that there are any grounds for applying tests based on statistical inference. Economists who attempt to estimate such models are misguided: they are observing correlations and drawing conclusions about mechanisms. Though they will find correlations, these will correspond to no causal mechanisms and will, therefore, be unreliable.

The key point in what is going on here is that a critical stage in the process – the transition from the theoretical to the empirical model – is informal. Theoretical modeling should be seen not as deriving a model that is then tested, so much as establishing that the mechanisms that are being hypothesized to operate in the empirical model are coherent. These mechanisms are what link the two types of model. The reason why this linkage remains informal is that important factors are unknown and have to be inferred from the data:
1. Precise details of the mechanism – functional form, lag structure, and so on
2. The quantitative importance and interactions between different mechanisms
3. Other mechanisms operating.
This comes across very clearly in cross-section models such as the Anand–Kanbur model cited by both Cartwright and Hoover in which,

$$H_{it} = \alpha_t + \beta Y_{it} + \delta E_{it} + \lambda_i + u_{it},$$

where H denotes living standards, Y *per capita* income, E social welfare expenditure, and u a random error term. Countries and time are denoted by i and t, respectively. There may be no formal model of the link between social welfare expenditure and living standards, but it is easy to construct possible mechanisms. Similarly, it is trivial to postulate a plausible mechanism linking income to living standards, or to postulate mechanisms whose operation is captured by the country- and time-specific effects, α_t and λ_i. It has been assumed that the interaction of these causes is additive (hence the very simple set of causal relations shown in Cartwright's figure 6.4) but if Anand and Kanbur had had reasons to do so, they could have explored other more complicated relationships.

The informal nature of the process whereby the empirical model is derived from mechanisms that might be operating means that there is the danger that the economist will be estimating a relationship that corresponds to no real-world causal mechanism. However, Cartwright goes too far in her rejection of such work. Two issues are confused. One is the claim that the standard econometric practices will often lead to the discovery of nonsensical correlations. This may or may not be true, but economists are well aware of the problem. It is, for example, one of the reasons for Hendry's (1993) emphasis on the superiority of general-to-particular modeling and the use of encompassing techniques. The point is that Cartwright's claim is an argument about the implications of certain econometric strategies, and to address it requires arguments very different from those offered. The second issue is the argument that in the absence of an underlying nomological machine, there is no reason to regard the data as having been generated by a probabilistic data-generation process. On this point, however, if we were to accept Cartwright's arguments, the conclusion should merely be that we can not assume that the data-generation process can *necessarily* be represented by a joint probability distribution over all relevant variables. It is entirely legitimate to regard the question as an empirical one that can be settled only case by case. Having said this, however, econometricians do sometimes assume that data must have been generated by some underlying probability distribution. Though not expressed in such language, Friedman and Schwartz's (1991) dispute with Hendry and Ericsson (1991) can be seen as a dispute over the appropriateness of this assumption (cf. Backhouse 1997, 166, 173).

Scientific claims, Cartwright argues at the beginning of her chapter, must be 'precise and unambiguous' (2002, 137). However, while precision and lack of ambiguity are laudable scientific objectives, and scientists should clearly strive for as much precision and clarity as possible, they are terms that must be defined *with reference to the subject matter concerned*. To expect that an economic science should achieve the same standards of precision as physics is inappropriate. In short, it could be argued that Cartwright's definition of a science rules out the possibility that economics can qualify.

There is a further puzzle over Cartwright's argument concerning precision, for her central argument is that there is a connection between the precision of scientific theories and their scope: "It seems to be in the nature of how we do exact science that what it can cover is very limited in scope" (2002, 150). There is an ambiguity here, as Hausman (1992) makes clear. Abstract (and hence precise) economic theories are limited in scope in the sense that they cover only a limited set of causal factors. On the other hand, such theories are, Hausman has argued, of maximal scope in the sense that the same theory applies to a wide range of different situations. It could, therefore, be argued that the abstract nature of economic theory and the problematic link between economic models and evidence arise because economists seek theories that are of very wide scope. If economists were content with theories of narrower scope, in the sense of theories that applied to a narrow range of situations, they could make assumptions that were much closer to reality.

To resolve this puzzle, we need to consider what is going on within economic theories in more detail. Economic theories certainly rest on finely honed, unrealistic assumptions. That is agreed. But assumptions can be honed in two different ways. One way is to use only assumptions that are of great generality.

We thus write that a consumer's maximization problem is:

$$\max U(x_1, \ldots, x_n) \text{ s.t.} \sum_{i=1}^{n} p_i x_i \leq 0 \tag{1}$$

where p and x denote prices and quantities of the n goods available to the consumer. The signs of the partial derivatives of $U(.)$ may be determined by assumptions such as that goods are gross substitutes or that external effects are absent but no more specific structure is imposed. On the production side, it might be assumed that firms maximize profits subject to a concave production function, but that is all. Such assumptions are, one assumes, unrealistic (the absence of externalities, imperfections of competition, and so on), but they are very general in that they do not tie the model down to any specific situation. Abstraction from specific circumstances is, at least in this type of theorizing, associated with the drive towards a theory of maximal scope – a theory that applies, at least in principle, to any economic situation.

Contrast this with the type of theorizing found in Akerlof's 'lemons' model (see Sugden 2002), where it is assumed that utility functions are of the form

$$U = M + \sum_{i=1}^{n} \delta x_i, \tag{2}$$

where M is the quantity of other goods consumed, x_i is the quality of the ith automobile owned, n the number of automobiles owned, $\delta = 1$ for group 1, and $\delta = 1.5$ for group 2. Whereas assuming utility function (1) can be viewed as abstracting basic features of consumers' behavior, function (2) is clearly a hypothetical, counterfactual example proposed purely for the purpose of illustrating a particular phenomenon. Function (2) is more specific but it is not specific in the sense of explaining a particular bit of the world. If we knew, for example, that utility functions for certain groups had certain specific forms, to assume one of those forms would be to produce a theory that was more limited in scope. This would, in Mäki's (1992) terminology, amount to horizontal isolation. In the case of Akerlof's utility function, however, we cannot regard the model as describing a particular situation: it is no more than an illustration of a point.

2 Models and stories

Morgan (2002) attempts to capture the informality surrounding the way in which models are used by arguing that stories form an integral part of models. This is valuable because it makes several important points:
1. Models need to be "used" if they are to contribute to any understanding of reality, and using models typically involves telling stories

2. The links between models and reality are provided through these stories which are less formal than the models in the sense that the logic underlying them is less rigorous
3. A model may be used in more than one story, providing it with multiple interpretations.

The idea that the use of models cannot be understood apart from stories helps us to understand, among other things, why theories develop the way they do. In the process of telling one story, the economist may find another story she wants to tell and be led into developing a new model in order to tell it better. At the same time, the economist may discover different stories that can be told using the same model. However, while referring to the informal arguments that surround the use of models as "stories" is one way to tackle the issue of how models are related to reality, there are some questions for which it is preferable to keep closer to more traditional terminology. One problem with using the concept of "stories" in this way is that it covers several things:

1. The interpretation of theoretical terms
2. Mathematical derivations that are left implicit
3. Causal sequences
4. Models that are more general than the one that is written down.

To illustrate this, consider a very simple model – the multiplier. The simplest version of the multiplier involves starting with an equilibrium condition for income,

$$Y = I + C = I + a + bY \qquad (0 < b < 1)$$

where Y is income, C is consumption, I is autonomous expenditure, a is autonomous consumption, and b the marginal propensity to consume. This can be solved for equilibrium income and the outcome represented on a graph, as in figure 9.1:

$$Y = \frac{1}{1-b}(I + a).$$

From this it follows that the multiplier $(\Delta Y / \Delta I)$ is $1/(1 - b)$.

We can then use the diagram to explain what happens if there is a rise in autonomous expenditure: when I rises to I', Y rises to Y', where

$$Y' - Y = \frac{1}{1-b}(I - I').$$

In Morgan's terminology, the model comprises the above equations and diagram, and the story is the discussion of what it means and how it can be used to explain the consequences of a rise in autonomous expenditure. The multiplier that is calculated and the change shown in the diagram describe

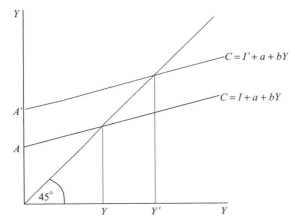

Figure 9.1 The multiplier

a comparative-static equilibrium, and the story is a dynamic one. However, the "story" comprises several elements:

1. The interpretation of the symbols (Y, I, b) as concepts such as "national income," "investment," "the marginal propensity to consume," and so on.
2. The mathematics that all economists know lies behind the model, but which is left unstated. For example, the consumption function can be specified as

$$C_t = a + bY_{t-1},$$

   in which case the model becomes a first-order difference equation, which can readily be shown to converge on the equilibrium defined by the model in a well-understood way.
3. The causal sequence that arises from introducing a shock (investment rises from I to I') and seeing what the consequences are for the level of income. This involves both the implicit mathematics (the difference equation) and claims about causation.
4. Elements of the causal process that are not captured in either the formal model, or in the mathematics that is understood to lie behind it. For example, the economist might bring in other variables that affect consumption, or discuss the interaction of stock-building and expectations during the transition from one equilibrium to another. In this sense, the story may be referring to an implicit model that the economist either can not solve (perhaps she does not even know how to write it down formally) or has chosen not to write down (perhaps because to do so would obscure the exposition or because she knows it would be familiar to her readers).

Though it is extremely suggestive, the term "story" conflates these four elements and unless it is very carefully used can easily obscure issues that more traditional terminology would make clear. For example, if we were to work with a distinction between "model" and "theory," where a "model" is a set of logical relationships between assumptions and conclusions, and "theory" comprises a body of claims about the real world (see, for example, Hausman 1992; Leijonhufvud 1997), this would lead naturally to a consideration of points 1 and 4 in the above list.

Similar remarks can be made about most other economic models. The supply and demand model discussed by Morgan, for example, involves symbols that can be interpreted in a variety of ways, it rests upon a well-understood dynamics that is often left implicit, it is used to tell causal stories, and it could be seen as demonstrating the coherence of a more general supply and demand model in which variables other than a single price and quantity occur, where functional forms are nonlinear. It may even be that the economist (like Alfred Marshall) believes that there are irreversibilities and other factors that cannot be modeled formally.

As evidence that implicit mathematical analysis is important in models such as the one in Meade (1937), note that the causal stories similar to those used in the multiplier were told long before Keynes, but it was only when convergence of the income–expenditure process had been proved that economists calculated the multiplier and took it seriously. Earlier generations of economists either denied that the multiplier could be different from unity, or else produced numerical examples that were hard to take seriously (see Backhouse 1995, chapter 6).

Thus, where Morgan argues that models are used in conjunction with stories, each informing the other, I suggest that the notion of a "story" is only one way to understand why models are believed to tell us something about reality. The need for stories as well as models helps explain why models cannot be taken on their own, but there is still value in persisting with more traditional terminology. Rather than talk about characters in a story it may be better to talk about the interpretation of terms in the model (as Backhouse 1997, 125–130), and instead of a story's plot we can discuss problems, solutions to problems, and causal mechanisms. The idea that models establish the coherence, and hence possible existence of, mechanisms that are then used to construct empirical models or otherwise explain what is going on in reality, provides a more precise explanation of how theoretical and empirical models are linked than does the idea that models need to be embedded in stories.

3   Models and evidence

Cartwright reaches a very skeptical conclusion concerning the possibilities for econometrics because she adopts a very strict view of what science involves. Scientific claims should be "precise and unambiguous." Where, as in economics, such claims are not possible, she concludes that scientific knowledge is impossible. However, a much more reasonable requirement for knowledge to count as scientific is that it be the result of systematic enquiry, undertaken with whatever degree of precision is appropriate for the particular field of enquiry. This opens up the possibility that there may be a middle ground between formal, exact, science and unscientific guesswork – that informal methods may none the less be systematic and hence qualify as scientific.

The Anand–Kanbur and Pissarides models, discussed by Hoover and Cartwright, provide good illustrations of this. The regression equation in the Anand–Kanbur cross-section study is not derived formally, but given the statement of the problem, most economists would write down a very similar equation. Similarly, the implicit rules for getting from Pissarides' theoretical equation to his empirical one are ones that any applied economist would understand. The theoretical model provides a list of variables that are believed to be significant, to which the economist (after thinking about the specific problem) adds a list of control variables designed to capture extraneous factors that are likely to be present (to capture what Mill would have described as the "disturbing causes"). Choice of functional form is partly limited by the available estimation techniques and is in part determined inductively from the data. Though there is still scope for the judgment (or prior beliefs) of the investigator to affect the outcome, there is a menu of well-known techniques to be used to decide whether the model is an acceptable fit.

Akerlof's 'lemons' model can be taken as another example. The aim of the paper, as its first and last sentence make clear, is to establish a general link between the quality of goods and uncertainty and to explore the implications of this link for the theory of markets:

This paper relates quality and uncertainty. The existence of goods of many grades poses interesting and important problems for the theory of markets . . . But the difficulty of distinguishing between good quality from bad is inherent in the business world; this may indeed explain many economic institutions and may in fact be one of the more important aspects of uncertainty. (Akerlof 1984, 7, 22)

Akerlof's paper does have an unusual structure, but there is a clear logic to it. He is interested in the *general problem* of the relationship between quality, information, and markets, and explores it though using an example. The example is chosen to isolate a specific mechanism, and hence can make some arbitrary simplifications. In that sense it is not intended as a general model. On the other hand, the mechanism that Akerlof isolates is intended to be a very general one, hence his list of examples – insurance, employment of minorities, dishonesty, and credit markets in underdeveloped countries. These are all examples where the same mechanism operates, but where other circumstances are different. Thus rather than a controlled experiment to show that asymmetric information is linked to the quality of used cars traded, we find a list of situations differing in all respects apart from the informational structure of the market.

Another example (see Backhouse 1997, 190–194) is Diamond's *On Time* (1994). His aim, like Akerlof's, is to explore a very general problem: the role of time in economic models. Diamond recognizes that the link between evidence and theory is weak (the facts he cites are "to be kept in mind" rather than related directly to the theoretical models either as assumptions or to compared with the models' predictions) but he nonetheless attaches importance to getting his facts right. He therefore cites a variety of studies to support what he believes to be the key assumptions in his models. For example, to support the claim that prices are sticky, he cites evidence on wholesale prices, magazine prices, and prices in mail-order catalogues. It is because prices appear to be sticky in each of these three, otherwise different, markets that he has confidence in the assumption of price stickiness. As in Akerlof's paper, evidence from a variety of markets is used to support a much more general theoretical claim. This can be likened to the process of replication in natural science, as understood in Cartwright (1991). It is not formal, but it is none the less systematic. Maybe economists ought to be *more* systematic, but to say that is not the same as claiming that economics is unscientific or that econometrics is impossible.

It is, therefore, possible to argue that in these examples empirical evidence is being used in an informal but nonetheless systematic way. What is going on in the way Diamond and other economists use evidence (for further examples, see Backhouse 1997, section 13.2) is analogous to the process of replication whereby, in experimental sciences, it is established that there are facts to be explained. If these facts were precise, quantitative laws, theorists would be able to incorporate them in their models. For example, if we knew that, in the USA, every percentage point rise in the growth rate of output would lower the unemployment rate by 1 percentage point (Okun's law), or that a 1 percentage point rise in unemployment would reduce wage inflation by 2 percentage points (the Phillips curve), we could use these numbers in our models. Our models would therefore be more precise and because of this would apply to only a limited domain. (This is the relationship that Cartwright sees between the precision and the scope of a model.) The significant feature of the process whereby economists establish facts, however, is that it does *not* establish such precise, quantitative numerical laws, but more general regularities and generalizations such as Okun's law or the Phillips curve. Okun's law is highly reliable, though the precise number varies from country to country, and the slope of the Phillips curve is generally negative provided that suitable "control" variables are used to control for the effects of changes in expectations of inflation and other variables affecting wage bargaining. It is because economists believe that broad generalizations such as these are much more robust than precise numerical relationships that theoretical models remain general in scope rather than relying on the numbers produced in econometric studies.

In citing a variety of examples where the same informational structure occurs but other aspects of the situation are different (Akerlof) and in citing a variety of empirical studies on otherwise different markets to show that prices may be sticky (Diamond), both authors are engaging in a process analogous to replication: establishing that there is a phenomenon that should be taken seriously, either as an assumption or as something to be explained. Despite the appearance that evidence is being used fairly casually, it is arguable that using evidence in this way does make sense in situations where precise, stable quantitative relationships are unlikely to exist. Both Akerlof and Diamond are using evidence in a systematic way that should be regarded as scientific.

4   Informal economic science

Economists' models tell economists something about the world, despite or even because they are based on counterfactual assumptions. Logical analysis of the structure of models and issues such as the ways in which economists use and argue about assumptions (as in Mäki 1994) takes us part of the way, revealing some of the ways in which assumptions are defended and used. Such an approach, however, does not go far enough, for to understand how models tell economists about reality we need to know more about how the various isolations involved are related to evidence about the world. Mäki (1992) has hinted that these links may be informal when he coined the phrase "storied isolation" – isolation that is achieved through telling a story. Morgan has shown that the significance of stories for understanding economic models goes beyond this.

The stories Morgan (2002) discusses are inherently informal compared with the models to which they relate. The point made is that not only should we recognize that informal stories are an integral part of the explanation of how models are used, but we should also explore whether there is a logic underlying the arguments used to justify and develop these stories (cf. Backhouse 1998). Two examples have been discussed in some detail: the use of mechanisms as a device for linking theoretical and empirical models; and the use of evidence from a variety of different situations to establish that there is a phenomenon that the economist needs to take seriously. Given that it is through these informal methods that evidence about the world is appraised and brought up against economic models, understanding these methods is essential if the relationship between models and reality is to be understood and critiques such as that offered by Cartwright are to be answered. Economics exists in the space between formal, mechanical logic and unscientific irrationality, but though Kuhn (1970) and

Lakatos (1977, 1978), with their emphasis on the importance of presuppositions and heuristics, drew attention to this years ago, we are still a long way from understanding how such informal but nonetheless scientific arguments might operate.

Note

This chapter was written after the conference, "Fact or Fiction: Perspectives on Realism and Economics" at the Erasmus University, Rotterdam, November 14–15, 1997, as a response to four of the papers presented there. I am grateful to Mary Morgan for helping me to clarify what I was trying to say in an early draft.

References

Akerlof, George (1984). *An Economic Theorist's Book of Tales*. Cambridge and New York: Cambridge University Press

Backhouse, Roger, E. (1995). *Interpreting Macroeconomics: Explorations in the History of Macroeconomic Thought*. London: Renoledge

(1997). *Truth and Progress in Economic Knowledge*. Cheltenham and Lyme, NH: Edward Elgar

(1998). If mathematics is informal, then perhaps we should accept that economics should be informal too, *Economic Journal*, 108, 1848–1858

Cartwright, Nancy (1991). Replicability, reproducability and robustness: a comment on Harry Collins, *History of Political Economy*, 23(1), 143–155

(2002). The limits of causal order, from economics to physics, see chapter 6 in this volume

Diamond, Peter (1994). *On Time*. Cambridge: Cambridge University Press

Friedman, Milton and Anna J. Schwartz (1991). Alternative approaches to analyzing economic data, *American Economic Review*, 81(1), 39–49

Hausman, Daniel M. (1992). *The Inexact and Separate Science of Economics*. Cambridge and New York: Cambridge University Press

Hendry, David F. (1993). *Econometrics: Alchemy or Science*. Oxford: Basil Blackwell

Hendry, David F. and Ericsson, Neil (1991). An econometric analysis of UK money demand in *Monetary Trends in the United States and the United Kingdom* by Milton Friedman and Anna J. Schwartz, *American Economic Review*, 81(1), 8–38

Hoover, Kevin D. (2002). Econometrics and reality; see chapter 7 in this volume

Kuhn, Thomas S. (1970). *The Structure of Scientific Revolutions*, 2nd edn. Chicago: Chicago University Press

Lakatos, Imre (1977). *Proofs and Refutations*. Cambridge and New York: Cambridge University Press

(1978). *The Methodology of Scientific Research Programs: Philosophical Papers, 1*. Cambridge and New York: Cambridge University Press

Leijonhufrud, Axel (1997). Models and theories, *Journal of Economic Methodology*, 4(2), 193–198

Mäki, Uskali (1992). On the method of isolation in economics, in Craig Dilworth (ed.), *Idealization IV: Intelligibility in Science, Poznán Studies in the Philosophy of the Sciences and the Humanities*, 26. Amsterdam and Atlanta, GA: Rodopi, 317–351.

(1994). Reorienting the assumptions issue, in Roger E. Backhouse (ed.), *New Directions in Economic Methodology*. London: Routledge, 236–256

Meade, James E. (1937). A simplified model of Mr. Keynes' system, *Review of Economic Studies*, 4(2), 98–107

Morgan, Mary S. (2002). Models, stories, and the economic world; see chapter 8 in this volume

Sugden, Robert (2002). Credible worlds: the status of theoretical models in economics, see chapter 5 in this volume

10   Truthlikeness and economic theories

Ilkka Niiniluoto

In a series of carefully argued and stimulating papers on realism, Uskali Mäki has pointed out that economic theories typically are unrealistic in two senses: by violating "the-whole-truth" and "nothing-but-the-truth" (Mäki 1989, 1992b, 1994b). He suggests that realism in economics can still be rescued by regarding theories as partially true descriptions of essences and as lawlike statements about tendencies. In this chapter, I defend realism by an alternative strategy: idealizational (or "isolational") statements are counterfactual conditionals (Niiniluoto 1986), and the concepts of truth and truthlikeness can be applied to them (Niiniluoto 1987). Further, false but sufficiently truthlike theories may be taken to refer to real entities in the world (Niiniluoto 1997, 1999).

1   Unrealistic assumptions in economics

Neoclassical economic theories describe business firms as rational calculating agents which maximize their profits on the basis of complete information about the quantities, costs, prices, and demand of their products. However, it is clear that such theories are unrealistic in several respects, among them the assumptions about perfect rationality and complete information. The internal structure of the firms and most aspects of their external relations are ignored in these theories. As Mäki (1992a) points out, even the core assumption

$$\text{Firms (or businessmen) pursue maximum expected returns} \qquad (1)$$

is problematic in two ways. First, the theory containing (1) suggests that the maximization of profit is the only motive of the producers, and by ignoring other relevant motives it violates the-whole-truth. Secondly, (1) involves an exaggeration, since in real life firms are satisfied with less than maximum returns, and thereby it violates nothing-but-the-truth.[1]

These features of typical economic theories have parallels in physical theories. As a description of freely falling bodies near the surface of the earth, Galileo's law $s = gt^2/2$ violates the-whole-truth: it is derivable from Newton's

214

mechanics by taking into account only gravitation and by ignoring all the other forces effecting the body. The derivation of Galileo's law also involves the false assumption that the acceleration due to gravitation of a moving body is constant (cf. Niiniluoto 1986). Moreover, Newton's theory itself should be corrected by Einstein's theory of relativity.

Mäki (1989, 1994a) makes a conceptual distinction between *realisticness* (a collection of attributes of representations like statements and theories) and *realism* (a collection of philosophical doctrines about science). He distinguishes various dimensions of realisticness (aboutness, observability, truth, empirical success, plausibility, partial truth, abstractness, and practical usefulness), and various doctrines of realism (ontological, referential, representational, veristic, methodological) (for related distinctions, see Niiniluoto 1986, 1995, 1999). Common-sense realism and scientific realism are then doctrines which descriptively assert, or normatively demand, that our folk beliefs and scientific theories have some realistic attributes.

I fully agree with Mäki that the use of "unrealistic" assumptions in scientific or economic theories does not alone warrant any anti-realist conclusions. But it is natural that the abundance of simplifying and idealizing assumptions in theories has nourished a temptation to anti-realist positions. In physics, this is illustrated by authors like Pierre Duhem, Bas van Fraassen, and Nancy Cartwright,[2] and in psychology by Gilbert Ryle. The corresponding meta-theoretical positions can be found also in economics (see Mäki 1989, 1992a). For example, Fritz Machlup advocates ontological anti-realism about neoclassical firms (*fictionalism*), and takes the theory of the firm to be a device for observational systematization without a truth value (*instrumentalism*).[3] Milton Friedman regards such theories as false statements, so that in this sense he is a veristic realist, but the theory may still be useful and accepted for prediction. In other words, economic theories are nothing but "predictive models." Mäki calls this view, which allows theories to have truth values but claims truth to be irrelevant to the aims of science, "methodological instrumentalism," while I have called it "methodological nonrealism." Its different variants are supported by Bas van Fraassen (empirical adequacy), and Larry Laudan (problem-solving capacity).[4]

But how could one defend any reasonable form of realism – in spite of the unrealistic features of physical and economic theories? It is evident that *naive* or *literal realism*, claiming that our theories are in fact completely or exactly true about the actual world, is excluded. So the position to be sought has to be a form of *critical realism*. In the following sections, I shall outline my favourite version of critical scientific realism (cf. Niiniluoto 1999), and at the same evaluate the related but somewhat different proposals of Uskali Mäki. I shall concentrate on three topics: truthlikeness (section 2), idealization and concretization (section 3), and theoretical reference (section 4).

2 Verisimilitude and legisimilitude

Mäki (1992a, 1994b) argues that several authors (Karl Popper, Milton Friedman, David Hendry, Nancy Cartwright) have conflated the notions of truth and the whole truth: if a theory fails to be noncomprehensive, it need not be false. Mäki points out that the failure to be comprehensive may be due to several reasons, such as linguistic and technical constraints in theory construction. In the special case, where exclusion is based on ignorance, the distinction between truth and the whole truth is, in fact, a classical issue in the history of epistemology: the advocates of coherence theories of truth in particular had difficulties in distinguishing errors of ignorance and errors of falsity. Perhaps the most notorious doctrines in this respect are Hegel's logic and Bradley's "degrees of truth and falsity" (see Niiniluoto 1987, 167–174).

Mäki (1994b) quotes Karl Popper as stating that any scientific model or theory is false, since it must "omit much" and "overemphasize much." I agree that it would be misleading to conclude the falsity of a theory merely from its omissions. But, as Mäki admits (1994b, 166), theories are false if they overemphasize. Thus, Popper's statement about omissions and overemphasis appears to make essentially the same point as Mäki in his distinction between violations of the-whole-truth and nothing-but-the-truth (see section 1). More generally, I think it would be unwarranted to make the charge that Popper in his overall philosophy of science makes the conflation between truth and the whole truth. Indeed, Popper's (1963) qualitative comparative definition of *truthlikeness* is based precisely upon this distinction: one theory A is more truthlike than another theory B if A has larger truth content (i.e. it should make fewer errors of ignorance) and smaller falsity content (i.e. it should include fewer false statements) than B.[5] This is often expressed by saying that Popper's notion combines the ideas of information and truth. But even more instructive terms are employed by Isaac Levi (1967) and Risto Hilpinen (1976) in their theories of inductive acceptance: the Popperian approach to truthlikeness combines in one concept the ideas of "relief from agnosticism" and "relief from error."

The same idea is preserved also in the *similarity approach* to truthlikeness, as developed since the mid-1970s after the refutation of Popper's definition (for details, see Niiniluoto 1987, 1998). First, the degree of truthlikeness of a statement or theory does not express its closeness to the whole truth about everything,[6] but rather its closeness to a *target* which is the most informative truth within a chosen conceptual framework L. In other words, the target t^* in language L is the logically strongest true statement that can be formulated in L. In this sense, truthlikeness is a "local" notion, relativized to some L and to truth expressible in L.

Secondly, a theory A in L can be understood as a set $C(A)$ of alternative "guesses" that can be formulated by "basic statements" in L. Theory A is true if the target t^* is included in $C(A)$, and A is maximally truthlike if $C(A)$ contains only t^*. In general, the truthlikeness of a theory A relative to target t^* depends on a weighted combination of two factors: the minimum closeness of the guesses in $C(A)$ from t^* (when this is small, theory A is *approximately true*), and the sum of all distances from $C(A)$ to t^*. These two factors explicate the ideas that a theory should get rid of the errors of ignorance and of the errors of falsity, respectively. Moreover, the "penalty" for an allowed mistake depends on its distance from the true target t^*.

The logical concept of truthlikeness can be used for defining scientific *progress*: a step from theory A to theory B is progressive if B has a larger degree of truthlikeness than A (Niiniluoto 1984). But, as the targets of genuine cognitive problems are unknown, this notion has methodological applications only if degrees of truthlikeness can be rationally estimated by the available evidence. Here the evidence may include both observations and background theories. My suggestion is to estimate truthlikeness by its *expected value*, relative to the epistemic probabilities of the alternative states of affairs. Thus, science is viewed as a cognitive enterprise of maximizing expected verisimilitude (Niiniluoto 1987).

The similarity approach is very flexible in the sense that the target may be chosen in different ways in different cognitive problems, and there are also dynamic ways of changing cognitive problems, e.g. by enriching the language. The relevant similarity or distance measures between basic statements depends on their structure. For quantitative theories (such as economic theories usually are), the distances can be defined by taking advantage of the mathematical representation of the relevant "state space."

It is important to observe that, for some purposes, the similarity account can be reformulated by taking the target to be a *real system* (structure) M^* in the actual world, and the "guesses" $C(A)$ made by a theory A are the *models* (structures, interpretations, states of affairs) where A is true (for this terminology, see Giere 1988). Then theory A is true in M^* if M^* is one of its models; A is approximately true in M^* if A is true in some model M that is "close" to M^*; and A is truthlike in M^* if the whole class of its models is "close" to M^* (cf. figure 10.1). Here the relation between the model of a theory and the real system is similarity, resemblance, or analogy (cf. Niiniluoto 1987, 1988).

If our interest is in finding truth about laws of nature, understood as "nomic necessities" valid in all physically possible worlds, rather than about contingent truths describing the actual world, then the cognitive problem is one of *legisimilitude* instead of *verisimilitude*. This terminology, proposed by Cohen (1980), makes a distinction between closeness to laws (Latin *lex, legis*) and

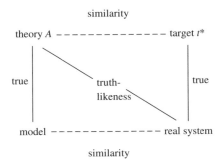

Figure 10.1   The similarity account

closeness to truth (Latin *verum*). The problem of legisimilitude can be solved by choosing as the target the strongest true lawlike statement in the relevant scientific language containing nomic modalities (see Niiniluoto 1987, chapter 11).

Mäki (1994b) suggests that the purpose of simplifications and idealizations in science may be to "isolate the essential or dominant features of the research object," and that a theory may be true about such a "part" of the world. In other words, even though theories may contain unrealistic assumptions, they are hoped to express *partial truths about essences*.[7] Mäki complains that the Popperian concept of verisimilitude is fruitless here (1994b, 166), and proposes that progress in economics should be analyzed in terms of *essesimilitude* or "closeness to the truth about essences or ontic cores in the economy" (Mäki 1991).

It seems to me that the similarity approach to truthlikeness, with a suitable choice of the target, gives a tool for assessing the "essesimilitude" of economic theories. Let L be the full language in which a theory A in economics can be expressed. A metaphysical realist, who advocates essences (cf. also Nowak 1980), should specify the sublanguage L_e of L which contains only the essential or core attributes. Then the essesimilitude of A can be defined as its closeness to a target sentence in L_e.

A more precise formulation of this account has to face an important complication, however. Suppose that the "essence" of free fall is acceleration due to gravitation, and the "essence" of economic behavior is maximization of expected utility. Then it may be the case that such situations, where a phenomenon is isolated in its "pure" form without "disturbing" additional factors, never occur in the actual world (even though we might be able to approximate or simulate them by means of artificial constructions). It thus seems to follow that such situations are not "parts" of the world after all, and therefore no suitable truth in L_e can be found as the target.

This problem can be solved in two interrelated ways. First, a realist may accept in his ontology *real possibilities* (potencies, causal powers, tendencies, propensities). A description of the actual world has then to be given in a modal language which can assign such potencies to individuals. The target for "essesimilitude" could then be the strongest true statement of this form – i.e. a sort of modal state description. Secondly, instead of describing potentially existing parts of reality, our theory may represent counterfactually existing "possible worlds."[8] Indeed, it seems in any case natural to think that scientific theories attempt to express general lawlike connections between kinds of entities in the world, and such laws entail counterfactuals. So the target should be a law, and thereby "essesimilitude" becomes a special case of legisimilitude. A systematic way of understanding this second proposal can be found in the method of idealization and concretization.

3 Idealization and concretization

The most comprehensive treatment of the method of idealization has been given by the Poznán School. Leszek Nowak (1980) initially applied this account to Marx's theory of value, but claimed also that the same method was used by Galileo in physics. Władislaw Krajewski (1977) expressed the approach in a general and easily readable form. In the 1990s, the book series *Poznán Studies* published already nine volumes of essays in idealization.

The starting point is typically an equation that expresses, for all objects x of certain kind, the functional dependence of a quantity $F(x)$ on a finite number of other quantities $q_1(x), \ldots, q_n(x)$. Let us assume, for simplicity, that $n = 1$, so that the initial equation has the form

$$F(x) = f_0(q(x)). \tag{T}$$

However, it is known in advance, or discovered later, that T excludes the influence of some other factors which are secondary relative to the primary or "essential" one, q. Assuming that there are two additional factors w_1 and w_2, the factual law T is then expressed as an *idealizational law*, which is conditional on the counterfactual assumption that the factors $w_1(x)$ and $w_2(x)$ have the value zero:

$$w_1(x) = 0 \text{ and } w_2(x) = 0 \rightarrow F(x) = f_0(q(x)). \tag{T_0}$$

In the next phase, the idealizing assumptions are removed one by one by *concretization* (factualization), i.e. by adding the factors $w_1(x)$ and $w_2(x)$ to the equation and by modifying the function f_0:

$$w_1(x) = 0 \text{ and } w_2(x) \neq 0 \rightarrow F(x) = f_1(q(x), w_2(x)) \tag{T_1}$$

$$w_1(x) \neq 0 \text{ and } w_2(x) \neq 0 \rightarrow F(x) = f_2(q(x), w_1(x), w_2(x)). \tag{T_2}$$

Moreover, it is required that Bohr's Correspondence Principle (CP) holds: the old theory should be obtained as a special case of the new theory, when some factors have a limiting value zero. In other words, this means that $f_1(q(x), z)$ should approach $f_0(q(x))$ as its limit, when z approaches 0, and $f_2(q(x), z, w_2(x))$ should approach $f_1(q(x), w_2(x))$, when z approaches 0.

Instead of Nowak's formulation of T_1, where the "realistic" condition $w_2(x) \neq 0$ is given in the antecedent of the conditional, it seems more natural to use the alternative

$$w_1(x) = 0 \rightarrow F(x) = f_1(q(x), w_2(x)), \tag{T_1'}$$

and similarly

$$F(x) = f_2(q(x), w_1(x), w_2(x)). \tag{T_2'}$$

(See Niiniluoto 1986, 1994a.) The law T_2' is then again factual like T (even though it may be based on hidden idealizations relative to even further omitted factors). As it asserts a law unconditionally, it entails Nowak's conditional T_2. Similarly, T_1' entails T_1. The advantage of this formulation is that T_2' entails T_1' and T_1' entails T_0, by CP: thus, concretization is the inverse of entailment. This allows us to think that the arrow $\rightarrow$ in the idealizational laws T_0 and T_1' is the operator for *counterfactual conditional* (cf. Lewis 1973). Hence, if T_2' itself is true, then T_1' and T_0 are true counterfactual conditionals.[9] In this case, the step from T_0 to T_1' and to T_2' leads us closer to the truth, as the latter theories in this sequence are more truthlike than the former ones. The same conclusion holds typically, if T_2' itself is only truthlike, but the truth is obtained from it by further concretization.

In his reply to Diederich (1994), who also proposes the formulations T_1' and T_2' (without referring to Niiniluoto 1986/1990), Nowak (1994) insists that concretization should not be understood as "an operation of deleting an idealizing condition," but rather as "replacing it with an appropriate realistic condition" (1994, 317). However, he mistakenly takes Diederich to claim that concretization is the relation of entailment (1994, 316). Moreover, Nowak (who refers to Niiniluoto 1986/1990) has failed to see the point of using counterfactual conditionals in the formulation of idealizational laws: he claims that, if b is the false condition that no other forces besides gravitation influence a freely falling body, then both conditionals

$$b \rightarrow s = gt^2/2$$
$$b \rightarrow s \neq gt^2/2$$

are true (1994, 319). This holds if $\rightarrow$ is the material implication, but not if $\rightarrow$ is a Lewis-type counterfactual conditional. The former of these conditionals not only "applies to the ideal world" (1994, 312), but is true (in Lewis' sense) in the actual world as well.

In typical applications of the method of idealization, the original law T is false, and the new factual law T_2' attempts to correct it. As Nowak emphasizes, this is compatible with the assumption that the most important or "essential" factors have been included already in T. Moreover, sometimes we may be able to deduce from the new theory T_2' that T is approximately true in some special cases. For example, the theory of relativity entails that bodies moving with very small velocities approximately satisfy Newton's laws, since then the effect of the finite velocity of light is negligible. In this sense, Newton's theory may be said to be a *partial approximate truth*. Similarly, an economic theory may be approximately true for some applications where, for example, the transactions costs are sufficiently small. Even though this resembles Mäki's view about theories as partial truths, it is not clear that the cases or applications almost correctly described by the theory are in any interesting sense "essential." For example, rigid bodies moving with a velocity close to zero are special only in the sense that they are familiar to us in our everyday life.

The applicability of the method of idealization and concretization to economic theories has been argued, besides Nowak (1980), also by Cools, Hamminga, and Kuipers (1994) with a case study (where CP holds). It should not be difficult to formulate neoclassical theories of the firm and Bayesian decision theories within this framework, since their unrealistic assumptions typically include various kinds of "negligibility conditions." Mäki (1992b, 1994b) discusses this approach in detail as the "method of isolation"; Nowak (1994) argues that the differences of opinion between him and Mäki are largely terminological.

What is important here is that sufficient attention should be paid to the logical form or structure of idealizational laws and theories. Mäki points out correctly that nothing-but-the-truth is violated when idealizing assumptions state that $w(x) = 0$ while in fact $w(x) \neq 0$, but he seems to imply that thereby the "isolative theory" itself also violates truth proper (Mäki 1992b, 341). Elsewhere he states that "when employing idealizing assumptions, isolative theories also violate nothing-but-the-truth," but adds that idealizations are usually called "assumptions" rather than "assertions" (Mäki 1994b, 152–153). This matter is clarified when we see that an idealizational law "contains" the false assumption $w(x) = 0$ only conditionally, not as its conjunct, and this is no obstacle to the possibility that the law may be true. By looking at T_0 we see that $w_1(x) = 0$ and $w_2(x) = 0$ are not asserted by it, but rather they are the antecedent of a counterfactual conditional, and this conditional may quite well be true or truthlike in spite of the falsity of its antecedent. This observation allows us to combine the method of idealization with scientific realism.

It should be added that the counterfactual formulation applies to genuine cases where the idealizing assumption is never true. For example, Newton's mechanics tells how physical bodies *would* move if the velocity of light *were* infinite. Still, Newton's theory is not a partial truth, since to transform it to a strict truth its laws have to be modified in the process of concretization. The situation is different with "quasi-idealizations" where the idealizing assumption is sometimes true (see Nowak 1980, 190). For example, a body may be moving in an almost perfect void, and the market may happen to be in equilibrium (see Mäki 1994b, 153). In such cases, T_0 may be a subjunctive conditional which expresses a partial truth about the unusual situations described by the antecedent condition.

4 Theoretical reference

A plausible holistic account of the meaning of theoretical terms leads scientific realism into trouble, since it appears to show that all false theories fail to be referring. Thomas Kuhn (1962) and Paul Feyerabend (1962) used this argument to attack realism in the 1960s. Causal theories of reference have been proposed as an alternative method of reference fixing for a realist, but these theories are not without their own problems. Hilary Putnam (1975) argued that also a descriptive cluster theory of reference with a principle of charity can be called to rescue realism. A similar suggestion was made by David Lewis (1970): theoretical terms can be taken to denote those entities which come "nearest to realizing the theory." It seems to me that the similarity theory of truthlikeness helps to make precise the idea of charitable theoretical reference, and thereby to undermine the scepticist meta-induction about the referential capacities of our theories (see Niiniluoto 1997).

In the following, we are assuming a typical situation where the language contains old and already interpreted terms, and a theory T introduces a new term t. How can the reference or denotation of this "theoretical term" t be fixed?

A scientific realist, who wants to defend reference invariance in spite of meaning variance, obviously has to reject the classical principle of descriptive theories of reference:

> (DR1) A term t occurring in theory T refers to object b iff b satisfies the claims of T containing t.

Namely, it would follow from DR1 that theory T cannot successfully refer to an entity if it is not strictly true about it. An attempt in this direction was made by N.L. Wilson in his *Principle of Charity* (Wilson 1959): the referent of a term is the object which makes true most of the beliefs of the speaker. Applied to scientific terms, and letting a theory T express the beliefs of the scientific community, this idea gives an alternative to DR1:

> (DR2) A term occurring in theory T refers to object b iff b satisfies the majority of the claims of T containing t.

However, it is doubtful whether DR2 covers typical cases where a theory is false but "close to the truth." When the theory is approximate or idealized, it need not be the case that most, or even any, of the statements of the theory are strictly speaking true. For example, a quantitative law may deviate from the true law at each point, but the law can still be truthlike.

A more plausible idea is sketched by Lewis (1970): if a theory T is not realized by any entity, it may still have a "near-realization" which realizes another theory T' obtained from the original theory T "by a slight weakening or a slight correction" (1970, 432). Then the theoretical term in T denotes the entity which is "the nearest near-realization" of the theory, if it "comes near enough." Thus,

> (DR3) Term t occurring in theory T refers to object b iff b satisfies the theory T' which is, among realizable theories, the closest to T.

A variant of DR2 and DR3 is obtained by saying that the theory T should be "approximately true" about its denotation (see Putnam 1975).

A weakness of the so far proposed accounts of charity is their reliance on intuitive notions, like "slight modification" or "approximate truth." As proposed in Niiniluoto (1997), a more precise formulation can be given by employing concepts developed in Niiniluoto (1987). Let $AT(T,b)$ be the degree of approximate truth of theory T relative to the "system" consisting of the object b, and $Tr(T,b)$ the corresponding degree of truthlikeness of T relative to b. Two new definitions of reference are thereby obtained:

> (DR4) Term t occurring in theory T refers to the actual object b which maximizes $AT(T,b)$.
>
> (DR5) Term t occurring in theory T refers to the actual object b which maximizes $Tr(T,b)$.

DR5 is more demanding than DR4, since a high degree of truthlikeness guarantees also a high degree of approximate truth.[10]

Both DR4 and DR5 include the special case where a theory refers to an object by giving a perfectly true description of it. But in general successful reference to actual objects does not presuppose the strict truth of the theory. Both definitions allow that Lorenz and Bohr in 1911 and in 1925 referred to the same electron – which, moreover, is still studied by contemporary physicists. Similarly, ideal gas theory, which by DR1 could refer only to nonexisting ideal gas, refers to real gas by DR4 and DR5.

DR4 and DR5 are still too liberal conditions, since they do not make sense of reference failure. For example, while in some special contexts "phlogiston" may be taken to refer to oxygen, phlogiston theory as a whole was so badly mistaken that its central theoretical term was not referring at all. A restricted methodological conception of successful reference is achieved by placing, depending on the context, a suitable lower bound or "threshold" to the values of $AT(T,b)$ and $Tr(T,b)$.

The ideas presented here can be applied, besides genuinely theoretical terms in advanced science, also to quite ordinary terms in our everyday language. For example, Lewis has evaluated the referential capacities of "folk psychology" which includes terms like "belief," "desire," "want," and "person."[11] Even though such "theories" are at best approximately correct, they may be taken to be referring according to DR4 and DR5.

If the notion of truthlikeness is applicable to theories in the social sciences, then the same holds for the theory of reference proposed here. In particular, the idea of charitable reference can be applied to economic theories. In this respect, many theories in economics resemble the ideal gas theory in physics. For example, in spite of the unrealistic assumptions of neoclassical theories of the firm, these theories may be sufficiently truthlike about real business firms.[12] In spite of unrealistic rationality assumptions, theories about the behavior of the "economic man" refer to ordinary human beings.

Let us illustrate our principles with the theory of innovation by Danny Miller and Peter H. Friesen (1982).[13] Their starting point is the observation that sometimes firms perform innovation only in response to serious challenges, while sometimes the natural state of innovation is excessively high. They postulate two models: the "conservative" firms are reluctant to innovation, but the "entrepreneurial" firms are aggressively pursuing innovations unless they are warned to slow down. This theory could be understood instrumentalistically so that the two "models" simply classify the firms in two subclasses. However, Miller and Friesen seem to favor a realistic interpretation, where "conservative" and "entrepreneurial" refer to two different types of propensities to innovate, and each "momentum" of this kind is "a pervasive force in organizations." However, no one hardly believes that this simple classification is yet the final truth about this matter. But even though the theory may be further developed and concretized in the future, its basic theoretical terms may be taken to refer to real behavioral characteristics of business firms.

It is a subtle question whether idealized decision theories refer to anything like really existing utility functions of human agents. The necessary and sufficient conditions for the relevant representation theorems are satisfied only in possible worlds that are close to the actual world (cf. Niiniluoto 1986). In this sense, quantitative real-valued utility functions do not exist in our world, but they are mathematical constructions that allow truthlike descriptions of rational human preferences and decision-making. One candidate for their actual reference might be money, which is a real quantity in the actual world, but the point of departure of classical utility theory was the observation that personal utilities differ from sums of money. An alternative suggestion is that theoretical utility functions refer to personal degrees of satisfaction (which have some kind of psychological reality) or to degrees of usefulness (which have some kind of technical reality) (see Hansson 1988), where the actual quantitative structure of such degrees is unsharp to some extent.

5 Conclusion

We have shown how theories with unrealistic, genuinely idealizational assumptions can be represented as counterfactual conditionals. For a scientific realist, this approach helps to show how such theories may be refer to real entities in the world and to give true or truthlike representations of such entities. The alternative realist strategy, proposed by Uskali Mäki, is partly but only partly vindicated, since theories involving quasi-idealizations, and theories restricted to applications where the influence of the idealized factor is negligible, may be partial approximate truths.

Notes

I am grateful to Professor Uskali Mäki for useful comments on earlier versions of this chapter.

1. Another illustration may be taken from cardinal utility theories: from "rationality axioms" one derives the existence of a utility function and a subjective probability function such that the rational agent's choices conform to the principle of maximizing expected utility (see, e.g. Gärdenfors and Sahlin 1988). Again it is clear that the classical axiomatizations (Ramsey, Savage) do not contain the whole truth, since they exclude some important aspects of decision making (e.g. risk aversion). Some of the axioms are structural conditions that limit the applicability of the theory (they thus resemble what Alan Musgrave 1981 has called "domain assumptions"), and some rationality axioms (e.g. the transitivity of preferences, the sure-thing principle) are often violated by real-life agents.
2. In her later work, Cartwright (1994) has acknowledged that she was "deluded about the enemy" in her *How the Laws of Physics Lie* (1983): what should be resisted is not realism but "fundamentalism" (i.e. the view of fundamental laws that are true and universally in force everywhere).
3. Similarly, Bayesian decision theory is often understood to state only that a rational decision-maker behaves *as if* she assigned numerical utilities to possible outcomes in conformity with the expected utility model, without implying that there are "real" utility functions. See Bengt Hansson's (1988) distinction between "formalistic" and "realistic" interpretations of expected utility theory.
4. For discussion of the related idea that simplicity is more important than truth, see Niiniluoto (1994b).
5. Technically speaking, "fewer" is explicated by set-theoretical inclusion.

6. Mäki (1991), p. 88, takes Popper to claim that science "should approach the true description of the whole of the actual universe." However, in speaking about "the whole truth" in his theory of truthlikeness, Popper in practice assumes that the set of all truths is relative to a given scientific language. In my approach, this consideration has been emphasized right from the beginning. I do not believe that there is any single privileged language which could cover the whole reality (see Niiniluoto 1984, 1987, 1998, 1999). Thus, every theory concerns only some aspect or fragment of the world. Even though the physicists are now searching for a "theory of everything," I find no good reasons to expect that all theories (e.g. in psychology, sociology, and economics) could be reduced to such a fundamental physical theory.

7. According to Mäki (1994b, 159), a *partial truth* is a representation which is true about a part or aspect of the world, but may fail to be true about other parts. A related syntactical characterization is the following (see Niiniluoto 1987, 175). Suppose that a theory T can be expressed as a conjunction $A \& B$. If A is false, then the whole T is false as well. But if the conjunct B is true, then T may said to be *partly true*.

8. It is also possible to apply the theory of truthlikeness in situations where the cognitive problem is defined relative to a counterfactual assumption b. In this case, the target t^* can be chosen as the strongest statement which would be true if b were true (see Niiniluoto 1987, 259–262). For example, if we restrict our attention to quantitative hypotheses that can be expressed by a linear function between two variables, and no such law is correct, then our target is the linear function that is closest to the true nonlinear law (1987, 287–289). Notice that in such a situation the counterfactual conditional $b \to t^*$ is true, and we could define a modified cognitive problem where it is chosen as the target. Cf. section 3.

9. According to Lewis (1973), a counterfactual conditional $p \to q$ is true in world w iff the p-worlds closest to w are also q-worlds. Thus, a counterfactual conditional may be true in the actual world, but this truth value is based on what happens in the closest possible worlds where the antecedent is true.

10. If the objective measure of truthlikeness is replaced by its estimate relative to evidence, new epistemic variants of DR4 and DR5 are obtained.

11. See O'Leary-Hawthorne (1994). (For this reference, I am grateful to Professor Philip Pettit.) O'Leary-Hawthorne also considers reformulations of DR3 on the basis of the suggestion of Lewis (1984), who claims that only an "elite minority" of entities are eligible to serve as referents: they are not "miscellaneous, gerrymandered, ill-demarcated," but rather "carved at the joints" in a natural way. This formulation seems to presuppose metaphysical realism, i.e. that there is a uniquely best way of carving the world into entities. Another view would allow that such carvings can be done in different ways within alternative ontological frameworks (cf. Niiniluoto 1987, 1999). Then rules like DR4 and DR5, which seem to contain quantification over all eligible entities, should be relativized to an ontological framework of acceptable kinds of entities.

12. Mäki (1999) has argued that Machlup's fictionalist view of the theory of firms is based upon his implicit acceptance of the descriptive theory of reference (cf. DR1).

13. Dr. Marja-Liisa Kakkuri-Knuuttila drew my attention to this interesting theory.

References

Brzeziński, J., F. Coniglione, T. Kuipers, and L. Nowak (eds.) (1990). *Idealization I: General Problems.* Amsterdam: Rodopi

Cartwright, Nancy (1983). *How the Laws of Physics Lie.* Oxford: Clarendon Press
(1994). Fundamentalism vs. the patchwork of laws, *Proceedings of the Aristotelian Society*, 93, 279–292

Cohen, L.J. (1980). What has science to do with truth?, *Synthèse*, 45, 489–410

Cools, K., B. Hamminga, and T. Kuipers (1994). Truth approximation by concretization in capital structure theory, in B. Hamminga and N. De Marchi (eds.), *Idealization in Economics.* Amsterdam: Rodopi, 205–228

Feyerabend, P. (1962). Explanation, reduction and empiricism, in H. Feigl and G. Maxwell (eds.), *Minnesota Studies in the Philosophy of Science*, 2. Minneapolis: University of Minnesota Press, 28–97

Gärdenfors, P. and N.-E. Sahlin (eds.) (1988). *Decision, Probability, and Utility: Selected Readings.* Cambridge: Cambridge University Press

Hamminga, B. and N. De Marchi (eds.) (1994). *Idealization in Economics.* Amsterdam: Rodopi

Hansson, Bengt (1988). Risk aversion as a problem of conjoint measurement, in P. Gärdenfors and N.-E. Sahlin (eds.), *Decision, Probability, and Utility: Selected Readings.* Cambridge: Cambridge University Press

Hilpinen, Risto (1976). Approximate truth and truthlikeness, in M. Przełecki, K. Szaniawski, and R. Wojcicki (eds.), *Formal Methods in the Methodology of Empirical Sciences.* Dordrecht: D. Reidel, 19–42

Krajewski, Władislaw (1977). *Correspondence Principle and the Growth of Knowledge.* Dordrecht: D. Reidel

Kuhn, Thomas S. (1962). *The Structures of Scientific Revolutions.* Chicago: University of Chicago Press

Kuokkanen, M. (ed.) (1994). *Idealization VII: Structuralism, Idealization and Approximation.* Amsterdam: Rodopi

Laudan, L. (1977). *Progress and its Problems.* London: Routledge & Kegan Paul

Lewis, David (1973). *Counterfactuals.* Oxford, Blackwell
(1984). 'Putnam's paradox, *Australasian Journal of Philosophy*, 62, 221–236

Mäki, Uskali (1989). On the problem of realism in economics, *Ricerche economiche*, 43(1–2), 176–198
(1991). Comments on Hands, in Neil De Marchi and Mark Blaug (eds.), *Appraising Economic Theories: Studies in the Methodology of Research Programmes.* Aldershot: Edward Elgar, 85–90
(1992a). Friedman and realism, *Research in the History of Economic Thought and Methodology*, 10, 171–195
(1992b). On the method of isolation in economics, in Craig Dilworth (ed.), *Idealization IV: Structuralism, Intelligibility in Science.* Amsterdam and Atlanta, GA: Rodopi, 317–351
(1994a). Reorienting the assumptions issue, in Roger E. Backhouse (ed.), *New Directions in Economic Methodology.* London: Routledge, 236–256

(1994b). Isolation, idealization and truth in economics, in B. Hamminga and N. De Marchi (eds.), *Idealization in Economics*. Amsterdam: Rodopi, 147–168

(1999). Representation repressed: two kinds of semantic scepticism in economics, in R. Scazzieri, R. Rossini Favretti, and G. Sandri (eds.), *Incommensurability and Translation: Kuhnian Perspectives on Scientific Communication and Theory Change*. London: Edward Elgar

Miller, Danny and Peter H. Friesen (1982). Innovation in conservative and entrepreneurial firms: two models of strategic momentum, *Strategic Management Journal*, 3, 1–25

Musgrave, Alan (1981). "Unreal assumptions" in economic theory: the F-twist untwisted, *Kyklos*, 34, 377–387

Niiniluoto, Ilkka (1986). Theories, approximations, idealizations, in R. Barcan Marcus, G.J.W. Dorn, and P. Weingartner (eds.), *Logic, Methodology and Philosophy of Science VII*. Amsterdam: North-Holland; reprinted in J. Brzeziński, F. Coniglione, T. Kuipers, and L. Nowak (eds.), *Idealization I: General Problems*. Amsterdam: Rodopi, 1990, 9–57

(1987). *Truthlikeness*, Dordrecht: D. Reidel

(1988). Analogy and similarity in scientific reasoning, in D.H. Helman (ed.), *Analogical Reasoning: Perspectives of Artificial Intelligence, Cognitive Science, and Philosophy*. Dordrecht: Kluwer, 271–298

(1994a). Approximation in applied science, in M. Kuokkanen (ed.), *Idealization VIII: Structuralism, Idealization and Approximation*. Amsterdam: Rodopi, 127–139

(1994b). Descriptive and inductive simplicity, in W. Salmon and G. Wolters (eds.), *Logic, Language, and the Structure of Theories*, Pittsburgh: University of Pittsburgh Press, 147–70

(1995). Is there progress in science?, in H. Stachowiak (ed.), *Pragmatik, Handbuch pragmatischen Denken*, Band V. Hamburg: Felix Meiner Verlag, 30–58

(1997). Reference invariance and truthlikeness, *Philosophy of Science*, 64, 546–554

(1998). Verisimilitude: the third period, *The British Journal for the Philosophy of Science*, 49, 1–29

(1999). *Critical Scientific Realism*. Oxford: Oxford University Press

Nowak, Leszek (1980). *The Structure of Idealization: Towards a Systematic Interpretation of the Marxian Idea of Science*. Dordrecht: D. Reidel

(1994). The idealizational methodology and economics: replies to Diederich, Hoover, Janssen, Jorland and Mäki, in B. Hamminga and N. De Marchi (eds.) (1994), *Idealization in Economics*. Amsterdam: Rodopi, 303–336

O'Leary-Hawthorne, J. (1994). A corrective to the Ramsey–Lewis account of theoretical terms, *Analysis*, 54, 105–110

Putnam, Hilary (1975). *Mind, Language, and Reality (Philosophical Papers, 2)*. Cambridge: Cambridge University Press

Ramsey, F.P. (1950). *Foundations of Mathematics and Other Logical Essays*. New York: The Humanities Press

Savage, J.L. (1954). *The Foundations of Statistics*. New York: John Wiley

van Fraassen, B. (1980). *The Scientific Image*. Oxford: Oxford University Press

Wilson, N.L. (1959). Substances without substrata, *Review of Metaphysics*, 12, 521–539

Part IV
The constitution of economic reality

11 Rational choice, functional selection, and "empty black boxes"

Philip Pettit

Those of us who have welcomed rational-choice theory as a way of doing social science have often sourced that enthusiasm in a critique of the functionalist theory that it supplanted (Elster 1979). But this dual attitude of enthusiasm and critique has proved hard, at least in my own case, to sustain. For it turns out that in order to vindicate rational-choice theory as a mode of explaining social patterns in general – social patterns beyond the narrow range of economic behavior – we have to recognize the legitimacy of explaining what I have described as the resilience of certain patterns of behavior (Pettit 1993, 1995). And once we allow the legitimacy of explaining resilience, then we can see how functionalist theory may also serve us well in social science; we lose the basis on which the rational-choice critique of the theory has mostly been grounded (Pettit 1996).

Putting the matter otherwise, there is a common problem that rational-choice theory and functionalist theory each have to confront. I call this the problem of the "empty black box." So far as I can see, both approaches are going to fail in face of this problem or they are both going to find resources for overcoming it; they are going to sink or swim together. Drawing on earlier work, I shall argue here that the problem can be overcome in the case of rational-choice theory but that the solution offered directs us to a parallel solution in the case of functionalist theory.

My chapter is in five sections. In the first I present the specter of the "empty black box" that haunts functional explanation in social science. In the second I show that there is a similar specter that haunts rational-choice explanation in social science. In the third I show that the specter can be dispelled in the rational-choice case by recognizing the propriety of explaining the resilience of social patterns as distinct from their emergence or continuity. And then in the fourth section I show that a similar move can be made to dispel the specter that hangs over functionalist theory. Finally, in the fifth section, I offer some general comments on the style of explanation exemplified in each case.

1   The problem for functional explanation

Functional explanation in biological science offers the obvious model on which to think about such explanation in social science. Why do we find such and such a trait in this or that sort of organism? Why do we find beating hearts, or echolocating devices, or tit-for-tat patterns of behavior, in this or that species or population? The answer given is that the trait serves a certain function: it circulates blood, or makes it easy to find food, or it helps individuals to achieve mutually beneficial cooperation. The very fact of serving such a function, the very fact of conferring the sort of benefit in question on its bearers, is meant to explain why the trait is found in individuals of the relevant type.[1]

Such functional explanation is tolerated in biological science, because it connects fairly obviously with the theory of natural selection. Suppose that a trait, T, is held to be functional in producing an effect, F, and that the disposition to produce F is regarded as offering an explanation for why we find T in relevant organisms. That picture of things becomes a plausible hypothesis under a paraphrase in terms of the mechanics of natural selection. The paraphrase, roughly cast, goes like this. The accidentally induced mutation whereby the gene for T appeared in the ancestors of the organisms in question gave those creatures an advantage over competitors in producing offspring, and in increasing the frequency of T in the population; it did this, in particular, so far as T-bearers manifested the effect, F. Why then do we find T in the population, or the species, or whatever? Well, because T produces F and because that gave T-bearers an advantage in the natural selection stakes: in short, because T is functional, so far as it produces F, because T has the function of producing F (Neander 1991a, 1991b).

The biological model of functional explanation suggests that the aim of functional explanation in social science is to explain why certain social traits are to be found in this or that society, or institution, or whatever, as the biological analog explains why certain traits are to be found in this or that species, or population, or whatever. And the availability of a natural selection mechanism to make sense of functional explanation in biology raises the question as to what sort of mechanism underlies functional explanation in social science. The "empty black box" problem is that for most functional explanations in social science there is no obvious mechanism to cite and that the explanations, therefore, are apparently baseless (Elster 1979).

Why do we find religious rituals in various societies? Because they have the function of promoting social solidarity (Durkheim 1948). Why do we find common ideas of time and space, cause and number (Durkheim 1948; see Lukes 1973, 442)? Because they serve to make mental contact and social life possible. Why do we find certain peace-making ceremonies in this or that culture? Because they serve to change the feelings of the hostile parties towards one another (Radcliffe-Brown 1948, 238–239). Why do we find social stratification – the unequal distribution of rights and privileges – in modern societies? Because it makes it possible to fill socially indispensable but individually unattractive positions (Davis and Moore 1945).

The problem with all of these bread-and-butter examples of functional explanation is that it is not clear why the fact that the trait in question has the functional effect cited explains why the trait is found there: explains why we find the relevant religious rituals, or peace-making ceremonies, or structures of social stratification. It is not clear what mechanism is supposed to operate in the "black box" that links the functionality of the trait with its existence or persistence. No one supposes that intentional design plays the linking role. The only mechanism that could do so appears to be a mechanism of selection akin to that which is invoked in biology; there may be other mechanisms possible in the abstract but they would not seem to fit these standard sorts of cases (Van Parijs 1981). And in most cases there is no evidence of a mechanism of selection having been at work. There are some examples, it is true, where functional explanation in social science can be backed up by a selectional story. Some economists say that the presence of certain decision-making procedures in various firms can be explained by their being functional in promoting profits and they back up that explanation with a scenario under which the firms with such procedures, being the firms which do best in profits, are the ones that survive and prosper: they are selected for the presence and effects of those procedures in a competitive market (Alchian 1950; Nelson and Winter 1982). But it is very implausible to think that such selectional mechanisms are available for social-functional explanation in general (Pettit 1993, 155–163). The "black box" which functionalist thinkers apparently have to postulate is in most cases empty.

2 The problem for rational-choice explanation

Rational-choice theory, as I understand it, is the attempt to use economic models of explanation in areas that go beyond what is traditionally seen as economic behavior. In order to see that there is a problem for such theory that parallels the problem raised for functionalist theory, it is necessary to look at the assumptions which economics makes about the way agents produce the behavior it seeks to explain: about the contents of the "black box" in the head of *homo oeconomicus*.

There are two sorts of assumptions that economists make about the minds of the agents with whom they are concerned. First, process-centered assumptions about the way in which desires or degrees of preference issue in action. And second, content-centered assumptions about the sorts of things that the agents desire: about which things they prefer and with what intensities.

As for process-based assumptions, the first thing to notice is that economists almost universally accept the relatively weak claim that whenever people act, they do so as a result of their own desires or utility functions. They do not act on the basis of moral belief alone, for example; such belief issues in action only if accompanied by a suitable desire. And they do not act just on the basis of perceiving what other people desire; the perception that someone desires something can lead to action only in the presence of a desire to satisfy that other person. Some thinkers toy with the possibility that agents may be capable of putting themselves under the control of something other than their own desires: for example, Mark Platts (1980) when he imagines that moral belief may motivate without the presence of desire; Amartya Sen (1982, essay 4) when he speaks of the possibility of commitment; and Frederic Schick (1984) when he canvases the notion of sociality. But economists are probably on the side of common sense in urging that all action is mediated via the desires of the agent (Pettit 1993, chapter 1).

How do people's desires lead to action, then, according to economists? The general assumption is that desires lead to actions via beliefs about the options available, about the likely consequences of those options, and so on. More specifically, the assumption is that that they lead to actions that serve the desires well according to such beliefs; in other words, that they lead to subjectively rational actions. There are different theories as to what it is for an action or choice to serve an agent's desires well, according to his or her beliefs: about what it is for an action to be subjectively rational. But the family of theories available is well exemplified by the Bayesian claim that an action is rational just in case it maximizes the agent's expected utility (Eells 1982).

So much for the assumptions that economists make about the way desires or preferences lead to action. What now of the assumptions that they make about the content of what human beings prefer or desire? The main question here is how far economists cast human beings as egocentric in their desires.

Many economists endorse what is sometimes known as "nontuism." They hold that people's desires in regard to others are not affected by their perceptions of other people's desires: utility functions are independent (Gauthier 1986, 87). Or they hold, more strongly still, that not only do people take no account of what others desire in forming their own desires in regard to others; any desires they have for what others should do, or for what should happen to others, are motivated ultimately by a self-centered desire for their own satisfaction (Gauthier 1986, 311). Economists endorse nontuism to the extent that various economic models assume that any good I do you is, from my point of view, an externality for which ideally I would want to extract payment: an external benefit that I would ideally want to appropriate for myself (or "internalize") (Gauthier 1986, 87). But this seems to be a feature of particular models and not an assumption that is essentially built into the economic way of thinking. And it is a feature that affects only some of the standard results of the theories in question, not all of them (Sen 1982, 93). I am not inclined to regard it as a deep feature of economic thinking. It may have little or no presence, for example, in the application of economic thought to social life outside the market.

But even if economics does not require people to be nontuistic, even if it allows that they may have noninstrumental desires in relation to others – perhaps desires that are affected by their perception of what the others desire – still it does generally assume that there is something egocentric about the desires on which people generally act. Economists assume that people's self-regarding desires are generally stronger than their other-regarding ones: that in this sense people are relatively self-regarding in their desires. Whenever there is a conflict between what will satisfy me or mine and what will satisfy others, the assumption is that in general I will look for the more egocentric satisfaction. I may do so through neglecting your interests in my own efforts at self-promotion, or through helping my children at the expense of yours, or through jeopardizing a common good for the sake of personal advantage, or through taking the side of my country against that of others. The possibilities are endless. What unites them is that in each case I display a strong preference for what concerns me or mine, in particular a preference that is stronger than a countervailing preference for what concerns others.[2]

The assumption that people are relatively self-regarding in their desires shows up in the fact that economists and rational-choice theorists tend only to invoke relatively self-regarding desires in their explanations and predictions. They predict that as it costs more to help others, there will be less help given to others, that as it becomes personally more difficult to contribute to a common cause – more difficult, say, to take litter to the bin – there will be a lesser level of contribution to that cause, and so on. They offer invisible-hand explanations under which we are told how some collective good is attained just on the basis of each pursuing their own advantage. And they specialize in prisoner's dilemma accounts that reveal how people come to be collectively worse off, through seeking each to get the best possible outcome for themselves.

The belief that people are relatively self-regarding shows up in other aspects of economic thought, too. It may be behind the assumption of economic policy-makers and institutional designers that no proposal is plausible unless it can be shown to be "incentive-compatible": that is, unless it can be shown that people will have self-regarding reasons for going along with what the proposal requires.[3] And it may be at the root of the Paretian or quasi-Paretian assumption of normative or welfare economics that it is uncontroversially a social benefit if things can be changed so that all preferences currently satisfied continue to be satisfied and if further preferences are satisfied as well. This assumption is plausible if the preferences envisaged are self-regarding, for only envy would seem to provide a reason for denying that it is a good if some people can get more of what they want for themselves without others getting less. But the assumption is not at all plausible if the preferences also include other-regarding preferences, as we shall see in a moment. And so the Paretian assumption manifests a further, deeper belief: that the preferences with which economics is concerned are self-regarding ones.

The Paretian assumption is not plausible – certainly not as uncontroversial as economists generally think – when other-regarding preferences are involved, for reasons to which Amartya Sen (1982, essay 2) has directed our attention. Consider two boys, Nasty and Nice, and their preferences in regard to the distribution of two apples, Big and Small. Nasty prefers to get Big no matter who is in control of the distribution. Nice prefers to get Small if he is in control – this, because he is other-regarding and feels he should give Big away if he is in charge – but prefers to get Big if Nasty is in control: he is only human, after all. The Paretian assumption suggests – under the natural individuation of options (Pettit 1991) – that it is better to have Nice control the distribution rather than Nasty. If we put Nice in control, then that satisfies Nasty – he gets Big – and it satisfies Nice as well: Nice's preference for having Big if Nasty is in control does not get engaged and Nice's preference for having Small – for giving Big away – if he is in control himself is satisfied. But this is clearly crazy: it means that we are punishing Nice for being nice, in particular for having other-regarding preferences; and this, while apparently attempting just to increase preference-satisfaction in an impartial manner. The lesson is that the Paretian assumption is not plausible once other-regarding preferences figure on the scene and so, if economists think that it is plausible – think indeed that it is uncontroversial – that suggests that they only have self-regarding preferences in view.

The upshot of all this, then, is that economists and rational-choice theorists present human agents as relatively self-regarding creatures who act with a view to doing as well as possible by their predominantly self-regarding desires. These desires are usually assumed to be desires for what is loosely described as economic advantage or gain: that is, roughly, for advantage or gain in the sorts of things that can be traded. But self-regarding desires, of course, may extend to other goods, too, and there is nothing inimical to economics in explaining patterns of behavior by reference, say, to those non-tradable goods that consist in being well loved or well regarded (Pettit 1990; Brennan and Pettit 1993). The economic approach is tied to an assumption of relative self-regard but not to any particular view of the dimensions in which self-regard may operate.

But does the egocentric picture fit? Are human beings rational centers of predominantly self-regarding concern? It would seem not. Were human agents centers of this kind, then we would expect them to find their reasons for doing things predominantly in considerations that bear on their own advantage.[4] But this isn't our common experience, or so at least I shall argue.

Consider the sorts of considerations that weigh with us, or seem to weigh with us, in a range of common-or-garden situations. We are apparently moved in our dealings with others by considerations that bear on their merits and their attractions, that highlight what is expected of us and what fair play or friendship requires, that direct attention to the good we can achieve together or the past that we share in common, and so on through a complex variety of deliberative themes. And not only are we apparently moved in this nonegocentric way. We clearly believe of one another – and take it, indeed, to be a matter of common belief – that we are generally and reliably responsive to claims that transcend and occasionally confound the calls of self-regard. That is why we feel free to ask each other for favors, to ground our projects in the expectation that others will be faithful to their past commitments, and to seek counsel from others in confidence that they will present us with a more or less impartial rendering of how things stand.

Suppose that people believed that they were each as self-regarding as economists appear to assume; suppose that this was a matter of common belief among them. In that case we would expect each of them to try to persuade others to act in a certain way by convincing them that it is in their personal interest to act in that way: this, in good part, by convincing them that they, the persuaders, will match such action appropriately, having corresponding reasons of personal advantage to do so. Under the economic supposition, there would be little room for anyone to call on anyone else in the name of any motive other than self-interest.

The economic supposition may be relevant in some areas of human exchange, most saliently in areas of market behavior. But it clearly does not apply across the broad range of human interaction. In the normal mode of exchange, people present each other with considerations that, putatively, they both recognize as relevant and potentially persuasive. I do not call on you in the name of what is just to your personal advantage; did I do so, that could be a serious insult. I call on you in the name of your commitment to certain ideals, your membership of certain groups, your attachment to certain people. I call on you, more generally, under the assumption that like me you understand and endorse the language of loyalty and fair play, kindness and politeness, honesty and straight talking. This language often has a moral ring but the terminology and concepts involved are not confined to the traditional limits of the moral; they extend to all the terms in which our culture allows us to make sense of ourselves, to make ourselves acceptably intelligible, to each other.

Consider how best an ethnographer might seek to make sense of the ways in which people conduct their lives and affairs. An ethnographer that came to the shores of a society like ours – a society like one of the developed democracies – would earn the ridicule of professional colleagues if they failed to take notice of the rich moral and quasi-moral language in which we ordinary folk explain ourselves to ourselves and ourselves to one another: the language, indeed, in which we take our bearings as we launch ourselves in action. But if it is essential for the understanding of how we ordinary folk behave that account is taken of that language, then this strongly suggests that economists must be mistaken – at least they must be overlooking some aspect of human life – when they assume that we are a relatively self-regarding lot.

The claim that ordinary folk are oriented towards a nonegocentric language of self-explanation and self-justification does not establish definitively, of course, that they are actually not self-regarding. We all recognize the possibilities of rationalization and deception that such a language leaves open. Still, it would surely be miraculous that that language succeeds as well as it does in defining a stable and smooth framework of expectation, if as a matter of fact people's sensibilities do not conform to its contours: if, as a matter of fact, people fall systematically short – systematically and not just occasionally short – of what it suggests may be taken for granted about them.

We are left, then, with a problem for rational-choice theory: that is, a problem for the use of economic method in explaining noneconomic behavior. We are left, in fact, with the problem of an "empty black box." The mind postulated in rational-choice theory is that of a relatively self-regarding creature. But the mind that people display towards one another in most social settings, the mind that is articulated in common conceptions of how ordinary folk are moved, is saturated with concerns that dramatically transcend the boundaries of the self. So how can we invoke the workings of the economic mind to explain behavior, when the "black box" at the origin of behavior does not apparently contain an economic mind?

Rational-choice theory is in the same pickle, so it transpires, as the functionalist theory it has often aspired to supplant. Functionalist theory is apparently committed to there being a history of functional selection at the origin of the behaviors and institutions that it explains, yet there is no functional selection in evidence. Rational-choice theory seems to be committed to there being a process of self-regarding motivation and deliberation at the origin of the behaviors and institutions to which it is directed, yet the mental processes in evidence among relevant agents are not particularly self-regarding in character.[5] In each case we are invited to believe that a "black box" mechanism is operating in a certain way when all the indications are that the "black box" is empty: or at least empty of the sort of mechanism that the theory postulates.

3   The solution with rational-choice explanation

The model of virtual self-regard

The problem of the "empty black box" that economists and rational-choice theorists face is not one of my invention (Hindess 1988). So far as rational-choice theorists have reflected on the problem, the general suggestion has been that people are implicitly, in the sense of unconsciously, self-regarding. Gary Becker (1976, 7) comes close to endorsing this model when he writes: "the economic approach does not assume that decision units are necessarily conscious of their own efforts to maximize or can verbalize or otherwise describe in an informative way reasons for the systematic patterns in their behavior. Thus it is consistent with the emphasis on the subconscious in modern psychology."

But the claim that people are all unconsciously self-regarding is not particularly compelling. We all admit that people profess standards from which they often slip and that their slipping does usually relate to an awareness, perhaps a deeply suppressed awareness, of the costs of complying with the standards. We all admit, in other words, that weakness of will and self-deception are pretty commonplace phenomena. But the suggestion here is that the whole of human life is shot through with this sort of failure: that what we take to be a more or less occasional, more or less localized, sort of pathology actually represents the normal, healthy state of the human organism. That is a fairly outrageous claim. Most economists and rational-choice theorists would probably be shocked to hear that the view of the human subject which they systematically deploy is about as novel, and about as implausible, as the picture projected in classical Freudianism.

The solution that I prefer for the problem facing rational-choice theory postulates, not that people are implicitly or unconsciously self-regarding, but that they are potentially or virtually so. Let it be granted that while actual self-regard may play a great part in market and related behavior, it has little or no deliberative impact on the ordinary run of nonmarket behavior: for example, in contexts of ordinary family or friendly interaction, in contexts of political decision, or in contexts of group behavior. This is a worst-case scenario from the point of view of an attempt to vindicate rational-choice theory. What I suggest, however, is that even under that worst-case assumption self-regard may still have an important presence: it may be virtually if not actually there; it may be waiting in the wings, even if it is not actually on stage.

Here is how self-regard might have a virtual presence in such contexts. Suppose, first of all, that people are generally content in nonmarket contexts – we can restrict our attention to these – to let their actions be dictated by the cultural framing of the situation in which they find themselves: by the habits or perhaps the whims underpinned by that framing. A friend asks for a routine level of help and, in the absence of urgent business, the agent naturally complies with the request; it would be unthinkable for someone who understands what friendship means to do anything else. There is an election in progress and, the humdrum of everyday life being what it is, the agent spontaneously makes time for going to the polls; that is manifestly the thing to do, under ordinary canons of understanding, and the thing to do without thinking about it. Someone has left a telephone message asking for a return call about some matter and the agent doesn't hesitate to ring back; even if aware that there is nothing useful they can tell the original caller, they shrink from the impoliteness, in their culture, of ignoring the call. In the pedestrian patterns of day-to-day life, the cultural framing of any situation will be absolutely salient to the ordinary agent and the ordinary agent will more or less routinely respond. Or so at least I am prepared to assume.

But that is only the first part of my supposition. Suppose, in the second place, that despite the hegemony of cultural framing in people's everyday deliberations and decisions, there are certain alarm bells that make them take thought to their own interests. People may proceed under more or less automatic, cultural pilot in most cases but at any point where a decision is liable to cost them dearly in self-regarding terms, the alarm bells will tend to ring and prompt them to consider personal advantage; and heeding considerations of personal advantage will lead people, generally if not invariably, to act so as to secure that advantage: they are disposed to do the relatively more self-regarding thing.

Under these suppositions, self-regard will normally have no actual presence in dictating what people do; it will not be present in deliberation and will make no impact on decision. But it will always be virtually present in deliberation, for there are alarms which are ready to ring at any point where the agent's interests get to be possibly compromised and those alarms will call up self-regard and give it a more or less controlling deliberative presence. The agent will run under cultural pilot, provided that that pilot does not carry them into terrain that is too dangerous from a self-interested point of view. Let such terrain come into view, and in most cases the agent will quickly return to manual; they will quickly begin to count the more personal losses and benefits that are at stake in the decision on hand. This reflection may not invariably lead to self-regarding action – there is such a thing as self-sacrifice, after all – but the assumption is that it will do so fairly reliably.

Under the model of virtual self-regard, most actions are performed without self-regarding consideration but that is true only so far as most actions happen to do suitably well in self-regard terms. The agent is genuinely moved by ordinary, culturally framed considerations but that is so only so far as those considerations do not require a certain level of self-sacrifice. Let the considerations push the agent below the relevant self-regarding level of aspiration – this will vary, no doubt, from individual to individual – and the alarms bells will ring, causing the agent to rethink and probably reshape the project on hand. Otherwise put, the model gives self-regard a filtering or policing role in relation to regular, culturally framed considerations. Those considerations will hold sway in ordinary contexts but only so far as the behavior produced in those contexts by those considerations satisfies a certain individually relative threshold of self-regard.

But is the model of virtual self-regarding control, in particular the scenario of the alarm bells, a plausible one? The question divides in two. First, is there any arrangement under which we can imagine that such alarms are put in place? And second, if there is, can we plausibly maintain that those alarms will reliably serve to usher self-regarding deliberation into a controlling position in the generation of behavior?

The alarms required will have to be informational; they will have to be signals that this is the sort of situation where the agent's advantage may be compromised, if habit or whim is given its head. So are there signals available in ordinary contexts that might serve to communicate this message? Clearly, there are. Consider the fact that a decision situation is nonroutine; or that it is of a kind where the agent's fingers were already burned; or that it is a situation in which the agent's peers – others who might be expected to fare about as well – do generally better than the agent. Those facts are going to suggest that in such unusual or such changed circumstances the behavior produced by the culturally framed considerations may no longer be satisfactory in self-regarding terms. Or consider the fact that while the contexts remain stable, the behavior of the agent is changing, owing to a certain drift in the effect of the culturally framed considerations or owing to their being disturbed by other factors. Those facts too are going to suggest the possibility that the behavior is not suitably satisfactory. Given that facts like these can serve as signals that the agent's personal advantage may be in especial danger, it is reasonable to assume that the alarm bells required in the model of virtual regard are going to be available.

The other question is whether it is plausible, given the availability of signals of this kind, to postulate that the signals will generally tip agents into a self-regarding sort of deliberation: a sort of deliberation that is normally sidelined in favor of fidelity to the cultural frame. This issue is wholly an empirical matter but it is an issue on which the weight of received opinion speaks unambiguously. It has been common wisdom for at least two thousand years of thinking about politics that few are proof against temptation and few, therefore, are likely to ignore signals that their self-interest may be endangered. Human beings may be capable of reaching for the stars but, except for some romantic strands of thought, all the streams in the Western tradition of thinking suggest that if there is opportunity for an individual to further their own interests, then they can generally be relied upon, sooner or later, to exploit that opportunity: all power corrupts. The main theme of the tradition is summed up in the lesson that no one can be entrusted with the ring of Gyges that Plato discusses: the ring that renders a person invisible and that makes it possible for them to serve their own interests with impunity, at whatever cost to the interests of others.

These lines of thought give support, therefore, to the picture described above. They suggest that it is very plausible to think that even where people pay no actual attention to relatively self-regarding considerations, still those considerations have a certain presence and relevance to how people behave. They are virtually present, in the sense that if the behavior rings the alarm bells of self-interest – and there will be plenty of such bells to ring – the agent will give heed and will tend to let self-regarding considerations play a role in shaping what is done.[6]

The explanatory relevance of virtual self-regard

The question which now arises, however, is how far the merely virtual presence of self-regard is supposed to legitimate the economic explanatory enterprise: the enterprise of explaining various patterns in human affairs by reference to rational self-regard.[7] If self-regarding considerations have a purely virtual presence in ordinary human deliberation – for the moment we continue to make this extreme assumption – then they are not actual causes of anything that the agents do. They may be standby causes of certain patterns of behavior: they may be potential causes that would serve to support certain patterns, were they not supported by culturally framed deliberation. But it is not clear how anything is to be explained by reference to causes of such a would-be variety. After all, explanation is normally taken to uncover the factors operative in the production of the events and patterns to be explained; it is normally taken to require a reference to actual causal history (Lewis 1986, essay 22).

This difficulty can be underlined by considering the explananda that economic investigation is ordinarily taken to be concerned with in the nonmarket area. These are, first, the emergence of certain phenomena or patterns in the past and, second, their continuation into the present and future. The explanation of the emergence of any phenomenon – say, the emergence of a norm or institution – clearly requires a reference to the factors that were operative in bringing it into existence. And the explanation of the continuation of any phenomenon, equally clearly, requires a reference to the factors that keep it there.[8] So how could a reference to virtual self-regard serve to explain anything? In other words, how can our model of the common-cum-economic mind serve to make sense of the explanatory claims of economics, in particular of the economics of nonmarket behavior: of behavior that is motored by the perception of what situations demand, under relevant cultural frames, not by considerations of self-regard?

The answer, I suggest, is that even in the unlikely event that self-regard plays no role in explaining the emergence or continuation of a pattern of behavior – we will return to that assumption in the concluding section – still it can be of great utility in explaining a third explanandum: the resilience of that pattern of behavior under possible disturbance or drift.

Imagine a little set-up in which a ball rolls along a straight line – this, say, under Newton's laws of motion – but where there are little posts on either side that are designed to protect it from the influence of various possible but nonactualized forces that might cause it to change course; they are able to damp incoming forces and if such forces still have an effect – or if the ball is subject to random drift – they are capable of restoring the ball to its original path. The posts on either side are virtual or standby causes of the ball's rolling on the straight line, not factors that have an actual effect. So can they serve any explanatory purpose? Well, they cannot explain the emergence or the continuation of the straight course of the rolling ball. But they can explain the fact – and, of course, it is a fact – that not only does the ball roll on a straight line in the actual set-up, it sticks to more or less that straight line under the various possible contingencies where disturbance or drift appears. They explain the fact, in other words, that the straight rolling is not something fragile, not something vulnerable to every turn of the wind, but rather a resilient pattern: a pattern that is robust under various contingencies and that can be relied upon to persist.

The resilience explained in this toy example may be a matter of independent experience, as when I discover by induction – and without understanding why – that the ball does keep to the straight line. But equally the resilience may become salient only on recognizing the explanatory power of the posts: this, in the way in which the laws that a theory explains may become salient only in the light of the explanatory theory itself. It does not matter which scenario obtains. In either case the simple fact is that despite their merely standby status, the posts serve to resolve an important matter of explanation. They explain, not why the pattern emerged at a certain time, nor why it continues across a certain range of times, but why it continues across a certain range of contingencies: why it is modally as distinct from temporally persistent.

The lesson of our little analogy should be clear. As a reference to the virtually efficacious posts explains the resilience with which the ball rolls on a straight line, so a reference to a merely virtual form of self-regard may explain the resilience with which people maintain certain patterns of behavior. Imagine a given pattern of human behavior whose continuation is actually explained by the cultural framing under which people view the relevant situations and by their habit of responding to that framing. Suppose that that pattern of behavior has the modal property of being extremely robust under various contingencies: say, under the contingency that some individuals peel away and offer an example of an alternative pattern. The factors that explain its actually continuing may not explain this robustness or resilience; there may be no reason, so far as they go, why the example of mutant individuals should not display a new way of viewing the situation, for example, or should not undermine the effects of inertia. So how to explain the resilience of the pattern? Well, one possible explanation would be that as the contingencies envisaged produce a different pattern of behavior, the alarm bells of self-interest ring and the self-regarding deliberation that they prompt leads most of the mutants and would-be mutants back towards the original pattern.

I said earlier that in all likelihood the thresholds at which people's alarm bells ring, and they begin to think in self-regarding terms, may vary from individual to individual. This means in turn that a pattern of behavior may be very resilient in some individuals, less resilient in others, and that the individual-level explanations of resilience may not have the same force; they may not support different predictions for different individuals. But this variation, of course, need not affect aggregate-level explanation. While allowing for individual differences in self-regard thresholds, for example, we may be confident that across the population as a whole a certain general pattern of behavior enjoys resilience in relation to a certain degree of drift or disturbance in the producing causes; people's thresholds may generally be low enough to ensure that self-regard will kick in and stablize the pattern.

The analogy with the rolling ball serves to show how in principle the model of virtual self-regard may leave room for the economic explanation, at the level of individual or aggregate, of behavior that is not actively generated by considerations of self-regard. But it may be useful to illustrate the lesson more concretely.

David Lewis' (1969) work on convention is often taken as a first-rate example of how economic explanation can do well in making sense of a phenomenon outside the traditional economic domain of the market. He invokes the fact that conventions often serve to resolve certain problems of coordination in explanation of such conventions; thus the convention of driving on the right (or the left) serves to resolve the coordination problem faced by drivers as they approach one another. But what is supposed to be explained by Lewis' narrative?

Lewis is clearly not offering a historical story about the emergence of conventions. And, equally clearly, he is not telling a story about the factors that actually keep the conventions in place; he freely admits that people may not be aware of the coordination problem solved by conventional behavior and may stick to that behavior for any of a variety of reasons: reasons of inertia, perhaps, or reasons of principle or ideology that may have grown up around the convention in question.

The best clue to Lewis' explanatory intentions comes in a remark from a later article when he considers the significance of the fact that actually conventional behavior is mostly produced by blind habit: "An action may be rational, *and may be explained by the agent's beliefs and desires*, even though that action was done by habit, and the agent gave no thought to the beliefs or desires which were his reasons for action. If that habit ever ceased to serve the agent's desires according to his beliefs, it would at once be overridden and corrected by conscious reasoning" (Lewis 1983, 181, emphasis mine). This remark gives support to the view that what Lewis is explaining about convention, by his own lights, is not emergence or continuance but *resilience*. He implies that the servicing of the agent's – as it happens, self-regarding – desires is not the actual cause of the conventional behavior but a standby cause: a cause that would take the place of a habit that failed to produce the required behavior in circumstances where that behavior continued to be what self-interest required. And if the servicing of self-regard is a standby cause of this kind, then what it is best designed to explain is the resilience, where there is resilience, of the conventional behavior.

But it is not only the Lewis explanation of conventional behavior that lends itself to this gloss. Can we explain American slave-holding by reference to economic interests (Fogel and Engerman 1974, 4), when slave-holders articulated their duties, and conducted their business in terms of a more or less religious ideology? Yes, to the extent that we can explain why slave-holding was a very resilient institution up to the time of the civil war; we can explain why the various mutants and emancipationists never did more than cause a temporary crisis. Can we explain the failure of people to oppose most oppressive states as a product of free-rider reasoning (North 1981, 31–32), when it is granted that they generally used other considerations to justify their acquiescence? Yes, so far as the free-riding variety of self-regarding reasoning would have been there to support nonaction, to make nonaction resilient, in any situation where the other, actual reasons failed to do so and alarms bells rang. Can we invoke considerations of social acceptance to explain people's abiding by certain norms, as I have tried to do elsewhere (Pettit 1990), when I freely grant that it is considerations of a much less prudential kind that keep most people faithful to such norms? Yes, we certainly can. Self-regarding considerations of social acceptance can ensure that normative fidelity is robust or resilient if they come into play whenever someone begins to deviate, or contemplate deviation, and if they serve in such cases to restore or reinforce compliance.

The upshot will be clear. We can make good sense of economic explanation, even explanation of non-market behavior, in terms of the model of virtual self-regard whereby the economic mind is reconciled with the common mind. That model recommends itself, then, on at least two grounds. It shows that the assumptions which economists make about the human mind, in particular about human motivation, can be rendered consistent with the assumptions of commonplace, everyday thinking. And it shows that so interpreted, the assumptions motivate a promising and indeed developing program for economic explanation: and explanation, not just in the traditional areas of market behavior, but across the social world more generally.

4 The solution with functionalist explanation

The model of virtual selection

But if we can have recourse in the rational-choice case to the notion of a virtual mechanism of self-regard – a mechanism that may not operate under actual circumstances but that would operate under relevant counterfactual conditions – then we can equally well help ourselves in the functionalist case to the notion of a virtual mechanism of selection. The idea would be this. Maybe there has not been any historical selection of a given type of institution for the fact that its instances have a certain beneficial effect. But still it might be worth noting that were the type of institution in question to be in danger of disappearing – say, under disturbance or drift – then a selectional mechanism would be activated that would preserve it against that danger. The institution is not the product of actual selection, so it may be assumed – again, this is the worst-case assumption from our point of view – but it is subject to virtual selection: it would come to be selected in any of a variety of crises that put it under pressure.

The idea here is familiar from biology and extends readily to social science. Suppose we say that a certain trait is adaptive or that the gene responsible for the trait increases the inclusive fitness of the bearer in a certain environment: roughly, it increases the propensity of the bearer to replicate its genes.[9] Just saying that a trait is adaptive does not amount to saying that it has actually been selected for in a historical process. After all, a trait might be adaptive or a trait might come to be adaptive owing to a change in the environment, without ever having played a role in causing its bearers to be selected. What has to be true if a trait is adaptive is that were it to be put under pressure – as it will be, of course, under ordinary evolutionary conditions – then it would cause its bearers to be selected: they would stand a better chance of replicating their genes than relevant competitors. Adaptiveness goes with being virtually, if not actually, favoured by selectional processes (cf. Bigelow and Pargetter 1987).

It is easy to imagine virtual selection at work in the social as well as the natural world. Imagine that golf clubs have emerged purely as a matter of contingency and chance: imagine that their popularity and spread has been due entirely to the brute fact that people enjoy swinging strangely designed clubs at a solid little ball and seeing how far and how accurately they can hit it. This is to suppose that golf clubs have not actually been selected for in anything like a history of competition with other institutions. Consistently with the absence of any such historical selection, however, what might well be the case is that golf clubs have certain effects – certain functional effects – such that were they to come under any of a variety of pressures, then the fact of having those effects would ensure that they survived the pressure. And if that were the case then it would be natural to say that though not the beneficiaries of actual selection, golf clubs do enjoy the favor of a virtual process of selection.

The story is not outlandish. For golf clubs do have certain effects that are functional from the point of view of members. They are expensive to run and so generally exclusive of all but the well-to-do. They are accessible from a city base. And they enable the well-to-do in any city or town to make useful business and professional contacts. What better way to establish a business or professional relationship than in the course of a relaxed round of golf? It is plausible, then, that were golf clubs to come under various pressures – were the cost of maintaining them and the cost of membership to rise, for example – still they might be expected to survive; we might not find people leaving the clubs in the numbers that such pressures would normally predict. The members of the clubs would be forced to reconsider their membership in the event of this sort of pressure but that very act of reconsideration would make the functionality of the club visible to them and would reinforce their loyalty, not undermine it. And were some members to leave then it would become clear to them, and to others, that they lost out in doing so.

As it is reasonable to postulate that people display a virtual, if not always an actual, self-regard, so this sort of example shows that it is quite plausible to think that social life is often characterized by virtual processes of selection. Among the institutions of the society, there are many that have functional effects. And while those effects may not give us ground for thinking that the institutions were actually selected for the effects, they may well give us ground for believing that the institutions would be selected under various counterfactual conditions. The institutions are not the beneficiaries of actual selection but they do benefit from virtual selection.

The explanatory relevance of virtual selection

We saw in the last section that where people are possessed of virtual self-regard, then that is enough to enable us to explain the resilience of various patterns of behavior and institutionalization by the fact that they rationally serve the self-regarding concerns of the agents involved. Thus we can explain on this basis the resilience of certain conventions, the resilience of political inaction during periods of repression, and the resilience of slave-holding in the ante-bellum south. And we can do so even in the event – the unlikely event – that the self-regard was never activated. The same explanatory lesson carries over to the present case.

The presence of a process of virtual selection enables us to explain the resilience of various behaviors and institutions by the fact that they have certain functional effects. Maybe we can not explain the historical emergence, or even the historical persistence, of golf clubs by reference to their functional effects for members; maybe there has not actually been any systematic selection of golf clubs for the fact of having such effects. But even in that surely unlikely case we can explain the resilience of golf clubs – as we may come to recognize that resilience in the first place – through identifying those functional effects. We can see that because of serving business and professional members in the way they do, golf clubs are fit to survive any of a variety of challenges; at least for the forseeable future, they are here to stay. The possibility can also be illustrated with some of the more traditional examples mentioned in the last section. Perhaps rituals emerged and survive in certain societies, or common ideas materialized and established themselves, for the most contingent of reasons. Still it may be that they are resilient by virtue of serving social solidarity or communication, since anyone inclined to give up on them would suffer an associated loss and would be drawn back in. Thus it may be possible to save the Durkheimian stories in question. And a similar analysis goes for the claim by Radcliffe-Brown, for it may well be that peace-making ceremonies are resilient to the extent that they mend the feelings of hostile parties for one another and that their resilience can be explained by how they function in that respect. Perhaps individuals in conflict would miss the ceremonies in the event of their having gone into decline and would seek recourse to them afresh. Or perhaps those in power in the society would see the loss associated with the decline and would insist on their restoration.

What of the example from sociology in which stratification is explained by its effect in securing high rewards for socially important but otherwise unattractive positions? This is more problematic, since everyone might notice the loss under widespread defection from stratification – assuming there is a loss – but there would seem to be a collective action predicament blocking them from individually doing anything about it. Even assuming the functionality of stratification, then, invoking that functionality will work as an explanation of the resilience of stratification only if there is some centralized agency like the government which we can expect to restore stratification under any pressures that lead to its temporary decline. Is it plausible to think that government will be disposed to do this? We need not offer a firm judgment. If it is plausible, then the functional explanation offered is a plausible account of the resilience of stratification; if it is not plausible, then the account fails.

Phenomena may be resilient so far as departures would activate rational-choice calculations and tend to inhibit or reverse those initiatives. But equally, so we now see, phenomena may be resilient so far as departures would activate a concern for certain functional effects and would tend in a similar fashion to lead to inhibition or reversal.

The sort of salvation that I am holding out for functionalist theory fits well, we should notice, with the tradition of functionalism in social science. Under the salvation offered to functionalists, the explanation they seek is the sort that would identify and put aside the features that may be expected to come and go in social life and that would catalog the more or less necessary features that the society or culture displays: those that are resilient and may be expected to survive a variety of contingencies and crises. The tradition of thinking associated with the likes of Durkheim in the nineteenth century and Parsons in the twentieth is shot through with the desire to separate out in this way the necessary from the contingent, the reliable from the ephemeral. The idea in every case is to look for the core features of a society and to distinguish them from the marginal and peripheral. Functionalist method is cast throughout the tradition as a means of providing "a basis – albeit an assumptive basis – for sorting out 'important' from unimportant social processes" (Turner and Maryanski 1979, 135).

It is also worth noticing, in passing, that when Cohen (1977) classifies Marx as a functionalist, the account that he gives would make good sense within the scheme of salvation on offer here. For Cohen Marx is committed to there being "consequence laws" which assert that various institutions are supported in existence by the fact of having certain consequences. If what we mean by those institutions being supported in existence is that they are resilient, then there need be no problem about how certain consequence laws may obtain. A consequence law will obtain precisely when the consequence is the sort of functional effect that is going to confer resilience on anything that systematically generates it.

5 A general perspective

The upshot of all this is that rational-choice and functionalist explanation have much more in common than may have been realized by proponents of either and, indeed, that the viability of each sort of explanation is secured only on a basis that is also likely to secure the viability of the other. Even if they do not enable us to explain the emergence or continuation of the behaviors and institutions they address, still both forms of theory can do well in explaining the resilience or stability of those social patterns. I turn in this final section to five general observations about the sort of explanation involved in the two theories and about their relationship.

First observation

The first thing I want to notice about the style of explanation in question is that it is not an esoteric form of accounting for how things are. Resilience explanation is illustrated by the staple of explanation in economics, biology, and even social science: the sort that invokes the notion – itself capable of many explications – of a *stable equilibrium*.

Equilibrium explanation does not show how a pattern emerged or why it is present but demonstrates that the pattern is more or less inevitable, at least in a certain context, by pointing out that any ways in which it is liable to be disturbed would lead to correction. An example is Fisher's explanation of the 1:1 sex ratio in many species (Sober 1983). Fisher's idea was that if a population ever departs from equal numbers of males and females, then there will be a reproductive advantage favoring parents who overproduce the minority sex and the 1:1 ratio will tend to be restored. Such an equilibrium explanation does not offer a distinctive way of explaining things – a distinctive *explanans* – but rather a way of explaining a distinctive *explanandum*. That the sex ratio is in stable equilibrium, or that any pattern represents such an equilibrium, is a way of saying that it enjoys a particularly high degree of resilience. Being in stable equilibrium, at least for a given context, is a limit case of being resilient.

When our rational-choice stories represent certain conventions, or patterns of political inaction, or forms of ownership, as resilient then they depict them, if not as stable equilibria, at least as possessed of the stability associated with many equilibria. And when our functionalist narratives display the functionality and fitness – the propensity to survive – of this or that institution, then they do much the same thing. Resilence explanations are not marginal forms of theoretical endeavor, then; they belong firmly in the mainstream of social science. They enable us to see that certain patterns of behavior and institutionalization are equilibrium patterns that people have learned or chanced upon and that being equilibrium patterns we can expect them to be proof against a variety of pressures.

Second observation

A second comment I want to make about the resilience explanation, however, goes in a different direction. This is that wherever we have a convincing explanation for the resilience of a certain behavior or institution, then we may often reasonably think that the explanation probably serves to make sense also of the survival of that pattern under past pressures. Once we notice that a convention is such that it would survive the reflections of the self-interested, calculating agent – that it is more or less proof against the test of such reflection – then we may well conjecture that this fact will probably have played a role in the past in ensuring the survival and persistence of the convention. And once we notice that an institution like a golf club has functional effects that make it similarly proof against various threats to its existence, then we may well conjecture that this functionality may have played a role in past times in securing the continuation of the institution. The lesson is that if we find resilience explanations, we may often be directed also to factors that explain the persistence of the patterns in question: not their day-to-day continuation but their past survival in the presence of specific dangers.

Third observation

A third observation bears also on another variety of explanation besides the explanation of resilience. It imposes itself on us when we ask whether the resources of resilience explanation, rational-choice or functional, also provide us with resources for explaining the nonresilience of certain patterns.

Suppose that the self-interested rationality, or the social functionality, are grounds for finding suitable patterns of behavior resilient. Does it follow that patterns of behavior that are neither rational nor functional in these senses will be nonresilient or fragile? Strictly no, it does not follow. For suppose that there are alternative patterns of behavior in some circumstances, such that they score equally well in terms of rationality and functionality, or do not engage with rationality or functionality. It may be that one such pattern will be more resilient than others so far as it engages with a virtual controller on a par with the mechanisms we have discussed here. It may be, for example, that the moral justifiability of one such pattern of behavior – and the unjustifiability of alternatives – will make it more resilient than the other.

We do not have to make any assumptions against the possibility of such a further source of resilience, except so far as it conflicts with the sources discussed here. We may think that the sort of controller envisaged will sometimes overdetermine the resilience of behavior that is already explained in rational-choice or social-functional terms. But we will have to think that the rational-choice and the social-functional mechanisms are the more powerful and that in cases of conflict that they will generally prevail. Otherwise there would seem to be no reason for singling them out and according them importance.

Fourth observation

But a question now arises about the relationship between rational-choice and functional explanation. While I may seem to have saved functionalist explanation by recourse to the same schema whereby rational-choice explanation is made safe, does not my account mean in practice that functionalist explanation is a variety of rational-choice explanation? Is that not indeed why there seems to be little cause to consider the possibility of the two sources of resilience coming apart? Take those counterfactual conditions that put a functional behavior or institution in danger, that thereby make the functional effects of the pattern salient to those involved and that generate fidelity to the pattern, as a result of that salience, among the agents involved. Can we not see these as nothing more or less than conditions where the alarm bells go off and where the fact that the behavior or institution presents itself, perhaps for the first time, as satisfying in self-regarding terms ensures that the agents will act to perserve it? And in that case, does the functional explanation not come across as just a special kind of rational-choice explanation? If a pattern is resilient as a result of its functional effects, so the line goes, it will be resilient for its satisfying the self-regarding concerns of relevant agents.

I am happy to admit that many functional explanations may prove to be rational-choice explanations of this kind, for they will still constitute an interesting category, by virtue of what distinguishes them from other rational-choice explanations: the focus on aggregate functional effects. But as a matter of fact functional explanations need not all be instances of rational-choice explanations, at least not in any straightforward sense. They may not conflict with rational-choice explanations in the sense of postulating patterns of intentional behavior that confound self-interest. But the factors that ensure the availability of the explanation may involve many dispositions in relevant agents over and beyond the self-regarding disposition invoked in rational-choice explanation.

Suppose that the following laws obtain in socio-political life, as I think they may do:

(1) Any outrageous crime will be given publicity by the media in a society like ours

(2) The public will react with outrage to such publicity

(3) The politicians will be obliged, on pain of reducing their chance of re-election, to register and endorse that outrage in the media

(4) The only way they can effectively do this in the television soundbite, or the newspaper headline, is by calling for, or promising, harsher penalties for the sort of crime in question

(5) If penalties for any category of crime are reduced then, however beneficial the reduction in overall crime rates, there will still be some outrageous offence committed, sooner or later, in that category.

Where such laws or regularities obtain, then we can say that a regime of harsh criminal penalties is functional in placating the outrage of the public in regard to crime. Suppose that such a regime is in place, no matter for whatever reasons. Let the regime be put in danger, say because some politicians come to office who have been persuaded by criminological findings that harsh sentencing is counterproductive. The fact that no more lenient regime will serve the function of placating public outrage as effectively as the existing one means, under our assumptions, that any attempt to introduce such a regime will fail; the society will return, sooner or later, to the harsher dispensation. Such a functional explanation conforms to the schema we sketched but it is not a straightforward rational-choice explanation. Perhaps the politicians respond rationally and self-regardingly in calling for harsher penalties. But the people do not respond particularly rationally when they feel and voice outrage. The functional explanation obtains in virtue of a variety of dispositions in relevant agents, some rational, some not.

Fifth observation

One final observation. I have argued that both functionalist explanation and rational-choice explanation have to make do, and can make do, with "empty black boxes." In many cases where such explanation is offered, there is no evidence of an actual process of functional selection or an actual process of rational choice. But while it is true that no actual process of selection or choice materializes in the "black box" assumed, what is the case under my story is that the box contains a mechanism that is set to go into action in the event of certain conditions being satisfied.

This means that though the "black boxes" are empty in one sense, they are not empty in another. Let the behavior or institution satisfy the self-interest of agents, and it will be actively chosen in the event that the alarm bells ring and the relevant agents go into self-regarding mode. Let it have certain functional effects, and it will be actively selected in the event of coming under this or that sort of challenge. The explanation of resilience that is involved in these cases does not require active process. But neither does it require any special magic.

To conclude, then. If we construct an image of social science in which rational choice and functional selection play the sorts of role envisaged here, then the emerging picture is distinctive but intuitive. We are invited to think that many patterns of human behavior are the product of the inventive, more or less irrepressible urge of our species to try out now this, now that, variety of action and interaction. Life is a kaleidoscope in which we take the motifs of the past and play around with them, searching out new words and tales, new modes of dress and dance, new forms of religious ceremonial, new varieties of technological accommodation, and so on. We are makers and creatures of fashion. We are exemplars of *homo ludens:* the playful human.

But while we are invited to recognize that in these respects life is an ever-changing kaleidoscope, our picture also introduces the idea that in any society, for any epoch, that there are some enduring and stable motifs. They may be ushered into being on the same spontaneous basis as all other forms of innovation and coordination but, once introduced, they stick. Within the parameters of the society or epoch in question, they serve the rational interests of individuals, or they sustain socially important functions, in a way that ensures their relative stability; it makes them more or less proof against the disturbance and drift that otherwise dominates the social kaleidoscope.

Notes

My thanks to those at the conference on "Fact and Fiction in Economics" at the Erasmus University, Rotterdam, November 14–45, 1997, for their helpful comments on an earlier draft of this chapter. And my thanks also to those who offered helpful comments when the paper was presented at the Columbia University Philosophy of Science Colloquium and at a discussion group in New York University, at the Jowett Society in Oxford, and at a seminar in Northwestern University. The chapter is an attempt to connect the strands of argument developed separately in Pettit (1995, 1996), and draws heavily on those articles. It is reprinted from the *Journal of Economic Methodology*, 7, 33–57 (2000), with the permission of the editors.
1. This reading of functional explanation in biology is not endorsed by everyone, of course (Cummins 1975). But it is the majority construal and it is the construal that is assumed in the argument against functionalist theory. Nor is our reading of functional

explanation entirely unambiguous: to explain why a trait is found in a certain sort of organism, to use my terminology, may be to explain why that sort of organism has it or why the sort of organism in existence is one with that trait (Sober 1984, 147–148). I try to abstract here from that issue.

2. Notice that this conception of self-interest is consistent with the recognition of a capacity on the part of ordinary agents to identify with entities beyond themselves. See Pettit (1997, chapter 8).

3. In fairness, however, I should note that this search for incentive-compatibility could be motivated – reasonably or not – by the belief that however other-regarding most people are, policies should always be designed to be proof against more self-regarding "knaves." See Brennan and Buchanan (1981).

4. Some might say that under the assumption that human beings are rational centers of predominantly self-regarding concern – this, in a Bayesian sense – we ought to expect that they would be, not only self-concerned, but also calculating: we ought to expect that they would think in terms of the ledger of probabilities and utilities that figure in Bayesian decision theory. I do not go along with this. Bayesian decision theory says nothing on how agents manage to maximize expected utility; it makes no commitments on the style of deliberation that agents follow. See Pettit (1991).

5. This problem may be dismissed by some thinkers on the ground that the literature on conditional cooperation shows how economically rational individuals may cooperate out of purely self-regarding motives (Hardin 1982; Axelrod 1984; Taylor 1987; Pettit and Sugden 1989). But that would be a mistake. This literature shows that economically rational individuals may come to behave cooperatively, not that they will come to think and talk in a cooperative way.

6. The picture of virtual self-regard may be modified by being made subject to certain boundary conditions. It might be held, for example, that the picture does not apply universally, only under certain structural arrangements: say, that it does not apply in family life, only in relations of a more public character. For related ideas see Satz and Ferejohn (1994).

7. Apart from the problem that I go on to discuss, there is an issue as to how, noncircularly, the economist is to tell the level of threat to self-interest at which an agent's alarm bells ring. I cannot discuss this problem here but would just note that it is parallel to the problem of determining an agent's aspiration level under Simon's (1978) satisficing model.

8. I ignore the requirements of potential explanation – fact-defective or law-defective explanation – as that enterprise is discussed by Robert Nozick (1974). It may be interesting to know how something might have come about or might have continued to exist under a different history, or under a different regime of laws, but the interest in question is not that which motivates ordinary economic attempts at explanation.

9. I ignore here the fact that as the fitness of a trait is normally understood, it is a function not just of how it would enable bearers to cope with certain contingencies that are taken as biologically relevant – these will not be all possible contingencies, of course – but of how probable those contingencies are.

References

Alchian, A.A. (1950). Uncertainty, evolution and economic theory, *Journal of Political Economy*, 58, 211–221

Axelrod, Robert (1984). *The Evolution of Cooperation*. New York: Basic Books

Becker, Gary (1976). *The Economic Approach to Human Behavior*. Chicago: University of Chicago Press

Bigelow, John and Robert Pargetter (1987). Functions, *Journal of Philosophy*, 34, 181–196

Brennan, H.G. and J.M. Buchanan (1981). The normative purpose of economic "science:" rediscovery of an eighteenth century method, *International Review of Law and Economics*, 1, 155–166

Brennan, H.G. and Philip Pettit (1993). Hands invisible and intangible, *Synthesè*, 94, 191–225

Cohen, G.A. (1977). *Karl Marx's Theory of History*. Oxford: Oxford University Press

Cummins, Robert (1975). Functional analysis, *Journal of Philosophy*, 72, 741–765

Davis, Kingsley and W.E. Moore (1945). Some principles of stratification, *American Sociological Review*, 10, 242–247

Durkheim, Emile (1948). *The Elementary Forms of the Religious Life*. New York: Free Press

Eells, Elleny (1982). *Rational Decision and Causality*. Cambridge: Cambridge University Press

Elster, John (1979). *Ulysses and the Sirens*. Cambridge: Cambridge University Press

Fogel, R.W. and S.L. Engermann (1974). *Time on the Cross: The Economics of American Negro Slavery*. Boston: Little, Brown

Gauthier, David (1986). *Morals by Agreement*. Oxford: Oxford University Press

Hardin, Russell (1982). *Collective Action*. Baltimore: Johns Hopkins University Press

Hindess, Barry (1988). *Choice, Rationality and Social Theory*. London: Unwin Hyman

Lewis, David (1969). *Convention*. Cambridge, MA: MIT Press

(1983). *Philosophical Papers*, 1. New York: Oxford University Press

(1986). *Philosophical Papers*, 2. New York: Oxford University Press

Lukes, Steven (1973). *Emile Durkheim*. Harmondsworth: Penguin

Neander, Karen (1991a). Functions as selected effects the conceptual analysis defense, *Philosophy of Science*, 58, 168–184

(1991b). The teleological notion of "function," *Australasian Journal of Philosophy*, 69, 454–468

Nelson, R. and Sidney Winter (1982). *An Evolutionary Theory of Economic Change*. Cambridge, MA: Harvard University

North, Douglass (1981). *Structure and Change in Economic History*. New York: Norton

Nozick, Robert (1974). *Anarchy, State and Utopia*. New York: Basic Books

Pettit, Philip (1990). *Virtus Normativa* rational choice perspectives, *Ethics*, 100, 725–755

(1991). Decision theory and folk psychology, in Susan Hurley and Michael Bacharach (eds.), *Essays in the Foundations of Decision Theory*. Oxford: Blackwell, 147–175

(1993). *The Common Mind: An Essay on Psychology, Society and Politics*. New York: Oxford University Press; paperback ed., with new postscript (1996)

(1995). The virtual reality of homo oeconomicus, *Monist* 78, 308–329; expanded version in Uskali Mäki (ed.), *The Economic World View*, Cambridge: Cambridge University Press, 2001, 75–97

(1996). Functional explanation and virtual selection, *British Journal for the Philosophy of Science*, 45, 291–302

(1997). *Republicanism: A Theory of Freedom and Government*. Oxford: Oxford University Press

Pettit, Philip and Robert Sugden (1989). The backward induction paradox, *Journal of Philosophy*, 86, 169–182

Platts, Mark (1980). *Ways of Meaning*. London: Routledge

Radcliffe-Brown, A.R. (1948). *The Andaman Islanders*. Glencoe, IL: Free Press

Satz, Debra and John Ferejohn (1994). Rational choice and social theory, *Journal of Philosophy*, 91, 71–87

Schick, Frederic (1984). *Having Reasons: An Essay on Rationality and Sociality*. Princeton: Princeton University Press

Sen, Amartya (1982). *Choice, Welfare and Measurement*. Oxford: Blackwell

Simon, Herbert (1978). Rationality as process and as product of thought, *American Economic Review*, 68, 1–16

Sober, Elliott (1983). Equilibrium explanation, *Philosophical Studies,* 43, 201–210

(1984). *The Nature of Selection*. Cambridge, MA: MIT Press

Taylor, Michael (1987). *The Possibility of Cooperation*. Cambridge: Cambridge University Press

Turner, J.H. and A. Maryanski (1979). *Functionalism*. Menlo Park, CA: Benjamin/ Cummings Publishing Van Parijs, Philippe (1981). *Evolutionary Explanation in the Social Sciences*. London: Taristock

12 The reality of common cultures

Shaun P. Hargreaves Heap

1 Introduction

Uskali Mäki's brand of scientific realism is, in his words, "hermeneutically enlightened" (see Mäki 1990). This chapter is concerned with whether scientific realism can survive the embrace of hermeneutics. The potential cause for concern is easy to see. Once it is conceded that the social world comprises people who interpret their place in that world, it seems that the relation between theory and reality so changes that the very idea of "science" is liable to alter beyond recognition and even possibly disappear. In particular, when theories help structure people's interpretations, the theories help shape the reality of the social world rather than report on it. Thus what seems like a bit of "enlightenment" can quickly turn into the social construction of reality (i.e. the social destruction of Reality with a capital R); and from here it is but a familiar short step to a thoroughgoing relativism as "facts" spin into "fictions."

I argue here against this concern over the descent into relativism. This is not because I side with the claims of relativism; rather I argue that hermeneutics is not the first step on the slippery relativist slope (and so I aim to lend succour to Mäki). While the hermeneutic turn may loosen reality's potential grip on theory, reality remains a source of friction. At the least, any theory concerning an aspect of the social world must be consistent with the fact that people are interpretative. One cannot loosen reality's grip hermeneutically without at the same time accepting this constraint because both flow from the fact that the world comprises people who interpret their place in the world. This may seem like a weak constraint, but I argue with the aid of an illustration that it can prove a significant check on admissable theories. In particular, with some relatively minor thickening of the type of interpretative activity that people engage in, I suggest in the next section that this constraint rules out the usual versions of the rational-choice model found in economics.

This argument naturally raises a puzzle about the rational-choice model. How has it proved so successful in economics and elsewhere when, if one grants the earlier argument, it seems to violate a reality constraint? Or to put this slightly differently, does this success of the rational-choice model undermine the argument for the hermeneutic turn? I address this question in sections 3 and 4. To be specific, I maintain the value of the hermeneutic turn by arguing: (1) that the success of the rational-choice model depends on its close connection to a model of action that does pass the hermeneutic-reality constraint and so the evidence of success is not necessarily inconsistent with the hermeneutic presumption; (2) that the rational-choice model is rather less successful than is sometimes supposed and, in fact, the hermeneutic turn actually supplies the resources for filling the gaps in this account of action.

2   Interpretative agents and rational choice

The starting point for my argument is the observation that, on some occasions, people like to make sense of their world and their actions in it. Of course, people often simply act and think nothing more about it, but they also occasionally like to be able to give an account of their actions. This seems uncontroversial (to most people, and not just anthropologists). In addition, I assume that the people are interested in this account for more than forensic reasons. They are interested in how the account of their behavior reflects upon themselves. They do not just want to know why they did something, they also want to know whether the action reflects well or otherwise upon them. This is possibly rather more controversial, but unless one wishes to deny that people commonly have feelings of shame, guilt or just plain embarrassment, it seems difficult to escape the conclusion that our interpretations are as much evaluative as they are explanatory.[1]

People need a standard by which they can make these judgments about the worth of their actions and this is the key to the hermeneutic constraint on theories. My claim is that the standards are *shared* and encoded in the behavior of (some) others and that this has consequences for the kind of theories of action that are admissable. In other words, judgments of self-worth depend on what anthropologists refer to as a "common culture" and only certain theories of action can form the building block of a common culture.

The common-sense support for this claim comes from a variety of sources. For example, the management theorist Charles Handy (1997) argues that it is very difficult to tell how well one is doing with respect to any evaluative criteria unless one can compare one's performance with that of others (see Hampshire 1989, for a more philosophical version of the same point). Consider for instance a standard of behavior that might be applied in relation to a relatively simple activity like running: speed. Here it is plain that there is no useful absolute standard of speed by which one's performance can be judged. Of course, one can record that one ran at 10 miles per hour, but was this fast or slow? One can make such judgments only by using the behavior and evaluation of others in similar circumstances as a benchmark; and the same seems likely to apply for more complicated standards involving ideas of honor and morality which are frequently used by people to judge the worthiness of their actions.

The deeper reason for supposing that the standard must be external to the individual comes from the analogy between the attachment of meaning to actions and the attachment of meaning to words. Both depend on rules for interpretation. In the one case these are linguistic rules and in the other they are what anthropologists describe as cultural rules. The difficulty with having a purely personal set of cultural rules is akin to the difficulty with having a private language. It turns on the impossibility of constructing a set of rules for judging behavior that are exhaustive. The infinite scope for the individuation of circumstances undermines the project of constructing rules for the application of rules. As a result an individual always has scope with respect to how to interpret a purely private set of cultural rules. This is problematic because it fuels the suspicion that the interpretations are simply self-serving and there is little satisfaction to be gained in judging that one's actions are worthy if it turns out that the standards can always be manipulated to produce this conclusion. The only way to avoid this suspicion is for the interpretation of the rules to occur in a manner that is external to the individual using the rules: that is, in this instance, by reference to what others do when they attach particular meanings to actions. Or to put this argument slightly differently, it makes sense to talk of acting in accordance with a rule only when there is a clear sense of what action would transgress the rule. Otherwise any action will conform with the rule and the rule will lose all content. But the only way that one can allow for incorrect yet sincere applications of the rule is to have a standard that is external to oneself.

The source of the argument is, of course, Wittgenstein and although it is controversial when applied as the private language argument to *all* meaningful concepts, it seems much less controversial as an observation about *some* concepts.[2] Thus the burden of my argument is that interpretative agents rely (at least some of the time) on shared rules or standards for interpreting their behavior: that is, they depend on a common culture.

To see how this may impose constraints on the kind of theories of action that can be coherently maintained, consider the economists' rational-choice theory of action. This comes in two forms. It is behaviorist in spirit when presented purely axiomatically. There is no account of why people act here, they simply act in a way that satisfies the axioms (or they don't); and action is rational or it is not. But without an account of why action in conformity with the axioms is rational, this provides little scope for agents to develop interpretations of their actions.

To exclude the rational-choice model on these grounds, however, would be a cheap shot because there is a psychologically richer variant of the model:

one where actions are taken to satisfy best the agent's preferences. The scope for interpretation here looks at once more promising as the agent could in principle go beyond the mere fact of consistency in behavior to reflect on how actions contributed to various types of preference-satisfaction. Indeed the great virtue of the richer pyschological structure is that, in principle, it is amenable to graduated judgments. For instance it seems possible to be more or less good at selecting actions which satisfy preferences whereas the axiomatic version admits only two categories of action: the rational and the nonrational. As a result, the preference-satisfying interpretation appears much better placed for the formation of the kind of evaluative judgments that contribute to a sense of self-worth. However, while this version is the more promising hermeneutically, it could not actually be used by agents to evaluate their actions in the manner I have just described because it depends on a standard that is intrinsically private. The problem is that a person's preferences are not directly observable and so there can be no public judgment of how well a person satisfies their preferences.

Of course, there will be odd occasions when a person may appear to violate preference-satisfying behavior altogether. For instance, in the absence of direct knowledge about an individual's preferences one can exploit the axiomatic approach and notice that intransitive behavior is not consistent with being a preference-satisfier. But this is a limiting case and tells us nothing about how well a person has actually satisfied their preferences, as transitivity is merely a condition for interpreting choice as preference-satisfying. Or to express the problem in a different way, the completeness axiom can not be satisfied in practice as people never reveal choices between *all* pairs of options and so the observation of transitivity among a limited set of options can not rule out the possibility of instransitivity involving nonobserved options. Furthermore, even in the limiting case when people act intransitively by revealing, say, xPy, yPz, and zPx, there are two alternative interpretations to the one that the person has failed to act in a manner that could be deemed preference-satisfying. Their preferences could have changed between the first and the last couplet; or a careful individuation of circumstances could reveal that the last choice was zPx', where x' is a close relative of x. So even in the case of intransitive behavior, it will not be clear whether an individual has actually failed to act in a manner that best satisfies their preferences.[3]

To summarize, a person will not be able to derive a sense of self-worth from knowing that others share his or her judgment that he or she has satisfied their preferences well (even supposing there was agreement that satisfying preferences was a good thing to do) for the simple reason that for something to be a source of shared recognition it must be publicly observable. In this way, the evaluative form of the hermeneutic condition demonstrates some bite, at least, with respect to theory-selection. It precludes the economists' standard rational-choice theory. This conclusion, though, raises an obvious puzzle.

It would be difficult to deny the success of the rational-choice model. It has been both helpful in directly explaining individual behavior in a range of circumstances and it has been indirectly helpful as a building block in models of aggregate behavior. Experimental evidence certainly reveals violations of the model, but it also supplies much evidence of behavior that is consistent with the model. Likewise aggregate models in economics may not be perfect predictors, but they enjoy some success. The puzzle is how to reconcile this explanatory success with the argument that people could not use the theory interpretatively.

3   The puzzling success of the rational-choice model

One way of resolving this puzzle is to argue that people use a theory of action for hermeneutic reflection which differs from the theory that actually best describes their behavior. Although it would be foolish to deny that people employ a variety of pyschological ruses to overcome inconsistencies of one kind or another, it seems difficult to stretch this point here. Can one imagine any pyschological mechanism that could paper over such an evident inconsistency between theory and reality? The alternative, obvious way of resolving the puzzle would be to doubt whether people actually engage in hermeneutic reflection. This would mean forsaking Mäki's "hermeneutic enlightenment." And while this has the advantage of avoiding the complications regarding what to make of science under conditions of "hermeneutic enlightenment," it runs in the face of what seems an uncontestable fact. As I alluded in n. 1, feelings of guilt and shame may be in retreat these days, but few would deny the experience of embarrassment from time to time! And embarrassment is constituted by an evaluative interpretation.

A third alternative avoids these difficulties. It turns on the idea that there is a variant of the preference-satisfying model that could satisfy the publicity requirement. If the common culture valued something like wealth accumulation or consumption, then as wealth and consumption are publicly visible, an individual could attempt to maximize something like wealth or consumption and derive a sense of self-worth from this behavior. This would then resolve the puzzle in the sense that people could engage in hermeneutic reflection using this wealth (or some such) maximizing model. The success of the preference-satisfying model, in turn, could be explained through its close association to the actual model of wealth maximization (or some such) employed by agents.

Indeed this argument has been powerfully made by anthropologists like Ernest Gellner (1997) to explain the apparent relevance of the wealth-maximizing model:

Far from down-playing identity in human motivation, I would go further and say that it is far more fundamental and important than desire. Human beings as such seldom have aims or desires, over and above a certain very basic and coarse minimum: avoidance of pain, death, hunger, thirst. Over and above this, the aims they do have are corollaries of the need to play out a given cultural role ... The contrary idea – that people pursue isolable identifiable "aims" whose attainment constitutes or leads to contentment – is engendered by a very distinct social condition, one special culture, namely our own: in a mobile, occupationally unstable economy with a society without important ascribed ranks, people do indeed pursue "wealth," because it happens to be the main or only means of securing status and power. (1997, 86)

In Gellner's terms people generate "identity," that is a sense of self-worth, through the pursuit of status and this happens to be achieved in our society through the accumulation of wealth. Thus it is the common culture of "modern" Western societies that makes wealth something worth pursuing and this in turn gives a peculiar relevance to the economic cousin of this model, rational-choice theory. In support of this argument, it is worth considering the actual applications of the rational-choice model that are responsible for the reputation of success.

I conjecture that a close examination would reveal that the examples of success often work with a specification of preferences that amounts to wealth maximization or its like. For example in the modeling of many choice settings under uncertainty it is commonly assumed that an individual's utility is a function of wealth; likewise it is assumed (albeit often implicitly) that the individuals who own firms have interests that are best served by the maximization of profits. So the success that needs to be explained is often *not* the success of a general preference-satisfying model but a particular model of wealth maximization (or its like).

This line of argument might help unravel the puzzle, but it begs a question about the value of the hermeneutic turn. What is the gain from adopting the anthropologists' approach rather than the economists'? For a culture that is individualistic like ours, what is the point in seeing this individualism as a cultural product when the bottom line in both cases is the fact that we are individualistic maximizers? Indeed the economic approach looks the more compact and the more flattering version of the two hypotheses in the case of wealthy societies since it avoids turning people into cultural dopes (even if it is slightly misleading in the preference-satisfying version).

In the remainder of this section, I want to sketch a couple of arguments for preferring the anthropological perspective to that of the economist in the case of wealthy societies. The key to the argument in favour of anthropology on this point is the fact that wealthy societies are not culturally homogeneous. Wealth or the ability to consume is not the only index for judgments of self-worth. There are others. For instance, people derive a sense of self-worth sometimes from acting in a manner that accords with what is a shared sense of "fairness," equally some people find that an identity which is "honorable" is a source of self-worth, and so on. These impulses may not be what is first associated with market capitalism, but nevertheless they survive in modern capitalist societies. The anthropologist Mary Douglas (1977, 292–293) makes this case most tellingly when discussing the activity of consumption:

> Consumption decisions are a vital source of culture . . . The shopper comes home with a selection of purchases. There are some things that will be kept for the household, some allocated to particular members of the family or, put aside for the children. Other things have been brought for the special pleasure of future guests . . . These sort of choices are the mainspring of culture . . . In the end, the consumer's choices should be seen as moral judgements about everything: about what a man is, about what a woman is, how a man ought to treat his aged parents, how much of a start he ought to give his children, how he himself expects to grow old . . . Let us forget that commodities are good for eating and clothing and shelter, and try instead the idea that commodities are good for thinking.

Thus, the anthropologists' approach differs from the economists' by being alert to the possibility of multiple cultural sources of worth in a way that the economists' tendency to naturalize individual wealth maximization is not; and this is a telling advantage when these other aspects of common culture contribute to economic behavior. I develop this point in the next section. For now it leads directly to the second reason for preferring the anthropological model.

In a society with various possible indices of self-worth (that is, plural sources of identity to use Gellner's way of putting it), it is possible to conceive of individuality in a rather different and plausibly more flattering way than the economic one. The economic version appears the more flattering at first (to individualist societies) because it seems to put the individual in charge of him or herself when the anthropological version makes the individual a cultural dope. However, the economic view does not provide an especially flattering view of the individual. The individual may be untainted by the hint of cultural determination but the individual is more computer than flesh and blood. In comparison, there is scope for an active sense of individuality in the anthropological world once it is recognized that society is not culturally homogeneous. An individual must position herself within the matrix of plural cultures. Cultural roles often conflict and so the individual must decide which is to take precedence. In this way she is involved in the choice of ends to pursue and not just the means to a given set of ends.

4   The limited success of rational choice

The other element in the reconciliation that preserves the hermeneutic side of the argument comes from a further consideration of the troubling "success" of the rational-choice model. I have already suggested that much of this success is actually consistent with the hermeneutic turn because it depends on some publicly observable objective like wealth or consumption maximization. In this section, I want to take this argument a stage further by suggesting that economics, far from being a success, is actually in many respects a failure.

In suggesting this I want to avoid sounding like the person who has been parading up and down Oxford Street for the last thirty years with a sandwich board proclaiming that "the end of the world is nigh." The danger is obvious since cries about the "crisis in economics" have also been heard only too regularly over the last thirty years. Towards this end, I think that a few signs of, rather than some clear demonstration of, a crisis-inducing failure is all that I need to destabilize the rational-choice end of the argument from this angle. (And I took some comfort at the time of writing from the fact that I appeared to be in the "good" company of the *Economist* magazine on this point: see its cover and leading article on the failure of economics in the issue of September 23, 1997.)

The clearest sign that the rational-choice model has failed comes from its application in strategic-choice settings. There are two key failures here for the purposes of my argument. In games with multiple Nash equilibria there is no well-accepted theory of equilibrium selection. This is particularly serious with respect to coordination and battle of the sexes games because they are ubiquitous in economic life. For instance, coordination games are at the heart of any economic interaction where the benefits associated with any action depend on the number of people within some group that also take this action. Technology choice is an obvious case in point, as are the many consumption decisions which have fashionable or bandwagon characteristics. Likewise the battle of the sexes game is at the heart of any market exchange where there is an element of bargaining.

The second failure in game theory is with respect to the prisoner's dilemma and here it is in a sense the opposite of the earlier one. Game theory is clear about what rational-choice individuals should do in these circumstances. The embarrassment is the frequent observation that they do not behave in this way: instead of defecting they frequently play the cooperative strategy.

To tie these failures back to the argument for "hermeneutic enlightenment," I contend that these failures are directly related to the inability to see that there are other cultural norms in addition to wealth maximization (or some variant of this). In other words, the appreciation of the hermeneutic turn, in effect, supplies the resources to fill these gaps in the rational-choice model. The potential here will be evident in the case of equilibrium selection in games with multiple equilibria as cultural norms give agents, so to speak, further reasons for action to those of pure wealth maximization and so they may help an agent when the logic of wealth maximization is indeterminate. Likewise, it is possible in prisoner's dilemma games that these further reasons may trump the reason supplied by wealth maximization and so explain the cooperative play.

And indeed this argument has been explicitly made in the growing literature that emphasizes the cultural sources of trust in economic relationships (e.g. Coleman 1988; Etzioni 1989; Casson 1991; Hargreaves Heap 1993; Fukuyama 1995).

These explanatory shortcomings of the rational-choice model can also feed through to create weaknesses in the prescriptions based on that model. The point here is that a prescription based on a simple rational-choice explanation of behavior will prove accurate only when the prescription has no effect on the influence of other cultural norms on behavior (for reasons that are analogous to the Lucas critique, see Frey 1992). The potential for prescriptive failure therefore depends on the relation between wealth-maximizing norms and the other cultural norms. I have argued in Hargreaves Heap (1989) that a competitive relationship exists between different norms in the sense that a norm depends for its existence on instantiations and an action can instantiate a norm only when it is clear that the action follows from that norm and not some other. Otherwise the message in an action becomes mixed, so as to speak, and instantiation does not occur.[4] As a result, and this connects with the earlier argument, in societies where wealth-maximizing norms predominate, nonwealth-maximizing norms are most likely to survive in two sets of circumstances: either where action is underdetermined by the logic of wealth maximization (as in the case of coordination and battle of the sexes games) or where the logic of wealth-maximizing calculation is clear, as in the prisoner's dilemma and where nonwealth-maximizing behavior is capable of an interpretation as something other than "irrational" behavior (again as in the prisoner's dilemma).

To see the potential for prescriptive failure under such an interactive relationship, consider an exaggerated version of what has happened in British universities with the drive towards accountability. British academics used to have a rather open-ended contract that gave them plenty of scope to "goof-off" under the guise of "doing research." I think it is no secret that some faculty did just that. Nevertheless large numbers conducted research under the influence of a collegiate academic norm that valued the pursuit of knowledge or understanding through teaching and research. An exclusively rational-choice understanding of this situation would not see the academic norm, it would just see the scope for "goofing-off" and some evidence of it and so would naturally recommend some tightening of the incentives towards research. Broadly speaking, this has been the consequence of the selective allocation of research funds using the research-assessment exercise. In effect, it represents the introduction of a payments-by-result system at the level of the university's budget and like many such payment systems it has had some quite perverse effects.

First, the actual benefits to research are likely to be less than the rational-choice-inspired policy-maker might have imagined because he or she will have overlooked the influence of the academic norm on research activity among those who subscribed to the norm. (As a matter of fact I doubt that the value of research actually increased sufficiently to offset the administrative costs of monitoring research in this way because while there is evidence that the process has increased research efforts quantitatively, it seems also to have detracted from the economic value of these efforts.) Secondly, "researching actively" is now less likely to instantiate the academic norm as it is an action that is more likely to be undertaken pragmatically for career reasons than was the case before the introduction of the research-assessment process. This undermining of the collegial academic norm has had further knock-on effects for behavior in nonresearch aspects of academic life as the norm has historically been important in guiding behavior in teaching and administration as well as research. In fact, new monitoring and reward systems have had to be introduced with respect to these activities as well. Naturally there is scope for argument over whether these other areas were also suffering from agency problems, with the result that the new monitoring system has also brought benefits. The point, however, is that a disregard for the role of academic norms leads to an assessment of policies where the benefits are exaggerated and the costs are understated.

5   Conclusion

One of the consequences of the hermeneutic turn is that it increases the potential scope of philosophical argument in the activity of social science. Philosophical reflection becomes not only relevant to the methodology of social science, it also plausibly contributes to a direct understanding of the reality of the social world. It makes sense to ask what philosophy can tell us about the natural scientists' approach to understanding subatomic particles, but it makes *no* sense to ask what philosophy can tell us directly about the nature of subatomic particles. In contrast, once it is accepted that, unlike subatomic particles, humans are interpretative agents, it can make sense to draw on philosophical arguments, for instance concerning the conditions under which humans can attach meaning to their use of words, to help build a picture of the nature of the social world.

The particular argument in the philosophy of language comes from Wittgenstein and it concerns the need for a standard in language usage that is external to an individual. I have used a variant of this argument that has individuals deriving a sense of self-worth, at least in significant part, from judging their actions with respect to a *shared* standard of behavior that comprises what anthropologists and sociologists refer to as those individuals' common culture. This sharing condition places constraints on the kind of theories of action that can be used by such interpretative agents. For instance, it precludes the standard rational choice model used in economics. Thus, while a bit of "hermeneutic enlightenment" gives new freedoms for theory in relation to reality, it need not presage a wholesale collapse into relativism. Indeed, it is not just that the charge of relativism does not stick. If some of the points in the last section are accepted, then the "hermeneutic enlightenment" offers a route for improving the explanatory and prescriptive power of economic theories; and what kind of realist could argue with that!

Notes

This chapter was prepared for the conference "Fact or Fiction: Perspectives on Realism and Economics" as the Erasmus University, Amsterdam, November 14–15, 1997.
1. To judge from both the political hustings and postmodern argument, feelings of shame and guilt are in retreat these days, but even postmodern argument typically admits that we still feel embarrassment!
2. See for instance, the philosopher Thomas Nagel (1986), who I draw on in this context because he is committed to Realism, when he makes the following comment:

> To mean anything in application to oneself in the first person . . . [concepts] must also be applicable to oneself and others on circumstantial and behavioural grounds that are not just privately available. This he [Wittgenstein] took to be a consequence of a general condition of publicity that must be met by all concepts, which in turn derives from a condition that must be met by any rule of whatever kind: that there must be an objective distinction between following it and breaking it, which can be made only if it is possible to compare one's own practice with that of one's community.
>
>   I am doubtful about the final "only" . . . But I do not wish to deny that the experiential concepts we use . . . more or less fit the pattern Wittgenstein describes. (1986, 22)

3. It would be possible to argue that social rules develop for interpreting when sequences of behavior are deemed to be preference-satisfying. This would concede that the activity of preference-satisfaction is necessarily social in character while preserving the possibility that people could derive a sense of self-worth from interpreting their action as preference-satisfying. For the purpose of the argument of this chapter, it is the social character of the rules that is the key concession to hermeneutics because it suggests that economics must necessarily be interested in something (i.e. the interpretative rules) that it has hitherto ignored. Nevertheless, there is also strong reason for supposing that the social rules for the interpretation of behavior would *not*, as a matter of fact, develop around sequences of individual behavior because such rules would require each individual to share an extensive memory of each individual's choices. For this reason the kind of rules that anthropologists have typically distinguished, which are discussed below, are much more intuitively plausible than a preference satisfying one.
4. See Pettit (1995) for a slightly different argument that comes to the same conclusion.

References

Casson, Mark (1991). *The Economics of Business Culture*. Oxford: Clarendon Press
Coleman, James (1988). Social capital in the creation of human capital, *Journal of American Sociology*, 94, Supplement, S95–120

Douglas, Mary (1977). Beans means thinks, *Listener*, 8 September
Etzioni, Amitai (1989). *The Moral Dimension*. London: Free Press
Frey, Bruno S. (1992). *Tertium datur*: pricing, regulating and intrinsic motivation, *Kyklos*, 45, 161–184
Fukuyama, Francis (1995). *Trust*. London: Allen Lane
Gellner, Ernest (1997). Reply to critics, *New Left Review*, 20, 81–118
Hampshire, Stuart (1989). *Innocence and Experience*. London: Allen Lane
Handy, Charles (1997). *The Hungry Spirit*. London: Hutchinson
Hargreaves Heap, Shaun (1989). *Rationality in Economics*. Oxford: Basil Blackwell
    (1993). Culture and competitiveness, in K. Hughes (ed.), *European Competitiveness*. Cambridge: Cambridge University Press
Mäki, Uskali (1990). Practical syllogism, entrepreneurship and the invisible hand, in D. Lavoie (ed.), *Economics and Hermeneutics*. London: Routledge
Nagel, Thomas (1986). *The View from Nowhere*. Oxford: Oxford University Press
Pettit, Philip (1995). Institutional design and rational choice, in R. Goodin (ed.), *The Theory of Institutional Design*. Cambridge: Cambridge University Press

13　Collective acceptance and collective attitudes: on the social construction of social reality

Raimo Tuomela and Wolfgang Balzer

1 Introduction

Many social and collective properties and notions are man-made in a collective sense. In particular, this holds true of social institutions of the general kind, such as natural languages, legal systems, and economic notions (e.g. money, market). Similarly, such social institutions as the school, church, government, leadership, and authority are collectively created and maintained. The resulting collectivity features (ontologically: ideas in people's minds and their collective activities) characterize the man-maintained parts of the social world.

In this chapter we will study "collectivity" in the sense that a feature of the social world can be regarded as collective as opposed to being private or personal. We argue in this chapter that collectivity is created through collective acceptance. We have elsewhere (in Balzer and Tuomela 1997b; Tuomela and Balzer 1999) offered a conceptually precise and partially formalized "Collective Acceptance" account of collectivity in a "constructivist" group phenomenon. The first two sections of the chapter will be concerned with the presentation of that account. The basic contribution of this chapter concerns the nature of collective attitudes and collective goals in particular (section 3). It turns out that our account of collective acceptance and collective goals throws some light on collective and public goods, which are notions of interest to an economist. However, our main interests in this chapter are not so much in the philosophical and conceptual problems related to economics but rather in the philosophy of social notions and social ontology. Accordingly, we will discuss not only collectivity but also the ontological nature of the social world. As to collectivity, it will be argued in section 3 that our "Collective Acceptance" account is able to give a neat characterization of the basic collectivity feature that all collective social phenomena or structures exhibit. We also discuss the ontology of the social world in a somewhat sketchy and programmatic manner and show that our general "Collective Acceptance" account can throw some new light on the issues at hand. The final section (section 4) accordingly discusses in which sense or senses the social world is man-made and in which sense it is not, and how all this relates to the reality of the social world.

Collective attitudes are needed to account for collective thinking and collective action. In Balzer and Tuomela (1997b) we have taken a first step towards a unified account of collective attitudes through the so-called "fixed-point approach."[1] In that investigation we relate collective attitudes to collective acceptance, argued to be a central notion in an adequate account of the collective features of social life. We argue that intentional collective acceptance can be explicated in terms of two kinds or rather "families" of collective attitudes: those of "we-intentions" and those of "we-beliefs." Collective attitudes are explicated as we-attitudes, and here the focus will be on we-intentions (or, equivalently, intended we-goals and we-beliefs, a brand of mutual beliefs). Collective goals – we-goals – are taken to satisfy an obvious collectivity condition concerning their satisfaction (see Tuomela 1995, 2000a). In this chapter, we show, among other things, that our theory of "Collective Acceptance" (of a suitable goal-expressing sentence) suffices to capture the notion of a collective goal in its fullest "group-sense." This "group-sense" will be called the "we-mode" sense as opposed to the "I-mode" sense of a we-attitude (or of any attitude, for that matter). A we-attitude is an attitude that an agent has such that she at least in the full and ideal case believes that the members of her group have the attitude and that there is a mutual belief about this fact in the group. A we-attitude can be held in the we-mode or in the I-mode. Intuitively speaking, we-modeness means the adoption of the group's perspective in contrast to a private, group-independent perspective.

2   The collective acceptance model of collective sociality

There are two important features of collectivity and the collective creation of some central aspects of the social world (emphasized by such authors as Barnes 1983; Searle 1995; Kusch 1996; and Bloor 1997). The first feature is that of the *performative* character of many social things (entities, properties). The second is the *reflexive* nature of many social concepts. Our account in section 3 adds a third feature to this list – the collective availability or *"for-groupness"* of collective items. From the point of view of the members of the collective this is partly explicated by the so-called "Collectivity Condition," a condition imposable on goals and other collective attitudes (see Tuomela 1998a, 2000a).

According to the "Collective Acceptance" account of collectivity – which we advocate in Tuomela and Balzer (1999) – certain entities get their collective (or, better, "collective-social") status by being collectively created. For example, almost any physical entity can become money owing to the fact that the members of the collective in question accept it as money. We are told that squirrel fur was once money in Finland. This was based on the members of the society regarding it as such. As soon as they ceased collectively to accept it as money and mutually to believe that it was money, squirrel fur lost its status and function.

We must distinguish between the collective creation of an idea, collectively holding and maintaining it, and finally collectively realizing it or carrying it out. In order to achieve conceptual clarity let us simplify the issues and metaphorically think that people have boxes in their heads for storing ideas (we assume these are sentences or sentence-analogs). Each such box has a compartment called "collective social reason" which in the present context can be taken itself to have two compartments: (1) collective intention and (2) collective belief ("acceptance belief"). We argue that collective social reasons – reasons for which collective social actions are performed – are special kinds of we-attitudes, or, more precisely, contents of such we-attitudes (see Tuomela 2000a, 2002, for a recent discussion). As the (collective) creation of an idea must result in people's holding and maintaining the idea at least for a while, the central notion here will be collective acceptance in the sense of coming to hold and holding an idea. Such collective acceptance amounts to coming to hold and holding a relevant we-attitude and to being disposed to act (especially to act collectively) to maintain the accepted item. Thus, if the idea is that squirrel fur is money, the acceptance of this thought entails that the participants hold a collective belief, a we-belief to this effect, and to being disposed to act suitably (e.g. relative to economic exchange activities) on this we-belief.

Our account concentrates on achievement actions which, if not intentional under the given description, are suitably based on individually intentional activity. Our somewhat idealized account resembles political contract theories in that it deals with what could have been the case rather than what actually was or needed to have been the case. Thus, for example, acceptance based on mistaken beliefs can be accepted to some degree. A child's acceptance (as correct) of propositions concerning her basic values can also be brought into play here. (We cannot go into detail here.)

Our account requires that actively holding an idea for the group (for the use of group members in a "we-mode" sense) is a collective action disposition which is realized as the performance of collective social action purporting to realize the idea, make it true (or correctly assertable), maintain it as true (or correctly assertable), depending on the case. This is the basic sense of collective acceptance. A related aspect is that the relevant kind of collective acceptance must be "for the group," for the participants as a group are in the full-blown case taken to be committed to what has been accepted and thus collective acceptance has a steering function.

Consider some examples. In a group there might be a (weak) we-goal to oppose a recent tax increase; this is the group members' goal and they believe that the others share this goal and believe that this is a mutual belief among them. Another example involving collective acceptance as we-belief would be one where the group members believe that the earth is flat, believe that others believe so, and also believe that this is mutually believed in the group. Collective acceptance in this kind of situation can in general be construed as acceptance either in the sense of *conative commitment* to a sentence or proposition A (intention to make A true or to uphold A, as in our example) or *doxastic commitment* to A (the acceptance belief that A is true; cf. Tuomela 2000b). Collective acceptance may vary in strength. In our example it is best taken as (weak) we-acceptance: each person comes to accept A (to have the goal or belief that A expresses, as the case may be), believes that the others accept A, and also believes that there is a mutual belief about the participants' acceptance of A. This we-acceptance can in principle be private acceptance (acceptance in the I-mode) or acceptance in the we-mode (basically: acceptance as a group member).[2] In the latter case also a collective commitment (we-mode commitment) to the goal as the group's goal must be involved, and we get the minimal intersubjective sense of accepting for the group (and the involved we-mode togetherness). Without the we-mode mutual belief there is not enough intersubjectivity and collective commitment for the applicability of the phrase "for the group" (in the sense wanted here) and for saying that the participants are attempting to see to it collectively that the accepted content will become or – as the case may be – stay satisfied. Acceptance "for the group" with collective commitment can accordingly be viewed in the present context as coextensive with acceptance in the we-mode: "We accept that s is correctly assertable for us in our group-related activities" is truth-equivalent with "We accept s in the we-mode." When accepting something for the group the participants in effect are collectively committed to observing a rule system which in general requires that the members perform certain actions (e.g. inferences) and permits the performance of some other actions.

Stronger forms of collective acceptance for the group are norm-based, institutional acceptance, and plan-based or agreement-based collective acceptance. An example of norm-based acceptance is the collective acceptance that driving when drunk is wrong and punishable, that anniversaries in a marriage ought to be celebrated, and perhaps also in some groups that squirrel fur counts as money. The last example is based on the social norm (the genesis of which we will not account for here) that everyone in the collective ought to treat squirrel fur as money. An example of plan-based or agreement-based collective acceptance is the group members' joint decision to elect a certain person as their leader. In general, rational acceptance for a group entails mutual belief in the acceptance, at least in "egalitarian" groups and in groups in which the normative structure in the group does not affect collective acceptance.

The following general thesis of collective sociality in a "constructivist" sense can now be presented (Tuomela and Balzer 1999).

> *Collective Acceptance Thesis* (*CAT*): A sentence A is *collective*
> (or *collective-social*) in a primary constructivist sense in a group g

iff the following is true for group g: (a) the members of group g collectively accept A, and (b) they collectively accept A iff A is correctly assertable.

In the analysans clause (a) is the assumption of the categorical collective acceptance of s while clause (b) is a partial characterization of the kind of collective acceptance that is needed here.

In logical terms:

> (CAT^*): A is *collective* (or *collective-social*) in a primary constructivist sense in g iff Forgroup($CA(g, A)$ & ($CA(g, A) \leftrightarrow A$)).

Here the "operator" CA represents collective acceptance, generally with collective commitment, by g for g of a sentence. Forgroup(g, A) means that A is correctly assertable for the group g in question (see Tuomela and Balzer 1999, for a discussion). We use the term "correctly assertable" here and regard "true" as the special case applicable to correctly assertable descriptive sentences. CA must be a performative achievement-expressing notion, and "acceptance" is general enough to cover both the creation and upholding of A and has achievement conceptually built into it. That a sentence is correctly assertable for g means, roughly, that the group members are collectively committed to the sentence and hence treat it as a premise in their various intellectual and practical activities in group contexts and when acting as group members. This kind of collective acceptance accordingly leads to action *qua a group member*, and is thus in a wide sense institutional and in the we-mode. (Collective acceptance with private commitments is possible in an instrumental sense, but in this chapter we will assume the presence of collective commitment throughout; see Tuomela 2000a, chapter 6, for a discussion.)

We wish to emphasize that, specifically, A can represent the content of a collective attitude here (e.g. A = We will achieve goal G). Then we speak of the correct assertability rather than the truth of A. In our example, in which A has the content of a we-goal to oppose tax increase, this goal is a full-blown collective goal if it satisfies (CAT). (This follows from the "theorem" proved at the end of section 3.)

Note that (CAT^*) is reflexive "in" A (within the scope of Forgroup): in order to determine whether A is correctly assertable for g one has to refer to A as occurring in $CA(g, A)$. For example, only collective acceptance of something as money (or someone as a leader, or of something as a new term in one's language, etc.) can make it money (etc.). Similarly, a relationship is not marriage unless collectively accepted in a society as a marriage, through marriage laws and weddings (see Tuomela, 2002, for the "Collective Acceptance" account of social institutions).

We say that, roughly, a sentence is collective-social in a derived constructivist sense if it is not collective-social in the above primary sense but presupposes for its correct assertability (for the group) that there are some relevant correctly assertable (for the group) sentences which are social in the primary sense. For instance, sentences using "power" or "wealth" are at least in some cases candidates for social sentences in our derived sense. Latent or unilateral social influence are social features of the social world that would not – and correctly so – be cases of even derivatively social features (not even if many agents were concerned). The same holds for "naturally" social emotions such as envy often is (cf. Tom envies John for the latter's new car).

3 Collective goals and collective goods

3.1

Collectivity is exemplified well in cooperative activity, which is the kind of activity our social life builds on. Cooperative collective action typically depends on collective goals, joint intentions, and other collective attitudes. In this section we will concentrate on collective goals of the full we-mode kind. We will below discuss their general features and, in subsection 3.2 their relationships to public and collective goods, and, finally in subsection 3.3, argue that they must indeed fulfill a special intuitive collectivity condition.

It can be argued that full-blown cooperation relies on collective goals (Tuomela 2000a). Cooperating (intentionally cooperating) means acting together intentionally either in the pursuit of an intended collective (or, more specifically, joint) goal or in the pursuit of an intended merely personal goal. Our writing a joint chapter or singing a song together are examples of cooperative joint action in the pursuit of an intended joint goal. In such joint action each participant cooperates by performing his part of the joint action. The joint or collective action with respect to which the agents cooperate may be a goal in itself or (inclusive "or") it can be a means for the agents to achieve their shared collective goal, when such a goal exists, or their merely personal (private) goals. Whichever of these three possibilities concerning further goals is realized, the joint action in question can in any case be regarded as at least a proximate goal – *telos* – that the agents share. Thus it is possible to say that when cooperating they share an intended collective goal – at least the goal to perform the same joint action with regard to which they cooperate.

The role of collective goals in cooperation – which in turn is central for the proper functioning of society – serves to illustrate the importance of collective goals on the whole. Although this has often been recognized and indeed is part of our common-sense thinking about the social world, theorizing in social science typically does not take collective interests and goals into account. A case in point is standard economic theory and most theorizing that relies on game theory.[3]

Let us now consider what distinguishes we-mode collective goals from shared I-mode goals. We can first notice that there is a togetherness element in collective goals. Arguably, it is built into the content of the "goal-holders'" goal-attitude. We will below consider this issue from the perspective of our *CA*-model. An intended collective goal is expressible in terms of sentences such as "We will achieve goal *G*" (Tuomela 1995, chapter 1, 2000a, chapter 2, for we-attitudes). Let this sentence, expressing collective intention to achieve *G*, be the sentence *A* in our earlier formula (*CAT**).

To make our problem more concrete, consider the example of some villagers trying to get street lights for their village. When this goal has been achieved (in accordance with whatever the participants have presupposed with respect to the goal satisfaction) every villager's collective goal of getting street lights will have been (nonaccidentally) satisfied. This indicates that a proper collective goal is a goal which, in contrast to shared I-mode goals, must satisfy the idea (which also full-blown joint intentions and joint goals satisfy) of "all for one and one for all." This is spelled out by the *Collectivity Condition* for goals.

> (*CC*): It is true on "quasi-conceptual" grounds that a collective goal *G* is satisfied for one of the group members holding it iff it is satisfied for any other group member.

The satisfaction of (*CC*) is an important feature of the collectivity of a goal. We also wish to emphasize that the satisfaction of a collective goal requires more than the mere coming about of the content state – it must come about by means of collective action as presupposed by the participants. They will collectively have to see to it that the goal is achieved, even if they need not all participate in concrete action.

The phrase "quasi-conceptual" means the following: owing to the fact that the participants have collectively accepted the goal as a collective goal, the goal has the conceptually necessarily simultaneous satisfaction of it as a conceptual feature. In other words, (a) a we-mode collective goal is a common goal which by its conceptual nature is simultaneously fulfilled for the participants, and (b) the simultaneous satisfaction-occurrences of the individuals' corresponding distributive (or "personalized") collective goals are *necessarily* connected owing to the collective acceptance already mentioned.

The participants can be said to construct collective goals by their conceptual activities, by their collective acceptances and allowances. In our street light example, they must collectively bring about the goal in order to satisfy it. What if only one of them provides the street lights or if they hire some persons or a firm to do it? This is of course quite acceptable, but it leads to proper satisfaction of the collective goal only if the participants somehow authorized the person to do it – or only if this is allowed by the collectively accepted presupposition of the collective goal. As indicated, one can have a goal (one and the same state or action) either in the I-mode, or in the we-mode. The central difference here is that the we-mode attitude brings about the satisfaction of the "Collectivity Condition" while the I-mode attitude does not.

Considering the characteristics of full-blown intended collective goals, they were claimed above to have satisfaction conditions which are collective in the sense of (CC). There is also the other collectivity feature that one person alone cannot have a collective goal. Thus somebody, say j, can have a collective goal G only if there is some different person, k, who also has it (or, minimally, is believed by i to have it). Thus both the *having* or holding and the *satisfaction* of a collective goal are somewhat special. Note however that we can define a notion of a shared I-mode goal which by its definition must be held by many people (cf. Tuomela 1995, chapter 1). Thus the mere attribution of a goal does not discriminate between we-mode and I-mode goals, but satisfaction does. As to satisfaction, you and I might have as our I-mode goals to go to the same opera performance, and mutually believe that we have these goals. It is central that these goals, although simultaneously satisfied, would not necessarily, in the sense meant of necessity, be concerned with our collective acceptance of the goal to go to the opera as our collective goal.

3.2

One may ask about the connection of collective goals to various types of "goods" that especially economics in particular is concerned with and that, more generally, social institutions can be assumed to generate. Public goods are often spoken of here. We will rather speak of collective goods (in a general sense) as achieved collective goal states – those intended states that come about when collective goals are satisfied. These goods can be step goods or they can be incremental ones, but this is immaterial for our present discussion.

Economists seem to use the notion of a collective good and public good interchangeably (cf. Nicholson 1992, 747). A public good is one which satisfies the two conditions of *indivisibility* of benefits (or, equivalently, *nonrivalry* of consumption) and the *nonexcludability* of benefits. "A good is nonrival or indivisible when a unit of the good can be consumed by one individual without detracting, in the slightest, from the consumption opportunities still available to others from that same unit." "Goods whose benefits can be withheld costlessly by the owner or provider generate excludable benefits" (Cornes and Sandler 1996, 8–9). A good is nonexcludable precisely in the case where it is not excludable. Consider the idealized notion of indivisibility. It seems best construed as a *quasi-ontological*, or to use the terminology of section 4 a *groupjective*, notion, for it concerns the existential nature of the good. Standard examples of such indivisible goods as national security, clean air, and sunsets are concerned with properties of an external good. For instance, national security is a groupjective item, something that owes its existence to collective acceptance (and is ontically real in that sense). Knowledge (such as that $E = mc^2$) can be regarded as a groupjective indivisible item. An invisible good can alternatively be real in a naturalistic, nonconstructed sense. Clean air is an example of such an indivisible good. In contrast, a loaf of bread is a divisible naturalistically real entity.

As to nonexcludability, we construe it as an enforceable *normative* notion. Thus a good is excludable for an agent in a collective g iff there is some agent in g who can be forbidden to consume this good, and the proscription here is enforceable by the authority controlling its use. A good which is indivisible but excludable is called a club good by economists (cf. a golf club permitting golf playing only to its members).

How does all this relate to our present account of collective goods? Nonexcludability clearly is independent of our notion of a collective goal: the benefits related to the achievement of a collective goal in principle can, but need not, be excluded for any collection of agents, including those who have actually brought about the wanted goal-state. Consider the following possibilities: (a) we-mode goal $\rightarrow$ indivisibility; (b) indivisibility $\rightarrow$ we-mode goal; (c) I-mode goal $\rightarrow$ divisibility; (d) divisibility $\rightarrow$ I-mode goal, with the arrow representing entailment. (a) is not true. We can have making a bowl of pea soup as our we-mode collective goal. The corresponding goal-state is a divisible one. How about (b)? It is not true either. A person can alone have securing world peace as his I-mode goal. Yet we can assume that world peace is indivisible. As to (c), an I-mode goal need not be divisible in view of the world peace example. As to (d), we may have as our collective goal to cook a meal for our group. The meal is divisible, and (d) is thus false. We have now seen that none of (a)–(d) is tenable. Thus we can see that the all the three dichotomies I-mode goal/we-mode goal, divisible/indivisible, and excludable/nonexcludable are extensionally different. Accordingly, the central goal notions in our theory are clearly different from the economist's notions of public good and club good.

3.3

In all, given the above discussion (and the additional considerations advanced in Tuomela 2000a, chapter 2, and Miller and Tuomela 2000), it seems reasonable to require that a full-blown collective goal satisfies the "Collectivity Condition" (*CC*). We have earlier argued that collectivity (or better, collectivity in a social sense) in its general sense essentially amounts to what (*CAT*) entails or what can be based on it. How is (*CC*) connected to (*CAT*)? What kinds of specific collectivity conditions do other collective attitudes satisfy? As to the latter, mutual belief does satisfy an analog of (*CC*) for shared sentences A without personal indexicals (e.g. "I"), if we define the satisfaction of a belief to be its truth. As to a plan-based joint intention (cf. Balzer and Tuomela 1997a), the answer is simple: Its content is a we-mode collective goal (e.g. joint action) which satisfies (*CC*). A shared intention in a weaker sense need not satisfy (*CC*), although it is true that when satisfied for one it is satisfied for all by the very definition of a shared we-attitude. The general concept of we-attitude does not entail that any we-attitude satisfies (*CC*), for its definiens might hold accidentally, not owing to the participants having constructively made it true.

Does (*CAT*), when applied to goals, entail (*CC*)? If yes, the collectivity condition that all collective goods (such as national security produced by the national defense system) satisfy might be given by (*CAT*). Let us start by considering an intended collective goal *G* as expressed by sentence *A*. Let us impose the condition on *A* that it satisfies (*CAT*) for *A* = We will (intend to) achieve goal *G*. Here we assume that collective acceptance is "for the group" in a strong enough sense to commit it to steer its behavior so that one can say after goal-achievement that the group brought it about that the goal content was satisfied; but, of course we do not initially assume that *G* satisfies (*CC*). We argue that this entails that the goal satisfies (*CC*) We argue that this entails that the goal satisfies (*CC*) and is a proper we-mode collective goal in this sense. Assume now *A*, that we have *G* as our goal (assume that "we" here consists of you and me). We need to show that it is necessarily the case that if *G* is satisfied for me it is satisfied for you, the necessity here being due to the "quasi-concept" or "collective acceptance" (*CA*) grounds.

The more precise argument to be given below does not (and should not) initially require a collective goal to satisfy (*CC*). We will now sketch an informal proof to the effect that collectively accepted collective goals will satisfy (*CC*) (cf. Tuomela, 2000a, chapter 2). The proof is formulated, for simplicity's sake, for a group *g* ("we") consisting of "you" and "me." We use "we will achieve *G*" to replace *A* in (*CAT*) – if preferred, the symbolism Goal(*g, G*) could alternatively be used to express the same as "we will achieve *G*."

> (1) Forgroup (We will achieve *G*) ((*CAT*).)
> (2) Forgroup (We will achieve *G* <->*CA*(*g*, We will achieve *g*) (*CAT*)) and the distributiveness of the Forgroup-operator.)
> (3) We will achieve *g* for our group (*G* is our common goal; from (1) and (3).)
> (4) Goal *G* is satisfied for me iff it is satisfied for you. (From (3)) and the standard understanding of we-sentences expressing a common goal, whether an I-mode or a we-mode goal.)
> (5) *G* is collective in the sense that (*CC*) is satisfied for *p*. (From (1), (2), and (4).)

The proof assumes that our group *g* is an informal group in which the group can have a goal if all its members have the goal. It shows that if we have accepted *G* as the goal for the group then *G* is not only our common goal in the garden variety sense but is a necessarily common goal owing to our having accepted it as our common goal. (4) shows the consequences of the underlying commonality assumption and collective acceptance for the group gives the necessity also needed for (*CC*) to be true. While the argument given assumes rather much and is thus somewhat shallow, it nevertheless seves to spell out in more detail the importance of (CA) for collectivity in the case[4] of goals and – in effect by the same token – joint and collective intentions.

What about the case of mutual beliefs (MB)? In this case collective acceptance amounts to MB (for the group) and the central formula (CAT) entails the truth of the sentence "$MB(A) \leftrightarrow A$" for the group. Taking belief here as acceptance belief, as before, this says that for the group it holds that A iff A is mutually accepted as true for the group. (Note, however, that there can also be mutual beliefs which are not acceptances-for-the-group.) The present section has thus basically shown *the applicability of (CAT) to all basic collective attitudes*: to the belief-family and the intention-family of concepts, which are directly relevant to collectivity (see Tuomela and Balzer 1999, for the latter claim). As a slogan, *the only (full-blown) notion of collectivity in the social world that a theorist needs is that provided by (CAT).*

4 On the reality of the social world

It follows from the "Collective Acceptance" account that the parts of the social world it applies to are socially constructed and man-made. This, however, needs qualifications. Let us consider the matter.

One can argue that reality is criterially connected to causality in the sense that an entity cannot be real unless capable of occurring in singular causal inquirer-independent contexts (in claims of the form $C(f, f')$, C standing for causation and f, f' being facts related to the entity in question). Here inquirer-independence is independence of an inquirer's mind or, put somewhat differently, the "ideally rational" scientific community's "mind" (attitudes, views). Roughly speaking, the inquirer-independence of causation can be understood here in the sense of causation in a world similar to ours but in which there are no (mind-possessing) inquirers. (Cf. Tuomela 1985, chapters 4–7, for a discussion of this and the appearance/reality distinction from the point of view of scientific realism.) Note that our present criterion for a mind-independent world "out there" of course allows that there are creatures possessing minds (e.g. intentions and beliefs) out there and thus mind-dependent things in that sense. It also allows that the things out there be describable and conceptualizable in various different ways. In addition to the two "levels" of (a) inquirer-independent reality out there and (b) the (ideal) scientific community's view – or, put differently, the standpoint of the ideal best-explaining theory – we must also deal with (c) a group's (any group's, large or small) point of view. From a group's point of view the social institutions and other collectively constructed and upheld things in that group are collectively mind-dependent in the sense of being dependent on the group's acceptance and thus its attitudes. Such group-dependent things can nevertheless be said to be "socially real" in the group (intersubjectively real and belong to the group's posited "public space"), and they are also real in the sense of being independent of an external inquirer's or best-explaining theory's point of view.

Criterion (a) of independence may be argued to be coextensive with (b), but one may still want to keep these criteria conceptually distinct. It can be noted that although group-dependent items can be regarded as "groupjective" (dependent on the "group's mind", as it were, and hence group members' minds) an item can still be group-dependent without in fact being dependent on any particular member's mind, because collective acceptance is compatible with such "exceptions." Thus ontological groupjectivity is distinct from ontological subjectivity and of course it is also distinct from epistemological groupjectivity that also comes to hold. (Epistemological groupjectivity more or less amounts to "epistemological objectivity" in Searle's, 1995, sense.).

Let us emphasize that group-dependent things are still objectively investigatable in the sense that they are inquirer-independent. This is the case even if we, as a thought experiment, let the group grow in size and become the class of actual and possible human beings. The inquirer's reflective stance towards an external, inquirer-independent world, which now includes also the class of all human beings, is still at least conceptually and metaphysically possible – at least if we are allowed to assume (scientific) realism. One underlying reason for this is that the method of investigation used – the scientific method – is idealized and normative and thus transcends the limitations of human beings.

Note that the group members generally (but not invariably) need to have right thoughts about money and school, etc. for example, when they act, but they need not of course think that by so acting they contribute to the maintenance and renewal of the institutions involved. To what extent false beliefs are possible is largely to be decided on functional grounds. As long as institutional activity is largely successful, false beliefs can be tolerated.

Note also that there are social entities and features which are not group-dependent in the sense of the *CA* account. These include nonconstructed things and states (such as presumably love and we-fear can be), which accordingly are mind-independent and objective in our full (a) sense.

Our "Collective Acceptance" model presupposes the distinction between sentences whose truth (or, more generally, correct assertability) is entirely up to the group members collectively considered (or indeed up to any human beings or beings capable of operating as the *CA*-account requires) and sentences whose truth is at least in part up to the way the inquirer-independent world causally is. This assumption of course presupposes that sense can be made of the causal processes occurring in the world out there. (Realists – such as we – are of course disposed to accept this.) Thus, according to this view, group members can collectively accept (for the group) the truth or correct assertability of some sentences, such as "Stars cause our fate to be what it is," without making it the case that those sentences are true in the standard sense. On the other hand, the truth of sentences like "A euro coin is money" is completely dependent on a relevant kind of collective acceptance. It cannot be refuted by any single person's refusal to accept that the euro coin is money.

While making a distinction between what is up to us collectively to achieve and what is up to nature is basically right, we think, considering the matter epistemologically, that it need not be assumed on *a priori* grounds. Here is a point which supports its *a posteriori* status. Assume that a group *g* collectively accepts, among other things, causal statements (e.g. that a bridge collapsed because of a heavy truck crossing it or that smoking causes cancer). Here we have embedded causality in a broader frame of collective acceptance by putting a nonsocial claim – a claim about a nonsocial causal connection – in the same "acceptance-box" as, say, the statement about stars determining our fate (a merely social claim). In more general terms, the embedding here proceeds as follows. We start with a comprehensive system of causal relations including relations of a purely social nature as well as other relations. In this system we can delineate the social causal relations as those which satisfy our *CA*-model. Now a good epistemic procedure should be able to distinguish between those collectively accepted causal connections which are not mind-independent in the intended sense from those which are. We conjecture that the scientific method (perhaps already our current view of it) is able to do the job. Thus, for instance, by means of theorizing and testing the constructed theories we are led to a warranted rejection of the claim that stars determine our fate, or that "*similia similibus curantur*" (the central claim of homeopathy), or that smoking is not a causal factor of lung cancer (up to now the central claim of the tobacco industry). This *a posteriori* method does (or tries to do) "from within" what the older metaphysical views do from an external point of view and in an *a priori* sense. Recall that the kind of *epistemic objectivity* under discussion can be achieved also with respect to group-dependent things, although of course relative to the assumed fact of collective acceptance and maintenance.

According to our "Collective Acceptance" account social institutions, *qua* collections of position-involving normative structures realized in social practices, can be causally effective ultimately only via the group members' minds and actions. This is because we need not assume that they ontically include other, more "holistic" elements, although the social institution concepts may well be irreducible primitives. Social institutions can have and often have causal impact via the participants' (in collective acceptance) thoughts and thus subjectively (in the group members' beliefs) *qua* social institutions, or at least their central nervous systems (in nonintentional cases). The "internalized" rights and duties related to institutional entities like money or institutional positions (like teacher), for example, can, accordingly, in this embedding involve causal connections independent also of the group members' minds.

In "nonnormative" cases (cf. leader, esteem, status) based on collective acceptance in the sense of mutual acceptance belief (the acceptance of something as true for the group) the analogous observation holds, for collective acceptance is always group-relative. That is, it relates the constructed and re-constructed things to the group and thus to the mental life of the group members (e.g. Tom is our leader only in so far as he is accepted by us as our leader).

Next, physical social artifacts such as church buildings, cars, chairs, books, and generally much of at least a city-dweller's environment and "public social space" and "social geography" should be mentioned. All these exist as causally effective entities. They can enter causal connections not only *qua* having suitable physical features but also, and in the present context in an important sense, *qua* being artifacts expressing normative or nonnormative collective practices (see Tuomela 1998b, for *qua*-causation).

Various unintended and unanticipated consequences (cf. the states of high inflation and unemployment, pollution of the environment) also belong to social artifacts broadly understood. It seems that they generally fall outside the scope of primary social things. Nevertheless, they often if not in general are collective-social in our derived sense.

Finally, there are social properties and relations which can be regarded as real in a more naturalistic sense and which correctly fall outside the scope of the *CA*-model. For instance, Tom's being jealous of Jane is (normally) an example of such a nonconstructed social fact. Another example is provided by some shared collective attitudes (or we-attitudes) in the I-mode (but not those in the we-mode) in the sense of Tuomela (1995, 2000a). A concrete example would be our we-fear that a lion will attack us.

The question "Is the social world real?" is not a very clear question, because the answer crucially depends on what is meant by the social world and by something being real. Basically, (1) a realist can regard the social world as real and objective in the mind-independence sense: the social world exists independently of an inquirer's mind or of the viewpoint of the inquirers' community. However, (2) a part of the social world is dependent on group acceptance, as emphasized. Yet this groupjective part of the world is ontically objective in the relative sense of being grounded (sometimes in a historically solid, permanent sense) in group acceptance. Accordingly, in order to be intelligible (in the sense of being correctly explainable) at least this part of the social world must be conceptualized as its inhabitants conceptualize it (squirrel fur may have been money for medieval Finns but not perhaps for others). Finally, (3) social and institutional artifacts such as cars, tables, and church buildings, *qua* physical entities are objectively real in sense (1) and *qua* social and institutional entities in sense (2) because they have been socially constructed along the lines of the "Collective Acceptance" account.

Notes

We wish to thank Kaarlo Miller for sharp comments on the final version. Thanks are also due to Pekka Mäkelä, and Petri Ylikoski for comments on an earlier draft. Owing to Wolfgang Balzer's illness, the present, considerably abbreviated version was written by the first author.

1. There are different approaches to the conceptual and logical nature of common knowledge and belief. One approach explicates common knowledge and belief by an infinite conjunction of ever-more complex combinations of individual attitudes, whereas in another approach, the *fixed-point* approach, this syntactical infinity is cut short by a finite fixed-point formula, that is, an impredicative construct in which the joint notion to be "defined" already occurs in the definiens. In the mathematical limit, these two approaches are equivalent, their difference relating to the basic conceptual-logical framework used. While the direct approach uses syntactical material exclusively referring to individuals and their relations, the fixed-point approach syntactically involves new, higher-order entities whose irreducibility indicates their independent status. In these approaches, differences may of course occur in finite iterations when different definitions are used.

2. In Tuomela (2000a) a precise criterion for the distinction between the I-mode and the we-mode is given. Without further clarification we will here state this criterion, termed ($ET*$), where ATT refers to a propositional attitude (e.g. $ATT =$ Goal) and CA to collective acceptance entailing collective commitment, and p is a sentence:

   ($ET*$): A sentence "We ATT-relate to p" expresses a g-attitude for group G in a situation iff in that situation, for group G, the sentence "We collectively accept that we ATT-relate to p" is true, and "We ATT-relate to p" entails and is entailed by "We collectively accept that we ATT-relate to p," understanding collective acceptance here to involve collective commitment to p. Put in logical notation, ATT (we, p) expresses a g-attitude for G in a situation iff, for G, CA (we, ATT (we, p)) and CA (we, ATT (we, p)) $\leftrightarrow ATT$ (we, p) in that situation.

3. See Tuomela (2000a, chapter 7). Let me mention that Soros (1998) is one of the critics of current economic theory who has spoken for the inclusion of collective goals and interests into economic theorizing. Although his work does not go into much detail, it succeeds in voicing concerns which the community of economists has tended to ignore.

4. Here is a somewhat different proof; we here again will formulate simple informal, "egalitarian" groups (groups without structure). We assume that group goal, G, is distributive so that if group g has G then every member j of G has it as her goal (we write G_j for this) and that goal satisfaction is similarly distributive. We can accordingly say that G is a goal, it is the members' common goal. Our proof starts without assuming that G satisfied the Collectivity Condition (CC). We show that the satisfaction of (CC) can essentially be based on the satisfaction of the formula (CAT):

   (1) Forgroup (We will achieve G). (From (CAT).)
   (2) "We will achieve goal G" ($= A$) is collectively available for the use of all group members. (From the meaning of the Forgroup-operator.)
   (3) The truth and satisfaction of G are both due to the CA-reason – the reason that G has been collectively accepted by g as its goal and thus that (1).
   (4) For the CA-reason it is true that g is satisfied for group g iff it is satisfied for every member – iff the corresponding personalized goal G_j is satisfied for every member j. (Distributiveness of common goal.)

(5) For the *CA*-reason it is true that G is satisfied for j (G_j is satisfied), then G is satisfied for any group member (G_k is satisfied). ((4).)

Therefore,

(6) Goal G satisfies the Collectivity Condition (*CC*). (Cf. Tuomela 2000a, chapter 6, n.3.)

References

Balzer, Wolfgang and Tuomela, Raimo (1997a). The structure and verification of plan-based joint intentions, *International Journal of Cooperative Information Systems*, 6, 3–26

(1997b). A fixed-point approach to collective attitudes, in G. Holmström-Hintikka and Raimo Tuomela (eds.), *Contemporary Action Theory, II: Social Action*. Dordrecht: Kluwer, 115–142

Barnes, B. (1983). Social life as bootstrapped induction, *Sociology*, 17, 524–545

Bhaskar, Roy (1989). *Reclaiming Reality: A Critical Introduction to Contemporary Philosophy*. London: Verso

Bloor, D. (1997). *Wittgenstein, Rules and Institutions*. London and New York: Routledge

Cornes, R. and T. Sandler (1996). *The Theory of Externalities, Public Goods, and Club Goods*, 2nd edn. Cambridge: Cambridge University Press

Giddens, Anthony (1984). *The Constitution of Society*. Cambridge: Polity Press

Kusch, M. (1996). The sociophilosophy of folk psychology, *Studies in History and Philosophy of Science*, 28, 1–25

Miller, K. and Raimo Tuomela (2000). What are collective goals?, manuscript

Nicholson, W. (1992). *Microeconomic Theory*, 5th edn. Fort Worth, TX: The Dryden Press

Searle, J. (1995). *The Construction of Social Reality*. London: Allen Lane, The Penguin Press

Soros, G. (1998). *The Crisis of Global Capitalism: Open Society Endangered*. London: Little, Brown & Co.

Tuomela, Raimo (1985). *Science, Action, and Reality*. Dordrecht, Boston, and Lancaster: D. Reidel

(1995). The *Importance of Us: A Philosophical Study of Basic Social Notions*, Stanford Series in Philosophy. Stanford, CA: Stanford University Press.

(1998a). Collective goals and cooperation, in X. Arrazola, K. Korta, and F. Pelletier (eds.), *Discourse, Interaction, and Communication*. Dordrecht: Kluwer, 121–139

(1998b). A defense of mental causation, *Philosophical Studies*, 90, 1–34

(2000a). *Cooperation: A Philosophical Study*, Philosophical Studies Series. Dordrecht and Boston: Kluwer

(2000b). Belief versus acceptance, *Philosophical Explorations*, 2, 122–137

(2002). *The Philosophy of Social Practices: A Collective Acceptance View*. Cambridge: Cambridge University Press

Tuomela, Raimo and Wolfgang Balzer (1999). Collective acceptance and collective social notions, *Synthèse*, 117, 175–205

14　Hayek and cultural evolution

Bruce Caldwell

1　Introduction

Realism has entered economics in diverse ways. One fairly common exercise is to provide a realist interpretation of the work of some famous economist. The economists whose works are reconstructed typically did not explicitly endorse realism, but rather elements of their work had aspects that permitted a realist reinterpretation.

The Austrian economist F. A. Hayek is a case in point. Both Tony Lawson and Steve Fleetwood have portrayed Hayek as an early, if imperfect, proponent of transcendental realism. Lawson argues that Hayek's views went through a "continuing transformation." He applauds Hayek's attack on positivism in the latter's wartime "Scientism" essay (Hayek [1942–44] [1952] 1979), but finds Hayek's alternative proposals there, which Lawson characterizes as a variant of hermeneutics, to be inadequate (Lawson, 1997, 149).[1] Elsewhere, though, Lawson claims that in Hayek's later contributions one can find an "at least embryonic acceptance of something like a transcendental realist ontology," hence the conclusion of Hayek's having undergone a continuing transformation (Lawson, 1994, 151). The suggestion that Hayek turned towards realism in his later work is addressed in greater detail in Fleetwood's *Hayek's Political Economy: The Socio-Economics of Order* (1995). Though he prefers a periodization of Hayek's work to Lawson's notion of a continuing transformation, Fleetwood agrees that after 1960 one can find ample evidence for what he calls "Hayek III's quasi-transcendental realism" (Fleetwood 1995, chapter 6). Fleetwood offers an extended realist reconstruction of Hayek's writings on the role of rules. Hayek viewed rules as a key part of a larger social structure, saw humans as rule-following animals, developed a cognitive psychology to explain rule-following behavior, and saw such behavior as resulting in a variety of spontaneous orders (Fleetwood 1995, chapters 7–10). I find some parts of Lawson's and Fleetwood's historiography troubling,[2] but their claim that certain aspects of Hayek's later work may be viewed as exemplifying some form of realism is quite convincing.

Fleetwood mentions but does not examine another area of Hayek's work, his theory of cultural evolution. In these writings Hayek makes a number of claims about how the extended market order might have come into being and about how it has been able to persist. These claims are about putative causal processes existing in our past and present, and as Jack Vromen (1995, chapter 9) has suggested, such ideas might well be used in a reconstruction of an evolutionary economic theory. They cry out for a realist reconstruction and assessment, but so far have gone unanalyzed.

One reason for their neglect is that Hayek's writings on cultural evolution are among his most controversial; as Fleetwood (1995, 165, n. 8) himself states, "this is a contentious area." Some representative criticisms include those of Gray (1986, 52–55); Steele (1987); Hodgson (1993, 153–157); Vanberg (1994, chapters 5, 6); De Vlieghere (1994); Witt (1994); Vromen (1995, 171–176); Shearmur (1996, 82–87): two who have defended him are Yeager (1989) and Boettke (1990). Given the number and distinction of the critics, before we think about providing a realist reconstruction of his ideas on cultural evolution, it seems mete first to assess the cogency of the most important of the criticisms. That is goal of this chapter.

The organization is straightforward. Section 2 provides a brief summary of Hayek's views on cultural evolution. Three major criticisms will then be outlined and evaluated. The first asserts that Hayek's endorsement of group selection as a mechanism for cultural evolution is inconsistent with his professed methodological individualism. The second suggests that Hayek's severe and uncompromising epistemological pessimism regarding our ability to shape institutions is a weakness, for it prohibits any attempt to improve society, and in particular to provide a better constitutional environment. The final criticism questions the adequacy of Hayek's explanation of how cultural evolution takes place. To show my hand a little, I will argue that the first criticism is less than persuasive, and that the second, though relevant if one is seeking to construct constitutions, is irrelevant to Hayek's own task of explaining the course of cultural evolution. The third criticism, however, points to what appears to be at least an incompleteness in Hayek's position, one that opens up avenues for further research that may be of interest to realists.

2   A summary of Hayek's position on cultural evolution

Cultural evolution refers to the evolution of a tradition of learned rules, norms, ethical precepts, and practices, "especially those dealing with several property, honesty, contract, exchange, trade, competition, gain, and privacy" (Hayek 1988, 12).[3] Our cultural heritage is neither genetically transmitted nor designed by a thinking mind, but emerged through "a process of winnowing and sifting, directed by the differential advantages gained by groups from practices adopted for some unknown and perhaps purely accidental reasons" (Hayek 1979, 155). The traditions that emerged allowed the development of a vast extended order, one capable of sustaining huge increases in population, an order that would have been considered fantastical to earlier humans existing under more primitive conditions.

Successful practices get passed on through tradition, learning, and imitation. Because acquired characteristics may be passed on, cultural evolution resembles Lamarckian rather than Darwinian evolution, and indeed this sort of evolutionary thinking is older than Darwin's. Cultural evolution also differs from biological evolution in that it can take place very fast, so that once begun "it swamps genetic evolution" (1979, 156).

Many of the rules and precepts take the form of prohibitions on our behavior, and aim at suppressing the "natural morality" (e.g. within-group solidarity, cooperation in the pursuit of group-approved goals, distrust of and aggressiveness towards strangers) that allowed earlier humans to function successfully in small groups. As a result, many constraints feel unnatural; they are resisted, even hated (1988, 13). In addition, rules were usually neither consciously adopted, nor adopted after a rational process of assessment of their consequences, simply because their wider effects were not then (nor even today) well understood. Many of these rules may well seem seem irrational to us. As such, Hayek characterizes them as lying between, and fitting uneasily with, both our instinct and our reason (1988, chapter 1).

The question arises: How did such unpopular prohibitions ever come to be adopted, and once adopted, how could they persist, given our natural aversion to them and the ever-present temptation to develop institutions and practices more consonant with our rationality? Hayek offers a straightforward answer: the groups that practiced them were better able to survive. In a phrase, "cultural evolution operates largely through group selection" (1988, 25).
Hayek himself provided this concise summary:

> the extended order resulted not from human design or intention but spontaneously: it arose from unintentionally conforming to certain traditional and largely *moral* practices, many of which men tend to dislike, whose significance they usually fail to understand, whose validity they cannot prove, and which have nonetheless fairly rapidly spread by means of an evolutionary selection – the comparative increase of population and wealth – of those groups that happened to follow them. (1988, 6, emphasis in the original)

3 Hayek and methodological individualism

A perennial issue in the secondary literature concerns whether Hayek's resort to group selection in his writings on cultural evolution is inconsistent with his advocacy of methodological individualism. Among those who have addressed the question are Gray (1986, 52–55); Boettke (1990); Hodgson (1993, 153–157);

Vanberg (1994, chapters 5, 6); Witt (1994); and Vromen (1995, 171–176). It is typically taken as uncontroversial that Hayek endorsed methodological individualism; people differ, though, over the consequences of this commitment for his group-selection arguments.

In what follows I will suggest that:

A   Direct evidence for Hayek's commitment to methodological individualism is scanty
B   To the extent that he can be characterized as a methodological individualist, the variant that Hayek supports is very different from the sort of methodological individualism that its critics typically attack, and
C   the sort of methodological individualism he endorses does not conflict with either evolutionary or group selection arguments.

A   What evidence exists to demonstrate Hayek's commitment to methodological individualism?

We might ask first: Does Hayek ever use the term "methodological individualism" in his writings? I could find only one instance of such usage, on p. 64 of his wartime methodological essay, "Scientism and the Study of Society," which was later published as part of the collection *The Counter-Revolution of Science* ([1952] 1979).[4] That said, Hayek does discuss issues relating to methodological individualism in a number of pieces. All the discussions were part of a project conceived by Hayek during the Second World War on "the abuse and decline of reason in modern times." The Abuse of Reason project was to include both methodological and historical components, with his essays "Scientism and the Study of Society" and "The Counter-Revolution of Science" constituting, respectively, sections of those two components. Another essay, "Individualism: True and False," was to serve as an introduction, and the book was to conclude with a discussion of the decay of reason under totalitarianism, which *The Road to Serfdom* contained "in popular form" ([1952] 1979, 9–11).

Hayek ultimately abandoned this grand outline. "Individualism: True and False" [1945] ended up being published with a group of other papers in 1948, and "Counter-Revolution" and "Scientism" were published together in 1952. Perhaps not incidentally, Hayek never again said anything about methodological individualism, even (as we will see) when it could have helped his case to do so. When the relevant texts are examined, we see further that Hayek's methodological individualism emerged within a very specific context. In the "Scientism" essay he opposed objectivism because he thought that social scientists should make reference to subjective beliefs of individuals to explain actions. He opposed historicism because he felt that the search for historical laws of change was chimerical. And he opposed collectivism because he thought that doctrines that posited the existence of social wholes independent of the people that created them were fallacious. In their place Hayek proposed that we follow the examples of men like Menger and the Scottish Enlightenment philosophers, who sought to reveal how various social institutions emerged as the unintended consequences of the actions of many individuals. In "Individualism: True and False" the same sort of story is told, but this time the French rationalists are added to his list of suspect groups.

One does not find in Hayek's writings a specific or sustained philosophical defense of methodological individualism.[5] He does not start from the doctrine. Rather, he compares what he considers to be the "best practice" (e.g. the analyses of people like Menger or Smith) with what he considers to be bad practice (e.g. behaviorism or historicism) and then constructs generalizations about what methods the different protagonists followed. To sum up: Hayek's writings on methodological individualism emerged at a particular point in time within a particular project, a project that he ultimately abandoned. I am not arguing that Hayek was not a methodological individualist; as we will see, he appears to have been one, of sorts. What I am questioning is the adequacy of accounts that assert, without further explanation or qualification, that Hayek endorsed methodological individualism. The textual evidence simply does not support such an assertion.

B   What kind of methodological individualism did Hayek support?

To the extent that Hayek endorsed methodological individualism, the doctrine he defended was of a particular and unique sort. One may see this by comparing his ideas with other variants. When one thinks of actually existing examples of methodological individualism within economics, a number of commitments come to mind (cf. Lange-von Kulessa 1997, 270–271). The neoclassical version starts from a standard set of assumptions. One begins with individual agents, either consumers or firms. The standard model of intermediate-level price theory assumes that agents are rational and that they have full information. In some versions (e.g. that of Chicago School economists) tastes and preferences are assumed to be unchanging. Other versions may assume further that agents are motivated only by their own narrowly defined self-interest, that their utility functions are independent of those of other agents. Critics of methodological individualism also sometimes note that the origins and content of people's preferences are left unexplained, even though it seems clear that these are affected by the institutional settings agents confront.

In his discussions of methodological individualism Hayek rejects almost all of these assumptions:

1. Hayek is quite explicit, for example, that the Scottish Enlightenment thinkers whose writings on individualism he endorses disavowed any notion of "the bogey of 'rational economic man'" ([1945] 1948, 11). To the contrary:

It would be nearer to the truth to say that in their view man was by nature lazy and indolent, improvident and wasteful, and that it was only by force of circumstances that he could be made to behave economically or carefully to adjust his means to his ends . . . The chief concern of the great individualist writers was indeed to find a set of institutions by which man could be induced, by his own choice and from the motives which determined his ordinary conduct, to contribute as much as possible to the need of all others; and their discovery was that the system of private property did provide such inducements to a much greater extent than had yet been understood. ([1945] 1948, 12–13)

2. Hayek's rejection of the full information assumption is well known. In this context he notes that dispensing with the full information assumption renders the question of rationality more or less moot: far more important than man's rationality is the "fact that he *cannot* know more than a tiny part of the whole society and that therefore all that can enter his motives are the immediate effects which his actions will have in the sphere he knows" ([1945] 1948, 14, emphasis in the original).
3. Hayek insists further that saying that individuals pursue their own interests does not imply that their behavior is necessarily "selfish." It simply means that people "strive for whatever *they* think is desirable" ([1945] 1948, 15, emphasis in the original).
4. He also asserts that "individualism true" is a theory of society. As such it is a misunderstanding to claim that it postulates or depends on the assumption of isolated or self-contained individuals for whom the larger society is irrelevant ([1945] 1948, 6).
5. Finally, Hayek has no patience with the view, associated principally with George Stigler and Gary Becker (1977), that tastes and preferences are stable.[6] If through their interactions in markets and other social institutions humans are constantly gaining new information, it seems hardly likely that their tastes and preferences would remain unchanged. As noted by Samuel Bowles (1998, 76), Hayek was a proponent of "endogenous preferences."

Of the various assumptions typically associated with methodological individualism, only two are apparently endorsed by Hayek. The first is that economists (as opposed to psychologists) need not concern themselves with the origins of individual tastes and preferences. There are good reasons for Hayek to defend this as a methodological principle. If one believes, as he did, that all manner of things may influence the formation of tastes, and further that as knowledge changes one's tastes change, it would be difficult indeed to imagine even how to begin the task.[7] Given that there is no presumption in Hayek's variant that tastes and preferences remain fixed, nor that they are formed by a narrowly defined self-interest, it seems quite reasonable that economists not burden themselves with investigating the origins of individual tastes. There are gains, after all, from the division of labor.

The second assumption is that, in explaining social behavior, one should start from individuals. In "Individualism: True and False" Hayek put it this way: "there is no other way toward an understanding of social phenomena but through our understanding of individual actions directed toward other people and guided by their expected behavior" ([1945] 1948, 6). In his "Scientism" essay he endorsed the same sort of idea in his chapter 4, which carried the title "The Individualist and 'Compositive' Method of the Social Sciences" ([1942–44], [1952] 1979, 61–76).

Even this apparently straightforward endorsement of methodological individualism raises questions, however. For if one looks at Hayek's economics, that is, his actual practice, it is difficult to find evidence of a sustained commitment to this sort of program. More often, Hayek engages in aggregate (market-level) analysis that is not explicitly related to the actions of individual agents. *For him, the individuals are there, but they are kept in the background.*[8]

The contrast is evident if one compares Hayek's analyses with mainstream microeconomics, where the starting point of the analysis is, in fact, the behavior of idealized individual consumers or firms. Hayek's strictures also fit better the work of another Austrian economist, Ludwig von Mises, who begins his "science of human action" with an examination of "acting man" ([1949] 1963, chapter 1). Now Mises' "acting man" was not *homo oeconomicus*, to be sure; like Hayek, Mises allowed his agents to choose whatever action happened to please them most at the moment of decision. But the point is that Mises, like his neoclassical counterpart but unlike Hayek, explicitly starts his analysis with the individual agent.[9]

Some critics of Hayek (e.g. Hodgson 1993, 153–157; cf. Caldwell 2001 for a critique of Hodgson's views) raise the issue of his methodological individualism because they dislike that doctrine as it has been used by mainstream economists. It should be clear from this section that, to the extent that Hayek endorses methodological individualism, his version has few similarities to the one usually encountered.

C   Does Hayek's methodological individualism preclude him from endorsing evolutionary or group selection arguments?

Geoff Hodgson, quoting Jon Elster, offers the following definition of methodological individualism: "the doctrine that all social phenomena (their structure and their change) are in principle explicable only in terms of individuals – their properties, goals, and beliefs" (Hodgson 1993, 153). If this definition is accepted, it implies that attempts to explain social phenomena that appeal to mechanisms operating either above or below the level of the individual are unacceptable. Group selection, which explains certain social phenomena (the persistence of certain social practices) as being due to the benefits they confer on a group, is inconsistent with it. So is sociobiology, since it explains the persistence of certain behaviors on the basis of their maximizing the chances of an individual's genes being passed on.

We have seen so far that, to the extent that Hayek may be characterized as a methodological individualist, his views typically differ from those of other proponents of methodological individualism. Whatever variant he may have endorsed, it was not of a form that would limit one to explaining social phenomena only in terms of individuals.

Hayek's long-standing support of group selection obviously argues against his accepting such a limitation on explanation. (His critics, of course, take it as long-standing evidence of his inconsistency.) But so do his views on sociobiology. Hayek criticized sociobiology in the first few pages of the "Epilogue" to *Law, Legislation and Liberty* (1979, 153–155; cf. 1988, 24). Had Hayek been a proponent of a methodological individualistic limitation on explanation, surely he would have used it to attack sociobiology. His argument against the sociobiologists was not, however, that they went below the individual to the level of the gene to explain the survival of certain practices. Rather, he faulted them for failing to see that there are *three*, not two, sources of values; that in addition to our genetic heritage and our rationally constructed institutions, there is our cultural heritage. Far from trying to delimit explanation, Hayek was willing to seek explanations for social phenomena on many different levels; he faulted the sociobiologists for being overly restrictive.

A second sort of objection might be raised by those who endorse a more mainstream variant of methodological individualism. The classic objection here, which was first raised in biology, is that group selection fails to explain how individually altruistic but group-beneficial behavior can persist in the face of free-riding by other nonaltruistic members of a group. In the language of game theory, this translates as the proposition that group selection works well enough for cooperation games (where what is advantageous to the group is also advantageous to the individual), but runs into problems when agents confront prisoner's dilemma situations (this translation is noted in Vanberg 1994, chapter 5; cf. Vromen 1995, 176–189).

Such an argument has considerable force if one believes that individuals always act to promote their own narrowly defined best interest. But Hayek's variant of methodological individualism allows for considerably more complex human responses, so is less susceptible to this objection.

We have shown that those who accuse Hayek of being a methodological individualist of the standard sort have not proven their case, and indeed we have suggested that much evidence exists against this view. But in a more positive vein, what may we conclude? In particular, how might we characterize Hayek's views?

My hypothesis is this: In his methodological essays in the 1940s, it is clear that Hayek did not like certain types of social explanations (historicist, behaviorist, and those that made reference to "social collectives") and preferred instead the sorts of individualist explanations offered by men like Menger and the Scottish social philosophers. It may well have been that in the early 1940s he thought that these types of explanations were sufficient to cover all social phenomena. But as he delved deeper into these matters, as he studied the earlier writers more thoroughly and simultaneously expanded his studies into such areas as psychology, he broadened his explanatory framework. By the late 1960s he was able to write passages like the following: "the *transmission* of rules of conduct takes place from *individual to individual*, while what may be called the natural selection of rules will operate on the basis of the greater or lesser efficiency of the resulting *order of the group*" ([1967a] 1967, 67), emphasis in the original).[10]

Clearly, there is a role for "individuals" in this account. And I think that one is on solid ground to say that Hayek remained to the end an ontological individualist. But it is also clear that he was willing to be eclectic in deciding which level was the proper one in attempting to provide a given social explanation. The footnote with which Hayek chose to open the article just cited makes the point well: "we shall occasionally use the pair of concepts 'order and its elements' and 'groups and individuals' interchangeably, although the former is of course the more general term of which the relation between group and individual is a particular instance" (Hayek [1967a] 1967, 66). This is not the way that a doctrinaire methodological individualist would begin an article.[11]

4   Are constitutional political economists also rationalist constructivists?

By the 1960s Hayek was developing a general framework for understanding the evolution of complex orders within a variety of phenomena, from the individual brain all the way on up to a society.[12] Central to the framework is that such orders typically arise as the result of the relevant elements following abstract rules. These rules are generally followed unconsciously, and the "agent" following them (even in cases where the "agent" is capable of speech) cannot explain what the rule is or why she is following it. Thus perception and pattern-recognition, the learning of language and of how to perform various skilled tasks, even many instinctive behaviors of animals arise from the following of (often simple, yet also often inarticulable) rules (Hayek, [1962] 1967, 43–65).

In this model "learning" may be viewed as a process in which an agent engages in a particular behavior, then corrects or reclassifies its perceptions or rules as a result of the outcome. Learning can be at the biological level (this might be carried on through an individual's particular genetic heritage, plus its species' hard-wiring), at the individual level, and at the social level (where what is learned is passed on in a society's institutions). An example of the last is the ability of markets to utilize dispersed knowledge, and to permit the discovery and transmission of new knowledge, this being the paradigmatic Hayekian case of how institutions promote the expansion of knowledge. Language too is both a part of what cultures transmit as well as something which enables (and shapes the content of) cultural transmission. Finally, cultural evolution itself is the process, often involving a competition among rules and institutions, by which the framework in which social interactions occur emerges and changes.

Within the process of cultural evolution, sometimes group-beneficial institutions emerge spontaneously, in that individuals in pursuing their own interests create them. The institutions are not intentional artifacts, they are rather (as Austrians, quoting Adam Ferguson, like to put it) "results of human action but not of human design" (Hayek [1967b] 1967, 96). The Scottish tradition focused on the emergence role of spontaneous social orders, and later the Austrian Carl Menger provided his own paradigmatic example with his conjectural history of the emergence of money. As noted earlier, game theorists would characterize such situations as coordination games. Once in place the institutions are self-enforcing, so that compliance is not generally a problem: Though free to do so, most people (even with no police in sight) would not drive the wrong way down a highway entrance ramp.

Sometimes, though, individual interests conflict with group interests, and prisoner's dilemma-type game situations result. It is important to note that even in prisoner's dilemma situations, cooperative behavior may emerge. Among sociobiologists kin selection has sometimes been invoked to explain this, but more commonly (especially when repeated encounters between agents occur) the notion of "reciprocity" may be utilized. Viktor Vanberg and James Buchanan (chapter 4 of Vanberg 1994) suggest that the advantages of reciprocal behavior can often be learned; indeed, it may even be the case that they may become to some extent biologically hard-wired. Reciprocity seems to work especially well in gaining compliance of what the authors call "trust-rules" (e.g. tell the truth; keep promises), because reciprocal relationships can form with individual encounters and violaters can be identified and then sanctioned, first by the person involved and later, as reputation spreads, by the group. Reciprocity works less well for so-called "solidarity rules" (e.g. don't drop litter; don't shirk) because violations involve not the relationship between two people but a person's relationship to a group, so the violators are less easily targeted. Additional incentives to guarantee compliance are often needed here.

Though reciprocity or other moral rules may reduce the need of an externally imposed enforcement mechanism, certain prisoner's dilemma situations are clearly aided by their addition. Here is where constitutional political economy comes into play. Constitutional political economy is the field that systematically studies social interaction, one which proffers general analyses of, and specific solutions to, situations in which enforcement mechanisms need to be constructed. How would Hayek feel about the move to constitutional political economy?

Over the years Hayek has been at least ambivalent (others would say inconsistent) about the move to constitutional political economy. In one of his first political efforts, a paper that foreshadowed *The Road To Serfdom* ([1944] 1976), Hayek talked about planning the "system of general rules" under which individuals act (Hayek [1939] 1997, 194). In 1960 he published *The Constitution of Liberty* where he restated the classical liberal case for laws that are general, prospective, known, and certain. He offered his own "Model Constitution" in the final volume of *Law, Legislation and Liberty* (1979, chapter 17). Finally, in *The Fatal Conceit* (1988, 36) he praised the work of property rights theorists, noting that it "opened new possibilities for future improvements in the legal framework of the market order." All of this is consistent with constitutional political economy.

But there is plenty of evidence pointing in the other direction, too. Hayek famously railed against what he called "rationalist constructivism," the view that we have both the ability and the obligation to reconstruct our institutions along more rational lines (e.g. Hayek [1964a] 1967, 85). This was not just a recent development: Though the phrase "rationalist constructivism" did not emerge in his writings until the 1960s, Hayek was complaining about the errors of "individualism false" ([1945] 1948, chapter 1), and about the "planning mentality" of the "men of science" ([1941a, 1941b] 1997) in the 1940s. But as time went on, this suspicion deepened, and Hayek seems increasingly to have been led to a profound epistemological pessimism. In his view, we simply cannot know enough to try to reshape our institutions. Reason properly used seeks to understand its own limitations; to think otherwise is to fall victim to the sin of hubris (e.g. 1960, 69–70).

This development is evident in Hayek's writings on cultural evolution, especially in his movement away from Menger and towards group selection when discussing the formation of institutions. Whereas Menger rationalized the formation of institutions that are the unintended consequences of self-interested human action, group selection allowed Hayek to discuss institutions that benefit the group but whose formation can not be attributed to the actions of self-interested individuals. This is the principle reason that someone like Vanberg, who is an advocate of both methodological individualism and of constitutional political economy, has so little patience with Hayek's use of group selection. He proposes a reconstruction of Hayek's thought, one that is more consonant with both methodological individualism and constitutional political economy (Vanberg 1994, 1; chapter 5, especially nn. 24, 25, and 31; chapter 6).

So what do we make of this tension in Hayek's thought? Is Hayek the epistemological pessimist being inconsistent when he proposes a model constitution?

One way to resolve the dilemma is to take Hayek's remarks as occupying different levels of generality, one being about rule design, the other about rule selection.[13] Rule selection takes place as new rules and practices are tried out, and as they either succeed or fail. Anyone, including Hayek himself, is free to put forward a proposal about how a new rule will improve things. Hayek's own proposed "rule designs" are informed by what he thinks has succeeded in the past. But Hayek the epistemological pessimist knows that there is no guarantee that they will be selected in new situations. Another solution is to see Hayek as accepting what might be termed as "piece-meal" or marginal changes to existing institutions (Hayek 1979, n. 50 might be cited as evidence for this view). His remarks on rationalist constructivism would then be seen as applicable only to the wholesale reconstruction of institutions.

Either of these solutions might allow Hayek to be interpreted as supporting the work of constitutional political economists, even as he voiced pessimism about rationalist constructivism. However, neither sheds any light on *how* Hayek reaches his conclusions about which institutions should be tinkered with, and which left alone. This is especially relevant given that his proposals (e.g. his model constitution) sometimes go far beyond tinkering, and that, as Jeremy Shearmur (1996, 83–87) has observed, at various points in his writings certain institutions (e.g. religion) are both praised and criticized.

For another line of defense, one might note that the world was a very different place when he first began writing about the dangers of rationalist constructivism. Despite his best efforts, for much of the twentieth century "planning" was not usually interpreted as meaning "constructing a viable constitution," but referred to a process both more extensive and more intrusive. In such a climate, Hayek naturally might emphasize the limitations of our ability to construct institutions. Though there may be much truth to this, it does not explain why Hayek seemed to become even-more pessimistic in his last works, which were written during a time when support for market solutions was increasing around the world.

Finally, it may well be that, at the end of the day, Hayek simply was less optimistic than constitutional political economists are about the viability of constructing institutions, even constitutions. Hayek's foundational belief was that the institutional framework of any society consists of a complex and intertwined set of practices, norms, and structures. These cannot simply be imposed on a new society. The transitions taking place in the former Eastern Bloc countries and in Western Europe may provide further evidence as to whether a Vanberg or a Hayek has the more plausible view.

If we are concerned with Hayek's views on cultural evolution, however, these issues, fascinating though they may be, are pretty much beside the point. We can see this by looking more closely at Viktor Vanberg's argument. Vanberg wants to reconstruct Hayek's ideas so that constitutional choice is permitted, and offers some interesting recommendations for how such a reconstruction might be accomplished. But in trying to do this, a subtle shift of the argument has taken place. Vanberg's claim is that, in situations of prisoner's dilemma, it is often the case that self-interested actions can lead to suboptimal outcomes, particularly in the absence of other constraints on behavior that a constitution might provide. This, then, is the rationale for adding constitutional choice to Hayek's analysis.

But this changes Hayek's question. In his writings on cultural evolution, what intrigued him were those institutions and practices that came into existence that were not evidently in the narrow self-interest of the parties engaging in them, the moral code being the principal case in point. The work of constitutional political economists addresses a different, more contemporaneous question: How can we change the environment in which rules are followed so that individual behavior is more likely to advance certain societal goals?

Hayek was suspicious about constructivist themes; as noted above, his epistemological pessimism might lead him to doubt Vanberg's project because he felt that we could never adequately foresee the actual consequences of our constitutional changes. But beyond that, Hayek was interested in explaining how institutions whose development didn't make sense given the prisoner's dilemma nevertheless came into being. Hayek's question is a positive one concerning the past, Vanberg's is a normative one concerning the present. Hayek's turn towards group selection may well be viewed as a mistake. But his question is an important one. It is a question that has intrigued many others, one that has so far not been well answered, and one that could be forgotten if Vanberg's integrative solution became widely accepted.[14]

5 The process of cultural evolution

Hayek credits genetic or biological evolution as the source of some human traits, namely our instincts (e.g. such things as solidarity and cooperation with other small-group members). He also notes that our reason is a later development, something that itself evolved through time. Finally, standing between our instincts and our reason, "logically, psychologically, temporally," is custom and tradition (Hayek 1988, 23). His theory of cultural evolution deals with the emergence of the last set of practices.

Any model of an evolutionary process must specify a unit of selection, a source of variation, a means by which variations may be passed on, and a selection mechanism.

In the opening chapter of *The Fatal Conceit* the unit of selection is variously described as rules, norms, habits, practices, structures, traditions, and institutions.

The mechanism of variation is harder to locate. One possible source is noted in the following sentence, one which echoes a theme of earlier work: "Competition is a procedure of discovery, a procedure involved in all evolution, that led man unwittingly to respond to novel situations" (1988, 19). He also mentions that "genetic evolution had probably also already endowed human individuals with a great variety of characteristics which were better adjusted to the many different environmental niches into which men had penetrated than those of any non-domesticated animal" (1988, 18). This suggests that humans themselves have long exhibited considerable variation, and that the force of competition among them, in response to changes in their environments, drove these diverse humans, however unwittingly, to experiment with new behaviors.

Hayek is succinct in describing the mechanism by which practices are transmitted: "rules are handed on by tradition, teaching, and imitation" (1988, 12).

He is equally unequivocal regarding the selection mechanism: "Cultural evolution operates largely through group selection" (1988, 25), that is, rules are "fairly rapidly spread by means of an evolutionary selection – the comparative increase of population and wealth – of those groups that happened to practice them" (1988, 6).

Hayek's presentation is informal, and his framework is very general. For example, not only is his list rather long, Hayek never provides definitions for exactly what gets passed on during the process of evolution.[15] When he comes to filling in the historical record, he notes that, because much of the evolution took place long ago and created little in the way of a fossil record, "we are reduced to reconstruct it as a sort of conjectural history in the sense of the Scottish moral philosophers of the eighteenth century" (1979, 156). Prior to *The Fatal Conceit*, much of what Hayek had to say about cultural evolution leaned heavily on those earlier conjectural histories, most of which took the form of "rational reconstructions" of the evolution of the institutions of capitalism. These references are still evident in *The Fatal Conceit*, but in the second and third chapters of the book he adds a number of new references to more contemporary work in economic history, philosophy, and anthropology. These are perhaps the strongest chapters in this oft-criticized book.

Before exploring the evolution of the institutions of capitalism, Hayek offers some important caveats that his critics have frequently overlooked. He notes, for example, that it would be wrong to conclude that "whatever rules have evolved are always and necessarily conducive to the survival and increase of populations" (1988, 20). So Hayek is no functionalist. He also states up front that his analysis "cannot prove the superiority of market institutions" (1988, 20–21), but only help us to understand how such an unpopular, but productive, set of institutions might emerge and survive. Finally, he decries the naturalistic fallacy: just because something survives, it does *not* in Hayek's opinion prove that it is necessarily "good" (1988, 27). He does point out, though, that since the traditions he describes have permitted large increases in population to occur, their removal would doubtless be accompanied by a massive reduction in our numbers.

We turn at last to group selection. Hayek's exposure to the idea probably dates back to the 1950s, and his enthusiasm for it seemed only to grow over time (Caldwell 2000). By *The Fatal Conceit* he obviously saw it as a necessary component for answering his central questions, namely: How did those rules of conduct, moral codes, and institutions of capitalism, practices that can make us so uncomfortable, that are repugnant to both our nature and to our reason, ever get established? And how is it that, once they got established, they not only persisted but thrived?

Hayek turned to group selection to answer these questions because (1) he didn't think (unlike, say, someone like Menger) that all such institutions could be explained as the outcome of self-interested individual action, and (2) he saw the only other alternative explanatory framework, that of sociobiology, as being too single-minded, too all-encompassing. Unfortunately, Hayek is as vague in his discussions of group selection as he is elsewhere; as Robert Sugden (1993, 399), who reproduces a number of passages from Hayek's work, dryly observes, "In the quotations which I have given, we can see hints of several quite different models of group selection, none of which has been developed."

The conclusion we must draw is evident: though Hayek's reconstruction of what actually took place in the process of cultural evolution is richly suggestive, it is also incomplete. He left much work for future generations of scholars to do.

That said, I for one would add that, in wanting to expand the explanatory framework, I think that Hayek's instincts were all to the good. It is simply too early to tell which of several possible explanatory frameworks, from group selection, to evolutionary psychology, to theoretical work in game theory and complexity theory, to the careful study of whatever historical or contemporary records might exist by anthropologists, economic historians, and the like, to the discovery and reconstruction of various causal social processes by realist philosophers of science, might yield the most fruit. Surely it is likely that it will be some combination of them. That a more interdisciplinary approach may be necessary if we are to make any headway with this problem is both exciting and methodologically significant, going as it does against the disciplinary specialization that has dominated social sciences in this century. And even better, the movement towards more interdisciplinary studies seems stronger now than ever.

What, then, is Hayek's legacy? He asked a key question: How did institutions that we often don't like, and which cannot be explained as the result of self-seeking human action, come into being and persist? He did not get far enough in trying to answer it, but researchers in many different fields are now taking up the challenge. We might also observe that in exploring questions that interested him, Hayek was always a fearless voyager into new fields and disciplines. That his question is on the table in the banquet hall of what promises to be a much more interdisciplinary social science might be considered as one of Hayek's final, and most important, legacies.

Notes

1. For alternative interpretations of Hayek's "interpretive turn" see Madison (1989, 1990), Burczak (1994).
2. For example, in Caldwell (1994) I take issue with the notion that Hayek ever endorsed hermeneutics.

3. This summary draws on a similar one provided in Caldwell (2000).
4. I am excluding those places where Hayek refers to the methodological individualism of others, like Menger or Schumpeter, as is the case for the references found in, for example, the index of Hayek (1992, 274).
5. Though see Lange-von Kulessa (1997, 274–276) for the claim that Hayek's later work in psychology may be interpreted as providing a foundation for his methodological individualism.
6. John Gray (1986, 47–55) details the considerable distance between the approaches of Hayek and Becker.
7. I attended a Conference on Behavioral Economics held at Princeton in May 1984, and one speaker presented a paper listing the factors that she thought might influence a person's choices. Her presentation consisted of reading the list. About twenty minutes into the "paper" most members of the audience were twisting and turning uncomfortably in their seats. The paper never appeared in the conference volume.
8. My interpretation conflicts with that of Birner (1999, 68), who claims that "In his economics and his methodology between the 1920s and 1950s, Hayek is a staunch defender of methodological individualism." Birner's chief evidence from Hayek's economics is his rejection of statistical aggregates (Hayek felt they masked changes in relative prices, which was an essential element of Austrian cycle theory) and his desire to make his cycle theory consistent with marginal value theory (1999, 56–57). This ignores the fact that Hayek's own cycle theory did not have the kinds of individualist foundations Birner commends, as Birner himself actually emphasizes: "Hayek was not interested in explaining the misperceptions that cause industrial fluctuations in terms of the workings of the minds of individual decision makers. What he wanted to do instead, was to investigate the systemic sources of misperceptions, i.e., the monetary system" (1999, 61). At a minimum, I think that this makes clear that different writers attach very different meanings to the term "methodological individualism."
9. This difference is a significant one. Hayek was prepared to accept the equilibrium construct when used to describe the choice of the individual. He viewed it as a tautology: the agent is always in equilibrium because the choice made always reflects the agent's preferences at the moment of choice. But in his famous 1937 paper, "Economics and knowledge,"(Hayek [1937] 1948) Hayek said that this could not get us very far towards understanding how societal equilibrium might emerge, which was for him the most significant question. Mises, on the other hand, thought that starting from acting man, one could via a "verbal chain of logic" end up reaching *a priori* true conclusions about society. The criticism of Mises in his 1937 article was implicit rather than explicit. Had Hayek explicitly started his analyses from the individual agent level, his split from Mises would have been more evident. This may explain his hesitancy to do so. For more on these matters, see Caldwell (1988); cf. Hayek (1994, 72–73).
10. See Caldwell (2000) for a fuller account of the emergence of Hayek's ideas on cultural evolution.
11. Both Vromen (1995, 172) and Lange-von Kulessa (1997, 279) make similar arguments.
12. Parts of this section draw from my review (Caldwell 1998) of Vanberg (1994).

13. Peter Boettke and Karen Vaughn made this point in a discussion at a Liberty Fund Conference on "Spontaneous Orders, Complexity and Liberty" held in Charleston, S C in March 1998.
14. Among others intrigued by the question are Jon Elster (1989, 115), who seeks the origin of norms that do not arise from the actions of self-interested agents, and Douglass North (1981, chapter 5), who inquires about the origins of "ideology," or self-sacrificial behavior, given the free-rider problem. Neither could answer his own formulation of the question. North, however, makes a claim that certainly would have distressed Hayek: that the impersonality of the extended order itself, rather than the pernicious writings of psychoanalysts and socialist intellectuals, may account for the undermining of the moral codes upon which its smooth functioning depend.
15. At the conference, Philip Pettit suggested that Richard Dawkins' ([1976] 1989 and 1982) work on "memes" might provide a good starting point for reconstructing this part of Hayek's theory.

References

Birner, Jack (1999). The surprising place of cognitive psychology in the work of F.A. Hayek, *History of Economic Ideas*, 7(1/2), 43–84

Boettke, Peter (1990). The theory of spontaneous order and cultural evolution in the social theory of F.A. Hayek, *Cultural Dynamics*, 3(1), 61–83

Bowles, Samuel (1998). Endogenous preferences: the cultural consequences of markets and other economic institutions, *Journal of Economic Literature*, 36(1), 75–111

Burczak, Theodore (1994). The postmodern moments of F.A. Hayek's economics, *Economics and Philosophy*, 10(1), 31–58

Caldwell, Bruce (1988). Hayek's transformation, *History of Political Economy*, 20(4), 513–541

(1994). Hayek's scientific subjectivism, *Economics and Philosophy*, 10(2), 305–313

(1998). Review of Viktor Vanberg, *Rules and Choice in Economics, Journal of Economic Methodology*, 5(2), 299–304

(2000). The emergence of Hayek's ideas on cultural evolution, *The Review of Austrian Economics*, 13(1), 5–22

(2001). Hodgson on Hayek: a critique, *Cambridge Journal of Economics*, 25(4), 539–553

Dawkins, Richard ([1976] 1989). *The Selfish Gene*, new edn. Oxford: Oxford University Press

(1982). *The Extended Phenotype*. Oxford: W.H. Freeman

De Vlieghere, Martin (1994). A reappraisal of Hayek's cultural evolutionism, *Economics and Philosophy*, 10(2), 285–304

Elster, Jon (1989). Social norms and economic theory, *Journal of Economic Perspectives*, 3(4), 99–117

Fleetwood, Steve (1995). *Hayek's Political Economy: The Socio-Economics of Order*. London: Routledge

Gray (1986), John. *Hayek on Liberty*, 2nd. edn. Oxford: Blackwell

Hayek, F.A. ([1939] 1997). Freedom and the economic system; reprinted in Hayek (1997, 189–211)

([1941a] 1997). Planning, science and freedom; reprinted in Hayek (1997, 213–220)
([1941b] 1997). Review of Polanyi and Clark; reprinted in Hayek (1997, 246–249)
([1944] 1976). *The Road To Serfdom*. Chicago: University of Chicago Press
([1942–44]). Scientism and the study of society; reprinted in Hayek ([1952] 1979, 17–182)
([1945] 1948). Individualism: true and false; reprinted in Hayek (ed.), *Individualism and Economic Order*. Chicago: University of Chicago Press (1948, 1–32)
(1948). *Economics and Knowledge*; reprinted in Hayek (ed.), *Individualism and Economic Order*. Chicago: University of Chicago Press
([1952] 1979). *The Counter-Revolution of Science: Studies on the Abuse of Reason*, 2nd edn. Indianapolis: Liberty Press
(1960). *The Constitution of Liberty*. Chicago: University of Chicago Press
([1962] 1967). Rules, perception and intelligibility; reprinted in Hayek (1967c, 43–65)
([1964a] 1967). Kinds of rationalism; reprinted in Hayek (1967c, 82–95)
([1964b] 1967). The theory of complex phenomena; reprinted in Hayek (1967c, 22–42)
([1967a] 1967). Notes on the evolution of systems of rules of conduct, in Hayek (1967c, 66–81)
([1967b] 1967). The results of human action but not of human design, in Hayek (1967c, 96–105)
(1967c). *Studies in Philosophy, Politics and Economics*. Chicago: University of Chicago Press
(1979). *The Political Order of a Free People*, vol. 3 of *Law, Legislation and Liberty*. Chicago: University of Chicago Press
(1988). *The Fatal Conceit*, ed. W.W. Bartley III, vol. 1, *The Collected Works of F.A. Hayek*. Chicago: University of Chicago Press
(1992). *The Fortunes of Liberalism: Essays on Austrian Economics and the Ideal of Freedom*, Peter Klein (ed.), vol. 4, *The Collected Works of F.A. Hayek*. Chicago: University of Chicago Press
(1994). *Hayek on Hayek*, Stephen Kresge and Leif Wenar (eds.). London: Routledge
(1997). *Socialism and War*, Bruce Caldwell (ed.), vol. 10, *The Collected Works of F.A. Hayek*. Chicago: University of Chicago Press
Hodgson, Geoffrey (1993). *Economics and Evolution: Bringing Life Back into Economics*. Ann Arbor: University of Michigan Press
Lange-von Kulessa, Juergen (1997). Searching for a methodological synthesis: Hayek's individualism in the light of recent holistic criticism, *Journal of Economic Methodology*, 4(2), 267–287
Lawson, Tony (1994). Realism and Hayek: a case of continuing transformation, in M. Colonna, H. Hagemann, and O. Hamouda (eds.), *Capitalism, Socialism and Knowledge: The Economics of F.A. Hayek*, vol.2. Aldershot: Edward Elgar, 131–159
(1997). *Economics and Reality*. London: Routledge
Madison, G.B. (1989). Hayek and the interpretive turn, *Critical Review*, 3(2), 169–185
(1990). Getting beyond objectivism: the philosophical hermeneutics of Gadamer and Ricoeur, in Don Lavoie (ed.), *Economics and Hermeneutics*. London: Routledge, 34–58

Mises, Ludwig von ([1949] 1963). *Human Action: A Treatise on Economics*, 3rd rev. edn. Chicago: Contemporary Books

North, Douglass (1981). *Structure and Change in Economic History*. New York: Norton

Shearmur, Jeremy (1996). *Hayek and After*. London and New York: Routledge

Steele, David Ramsay (1987). Hayek's theory of cultural group selection, *Journal of Libertarian Studies*, 8(2), 171–195

Stigler, George and Gary Becker (1977). De gustibus non est disputandum, *American Economic Review*, 67, 76–90

Sugden, Robert (1993). Normative judgments and spontaneous order: the contractarian element in Hayek's thought, *Constitutional Political Economy*, 4(3), 393–424

Vanberg, Viktor (1994). *Rules and Choice in Economics*. London: Routledge

Vromen, Jack (1995). *Economic Evolution: An Enquiry into the Foundations of the New Institutional Economics*. London: Routledge

Witt, Ulrich (1994). The theory of societal evolution: Hayek's unfinished legacy, in Jack Birner and Rudy Van Zijp (eds.), *Hayek, Co-ordination and Evolution: His Legacy in Philosophy, Politics, Economics and the History of Ideas*. London: Routledge, 178–189

Yeager, Leland (1989). Reason and cultural evolution, *Critical Review*, 3(2), 324–335

15   Putting evidence in its place: John Mill's early struggles with "facts in the concrete"

Neil De Marchi

1 Overview

Experience versus assumed behavior

Mill was a realist in the most fundamental sense: he believed in the existence of an external world. Since he also believed that our knowledge of facts or phenomena is received via sense impressions, he had to show that there is indeed a reality independent of these. His approach to that problem remained much the same over time, though he experimented with various forms of words for articulating it. Basically it held two elements. First, not all sensations are fleeting. They can, and some do, retain the same properties under changed circumstances, even though those changes may affect appearances. For sensations having such persistent properties Mill adopted the Kantian label "perdurable." Second, impressions and memories are personal but not necessarily individual: they may be common to vast numbers of individuals. That there are perdurable and public possibilities of sensation seemed to Mill sufficient to back his claim that there is an external world.[1]

I will not probe Mill's grounds for realism. Rather, taking his realist convictions as fixtures of his mental apparatus, my aim here is to examine afresh his move in the early 1830s to portray inquiry in political economy as unavoidably *a priori*. He defined this phrase in his famous 1836 essay on method, "On the Definition of Political Economy; and on the Method of Investigation Proper to It." *A priori* reasoning is "reasoning from an assumed hypothesis" ([1836b] 1967), *Works* IV, 325). That characterization was purposely strong: Mill wanted it understood that "experience" is not a valid alternative to "abstract" or "hypothetical" reasoning in political economy or the other moral sciences. The implied tension – what business could an avowed realist have denying the importance of "experience"? – is easily enough dissolved with careful exposition and precise terminology, and Mill himself supplied most of what was needed in those directions. But why did he set up such a strong opposition in the first

304

place between "facts in the concrete" and "abstract reasoning" (329)? What was it about experience that had come to trouble him so?

Two cheers for "facts in the concrete"

Mill gave answers to these questions in his 1836 essay. A single argument covered them both, and the reasoning is familiar. The problem with concrete experience in human affairs is that (1) there are so many causal factors operating; moreover, (2) these are "never perfectly known to us," (3) most of them we cannot directly observe, and (4) for those we can, it is hardly ever in controlled conditions (327–328). These difficulties add up to a powerful case for *not* starting with experience: if facts in the concrete are uninterpretable, clearly they cannot be independent building blocks of knowledge. Nonetheless, there is a difficulty with taking Mill's answer as his final – better, his representative – word. In two important essays published shortly after 1836 he spoke of concrete experience in much more positive terms.

One of these was a carefully wrought statement of 1838 on Bentham – Mill's own early mentor. There he singled out, as Bentham's great contribution to human philosophy, the introduction of the "method of detail." The method, Mill explained, comprised the practice "of never reasoning about wholes until they have been resolved into their parts, nor about abstractions till they have been translated into realities" ([1838] 1969, 86; cf. 830). Accepting Bentham's view, as Mill seems to have done, implies that there are corresponding concrete counterparts to theoretical entities, and that translation mechanisms exist for moving from one to the other – in either direction. It follows, too, that any translation problem must be of a practical sort: for example, a translation would necessarily be partial, and relatively useless, if we are unaware of key causes. Still, there is no hint here that Mill had any objection of principle to working with "realities" – quite the contrary, in fact.

In the other essay, a friendly review of Thomas Carlyle's *French Revolution* ([1837] 1985, *Works* XX, 133–166), Mill had already gone farther in the direction of this conclusion. At one point in his review he inserted comments that put a different spin on his own recently published views on method. What is the role of general principles, he asked. When the object of our interest is "out of our reach" – cannot be observed – "we must follow general principles." But why, exactly? Because doing so will reduce the likelihood of our going wrong, and we are "almost certain not to go *so far* wrong," as we should without them (200, emphasis mine).

This warning about going wrong is in part exactly the same as the one Mill gave to would-be *users* of theory in the 1836 essay itself. General principles are abstracted from multiple occurrences and as such are only approximately true of any single instance. In the words of the review, a general principle is "a mere approximation to truth; an approximation obtained by striking an average of many cases, and consequently not exactly fitting any one case" (199; cf. "On the Definition," *Works* IV, 326). A wise person, intending to apply a principle, therefore looks for what may be missing from it, or seeks the several principles perhaps involved in the situation of interest. But once allowance for this aspect of the warning has been made, we are still left, as in the Bentham essay, with a basically pragmatic argument against working with observations. Error is possible even with theory, only the chance of error is less.

There is more involved here than simply reducing the choice of methods to the pursuit of least error. Mill, in his review, seems actually to be looking for a way to place observation in the foreground. He tells the reader that if the object of our interest is unobservable then speculating without principles means that we are adrift "on the boundless ocean of mere conjecture." However, "when we are not driven to guess, when we have means and appliances for observing, general principles are nothing more or other than helps towards a better use of those means and appliances" (161). Without telling the reader what these might be, Mill goes on to extoll Carlyle's concreteness. And at this point he almost turns his review into a test application of Bentham's method of detail. "Mr. Carlyle brings the thing [the Revolution] before us in the *concrete* – clothed not indeed in *all* its properties and circumstances, since these are infinite, but in as many of them as can be authentically ascertained, and imaginatively realized" (158, emphasis in the original). Whatever he may have meant by these phrases, the thrust of Mill's thought is clear.[2] General principles are "not intended to dispense with thinking and examining, but to help us to think and examine," to help us to know "which end to begin at, what points to enquire into" (200–201). In short, they are aids to observation.

One might argue that all the differences here are matters of emphasis only. Yet the more measured tone and altered emphases are sufficiently clear to warrant the question: which account should we take as indicative, that of the essay on method, or that found in writings such as these essays, and still others like them?

The argument in brief

The more measured Mill is at one with the Mill of an extraordinarily clear and methodologically sophisticated investigation of the mid-1820s, an essay entitled "Paper Currency and Commercial Distress" [1826b]. Even more so than the review of Carlyle, this essay can be read as an application of the method of detail. Set against it, and the two essays I have cited from 1837 (the Carlyle) and 1838 (the Bentham), the author of the 1836 essay on method appears almost aberrantly strident in favor of reasoning "from assumptions, not from facts" (*Works* IV, 325). I will try to account for this uncharacteristic stridency. However, my main aim here is to enlarge the interpretative space, thereby facilitating the recovery of nuances that seem to be validated by Mill's own embrace of them both prior to and subsequent to the 1836 essay. My approach complements the numerous existing treatments that focus on the essay of 1836 in isolation.

I shall argue that the appearance Mill gave in 1836, of having quite rejected empirical inquiry as a way to gain moral–scientific insight, was more than that, though it does have a lot to do with the questions he was asking at the time. One of these was whether we can expect *certainty* from examining facts in the concrete. This was a demanding criterion to apply, but relative to that standard he found history, and nonexperimental evidence more generally, wanting. Mill's negative judgment, however, also marked the end-point of a decade-long evolution, during which he at first entertained at least limited possibilities for empirical evidence – a position he also never quite gave up.

Mill's starting position owed a great deal to Bentham's method of detail and his writings on legal evidence. Precisely because certainty is rare, Bentham urged, we should refine our methods for grasping degrees of belief, or of the "probative force" of witness testimony. He also employed the notion of a judge able to detach from his own sense impressions, and in this way cause his observation to stand for that of many independent witnesses. Mill was drawn to this latter notion, the more because his willingness to follow Bentham's "probabilistic" inclinations increasingly vied with drawbacks he detected in evidence-based reasoning. History was particularly problematic. Complexity and the absence of experiment were part of the problem. Another element burdening all histories, according to Mill, is that we are able to know the present much more completely than past periods or events. A third strand, not especially related to history, is the inherent conservatism of any method based on the close examination of instances. The approach requires no separate examination of the existing framework, or body of rules or precedents, supplying the principles to apply to any particular instance. Mill was especially conscious of this conservative bent in English law.

For a long time, nonetheless, as we have seen, Mill was prepared to grant that in certain instances facts clothed in all their complexity can be analyzed satisfactorily, by linking them, through analogy, to other events, already explained by a known cause or causes. Finding the resemblance, or the common characteristic(s) of the cases is, in the language of Mill's "Early Draft" of his *System of Logic*, written between 1830 and 1833 ([1873] 1981, *Works* I, 167, 191, 229), "a mere short hand registration of facts known" (1974, *Works* VIII, 1103). It is not a true induction, that is, an inference from facts known to facts unknown (1103); nor can it yield generalizations. Even so, such "analogical reasoning" may be a valid step towards generalization; for, in the right conditions, it is likely, even if not certain, that the ultimate generalization reached will be found *not* to exclude the instance under examination (1100). We will examine more closely how this likelihood is established.

Over the course of the 1820s Mill more than once expressed disappointment that the public was much less willing to acquiesce in knowledge obtained in moral and social science, as compared with physical science. In the former sphere, people looked backward, to the "wisdom" of antiquity, a standard that would have seemed ridiculous applied to physical science. But why was the public so willing to accept the improvements wrought in physical science? For Mill the answer lay in the certainty of knowledge in that sphere, a certainty he ascribed to the method of inquiry adopted. He concluded that progress towards certainty in moral and social science would come only with an understanding of the proper method of inquiry there too. As noted earlier, against this standard, evidence, facts in the concrete, hence history and nonexperimental evidence, showed up badly, and Mill's writings increasingly detail and portray their weaknesses. This is the immediate background to his 1836 essay on the method of political economy.

With this summary evolution before us, it is time to re-trace Mill's steps more slowly.

2   Facts in the concrete

When is an instance analyzable?

Mill's 1826 essay, "Paper Currency and Commercial Distress," was addressed to the "practicals," as he dubbed men of affairs, politicians, and writers who sought to determine every question by a direct induction from a particular case, or on the basis of a few convenient facts. Here Mill argued against the practicals' notion that paper currency, and, in particular, small notes issued by the country banks, was responsible for the speculation of 1824–1825, and the crisis of 1826. He did so using a mixed method. On the one hand he reasoned from "the nature and properties of currency and trade," while also hinting that perhaps this is not as straightforward as one might prefer. That is to say, (a) it is not as simple as showing the theory's discordance with the facts, and (b) is "more laborious in the process," though in the end both approaches are equally conclusive ([1826b] 1967, *Works* IV, 80–81). In any event, Mill also adduced facts to disprove the practicals' explanation, and seems to have regarded the in-principle and the in-fact methods as complements.

The deliberate mix appears to have been an acknowledgment on Mill's part that facts, if they are to have meaning, must be attached to some principle or generalization. Principles supply the analogy by which instances can be linked. Moreover, principles, or laws, make it possible to explain particular events. However, none of this works in reverse. Isolated facts, the 1826 essay suggested, can "negative an alleged cause," but they do not enable us "to assign the real one" (102). This asymmetry embodies important limiting conditions on the study of instances. Nonetheless, that there are some instances in which it is possible to untangle the mess of numerous, often veiled, and complexly interwoven causes operating upon real events, also sets a limit on the scope of the 1836 proposition that political economy "reasons . . . and must necessarily reason, from assumptions, not from facts" ([1836b] 1967, *Works* IV, 325).

But what determines whether a single event is analyzable by the method of resemblance, or analogy? Mill laid down the conditions in his *A System of Logic*, not before, so we have to read backwards to the instances he adduced in the years prior to 1843. I summarize his discussion in chapter XX of book III of the *Logic*, on Induction. Comparing two events, *A* and *B*, argument by analogy amounts to proposing that, because some property *p* belongs to *A*, and *A* and *B* share certain other properties, it is likely that *p* will also be found to belong to *B*. The likelihood depends, at a minimum, on the known resemblances not *preventing* the occurrence of *p*, though *p* itself need not be a determinative property ([1843] 1973, Works VII, 554–555). Likelihood also requires that, on an average of all cases, there will be "a competition" between known points of agreement and known points of difference. In other words, the larger the proportion of properties that is known, the smaller will be the share of unknown properties, and the higher the "probability" that *B* will share property *p* (555). Mill went on to state that likelihood thus presupposes "tolerably extensive" knowledge of the events in question – without knowing the size of the denominator, for example, we could not be sure that the *proportion* of known resemblances is large. He concluded that the argument from analogy can approach "very near to a valid induction," but only where the area of resemblance is "very great" (559); that is, where we already know that *A* and *B* are "adjacent" – alike in nine out of ten known properties, say.

Mill clearly thought the problem situation discussed in his 1826 essay met these conditions (even if they were not made explicit at the time). So too in the case of the French Revolution. Not, it must be emphasized, that he thought it possible ever to fully describe a practical situation – compare his comment quoted above from the review of Carlyle – but in these two instances he felt that a reasonable judgment as to what took place really was possible. It will be useful to look more closely at these, and some other instances.

Illustrations: 1 – paper currency and commercial distress

Mill set out first to characterize the commercial distress by analogy with known cases. He was able to do this with help from Thomas Tooke's meticulous investigations into recent price history, *Thoughts and Details on the High and Low Prices of the Last Thirty Years* (1823). As to the nature of the speculative fever and subsequent crash, one need look no further, Mill suggested, than to a prior build-up in stocks of goods. This, combined with some reports of actual shortages, had fed expectations of scarcity and induced anticipatory price increases. Combined with the use of credit, these expectations came to be broadly held, extended themselves to goods other than those affected by the reported shortages, and influenced others than the experts – merchants and brokers in the know about specific commodities ([1826b] 1967, *Works* IV, 74–77, quoting Tooke). Thus described, the speculative build-up in 1824–1825, preceding the crisis and revulsion of 1826, appeared to be sufficiently close to the general experience known as "overtrading" to be classed as an instance of that general phenomenon. Mill appealed to parallel experiences in 1810–1811 and 1815–1816 as confirmation.

Having characterized the events in question Mill turned to detailed facts, not to ascribe true causes, but to negative false alleged ones. Practical men (here politicians), as noted, blamed the speculation on an overissue of paper currency, and in particular of small notes issued by country banks. At this point Mill invoked "the nature and properties of currency and trade" (80). It is impossible, he argued, that there could be an overissue of paper currency under conditions of free trade and free international movement of gold. Under those conditions Hume's price–specie flow mechanism will apply: an expansion of the paper issue will induce inflation, exports will suffer, the exchanges will fall, and gold will leave the country. The amounts of gold and paper in the currency thus vary inversely, but no change in the overall stock of currency (paper *plus* gold) can occur. This bit of general thinking guided Mill in his reading of the facts.

He acknowledged that the paper portion of the currency had increased, but added that this increase dated from at least 1822, well before the speculation of 1824 began in earnest. He also acknowledged that the country banks were chiefly responsible. But he pointed out that this is a normal process: these banks invariably issue more notes when there is a rise in the price of agricultural produce, because farmers wish to buy in and hold corn till they think the rise has ceased. They can readily obtain bank loans by offering their corn as collateral. At the same time, no such process as that just described would occur if there were no restrictions on the importation of foreign corn. Applying the mechanism outlined above, restrictions on corn imports prevent the substitution one would expect between paper issue and gold when agricultural prices rise, since the opportunity is strictly limited of bringing in foreign corn in exchange for gold. The normal mechanism safeguarding the nation against speculation and inflation owing to an increased paper issue is thus made ineffective: even if domestic corn prices rise, the paper issue can expand, and without loss of gold. But the phenomena observed are not owing to deficiencies of the paper currency – a supposed inherent tendency to overissue – or to careless practice by the country banks. All can be explained in terms of the corn laws, in combination with normal practice by those banks. Nor would placing restrictions on those banks prevent what had happened from happening again (86–88). Mill went into other details of the opposition beliefs, but this suffices to show that, by a judicious mix of theory and observation, he could dismiss the practicals' chief contentions.

In this instance, then, the events under examination, and selected test cases, proved to be adjacent. Mill was also able to use to good effect the distinction between material properties (the corn laws) and those without causative influence (paper currency in and of itself). And it is clear that he had amassed a very considerable knowledge of the relevant facts.

Illustrations: 2 – price movements

Mill had used Tooke's *High and Low Prices* in an earlier analysis, "War Expenditure" ([1824], *Westminster Review*, July 1824, *Works* IV, 3–22). There he aimed to show that price movements during the preceding three decades could not be accounted for in any degree by war expenditure, but were due in lesser degree to alterations in the currency, and mainly to seasonal factors. As in 1826, the method was mixed. Without going into details, examination of the material facts of the period disclosed its character, while theory supplied strong expectations as to what we should observe in such circumstances. More detailed facts were invoked to illustrate the theory and at the same time disconfirm the hypotheses of those who affirmed the chief causes to have been war expenditure and changes in the currency.

Illustrations: 3 – whether oaths are effective

In newspaper articles almost contemporary with this analysis Mill also explored a noneconomic instance in which he believed the circumstances were right for analyzing facts in the concrete. The instance involved sworn oaths, and the issue was whether or not they are effective in securing true testimony. In articles that appeared in the *Morning Chronicle* of 8 February 1823 and 25 July 1823 ([1823a], [1823b] 1986, *Works* XXII, 12–15, 30–33), Mill showed himself aware of the problem of composition of causes. He also discussed in simple form what he would call in his *A System of Logic* the "method of difference" (see [1843] 1974, *Works* VII, 391). The method, as Mill used it to analyze oaths, works as follows. Cause *O* (oaths), in conjunction with causes *L* (the law) and *PE* (popular enthusiasm), seems to be attended by true testimony. Truth is observed to be violated, however, when *O* alone is operative. Thus truth cannot be attributed to the swearing of oaths:

If we find that one of the causes, when unsupported by the others, is not followed by any degree of the effect in question, we shall be intitled to conclude, that in all those cases in which the effect really takes place, it is to the other causes, and not to this one, that it ought to be attributed. ([1823a] 1986, *Works* XXII, 13)

This analysis is exactly what Mill tried, in less explicit fashion, in eliminating certain proposed explanations of price movements post-French Revolution, and of the speculation and revulsion of 1824–1826.[3] Only, as he was to note in the *Logic*, reasoning from resemblance between instances is a method used because "There have been no opportunities of putting in practice the Method of Difference" or any other experimental method ([1843] 1973, *Works* VII, 555). When circumstances allowed it, we may infer, the Mill of the *Logic* preferred the certainty associated with the method of difference. There is no evidence that he made such a sharp distinction in the mid-1820s, though he knew that the only genuine certainty in reasoning from facts lay in their capacity to falsify alleged causes.

Illustrations: 4 – Carlyle's French Revolution

I pass quickly over the case of Carlyle's *French Revolution*, since Mill offered no justification for why he thought those events, complex and clothed in unique circumstances as he believed they were, could be characterized, and causes assigned. Mill's reasons might perhaps be gleaned by contrasting his review of Carlyle's history with what he said of numerous other histories, most of which he viewed negatively. His own political theory is also relevant here, as are the essays he published in a five-part series, "The Spirit of the Age," ([1831a], [1831b] 1986) which appeared in the *Examiner* between January and May 1831, though it remains unclear how he and Carlyle came to agree on causes given their differences on method. In any event, here I simply accept the causes Carlyle assigned, though it was uncharacteristic of Mill even to allow that causes could be positively assigned in a unique and complicated historical instance.

Carlyle adduced two causes, one each for the revolution itself, and for its failure to usher in a new order of society in France. The great cause of the revolution he ascribed to a gradual abdication by the king and nobles, and by the clergy, of their responsibility to provide that "guidance" which alone guarantees willing obedience on the part of a people (*Works* XX, 158–159). This "theorem," Mill wrote, is "true as far as it goes, and [wants] little of being as complete as any theory of so vast and complicated a phenomena can be." That the revolution failed to fashion a new order Carlyle explained as due to the people not having deep "convictions to base such order of things upon" (159).

Mill's review of Carlyle's *French Revolution* offered only a summary display of the method of resemblance. Yet, in combination with the other instances we have noticed, it shows us a Mill who, prior to and after his essay on method, believed a direct interrogation of the facts is sometimes useful. However, as we will now see, the role he assigned to this method diminished steadily. The erosion was most obvious in the case of history.

3 The limited uses of history

The best history is analysis of the present

Mill was interested in history, as he was interested in the law, because it represented an important way of marshaling human experience to the end of effecting change and improvement. But from the start he was critical of the two standard modes of writing histories: the old, or novelistic mode, which strove after vividness of conception and emotional effect; and the modern, in which narrative was used only for polemical purposes, to illustrate and instruct in the (alleged) laws of human nature and of human society, but which often failed because of partiality ("Mignet's French Revolution" [1826a] 1985, *Works* XX, 3–4). A "true and living picture" of the past is essential, Mill would later acknowledge; but it requires that the facts be "authentically ascertained," and also that people, events and causes be "imaginatively realized." Carlyle was the measure here (see n. 2 above). Just as essential, according to this later view, is history constructed as "a progressive chain of causes and effects." This demands accounts of states of society and of the human mind, and of their "filiation" ([1837] 1985, *Works* XX, 225). Explaining the filiation of states was the "ultimate and highest" stage in moving to a new "science of history," towards which the French had contributed the most. The task here was to go beyond understanding each state, and to show how each "produced" the one that followed it, according to the laws of human nature and of the "outward world" (225).

In the mid-1820s, however, Mill had little notion of this ultimate stage in constructing history. The first glimpse we catch of it is in his series, "The Spirit of the Age" ([1831a] 1986). From those essays it is clear that he had moved beyond romantic and polemical histories, to a view according to which understanding "states" was the important focus. This was the second of the three stages through which history must pass to become truly scientific, the first being to reconstruct events through the eyes and minds of contemporaries, eschewing anachronisms. In discussing this second stage Mill identified a serious weakness affecting all history writing. For the fact is, he observed, that we cannot know a past age anything like as well as we can know the present ("Spirit of the Age, I" ([1831a] 1986, *Works* XXII, 230). Only universal experience, summarized abstractly, as principles, yields true knowledge, but to derive these principles from a study of the past is well-nigh impossible. The reason is that the necessary materials simply are not available. One may learn, "in a morning's walk through London," more of the history of England in the nineteenth century than all the available histories teach of the other eighteen. For each of us can pick up, through the senses, a host of "obvious and universal facts." The trouble, however, is that these facts, being so obvious, "it seldom occurs to any one to place [them] on record" ([1831a] 1986, *Works* XXII, 230; cf. *Works* XX, 224). Thus it comes about that even true histories never teach general rules or, if they do, it is only because of "the notice bestowed by contemporaries on some accidental *exception*" (230, emphasis mine). The present, by contrast, "affords a fund of materials for judging, richer than the whole stores of the past, and far more accessible" (230).

Good history, but without a method of induction

Good history is possible, Mill had allowed in an 1828 review of Sir Walter Scott's *Life of Napoleon* ([1828] 1985). Even the best, however, does not advance us beyond the probabilistic knowledge available by reasoning through analogy. And that best requires an enlarged mind, matched by universal experience, plus skill in "the art of connecting facts into principles, and applying principles to explanation of facts" ([1828] 1985, *Works* XX, 56). These are high requirements. Indeed, the historian who is "fit for his office" must be "a *philosopher*." A philosopher, nonetheless, without any *method* for discovering principles.

The closest Mill came to enunciating a method for generalizing at this point was to invoke Bentham's argument that a good judge, called upon to render judgment in the absence of testimony, may project himself into the character of a multitude of witnesses. How does this work? In effect the judge's senses "are detached from his person, erected into so many independent persons, and in that character introduced as witnesses" (*Rationale* [182], vol. I, book I, chapter XII, 252). Mill combined this with Bentham's notion of measuring probative force in "degrees" of belief. In this matter Bentham had argued that legal judgments might be improved if, in giving and receiving testimony, we could get beyond the crude, all-or-nothing language of "I know–I believe" and their opposites (vol. I, book I, chapters V and VI).[4] But a judge, having heard testimony – even if in the form of his own observation and "internal perception" – reaches a decision based on a rich knowledge of human nature and after making allowance for the circumstances affecting the testimony (chapter V). In similar manner, to elicit "real facts," and distinguish them from "vague, scanty or conflicting, testimony," the historian should display both the enlarged views of a philosopher, and be "practised in striking the balance between opposing testimonies, or between testimony on the one side and probability on the other . . . [should] be, to sum up this also in a word, a consummate *judge*" ([1828] 1985, *Works* XX, 56, emphasis in the original).

So far we have seen Mill urging that history has limited access to the necessary enlarged experience of the past, without which generalizations can scarcely be expected. He also posed the same difficulty in another way. Historians are less likely to discover generalizations when common experiences are passed over, and all that is left to guide them to the rules they seek are occasional exceptions, noticed and recorded as a matter of happenstance. Mill's review of Scott's *Napoleon*, in addition, seems to confirm that he regarded historians' attempts at generalization as subject to the same limitation as reasoning through analogy: bound to be probabilistic, or less than certain. A third limitation emerges in the text of a speech Mill delivered to a meeting of the Utilitarian Society, in 1827, on "The Use of History" ([1827] 1988). Here we encounter for the first time the complexity argument that occupies such an important place in Mill's 1836 essay on method, where he promoted *a priori* reasoning.

Complexity, and lack of experiment

Mill's speech in effect ruled out reasoning through analogy in the case of history; for "in history no one instance can be a rule for another": circumstances are never repeated. "Even those circumstances which we know to exist are never in any two cases the same: and besides these there may be a hundred others which we do not dream of" ("Use of History," *Works* XXVI, 394). If it is said that all we need to know is that the "material circumstances" are the same, the answer is that we do not in fact have any way of knowing even this:

We see the results, only in the gross: We see that under particular laws the people are or seem contented and tranquil, that under particular systems of commercial policy the country seems prosperous . . . But do we see how many hidden causes have contributed to this result, or is there any one circumstance in the physical moral or political state of a nation which without other evidence than this we could boldly pronounce to be totally unconnected with it? (394)

The experimental method offers a way around these difficulties; however, experimentation is not available to us in the political world:

the great instrument by which we have penetrated the arcana of the physical world fails us in the political, *at least when history is our guide*. We cannot there combine and vary the circumstances as we will, we must rest content with the few and unsatisfactory experiments which nature has made. (394, emphasis mine)

The upshot is that, in "any system of politics which has only history for its basis," there is the same lack of certainty as in the one branch of physical science where we have "nothing better than history to go upon," namely, geology.

The importance of being certain

Certainty, we may assume, was always important to Mill, but in this 1827 speech for the first time he invokes it as a criterion for ruling out one whole approach to gaining useful knowledge. History, for all the reasons listed, but chiefly because of complexity combined with the unavailability of experimentation, is virtually useless, except as a means of saving the deeds of the great from oblivion (395; cf. "Sedgwick's Discourse" [1835] 1969, *Works* X, 44). Notice that this same condemnation was not yet extended to a political economy based on experience, though that may merely reflect the fact that political economy was not the subject of the 1827 speech. Mill states in his *Autobiography* that he drafted his essay on method in political economy in 1830 and 1831; and that, aside from a partial revision in 1833, the draft was about the same as the version first published in 1836 ([1873] 1981, *Works* I, 167, 189). The essay invokes the same or similar arguments against experience, including absence of certainty. But why was certainty suddenly such an overt concern? Why did it suddenly assume greater importance than probabilistic reasoning?

The exact timing is less critical than the fact that probabilistic reasoning was supplanted. The shift was gradual, but in any event, certainty was bound to come to the fore. For certainty was connected with success – or lack of it – in the reform movement to which Mill was committed. He had shown awareness of the linkage from the early 1820s, and by 1831 he had it fully worked out. I mentioned earlier his distress at the unwillingness of the public to submit to the authority of the findings of moral and political inquiry. This unwillingness, Mill believed, blocked broad acceptance of reform in society and in its institutions (e.g. "Old and New Institutions," [1823c], *Morning Chronicle*, 17 October 1823, *Works* XXII, 73). It was different with physical science, and the difference turned on certainty in the results. With certainty in the findings of moral philosophy, reform, presumably, would be that much easier to achieve.

Mill's recognition of this connection went along with a conviction that secure, certain findings in any science stem from using the proper method of inquiry. Certainty, then, would be ascribed to the findings of moral and social philosophy only when the method of investigation proper to that sphere had been grasped and applied (e.g. "Spirit of the Age, II," *Examiner* 23 January 1831, [1831b] 1986, *Works* XXII, 239–40).

In a notice of astronomer William Herschel's *Discourse on the Study of Natural Philosophy* (1930), written in the midst of his "Spirit of the Age" series, Mill set out all these links. In physical science, "by universal acknowledgement, the greatest number of truths have been ascertained, and the greatest possible degree of certainty has been arrived at" ([1831c] 1986, *Works* XXII, 285). By contrast "uncertainty . . . hangs over the very elements of moral and social philosophy," in turn proving, that "the means of arriving at the truth in those sciences are not yet properly understood" (285).

The opposite to the method of physical science was the worship of ancient "wisdom," which is what Mill fancied he saw being applied in political and moral philosophy. But not only there; something similar also governed the law.

In fact, to Mill the practice in English law of depending on "precedents and cases" embodied exactly what must be overthrown if a spirit of reform was to take hold.

Forming judgments based on cases is just like reasoning though analogy; it involves applying a general rule to each particular new instance. Bentham thought of it as a purely intuitive procedure. Mill pointed to four specific problems. First, the basis for the rules used in English law is not universal experience but a few cases – the same weakness Mill detected everywhere among practicals. In addition, to appeal to precedent was to abdicate responsibility for erecting a general rationale for decision-making; it was simply "to take the opinions of the 'constituted authorities' for gospel" ("Technicalities of English Law," *Morning Chronicle* 18 September 1823, [1823c] 1986, *Works* XXII, 62). Third, there is nothing invariable (read dependable) about rulings, since the authorities differed, as did judges among themselves, in choosing from among authorities ("Practicability of Reform in The Law," *Morning Chronicle* 8 October 1823, [1823d] 1986, *Works* XXII, 71–72). Finally, in the English system, practicing lawyers must accumulate a huge store of detailed and specific information, leaving them with neither time nor the mental energy to compare their system against alternatives used elsewhere. Thus even if they wished to accept responsibility for making a comparative assessment, in practice they could not (speech, "The Influence of Lawyers" [1827?], 1988 *Works* XXVI, 387–388). These elements combined to engender a deep-rooted conservatism in English law and among legal practitioners.

4   Passage to the *essay on method*

Sidestepping the problem of induction

If history would not do, and if experimentation is unavailable in political inquiry, where was Mill to look for the moral and social philosophical equivalent to the method that produced such enviably secure findings as those of physical science? Mill viewed the availability of experiment there as crucial to abstracting the common elements from a wide variety of instances, the process called "generalization." The various experimental methods he would later describe in his *Logic* (book II, chapter VIII) were intended to identify actual procedures for arriving at satisfactory generalizations. However, in his *Autobiography*, Mill states that during the years 1830–1833, when he was preparing a first draft of the *Logic*, he had no theory of induction (*Works* I, 167, 191). His early, informal recognition of the method of difference, noticed above, though important, did not amount to a general view of the subject. By 1833, he states, "I had come to the end of my tether: I could make nothing satisfactory of Induction, at this time." Boxed in, he set aside the draft of the *Logic*, letting it lie until 1838 (191, 229).

Taking this account at face value, consider Mill's situation. At the same time as he began the *Logic* he started on drafts of five essays in political economy, one of which was the essay on the definition of the subject and the method proper to it. He already knew that, no matter how he defined political economy, the method he sought must live up to the certainty enjoyed by the findings of physical inquiry. He had explored reasoning through analogy, but concluded that it fell short of the certainty he desired and judged necessary if a desire for social reform was to become widespread. And he had decided that history is virtually useless as a way to understand commercial policy, affluence, or the political state of a nation (*Works* XXVI, 394). Moreover, experimentation is not available in those areas of inquiry. So, he was in need of certainty but lacked the methods available to physical science, was without ways of discovering true generalizations. Yet it is these that give us the "tendencies" or capabilities for producing effects; they describe causes. This last is taken from the published version of the essay on method, but the rest simply summarizes what Mill had concluded for himself by the early 1830s, traces in the evolution of which we have been following.

What means did Mill possess for getting what he needed? Most importantly, he had Bentham's insight, noticed earlier, that a judge, given the responsibility of coming to a decision without "evidence" (that is, without testimony), uses his own observation which, it must be supposed, is adequate ("sufficient") but, aside from that, detaches his senses from his own person. His senses are thus "erected into so many independent persons, and in that character introduced as witnesses" (*Rationale* [1827], vol. I, 252). Bentham had also spoken of "the judge as legislator" since, "under unwritten law," that is his character and role (67). Mill borrowed and used both ideas, in his 1827 speech "The Use of History" – the very same year in which his edition of Bentham's *Rationale of Judicial Evidence* was published. There he proposed that the most statesmanlike of legislators must know "the causes, rules or influences which govern the actions of mankind," plus "those other principles of human nature upon which depends the influence of the social arrangements over their happiness" (*Works* XXVI, 393). Then, addressing the unstated problem that we lack methods for generalizing from experience (evidence), he added:

These principles are far from being obscure or mysterious; they are such as a diligent study of our own minds, together with a careful observation of a few others, are adequate to disclose to us. For it is sufficient to him who designs laws and constitutions, to know those things in which all mankind agree." (393)

These novel assertions were alluded to a second time, and applied specifically to political economy, a few years later, in one of the essays in the "Spirit of the Age" series, written concurrently with the drafting of the five essays on political economy, including the essay on method.

In "The Spirit of The Age, II," Mill noted that, "it is not every one . . . who has had sufficient experience of mankind in general, and has sufficiently reflected upon what passes in his own mind" to get at the "the most important moral and political truths." But this is not a barrier. "There is . . . a great number of important truths, especially in Political Economy, to which, from the particular nature of the evidence on which they rest, this difficulty does not apply" (*Works* XXII, 243).

It is worth pausing to appreciate the transformation Mill achieved with this insight. He had been in search of methods of induction that would yield general principles. In political and economic inquiry the principles needed are none other than the laws of human nature. And now, at a stroke, by drawing on Bentham (and indirectly, on Adam Smith's Impartial Spectator, which supposed a similar sort of projective capability), Mill was able to abandon what had come to seem a hopeless search, and had positioned political economy within the realm of the deductive sciences. For, once the necessary laws are in hand, inquiry can properly switch from induction to deducing the consequences of the known laws under specified circumstances.

What was it about political economy that its laws appeared to Mill to be open to discovery by the truncated method of generalizing directly from what passes in one's own mind? For an answer we must turn for the first time to the 1836 essay itself. Mill prefaced his remarks on method by a long discussion of the definition of the subject. The modern reader is inclined to skip this section – about a third of the whole – as unnecessary, but that is a mistake. The discussion on definition prepared the way for Mill's sidestepping maneuver. Political economy, he determined, deals with a circumscribed range of human desires. Human beings are treated only as desiring to possess wealth, and having the ability to judge the relative efficacy of means to that end (*Works* IV, 321). Within such a narrow area of human motivation and decision, it seemed to Mill reasonable to suppose that what we know of ourselves and of a few others will tell us about as much as an enlarged and truly universal experience.

There was allowance made for two "perpetually antagonizing principles," equally uncontroversial: a general aversion to effort, and a preference for present enjoyment (321). Mill also brought within the expositions of standard results in political economy corrections resulting from different motivations (the principle of population is given as an example: 321, 323). But with this he was satisfied. He insisted that the limited figure he assumed, though obviously a fiction, was misleading only in being not *fully* descriptive of real people; so, importantly, no other distortion was introduced by this incompleteness (322–323). To be sure, care must be exercised in applying the results of abstract political economy to particular situations, involving particular persons. A thousand details might have to be considered at this stage to avoid mistakes (330). But otherwise the picture of the behavior deduced "from an assumed hypothesis" – humans desire only to acquire wealth – is "the nearest to the truth" of any equally simple alternative (323). Moreover, in the face of complexity, and lacking experiment, there is no other way of proceeding that will yield results having "as much certainty as . . . the most demonstrative parts of physics" (329).

Mill's achievement is stunning: demonstrative certainty is achieved, but without the experimental methods of physical science. I have not been able to show that Mill anticipated the 1836 essay in many of the details and qualifications just listed. But that is not surprising. The refinements of the essay were worked out during intense drafting, and no doubt revision following the responses of friends. And, in any event, the truly big step was the one we have been able to catch Mill edging towards: the abandonment of evidence in favor of reasoning from assumptions.

5 Conclusion

It remains to summarize and, in the process, address more directly the question with which we began: did Mill actually abandon experience in his 1836 adoption of *a priori* reasoning in political economy? I began by positing an apparent conflict between the two. The conflict seemed real enough because of instances in which Mill returned to facts after asserting in his essay on method that reasoning from assumptions is the only way forward in social philosophy.

In fact, Mill abandoned not experience, but history. The decade preceding the drafting of his essay on method is a register of his growing disenchantment with history. For a time he was satisfied with reasoning through analogy, while recognizing that it is no substitute for true induction, and that inferred resemblances are never certain. Single instances, like individual facts, can demonstrate nothing positively, but are useful for negativing alleged causes. They are good also for confirming or illustrating a known principle. Moreover, and in combination with principles, a very persuasive case can sometimes be made for preferring one interpretation of events above alternatives, based on a close examination of the material facts. Finally, knowing many details helps keep one from mistakenly applying a theory where it is not appropriate.

As certainty came to seem more important – not least because, without it, public acquiescence in the findings of social inquiry would be lacking, and the cause of reform suffer – Mill began to be more critical towards history. Pushing him hard in this direction was a growing sensitivity to the problems of complexity (multiplicity of causes) in the absence of experiment, and an emerging, and appealing, redefinition of history. He foresaw a new, scientific history, engaging in attempts to understand states of society, and the laws according to which one state succeeds another. This would do away with histories of political events, meant to teach lessons but often so biased as to be useless. But even a renewed history could not overcome the problems of complexity and lack of experiment. Mill emphasized, in addition, the difficulty that no past state or event can be grasped as fully as the present. This is a matter of not having the necessary information. A contemporary observer has access to numerous facts of common experience, but these are rarely thought significant enough to record. What tends to be recorded is the exceptional occurrence. Sometimes an imaginative historian might infer the rule lying behind a recorded exception, but in this way history also becomes beholden to happenstance.

Faced with all these difficulties, Mill despaired of history as a model for social inquiry. He turned instead to the methods of physical science, known for their success in producing secure results. Only, he lacked a satisfactory understanding of inductive (experimental) methods and, even had he had this, experiment, he knew, is unavailable in the social sciences. In political economy, therefore, Mill elected to bypass induction by seeking the principles of the subject, which is to say, the laws of human nature, directly in knowledge that each of us possesses from what passes in our own minds. This includes an awareness of our own desires and, since we know ourselves under various circumstances, it is also a sort of experimental knowledge. To keep things manageable Mill selected a few undeniably active and common desires, principally the desire for wealth, and treated these few as the whole. He thereby secured certainty, since one can reason demonstratively from assumed premises, but his model of the active agent is incomplete, descriptively false. Nonetheless, such *a priori* analysis, true only in the abstract, can, he believed, be filled out with particulars by anyone wishing to apply the results to specific persons and circumstances.

The model for social scientific inquiry Mill adopted in his 1836 essay on method was the result of a set of choices. One of these – the one most obvious in the light of the list of characteristics just given – has him pursuing certainty, purportedly via the method of the physical sciences, yet without its essential ingredient, a procedure for making generalizations, or what he would later call Methods of Experimental Inquiry. This left him with an obligation to explain how ratiocination, the one bit of physical science method that he did end up using, connects with induction. I shall say more on this in a moment.

Another of Mill's choices, and the one I have stressed throughout, involved him in rejecting history while maintaining an essential role for particulars. The particulars of individual experience were slighted – necessarily so – in the process of discovering general principles, the laws of human nature. But so was that enlarged experience he talked about so often in the 1820s, knowledge of many instances and varieties of circumstance. In effect, history as the source of such instances and variety was rejected in favor of the knowledge that each of us has of and within ourselves. Enlarged experience, however, was retained as a quality necessary to apt applications of theory. And this was just one of three roles retained for history: illustrating or confirming a principle, falsifying an explanation, and keeping us from error in applications. Mill's post-1836 re-assertions of the importance of facts – his review of Carlyle's *French Revolution*, and his selective appreciation of Bentham – fit these rather specific roles of factual inquiry.

Carlyle's success in accounting for the French Revolution confirmed a general principle – that voluntary obedience is given by a people when they feel responsible guidance being given by those set over them. If the revolutionary period itself is viewed as a distinct state of society, the same principle might even be interpreted as a law accounting for the emergence of this state from that which preceded it. But Carlyle did not discover the principle, nor was the historical method capable of doing so, for all the reasons adduced by Mill over the course of the 1820s.

Mill's appreciation of Bentham's method of detail, on the other hand, was based on the negative protection it afforded; for "error lurks in generalities." Bentham held, and Mill accepted, that only by tracing every abstraction, every generalization, back to the facts it summarizes and expresses, can philosophy be kept from descending into vague phrases, empty of reasons (*Works* X, 84).

In Carlyle's case, Mill certainly valued the way a complex event had been grasped and portrayed, by the author's imaginative projection of himself into the minds and events of the period. This was exactly what was required in stage two of the progression toward the new history, in which states of society at a point in time were to be grasped. In the case of Bentham, and aside from the negative value of the method of detail, Mill had to have sensed that the method was just a particular application of his own belief that all reasoning is from particulars to particulars. Thus there can be little doubt that Mill continued to adhere to the primacy of facts, for the specific roles that they could properly play, at the same time as he progressively curtailed any positive value that they might have in constructing generalizations.

That is what my two examples post-1836 point to, then, and there is no inconsistency in Mill's having continued to embrace experience, rightly understood, after insisting upon the sole efficacy of abstract reasoning in political economy. In fact there is a persistent strain in his writings, a quietly stated reiteration of the thought that abstract reasoning and facts are mutually dependent. We pick it up first in the mid-1820s, in his deployment of what I have called the "mixed method" used to account for commercial phenomena. That very term is then introduced, in the 1836 essay, and again in the *Logic* (*Works* IV, 325; VII, 453 and book III, chapter XI), where Mill explains that it stands for the combination of induction and ratiocination, and that *both* are properly part of the so-called Deductive Method. In 1836 and 1843 Mill used "*a priori*" and "Deductive" as interchangeable expressions.

Up to this point, and in successive editions of the *Logic*, Mill represented the complementary aspects of the Deductive Method as comprising a sequence of stages in inquiry: induction, followed by ratiocination, followed by verification.

But there is a slightly different account offered, in the *Examination of Sir William Hamilton's Philosophy* ([1865] 1979), where the stages are linked recursively or, as Mills chooses to portray it, organically. Here ratiocination is credited with actually assisting, and strengthening, induction. If we may take this as representative of Mill's mature thinking, it seems clear that his retention of facts as primary and foundational, *and* his convictions about the *a priori* method, worked entirely hand in glove, a certain rhetorical stridency in the 1836 essay notwithstanding. That is my conclusion, so it is fitting that I close with Mill's organic account of the interaction of induction and ratiocination.

Mill's 1865 exposition begins with an encomium to mathematical investigation. Mathematics (by which, he tells us, he means always *applied* mathematics), supplies the "only sufficiently perfect type" of scientific investigation, whether physical or moral (*Works* IX, 481). How so? It is not, we are assured, that mathematics is "directly applicable" to the moral and social sciences. What mathematics does, however, is add certainty to "theorems drawn from specific experience, when they can be affiliated as corollaries on general laws of nature – a certainty more entire than any direct observation can give" (481–482). It does this in at least two ways. First, by showing how "one truth sums up a multitude of others, and explains them, special truths being merely general ones modified by specialities of circumstance" (481). Second, by "making us acquainted with points of resemblance which could not have been reached by direct observation," as when "the inaccessibility or unmanageableness of the phænomena precludes the necessary experiments" (480).

But in precisely these ways, Mill continues, applied mathematics, "the great instrument of Deductive investigation . . . comes to be also *the source of our principal inductions*" (480, emphasis mine). This is because, as stated, when special cases are subsumed under a general law, certainty is added to the narrower inductions which form the materials of the generalization itself. It is not quite clear how this happens, though Mill seems to hold that the very process of fitting cases or instances under a general rule increases depth of insight, enabling the narrower inductions themselves to be viewed differently. Thus, with the aid of applied mathematics, "apparent exceptions" are freshly perceived, as confirmations; and "superficial inconsistencies" are reconciled (482). In addition, since mathematics enable us to "disentangle the phænomena of complex cases – explaining as much of them as can be so explained, and putting in evidence the nature and limits of the irreducible residuum" – they also "suggest fresh observations preparatory to recommencing the same process with additional data" (481).

In short, ratiocination is crucial, not just because it is the only practical way to proceed in social science, but because it actually has a special enabling function with respect to induction. That was at best only hinted at in the 1836 essay, however, and it takes us way beyond the bounds I originally set for myself,

of tracing his grapplings with history during the decade preceding his drafting
of that essay. My hope was that knowing of his struggles might help explain
why the essay took the character it did, including why Mill was so strident
there in behalf of ratiocination. I also felt it necessary to examine his attitude to
history in order to understand why he retained certain roles for experience after
1836. Clearly these are not the only routes to recovering context, and more
such explorations will be needed if economic methodologists are to effect their
own version of an escape from history. In this case, the escape will be from
a history of interpretation shaped by Mill's ambition, that his essay "should
become classical and of authority," which has encouraged its study as an object
of timeless, contextless, lapidary splendor. [5]

Notes

I am grateful for comments received on earlier, very different versions, from audiences
in Durham, NC, Rotterdam, and Cambridge, England. Thanks to Mary Morgan, Harro
Maas, Roy Weintraub, and Jukka Pekka Pimies for particularly provoking questions.

1. Here I draw heavily on Alan Ryan's superb introduction to the edition, in *Collected
   Works of John Stuart Mill* (hereafter *Works*), of Mill's *An Examination of Sir William
   Hamilton's Philosophy* ([1865] 1979, *Works* IX, esp. xxxviii–xlix). Pertinent statements by Mill are of course scattered throughout this long work, but chapters X and
   XI (plus appendix), and chapter XIII, are especially useful for understanding his realism. The term "realist" as used here, however, would have seemed quite strange
   to Mill. His opponents adhered to "the Realistic theory," whereas he stood for the
   Psychological theory of matter (see 196–198).
2. For "imaginatively realized," the more elusive phrase, see Mill, "Michelet's History
   of France," ([1844] 1985, *Works* XX, 224–225). There Mill writes, with reference to
   Carlyle, that recapturing a former age as it was experienced by those living through
   it, requires in the historian "some of the characteristics of the poet. He has to 'body
   forth the forms of things unknown.' "
3. Mill's analysis of the efficacy of sworn oaths parallels, though it incorporates one
   more cause, than Bentham's discussion in his *Rationale of Judicial Evidence*, 5 vols.,
   edited by Mill (1827: vol. I, book II, 375–376).
4. Bentham argued that testimony stated in these terms is automatically assumed to be
   at its maximum of persuasive force. But if in a particular instance all the witnesses are
   equally forceful and equally trustworthy, then the judge in the case must be guided
   merely by the numbers of witnesses, the testimony of each having the appearance
   of complete demonstration – positive or negative (*Rationale*, vol. I, 60). Instead,
   let the force of persuasion be graduated along a scale, say from 0 to 10. Assume
   three witnesses each of whom expresses positive belief in a fact, with a strength of
   persuasion equal to 1. Let there be two other witnesses, on the negative side, each
   setting the degree of their belief at 10. In the absence of the supposed scale the judge
   must decide, 3 to 2, for the existence of the fact; with the scale, however, the weight
   of belief clearly indicates against it (77–78). Here judging by numbers of witnesses
   alone would result in misdirection.

5. The implied criticism here is one I accept of some of my own past work. For a useful, if controversial, reminder of a need to integrate the 1836 essay with the study of Mill's other writings, see Hollander and Peart (1999).

References

Bentham, Jeremy (1827). *Rationale of Judicial Evidence, specially applied to English Practice*, ed. J.S. Mill, 5 vols. London: Hunt & Clarke

Hollander, Samuel and Sandra Peart (1999). John Stuart Mill's method in principle and practice: a review of the evidence, *Journal of the History of Economic Thought*, 21, 369–397

Mill, John Stuart ([1823a] 1986). Free Discussion, Letter II, *Morning Chronicle*, 8 February; reprinted in *Newspaper Writings, December 1822–July 1831*, vol. XXII, *Collected Works of John Stuart Mill*. Toronto: University of Toronto Press, 12–15

([1823b] 1986). Judicial Oaths, *Morning Chronicle*, 25 July; reprinted in *Newspaper Writings*, vol. XXII, *Collected Works*, 30–33

([1823c] 1986). Technicalities of English Law, *Morning Chronicle*, 18 September; reprinted in *Newspaper Writings*, vol. XXII, *Collected Works*, 60–62

([1823d] 1986). Practicability of Reform in The Law, *Morning Chronicle*, 8 October; reprinted in *Newspaper Writings*, vol. XXII, *Collected Works*, 70–72

([1823e] 1986). Old and New Institutions, *Morning Chronicle*, 17 October; reprinted in *Newspaper Writings*, vol. XXII, *Collected Works*, 72–74

([1824] 1967). War Expenditure, *Westminster Review*, II (July), 27–48; reprinted in *Essays on Economics and Society*, vol. IV, *Collected Works*, 3–22

([1826a] 1985). Mignet's *French Revolution, Westminster Review*, V (April), 385–398; reprinted in *Essays on French History and Historians*, vol. XX, *Collected Works*, 3–14

([1826b] 1967). Paper Currency and Commercial Distress, *Parliamentary Review. Session of 1826*. London: Longman, Rees, Orme, Brown, & Green, 630–662; reprinted in *Essays on Economics and Society*, vol. IV, *Collected Works*, 73–123

([1827] 1988). The Use of History. Speech to London Debating Society; printed in *Journals and Debating Speeches*, vol. XXVI, *Collected Works*, 392–397

([1827?] 1988). The Influence of Lawyers; printed in *Journals and Debating Speeches*, vol. XXVI, *Collected Works*, 386–391

([1828] 1985). Scott's *Life of Napoleon, Westminster Review*, IX (April), 251–313; reprinted in *Essays on French History and Historians*, vol. XX, *Collected Works*, 55–110

([1830–1833] 1974). Early Draft of the *Logic*, appendix A in *A System of Logic, Ratiocinative and Inductive*, vol. VIII, *Collected Works*, 961–1110

([1831a] 1986). The Spirit of The Age, I, *Examiner*, 9 January, 20–21; reprinted in *Newspaper Writings*, vol. XXII, *Collected Works*, 227–234.

([1831b] 1986). The Spirit of The Age, II, *Examiner*, 23 January, 50–52; reprinted in *Newspaper Writings*, vol. XXII, *Collected Works*, 238–245

([1831c] 1986). Herschel's *Preliminary Discourse, Examiner*, 20 March, 179–180; reprinted in *Newspaper Writings*, vol. XXII, *Collected Works*, 284–287

([1835] 1969). Sedgwick's *Discourse, London Review*, I (April), 94–135; reprinted in *Essays on Ethics, Religion and Society*, vol. X, *Collected Works*, 33–74

([1836a] 1977). State of Society in America, *London Review*, II (January), 365–389; reprinted in *Essays on Politics and Society*, vol. XVIII, *Collected Works*, 93–115

([1836b] 1967). On the Definition of Political Economy; and on the Method of Investigation Proper to It, *London and Westminster Review*, IV and XXVI (October), 1–29; reprinted in *Essays on Economics and Society*, vol. IV, *Collected Works*, 309–339

([1837] 1985). Carlyle's *French Revolution, London and Westminster Review*, V and XXVII (July), 17–53; reprinted in *Essays on French History and Historians*, vol. XX, *Collected Works*, 133–166

([1838] 1969). Bentham, *London and Westminster Review*, 7 and 29 (August), 467–506; reprinted in *Essays on Ethics, Religion and Society*, vol. X, *Collected Works*, 77–115.

([1843] 1973, 1974). *A System of Logic, Ratiocinative and Inductive*, vols. VII and VIII, *Collected Works*

([1844] 1985). Michelet's *History of France, Edinburgh Review*, LXXIX (January), 1–39; reprinted in *Essays on French History and Historians*, vol. XX, *Collected Works*, 219–255

([1865] 1979). *An Examination of Sir William Hamilton's Philosophy*, vol. IX, *Collected Works*

([1873] 1981). *Autobiography*, in *Autobiography and Literary Essays*, vol. I, *Collected Works*, 4–290

Ryan, Alan (1979). Introduction to *An Examination of Sir William Hamilton's Philosophy*, in vol. IX, *Collected Works*, vii–lxvii

Part V
The institutions of economics

16　You shouldn't want a realism if you have a rhetoric

Deirdre N. McCloskey

Uskali Mäki and I taught a course at Erasmus in the Autumn of 1996 called "The words of science." It had a dozen or so bright undergraduates, many with philosophical backgrounds, some with economics. We started with classical rhetoric, as represented for example in Michael Billig's work on social psychology *(Arguing and Thinking* 1987), moved on to the modern rediscovery of rhetorical ideas in Austin and Searle and the like, then to the (mainly British) sociologists of science who call themselves The Sons of Thomas Kuhn. We ended with the daughters, such as Helen Longino. Rhetoricians all were these students of science, though only a few of them notice their connection to the Greek sophists and to the rhetorical tradition that ruled education in the West until the seventeenth century.

It was a wonderful experience to be trapped in a room with Uskali Mäki for several hours a week, forced to explain yourself! Uskali Mäki and I have disagreed on Realism, but it is a tribute to his attitude – which I shall argue is not Realist–that he was willing to converse. And converse. And converse. He has always been willing to converse, an open-mindedness I do not find universal among people trained in analytic philosophy. Clark Glymour amused many of his colleagues by beginning his *Theory and Evidence* (1980) with the following *jeu d'esprit*, an example of openness to ideas in analytic circles: "If it is true that there are but two kinds of people in the world – the logical positivists and the god-damned English professors – then I suppose I am a logical positivist" (Glymour 1980, ix). Most Anglo philosophers find this funny, which is a measure of how far they have strayed from the love of truth. I asked John Searle in the presence of graduate students once if he had read Hegel. John replied cockily, in defiance of the opinion of hundreds of highly intelligent people since Hegel wrote, that he had not read a page and proposed never to do so. The graduate students laughed in appreciation of this convenient advice for avoiding work. Another and more tolerant philosopher, Stanley Rosen, noted that "the typical practitioner of analytic philosophy" succumbs "to the temptation of confusing irony for a refutation of opposing views" (Rosen 1980, xiii). Not Uskali Mäki. It makes him a strange sort of realist.

Uskali Mäki and I tried to persuade each other all term long, with no mere irony to refute opposing views, and the students I think benefited from our genial quarreling. Teaching ought more often to be done in pairs. We teach our students in philosophy courses the style of what might be called the Rationalist Monologue (I refer to the parallel style on which the Sons and Daughters of Thomas Kuhn heap scorn, the Empiricist Monologue). "Here in a nutshell is what was said by Kant (or Austin or Mäki or McCloskey, in descending order of philosophical sophistication), but any fool can see that it's wrong, for such and such a reason; next topic!" With two views in tension this doesn't work, and the students learn to treat opponents with the respect that allows learning, as opposed to the smart-aleck conviction that we Know and they Don't – and so there's no point in reading a page of Hegel or the god-damned English professors. It's harder to treat X as a strawman suitable for demolition when he's standing there saying, "No, it's not quite as simple as that. Allow me to show you" (seizes chalk).

Our course was about philosophical rhetoric. That we gave it at all makes my first point. Philosophers should start seeing themselves – and seeing scientists, and busdrivers, and friends – as rhetors, as people engaged in sweet or not so sweet persuasion. Rhetoric gives a place to stand to see how we are persuading. It is better than thinking that there is one and only one way of making an argument, and that we already know what it is. The study of the philosophical tradition in the West suggests that How We Persuade is not fixed for all time. Plato persuaded with dialogues; modern philosophers require first-order predicate logic. In fact How We Persuade has not been fixed in philosophy for any thirty-year stretch in the history down to the present. Whether this or that argument is knock-down is always under negotiation. It's what philosophy is about, this "rhetoric."

Imagine the figures of speech stuffed into a storeroom: twelve dozen appeals to authority here, a gross of syllogisms there, 157 metaphors (few of them fresh) on the top shelf, a worn-out argument from self-refutation (evidently heavily used) close to the door, a dozen slippery-slope arguments squashed in behind the metaphors, and one argument from design, with dust accumulating on it, over by the little window. These and others are available for use. A community of persuaders such as philosophy will at one time make large use of the argument from design, say, and little use of appeals to the character of The Scientist; at another time it will use a different bundle, having put the used ones back in the storeroom. None of the items are epistemologically privileged. I am denying, in other words, that there is a timeless Good Argument for anything. To be proud that you achieve human persuasion by using self-refutation arguments and *ad personam* attacks on literary people as against story telling and Pascal's reasons of the heart does not make much sense, considering that the bundle of figures used is not permanent. Today's user of an argument from verifiability will be tomorrow's user of an appeal to authority.

Philosophy differs from history or physics in two respects. It uses for a while a somewhat different selection than these other sciences from the common store of figures of speech. Much overlap can be expected. And it studies different objects. A science is a class of objects and a way of conversing about them, not a way of knowing Truth now and forever.

You can begin to learn about the rhetoric in philosophy from philosophers like Jeff Mason, *Philosophical Rhetoric* (1989), or Martin Warner, *Philosophical Finesse: Studies in the Art of Rational Persuasion* (1989), or on a more modest level from John Passmore, *Philosophical Reasoning* (1970), Anthony Weston, *A Rulebook for Arguments* (1992), or Mark Woodhouse, *A Preface to Philosophy* (1984). Or you can recur to Aristotle's *Rhetoric* (trans. Kennedy 1991), which most analytic philosophers know they disdain (Plato told them to do so, before the letter), though few of them have read a page of it. And then you can read in the half of the Western tradition that is rhetorical as against philosophical: formal treatises by Cicero (trans. Sutton 1942), Quintilian (trans. Butler 1920), Adam Smith (yes!) (1748–1751), Perelman and Olbrechts-Tyteca (1958 [1969]), Booth (1993), together with the poets and novelists and tellers of tales. Uskali Mäki is unique among analytic philosophers of my acquaintance in actually having done some of this homework. It amazes me.

My argument for such a supplement to philosophical education is the oldest educational argument in philosophy. It is that one has a rhetoric implicitly, and might as well be aware of it. Recognize the argument? When Simon Blackburn, sometime editor of *Mind*, visited the University of Iowa some years ago he gave a speech to a large audience on the old theme that one has a philosophy implicitly, and might as well be aware of it. Therefore the department of philosophy at every university should be large and all students regardless of field should be obliged to take courses in it. My philosopher colleagues at Iowa had evidently told Blackburn that down the street was this awful group of nonphilosophers gathered in the Project on Rhetoric of Inquiry ("Poroi": Greek for "river fords," or more generally "ways and means"; thus "aporia," the state of not knowing the way forward). So Blackburn made a few sneering remarks about the rhetoric of the god-damned English professors. I rose (Donald was always doing that, heatedly), and said, "Dr. Blackburn: You have used the argument that philosophy is foundational because we have to have a philosophy anyway. Do you grasp that in making such an argument you have shown that rhetoric is foundational, too, because it is the art of argument, which we must all have anyway?" Blackburn did not grasp what Donald said, and could only repeat Plato's aristocratic calumnies against rhetoric, but the Iowa philosophers were satisfied that their local monopoly of philosophical reflection on campus had been defended from the barbarous Poroivians.

* * *

So my first point is that philosophers would do better to grasp rhetoric. My second point is that it is really true that Realism and Truth are not Really True.

If you are properly socialized in the speech community of modern analytic philosophy you will at once leap forward toting the Philosopher's Friend, the Argument from Self-Contradiction, the rhetorical device of catching someone being committed to X at the very moment of arguing against X. Here $X =$ Truth and The Real. I just said that it is true there is not Truth. You fancy I am caught in a contradiction (if you do not notice the distinction between pragmatic small-t truth and reified Large-T Truth).

All right, let's suppose you *have* caught me. Call it the Philosopher's Tu Quoque, "you also." It is the standard and indeed the sole argument by philosophers against what they imagine "relativism" to be. Philosophers believe that the Philosopher's Tu Quoque is decisive.

(It is not, of course, because it is not valid. I mentioned small-t and Big-T. That's one rebuttal: the alleged Tu Quoque depends on an equivocation of Truth for truth. And as Richard Rorty and others have noted, "The world is out there, but descriptions of the world are not", Rorty 1989, 5, which is to say that the tu quoque argument equivocates between realism in ontology and realism in epistemology; but set these aside.)

The tu quoque is: You, oh relativist, in asserting the truth of relativism must acknowledge a standard of Truth. Gotcha. All such reasonings must confront, however, another tu quoque: that you, oh philosopher, are in turn arguing rhetorically. Gotcha yourself. Yer mudder wears combat boots. The argument is the Rhetorician's Tu Quoque. I used it on Blackburn. A philosopher is committed to rhetorical thinking at the very moment of arguing against rhetoric and advocating less reading of Hegel. It is the serious point behind Cicero's witticism in *de Oratore* (I, 11,47) that Plato was the best rhetorician when making merry of rhetoric. Bacon, Descartes, and Hobbes turned against their rhetorical educations, but of course inconsistently (cf. Amelie Rorty 1983; and France 1972, chapter 2). They used metaphor at a rhetorical level to attack metaphor at a philosophical level, and story to attack story . But I argued earlier that the levels are not distinct, that there is no meta-linguistic level of "philosophical Truth" distinct from the arguments appropriated by philosophers from the storeroom. As the rhetorician of science Henry Krips observes about Boyle's *New Experiments Physico-Mechanical* (in 1660, after decades of rhetoric against rhetoric):

On the one hand, a text cannot be rhetorical if it is to conform to the collective scientific norm which favors proper method (say, reason and evidence) and disavows rhetoric.

On the other hand, the text must be rhetorical if it is to fulfill its essential function of persuading readers who do not have at their disposal the evidence needed to justify the text's knowledge claims. (Krips 1992, 10)

I would only amend Krips' formulation by saying that reason and evidence should be construed as parts of rhetoric. Kreps is equivocating, as American rhetoricians these days often do, between Little Rhetoric (mere tricks) and Big Rhetoric (the available means of uncoerced persuasion, as Aristotle defined it, among them various appeals to reason and fact).

Bruno Latour contradicts the Philosopher's Tu Quoque as follows:

Those who accuse relativists of being self-contradictory . . . can save their breath for a better occasion. I explicitly put my own account [of French science] in the same category as those accounts I have studied without asking for any privilege. This approach seems self-defeating only to those who believe that the fate of an interpretation is tied to the existence of a safe metalinguistic level. Since this belief is precisely what I deny, the reception of my argument exemplifies my point: no metalinguistic level is required to analyze, argue, explain, decide, or tell stories. Everything depends on what sort of actions I take to convince others. This reflexive position is the only one that is not self-contradictory. (Latour 1984 [1988], 266)

This nonself-contradictory position is mine, too, and Wittgenstein's, Austin's, Putnam's, Rorty's, Feyerabend's, and that of modern sociologists and rhetoricians of science. There does not exist a safe meta-linguistic level. The only noncontradictory way to deal with this unfortunate fact is to stop making arguments–such as the Philosopher's Tu Quoque, Realism, and belief in Truth – that unconsciously depend on the existence of a safe metalinguistic level.

In his *How to Do Things with Words*, for example, Austin wrote:

Suppose that we confront "France is hexagonal" with the facts, in this case, I suppose, with France, is it true or false? . . . It is good enough for a general, perhaps, but not for a geographer . . . "True" and "false" . . . do not stand for anything simple at all, but only for a general dimension of being a right or proper thing to say . . . in these circumstances, to this audience, for these purposes and with these intentions. (Austin 1975, 143,145)

In commenting on this passage the literary critic Stanley Fish makes the point here about Realism and Truth: "All assertions are . . . produced and understood within the assumption of some socially conceived and understood dimension of assessment. The one thing you can never say about France is what it is really like, if by 'really' you mean France as it exists independently of any dimension of assessment whatever" (Fish 1980, 198–199). Physicists say similar things about the realest of realities. In mathematics Beltrami's proof in 1868 (a proof that Lobachevskian geometry can have no possible self-contradictions if Euclidean geometry has none) has been taken as the model of how to go about such tasks. The task is to link one discourse with another (even a discourse about Facts).

The social and persuasive character of persuasion is, after all, routinely sensible, something on which we act daily. We look naturally for social standards with which to make judgments, quantitative or not. Does your son have big feet? Well, how many fourteen-year-olds have American size thirteen shoes? Reporting "size thirteen" without some conversational context would not advance the discussion. Is "Ode on a Grecian Urn" a good poem? Well, compare and contrast it with one hundred randomly selected poems. Decisions such as these cannot be made independent of the conversations of humankind. We decide what are big feet, good poems, or satisfactory philosophical arguments. The criteria are social, not solipsistic. They are written in conversations, not in the stars.

The social character of scientific knowledge does not make it arbitrary, touchie-feelie, mob-governed, or anything else likely to bring it into disrepute. It is still, for instance, "objective," if that is a worry. In vulgar usage the objective/subjective distinction beloved of Western philosophy since Descartes means discussable/undiscussable. But even "objectivity" has a necessarily social definition: we know that the yield of corn in the Middle Ages was objectively low because we converse with people who agree with our evidence and our calculations and our standard of comparison validating the word "low." Nor are such human standards peculiar to the human sciences. The mathematician Armand Borel notes that "something becomes objective . . . as soon as we are persuaded that it exists in the minds of others in the same form that it does in ours, and that we can think about it and discuss it together" (1983, 13). A scale of particle durations, star sizes, or electrical activity of the brain depends on being able to "discuss it together." The scale, to repeat, is of humans, not of God.

* * *

Now after all this talk, which I hope is boring and obvious (because if it is for you I think you are conceding my case), I want to make a concession to Realism. We are all realists *of one kind or another.* Well, truthfully, this isn't really a concession. It's an illustration that, really, the conversation of philosophy is rhetorical all the way down. We are realists of whatever sort because we all want to be able to use the rhetorical turn, "Such and such is *really* the case, true." We want to write history, for example, *wie es eigentlich gewesen.* Since there is no known test for whether as historians we are really in touch with *das Wesen* of the battle of Gettysburg, merely whether we have this or that fact about it right, the number of facts being numberless and the only test for their relevance being the rhetoric of some human conversation, the "really" refers to our rhetoric. It refers to our persuasions about the world, not directly to the world itself.

We are all realists, then. The warrants for reality that I have in mind go this way: "*X* is really true" amounts to saying, "Our conversations about this matter usually result in saying *X*"; and that in turn, I am about to argue, amounts to saying, "In our rhetorical community one *should* at least admit *x*." The kind of realist I am is an Ethical Realist. By this I do not mean that I am good and you, if you do not agree with me, are bad. I mean that Reality, capital-R, is not material but ethical.

Now of course we all admit, whatever our philosophical convictions, that the table is real (small-r) and that if we step heedlessly into a street near Erasmus University, for example, we are likely to get run down by either a car or a bicycle or a tram. I don't think the philosophical disagreements are really (there it is again, signaling a feature of our speech community) about the quotidian world of the Oostzeedijk in Rotterdam on a busy Monday morning. Material realists are fond of invoking the Oostzeedijk to criticize other philosophers. They say, "You would not survive for a moment out there without believing in our kind of Realism." But philosophers are not any better at navigating the Oostzeedijk or the New York Stock Exchange than other people, so it must be that their remarks about What Is are about non-practicalities. (Or else they are simply confused. I am appealing here to a sympathetic reading of them all, both Material and Ethical Realists.) If we converse on the assumption that Irrealists, who after all include many thoughtful people, are not just confused or insincere, they must have something other in mind than denying the bumpiness of trams and tables and the like. I say it's ethics, and I say it's good.

An ethical realist says that what we Know is not the Objective World. She points out that there is no way to connect ultimate epistemology with ultimate ontology – except by assumption. She therefore wants to abandon this 2,500-year-old project as, on the evidence, a bad idea, a messing with ultimates that has not worked out. The Material Realist wants to carry on, trying to imagine a bridge from a pragmatic and sensible position about small-r reality to his favored ontology, Reality. "This is Reality with the big R, reality that makes the timeless claim, reality to which defeat can't happen" (James 1907 [1949], 262). I repeat: James and I, like you, live squarely in a world of reality, small-r, a world in which Eastern Iowa is hillier than Eastern Massachusetts and in which the American Internal Revenue Service and the Drug Enforcement Agency have unconstitutional powers. What is at issue here is the philosopher's construct, Reality, a thing deeper than what is necessary for daily life. The Real may or may not exist, like Truth. I don't know, though God I reckon does. In contrast to the Material Realists, I claim only to know about the small-letter reality and truth that we humans might know.

I do know from the history of philosophy that, unfortunately, there does not seem to be any way of getting from Truth in epistemology to Reality in ontology. We all wish there was, and many thinkers since Plato have floated logs and tossed bricks into the river to build a bridge between the two. But empirically speaking the bridge looks a hopeless job. If you try to walk across the few finished pieces, you fall right in. The construction time has exceeded that of a new defense system, two-and-a-half millennia and counting. As an empirical scientist I have to conclude that further investment in the bridge should be given a low priority. As Richard Rorty put it, "It might, of course, have turned out otherwise. People have, oddly enough, found something interesting to say about the essence of Force and the definition of 'number.' They might have found something interesting to say about the essence of Truth. But in fact they haven't" (Rorty, 1982, xiv).

To this the Material Realists are liable to claim that their notions of Truth and Reality and a Brooklyn Bridge between the two are necessary to prevent "permissiveness" and, as they invariably put it, "anything goes." The fears about "permissiveness" and lack of discipline are surprisingly neurotic and authoritarian. As James observed, "The rationalist mind, radically taken, is of a doctrinaire and authoritative complexion: the phrase 'must be' is ever on its lips" (James 1907[1949], 259). I wonder if Material Realists can hear how much they sound like a Monty Python skit on sado-masochism when they talk about "discipline," and "permissiveness," and how things "must be." John Cleese as The Philosopher.

But, look: the Material Realist is indignant about the Sophists and James, and Rorty, and McCloskey. He is making an *ethical* claim, that it is *bad* to not be a Material Realist. *Tu quoque.*

The ethical realist takes the indignation of the philosophers seriously and concludes that what we Know is above all, indeed only, right and wrong. We cannot Know in the lofty, philosophical sense that the world exists, but we have no doubt that we *should* believe this or that about it. It's the "should" part that shows our ethical realism. The vehemence with which Realists argue, it seems to me, shows the fount of their conviction to be ethical.

I have been saying this sort of thing for a long time, but have only recently started to grasp (in Dutch *begrijp*, as against mere *verstaan*) what I was saying. Probably I am still muddled. In the first edition of my book *The Rhetoric of Economics* (1985; 2nd edn., 1998) I wrote (forgive the length of the quotation; I still believe what I said then, and it is strictly relevant):

You are more strongly persuaded that it is wrong to murder than that inflation is always and everywhere a monetary phenomenon. This is not to say that similar techniques of persuasion will be applicable to both propositions. It says merely that each within its field, and each therefore subject to the methods of honest persuasion appropriate to the field, the one achieves a greater certitude than the other. To deny the comparison is to deny that reason and the partial certitude it can bring applies to nonscientific subjects, a common but unreasonable position. There is no reason why specifically "scientific" persuasiveness (well, actually pseudoscientific: "at the .05 level the coefficient on M in a regression of prices of 30 countries over 30 years is insignificantly different from 1.0") should take over the whole of persuasiveness, leaving moral persuasiveness incomparably inferior to it. (McCloskey 1985, 45–46)

I was reflecting Wayne Booth's demonstration that to make ethics into "mere" opinion is a mistake (Booth 1974). Then I discovered that other people had said approximately the same thing. Hilary Putnam, for example, averred that "to claim of any statement that it is true ... is, roughly, to claim that it would be justified were epistemic conditions good enough" (Putnam 1990, vii, italics omitted). He later elaborates:

In my fantasy of myself as a metaphysical super-hero, all "facts" would dissolve into "values." That there is a chair in this room would be analyzed ... into a set of obligations to think that there is a chair in this room if epistemic conditions are (were) "good" enough ... What I do think, even outside my fantasies, is that fact and obligations are throroughly interdependent ... To say that a belief is justified is to say that it is what we ought to believe; justification is a normative notion on the face of it. (Putnam 1990, 115)

Such a definition of knowing has nothing to do with "privilege" as Uskali Mäki has claimed (Mäki 1993, 33); it has to do with ethics, Ethical Realism. As Austin said, truth has to do with "being a right or proper thing to say."

Realism is a social – that is, a rhetorical, that is an ethical – necessity for the sciences. "For the presence of unforced agreement in all of them gives us everything in the way of 'objective truth' which one could possibly want: namely, intersubjective agreement" (Rorty 1987, 42). Or Stephen Toulmin: "Men demonstrate their rationality, not by ordering their concepts and beliefs in tidy formal structures, but by their preparedness to respond to novel situations with open minds" (Toulmin 1972, vii). Such a definition of "rationality" would cast the "rational reconstruction of research programs" into another and ethical light. As Rom Harre puts it, "To publish abroad a discovery couched in the rhetoric of science is to let it be known that the presumed fact can safely be used in debate, in practical projects, and so on. Knowledge claims are tacitly prefixed with a performative of trust" (Harre 1986, 90; cf. Gilbert Harman's notion that authoritative statements are ones that we accept on behalf of some group, since "learning about the world is a cooperative enterprise," Harman 1986, 51). That "'I do not do it alone, we do it together'" in a process that never comes to a full stop, does not mean that ethical criticism need be capricious or merely 'subjective' ... Theorists of most other disciplines are by now acknowledging similar co-dependencies of all inquiries" (Booth 1993, 385).

Then in the fall of 1997 I started to read C. S. Lewis again. As a bookish adolescent I had read *The Screwtape Letters* (1942), and much later as an adult his autobiography, *Surprised by Joy* (1956). Lewis was a professor of literature at Oxbridge, a writer of children's books, and a Christian apologist, specifically Anglican, active in the 1940s and 1950s. In *Mere Christianity* (1952, based on lectures published 1943–1945) Lewis was arguing for the existence of a Moral Law, beyond convention or evolutionary prudence, and points out that:

there is one thing, and one only, in the whole universe which we know more about than we could learn from external observation. That one thing is Man [Humanity, if you please!] ... In this case we have, so to speak, inside information; we are in the know. And because of that, we know that men find themselves under a moral law, which they did not make, and cannot quite forget even when they try, and which they know they ought to obey . . . Anyone studying Man from the outside as we study electricity or cabbages, not knowing our language, . . . would never get the slightest evidence that we had this moral law . . . His observations would only show what we did, and the moral law is about what we ought to do. (Lewis 1952 [1996], 35)

We do not know about Reality, the essence, the *Wesen* – the "more . . . than we could learn from external observation" – in a way that would elevate it above mere pragmatic reality, small r. But we *do* know, Lewis is arguing, the extra-behaviorist fact about our ethical selves. I think therefore I judge.

As you would expect, on the same page Lewis drew theistic conclusions from the fact of the moral law: "We want to know whether the universe simply happens to be what it is for no reason or whether there is a power behind it that makes it what it is . . . There is only one case in which we can know whether there is anything more, namely our own case. And in that one case we find there is." Eerie. But the way I am using Lewis' argument (he elaborates it on pp. 17–39; Lewis was not the originator of the argument, I believe it is found in Augustine, for example) does not depend on a belief in God. A prejudice against belief in God need not stand in the way of admitting Lewis' original observation: what we Know is ethical.

What we know together as reality is what we should agree on for practical purposes. What we Know as Reality, if we know anything at that exalted level (and the project of Material Realism as I understand it is to claim such a Knowledge), is only ethical. Ought, not Is.

Lewis himself did not deny the truths of science, and neither do I. He and I would agree, I think, that the truth of the latest quark or astrophysics is on a level with the truth of traffic on the Oostzeedijk, and does not present any special problem of epistemology. It's wonderful stuff, this science, but when philosophers start claiming it to be Reality they are making a claim beyond what the scientists themselves have to Know to do their good work. After all, many distinguished physicists (Newton, to take one example) have been theists, who speak of Knowing beyond the inverse square law. It is not the case, as Material Realists sometime claim in their hotter moods, that the Oostzeedijk and the Orion Nebula *imply* their metaphysics.

* * *

There has always been something puzzling about the subjective/objective split beloved of Western philosophers since Descartes. It is: I cannot know your subjective experience (for example, I cannot feel your pain); and I cannot Know what is the case in the objective world, since all manner of Kantian frameworks-for-seeing intervene. Dividing up the world of discourse into subjective and objective therefore does not seem to get very far. It's dividing up a null set.

Suppose we divide the world of discourse another way, into unknowable subjectivities and objectivities on the one hand, and the Conjectivities on the other, the things we Know together. I think such a move, a late linguistic turn, would be more fruitful. It would not obviate any agreements our persuasion had arrived at about rolling balls down inclined planes or the standard of taste in literature. It would merely put these two and others in conversation, if that was thought ethically wise or useful. It would make science and religion defend themselves openly, instead of claiming Reality as their exclusive yet mutually negating realms. It would admit that we have minds and morals, that we are rhetorical creatures, sweetly persuading–like my friend Uskali Mäki, who is not *really*, you see, a Realist.

References

Aristotle (1991). *Rhetoric*, trans. George A. Kennedy. New York: Oxford University Press

Austin, J. L. (1955 [1965, 1975]). *How to Do Things with Words*, 2nd edn., J. O. Urmson and M. Sbisà (eds.). Cambridge, MA: Harvard University Press

Billig, Michael (1987). *Arguing and Thinking: A Rhetorical Approach to Social Psychology*. Cambridge: Cambridge University Press

Booth, Wayne C. (1974). *Modern Dogma and the Rhetoric of Assent*. Chicago: University of Chicago Press

(1988). *The Company We Keep: An Ethics of Fiction*. Berkeley and Los Angeles: University of California Press

(1993). Ethics and criticism, in A. Preminger and T. V. F. Brogan (eds.), *The New Princeton Encyclopedia of Poetry and Poetics*. Princeton: Princeton University Press, 384–386

Borel, Armand (1983). Mathematics: art and science. *Mathematical Intelligencer*, 5(4), 9–17

Cicero, Marcus Tullius (1942). *De Oratore*, trans. E. W. Sutton, vol. 1. Cambridge, MA: Harvard University Press

Fish, Stanley (1980). *Is There a Text in This Class? The Authority of Interpretive Communities*. Cambridge, MA: Harvard University Press

France, Peter (1972). *Rhetoric and Truth in France, Descartes to Diderot*. Oxford: Clarendon Press

Glymour, Clark (1980). *Theory and Evidence*. Princeton: Princeton University Press

Harman, Gilbert (1986). *Change in View: Principles of Reasoning*. Cambridge, MA: MIT Press

Harre, Rom (1986). *Varieties of Realism: A Rationale for the Natural Sciences*. Oxford: Basil Blackwell

James, William (1907 [1949]). *Pragmatism: A New Name for Some Old Ways of Thinking, together with four essays from The Meaning of Truth (1909)*; reprinted, with original pagination of the 1907 edn. New York: Longmans, Green

Krips, Henry (1992). Ideology, rhetoric and Boyle's new experiments, unpublished manuscript for "Narrative Patterns in Scientific Disciplines," April 27–30, Cohn

Institute, Tel Aviv University; Edelstein Center, Hebrew University; and the Van Leer Jerusalem Institute

Latour, Bruno (1984 [1988]). *The Pasteurization of France*, trans. A. Sheridan and J. Law. Cambridge, MA and London: Harvard University Press

Lewis, C. S. (1952 [1966]). *Mere Christianity*. New York, Simon & Schuster (the text quotes from the 1996 edn.)

McCloskey, D. N. (1985). *The Rhetoric of Economics*. Madison: University of Wisconsin Press (2nd edn., 1998)

Mäki, Uskali (1993). Two philosophies of the rhetoric of economics, in Willie Henderson, Roger E. Backhouse, and Tony Dudley-Evans, *Economics and Language*. London: Routledge, 23–50

Mason, J. (1989). *Philosophical Rhetoric*. London: Routledge

Passmore, John (1961). *Philosophical Reasoning*. London: Duckworth (2nd edn., 1970)

Perelman, Chaim and Olbrechts-Tyteca, L. (1958 [1969]). *The New Rhetoric: A Treatise on Argumentation*, trans. J. Wilkinson and P. Weaver. Notre Dame: University of Notre Dame Press

Putnam, Hilary (1990). *Realism with a Human Face*, James Conant (ed.). Cambridge, MA: Harvard University Press

Quintilian, Marcus F. (1920). *Institutio Oratoria*, trans. H.E. Butler. Cambridge, MA: Harvard University Press

Rorty, Amelie Oksenberg (1983). Experiments in philosophic genre: Descartes' *Meditations*, *Critical Inquiry*, 9, 545–565

Rorty, Richard (1982). *Consequences of Pragmatism (Essays: 1972–1980)*. Minneapolis: University of Minnesota Press

(1987). Science as solidarity, in John Nelson, Allan Megill, and Donald N. McCloskey (eds.), *The Rhetoric of the Human Sciences: Language and Argument in Scholarship and Public Affairs*. Madison: University of Wisconsin Press, 38–52

(1989). *Contingency, Irony, and Solidarity*. Cambridge: Cambridge University Press

Rosen, Stanley (1980). *The Limits of Analysis*. New York: Basic Books

Smith, Adam (1748–1751). *Lectures on Rhetoric and Belles Lettres*, J. C. Bryce (ed.), Glasgow edn. Oxford: Oxford University Press

Toulmin, Stephen (1972). *Human Understanding: The Collective Use and Evolution of Concepts*. Princeton: Princeton University Press

Walton, Douglas N. (1985). *Arguer's Position: A Pragmatic Study of* Ad Hominem *Attack, Criticism, Refutation, and Fallacy*. Westport, CT: Greenwood Press

Warner, Martin (1989). *Philosophical Finesse: Studies in the Art of Rational Persuasion*. Oxford: Oxford University Press

Weston, Anthony (1992). *A Rulebook for Arguments*, 2nd edn. Indianapolis and Cambridge: Hackett

Woodhouse, Mark B. (1984). *A Preface to Philosophy*, 3rd edn., Belmont, CA: Wadsworth

17 The more things change, the more they stay the same: social realism in contemporary science studies

D. Wade Hands

1 Introduction

The demise of the so-called Received View within mainstream philosophy of science and the subsequent Kuhnian and Quinean revolutions have left contemporary science theory in a state of relative disarray. While there are many different responses to this malaise – evolutionary epistemology, various naturalisms, and the revival of pragmatism, for example – the one that will be examined here is an approach to scientific knowledge that has evolved independently of such philosophical developments. The approach is constructivism, or the sociological turn, and while it remains controversial, it is certainly one of the main competing frameworks within contemporary science theory. Although a wide range of different programs fall under the broad constructivist rubric, some common themes clearly emerge from all of these different approaches. Most importantly, constructivism replaces armchair *a priori* philosophy, but unlike certain naturalistic approaches, it replaces it with inquiries into the *social* characteristics of the knowledge production (and legitimization) process. According to constructivists, science is fundamentally social, and for many this means that science, and scientists, should be studied in essentially the same way that one would study any other social or cultural phenomenon: using the tools of the human and social sciences. Both the philosophy of science and the self-descriptions of those within the scientific community tell us that legitimate scientific beliefs are determined exclusively by nature: that the "scientific method" is a procedure that allows privileged access to the voice of nature. While this "nature did it" view of scientific knowledge is widely accepted within contemporary scientific culture, it is equally clear that all cultures employ similar strategies in defense of their guiding beliefs. The relevant issue for the sociologist is to unpack the social construction of – and the social interests, causes, and functions behind – such cultural strategies. For the sociology of scientific knowledge, the objective is to understand the role that such strategies play in sustaining the culture of (or particular cultures within) science. For some constructivists the resulting inquiry is purely descriptive; for others it is important because of its anti-normative (or debunking) effect; and for still others understanding these social relationships are (like the method of traditional philosophy of science) the key to understanding the unique cognitive virtues of the scientific culture.

The purpose of this chapter is neither to praise nor to denounce the sociological turn, but rather to challenge a cognate claim about the impact of such developments on the *philosophy of social science*. It is often suggested because the concerns of "the philosophy of" the special sciences were derived directly from the concerns of the Received View (or its Popperian analog), and since recent developments such as constructivism have radically transformed the way we think about scientific knowledge, that all of the traditional questions in these special philosophical fields have lost their significance for (and should disappear from) contemporary science theory. In the halcyon days of what Philip Kitcher (1993) calls the Legend view of science, there was a rough consensus about the essential features (and cognitive virtues) of natural science, and the important questions in the philosophy of social science were most often couched in the language of subordinate conformity to that consensus. The most common question in the philosophy of social science was: "what do social scientists have to do in order to live up to the proper standards for scientific inquiry?" Traditional debates within the philosophy of social science, such as the question of methodological individualism vs. social holism, were reduced to the issue of which approach would most easily allow the relevant social science to most effectively employ the (known) method of the natural sciences. But are such questions still relevant? Since the constructivist turn and other developments within contemporary science theory have thoroughly disrupted the traditional view of the natural sciences, have not these same developments also rendered otiose all of the substantive debates within the philosophy of social science that were based on that traditional framework?

I claim that the answer to this question is in fact "no," and defending this negative answer is the main purpose of this chapter. I will argue that one of the most important questions in traditional philosophy of social science – the question of the character and explanatory status of social entities – has not only not vanished, it has re-emerged as an important and contentious (if often unrecognized) issue in the current debates among constructivists. Not only does this traditional question – what I will call the question of *social realism* – play a role in recent debates, it also influences how one views the relevance of the social science of economics to the study of scientific knowledge in general. The argument will focus on one particular episode in the sociological literature where social realism has been a major point of contention: the so-called "epistemological chicken" debate involving Harry Collins and Stephen Yearley (1992a) and a number of other contributors to contemporary science studies.[1]

I have one remark, or perhaps a disclaimer, to make before embarking on this discussion of constructivism and social realism. Since the chapter focuses on how particular general themes emerge from within the constructivist literature and how these themes relate to the role of economics within contemporary science studies, I have consciously avoided getting enmeshed in the myriad of traditional controversies about the different philosophical concepts that travel under the headings of individualism, holism, realism, etc. My reluctance to take a position on such controversies is certainly not that I find such topics unimportant – in fact, the main point of the chapter is that such controversies continue to be intellectually significant (the social turn has actually given them a new lease on life) – it is simply that this particular chapter does not have anything of substance to add to these traditional philosophical debates. This chapter does not purport to settle – or even take any particular position on – the traditional controversies within the philosophy of social science; the purpose of this chapter is simply to make a convincing case that such debates are still alive – actually rejuvenated – and to demonstrate that such issues have something substantive to do with the relationship between economics and the science studies wing of contemporary science theory.

2   Social realism and epistemological chicken: the opening volley

The sociology of scientific knowledge (SSK) consists of two initial waves of literature – first- and second-generation SSK – with the various post-chicken-debate contributions forming an ongoing, third generation, of literature. The first generation appeared in the 1970s and early 1980s and contained two separate, but intertwined stems: the Strong Program and social constructivism.[2] The second generation was a more diverse, and frequently more radical, body of literature that expanded on, and often reacted to, the main themes of these earlier programs. Two of these second-generation programs are the actor network theory (ANT) of Bruno Latour (1987, 1992, 1993), Michel Callon (1986), and others (Callon, Law, and Rip 1986); and the reflexivity (or hyper-reflexivity) school of Malcolm Ashmore (1989) and Steve Woolgar (1988). One of the main points of contention in the literature is whether this second generation was successful in solving some of the problems associated with the Strong Program and social constructivism – whether the second generation moved SSK forward – or whether it actually created more difficulties for the constructivist approach.

One point of agreement among most of those writing in SSK is the identification of "scientific knowledge" with "the beliefs of those within the scientific community." Scientific knowledge is not some special class of sentences or representations that have been certified as knowledge by nature, or by compliance with rules set down by philosophers of science; scientific knowledge is simply the set of beliefs that are held by scientists as a result of their membership in the (or a particular) scientific community. For most of those writing within SSK, the main goal is to provide a socially based understanding, account, or explanation, of the scientific beliefs that are held by the (or one particular) scientific community. The Strong Program maintains that scientific beliefs are determined by the "social interests" of the scientific community – scientists' place in the overall pattern of social relationships – while social constructivists generally give scientific beliefs a more local or site-specific explanation, but both approaches (as well as most second-generation authors) consider the social determination of the beliefs of scientists to be the main subject for the sociological approach to scientific knowledge.

Since those writing in SSK generally see society, and not nature, as the agency responsible for scientific knowledge, they are often accused of endorsing a radical form of *relativism*; scientific knowledge is not about the world "out there," but is merely about the scientific culture ("in here"). Different scientific cultures, like different societies in general, will have different beliefs, and since each is consistent with, or determined by, the particular culture in which that belief has emerged, there is no external, objective, way to choose between different scientific beliefs. Scientific knowledge, according to this reading of SSK, is relative to the particular scientific culture that produces it, and is thus no different from any other set of culturally determined beliefs.

A related, but separate, issue is the problem of *reflexivity*. Since sociology claims to be a type of scientific inquiry, the argument that social interests or social conditioning determine the beliefs of scientists, seems to imply that these same social factors also determine the beliefs of those doing SSK. If the arguments of SSK can be applied to SSK – and according to many (Bloor 1991, 7) they should – then doesn't that application undermine what these sociologists have to say about natural science? If sociologists can uncover the "nature of the case" within the social domain, then why shouldn't natural scientists have the same ability within the natural domain? In either case, reflexivity seems to be a serious problem; in the words of one critical philosopher "this sort of sociology pulls itself down by its own boot straps" (Rosenberg 1985, 380).

These two problems, relativism and reflexivity, became the two main organizing issues for the second-generation literature in SSK; exactly how each new program reacted to, or circumvented, these two difficulties often defined the program in question. This is particularly the case for the two second-generation programs most directly indicted by the chicken debate: the "reflexivity school" and "actor network theory" (ANT). The *reflexivity school* of Ashmore, Woolgar, and others, is so named because these authors consider reflexivity to be the main contribution of the sociological approach. For them reflexivity not a problem; it is an opportunity. It provides the fulcrum to overturn all of our traditional conceptual categories and ways of thinking about knowledge, to transcend our tired old representational ways; pushing reflexivity to the limit, exploring its most unsettling implications, creates, according to the reflexivity school, the opportunity to explore the critical "dynamic of iterative reconceptualization" (Woolgar 1992, 333). The ANT of Callon, Latour, and others, provides a very different view of science.[3] Roughly, ANT wants to bracket the entire debate over society vs. nature determining scientific knowledge. For ANT there are just "actants" (any entity that has the ability to act) in science; and these actants continually shift between being predominantly natural and being predominantly social. Science is a field for the interaction of these two constantly renegotiated sets of actants – human and nonhuman agency – and the products of science are a result of the interaction of these two forms of agency (and cannot be reduced to either one).

The central thesis of Collins and Yearley's "epistemological chicken" (1992a) is that second-generation programs such as the reflexivity school and ANT have led SSK down a dangerous road that will ultimately lead to the destruction of the entire sociological approach to scientific knowledge. Each new development within SSK has been more radical and more relativist; the result of which has been "an escalation of skepticism which we liken to the game of chicken; in this case the game is epistemological chicken" (Collins and Yearley 1992a, 302). The impact of this game has been to effectively undermine the critical relevance of SSK and leave the sociological study of science without any means for critically engaging either mainstream philosophy of science or the scientific community itself. While the authors (and most readers) of these second-generation studies consider their position to be quite radical, Collins and Yearley argue that it is actually rather *conservative*:

As we ... explain, the philosophy may be radical, but the implications are conservative. Where there are no differences except the differences between words there are no surprises left – no purchase for skeptical levers to shift the world on its axis. (1992a, 303)

While there are substantive differences among the various second-generation authors and approaches – in particular, the path taken by reflexivists is clearly different from the path taken by actor network theorists – the final destructive destination is essentially the same:

In sum, following the lead of the relativists, each new fashion in SSK has been more epistemologically daring, the reflexivists coming closest to self-destruction. Each group has made the same mistake at first; they have become so enamored of the power of their negative levers on the existing structures as to believe they rest on bedrock. But this is not the case. Though each level can prick misplaced epistemological pretentions, they stand in the same relationship to each other as parallel cultures; ... while SSK showed that science did not occupy the high ground of culture, the newer developments must be taken to demonstrate ... that there simply is no high ground. (1992a, 308)

Collins and Yearley argue that the greatest failure of these newer approaches to SSK – and the main reason why they can not critically engage philosophers or scientists – is that they do not provide any *explanation* for why one particular scientific theory (or lab, or research program) was successful while others failed. The reflexivists and ANT theorists both "supply an elaborate vocabulary for describing the means of knowledge making, but the vocabulary does not allow explanations of why certain knowledge claims are accepted and others are not" (1992a, 322). If SSK is to provide an effective counterargument to the nature-as-explanans of philosophers and scientists, then sociologists will need to provide an alternative explanation of scientific success and failure: not just redescribe scientific activity in interesting and entertaining ways.

Collins and Yearley's solution to the political and explanatory impotence of recent SSK is to return to the field's disciplinary roots in social theory; to employ the social scientist's "special understanding of social life" (1992a, 321); and *be social realists*. Their defense of social realism is straightforward. Natural scientists are realists about the aspects of nature they study, and social theorists should be (and with the exception of certain contributors to SSK, are) realists about the aspects of society they study. The explanations of natural scientists involve things like electrons and genes, while the explanations of sociologists involve things like social structure and social interests; and that is "all there is to it" (Collins and Yearley 1992b, 382):

Natural scientists, working at the bench, should be naïve realists – that is what will get their work done. Sociologists, historians, scientists away from the bench, and the rest of the general public should be social realists. Social realists must experience the social world in a naïve way, as the day-to-day foundation of reality (as natural scientists naïvely experience the natural world). (Collins and Yearley 1992a, 308)

If SSK is to provide an alternative, social, explanation of the beliefs of scientists, then those doing SSK should be social realists and provide an alternative, social, *explanation* of such beliefs. Of course, other things should go on in SSK besides explanation, but if the field is to fulfill its critical mission, then the prevailing research strategies must "leave room for explanation" (1992a, p. 323), and the purely redescriptive frameworks of reflexivity and ANT do not. Note that while Collins and Yearley's version of SSK is relativistic in the sense that the explanation of what occurs in science, or at a specific scientific site, is "relative to" the social context and social conditions, it is not relativistic in the sense that any explanation is just as good as any other. From a social realist perspective there are good explanations for why a particular theoretical strategy within science (or perhaps even the scientific form of life in general) triumphed over other theoretical strategies, but those explanations are to be found in the social conditions of that scientific theorizing, and not in the inherent characteristics of an unconditioned nature.

3 Social realism and epistemological chicken: other responses

One of the many authors that has offered an alternative response to the issues raised by the chicken debate is Andrew Pickering. Although Pickering edited the volume that contained Collins and Yearley's original paper, his most important contribution to the debate came later in the presentation of his own "Mangle of Practice" (1995) approach to science and scientific knowledge. Pickering's mangle borrows heavily from the second-generation literature, particularly ANT, but his main focus is on the relationship between the "material world" and SSK. Even before the "Mangle" was fully articulated, Pickering had emphasized material "resistances" to scientists' construction and endorsed a "pragmatic realism" based on the "dialectic of resistance and accommodation" (Pickering 1990, 702). The dialectic of resistance and accommodation, while denying the traditional representational view of scientific knowledge, is broadly realist in its metaphysical focus; scientists engage the material world and construct knowledge, but the material world resists in various ways, frustrating the scientists' intentions, and these resistances must be accommodated:

This dialectic of resistance and accommodation in material practice sure justifies calling the resulting picture of scientific practice a realist one. But, I repeat, "realist" here means something different from "realist" as it appears in the standard realism debate. It points to a constitutive role for "reality" – the material world – in the production of knowledge, but it carries no necessary connotation of correspondence (or lack of correspondence) for the knowledge produced. (1990, p. 706)

The "Mangle" has expanded this basic argument, but Pickering's focus on social constructivism with a role for the material world remains the same. The term "mangle" comes from the British use of the term (as a noun) for a clothes wringer: although the more common American usage, as a verb, works equally as well to capture the basic idea:

The practical, goal-oriented and goal-revising dialectic of resistance and accommodation is, as far as I can make out, a general feature of scientific practice. And it is, in the first instance, what I call the *mangle of practice*, or just the mangle. I find "mangle" a convenient and suggestive shorthand for the dialectic because, for me, it conjures up the image of the unpredictable transformations worked upon whatever gets fed into the old-fashioned device of the same name used to squeeze the water out of washing. (Pickering 1995, 22–23, emphasis in the original)

Pickering's mangle, like ANT, does not rely on a single form of agency: "the mangle and the actor-network insist on the constitutive intertwining and reciprocal interdefinition of human and material agency" (1995, 25–26). What makes the mangle substantially different from ANT is Pickering's insistence on the performative, rather than representative, idiom. Conceptual structures and the other social aspects of science are representational but they also sustain specific human practices and performances. Various resistances are encountered during these performances and material agency emerges (temporally) in the context of these practices. Material agency acts for Pickering, but it acts within the context of specific culturally conditioned practices. The performative idiom forces us to think of science as "doing things," but it is not just we (humans) that are doing things – it is not just social agency – nature is doing things too and this material agency becomes manifest in resistances that emerge when the cultural structures and material performance fail to cohere and require accommodation: "in scientific culture, particular configurations of material and human agency appear as interactively stabilized against one another" (1995, 145). Pickering thus allows for the world to act (material agency) in a way that he argues many in SSK (social realists in particular) do not, without giving nature in any sense "free rein" (as in the traditional accounts of philosophers of science and the scientists themselves). This performative realism, according to Pickering, evades both horns of Collins and Yearley's dilemma (social agency or natural agency); it "recognizes material agency as that with which scientists struggle (unlike SSK), without acceding to scientific accounts of such agency" (1995, 53). Pickering, like Collins and Yearley, seeks an alternative social explanation for why certain scientific beliefs have triumphed over others, but his explanatory framework is quite different: both the social and the realism are different.

Yet another solution to the problems posed by the chicken debate has been offered by defenders of the Strong Program (Barnes, Bloor, and Henry 1996). These authors also focus on the role of nature within the social studies of scientific knowledge, but their concerns are philosophically more traditional; they emphasize the role of "objective reality" in the determination of scientific beliefs. They criticize sociologists who practice what they call "methodological idealism" – acting as if "the natural world, and our experience of it, played no significant role in the production of knowledge" (Barnes, Bloor, and Henry 1996, 13) – and repeatedly cite Collins' social realism as a primary example of such methodological idealism (1996, 14–15, 73–77).

The way to control such idealism is of course to let nature back into the sociological analysis of science, and this, according to Barnes, Bloor, and Henry is exactly what the Strong Program (unlike social realism) does. They start from the traditional assumption that "at the basis of knowledge there lies a causal interaction between the knower and reality" (1996, 1), and end by admitting that "there is nothing epistemically radical about the approach being taken" (1996, 200):

No plausible sociology of knowledge could deny a role for such basic, material and causal factors in the process of belief formation: sometimes theories work, and we are impressed by this. To deny this would be to adopt a from of idealism in which the world is understood as an emanation of our beliefs, rather than as a cause of them. (1996, 32)

So how can the Strong Program manage this? How can they allow the agency of nature, maintain a relatively traditional epistemological stance, and still offer a *sociological* account of scientific knowledge? The answer lies in their particular version of *empiricism*: a version which, for want of a better term, I will call *social empiricism*. Humans, like other animals, have developed "reasonably reliable and tolerably non-frustrating routines for interacting with the environment" (1996, 32), but in humans this information-processing ability always has a social component. This empirical-processing method requires *social calibration*; it produces reliable knowledge only when it is certified by coherence with the observations made by other members of the relevant epistemic community:

Observers, like instruments generally, only yield up reliable knowledge when they are working properly. If we ask where the criterion of properly functioning comes from, we find that it lies in the coherence of the individual observer or instrument with other relatively similar ones. However self-evident or subjectively convincing an observation seems to the observer, it is only counted as genuine or veridical if it coheres with the generality of other readings. Individual and internal criteria don't outweigh collective ones. The standard implicit in treating an observation as genuine or reliable means that there is a social criterion to be satisfied before something can even count as a genuine observation for its users. (1996, 16)

This is clearly a brand of empiricism, but it is a *social empiricism* and not the individualistic empiricism of the Received View. This social empiricism allows the Strong Program to be epistemologically rather traditional (at least relative to second-generation programs like the reflexivity school and ANT) and yet retain a fundamentally sociological theory of scientific knowledge. Since a "social criterion" must be satisfied for an observation to be genuine and reliable, the opportunity clearly exists for sociologists to explain why a particular social criterion is in effect and what social function, or interests, or structure, it serves. Again, like Collins and Yearley, and also Pickering, these defenders of the Strong Program seek an alternative social explanation for the success of certain theoretical strategies within science – an explanation that can effectively compete with those offered by philosophers of science and the scientists themselves – but it involves different versions of both realism and the social.

Despite their substantive differences, all of the parties involved in the chicken debate end up defending specific theoretical strategies regarding the proper "social explanation" of the beliefs of those within the scientific community. In particular, each approach endorses certain specific commitments about the proper characterization of "the social" within the social studies of science. For Collins and Yearley the relevant social factors seem to be the structural and functional social relations that have been the focus of most twentieth-century (nonMarxist) social theory. For the ANT theorists the social is much more transitory; the relevant agents are individuals – scientists, fishermen, scallops (Callon 1986), Door-Openers (Latour and Johnson 1988) – and the way that these individual actants exhibit particular forms of social and natural agency within the context of various social networks is the main focus. For Pickering the social framework seems to be Marxist in orientation with material relations determining (though not mechanically, or teleologically) the configuration of social relations and the effective modes of accommodation. The Strong Program grounds its approach in empiricism, but it is not traditional (individualistic) empiricism, it is a version of social empiricism that owes more to Durkheim than to Hume or Mill. These are all different roles for, and characteristics of, the social within the sociological study of scientific knowledge and they are certainly all open to critical examination; the point is that each of these positions is simply a variant of an established explanatory framework within traditional philosophy of social science. Each of these stories about the identity of "the social" within science studies reflects a particular tradition within social theory, and the various arguments that might be (and have been) presented to defend one of these characterizations against another simply represent a new forum for rehashing the traditional arguments for and against these various traditions within social theory. SSK has raised the ante, in the sense that what is at stake now is our understanding of knowledge and the knowledge-acquisition process in general, rather than some more narrow topic in social science – like say the function of the caste system, the impact of a fully-anticipated monetary expansion, or the origin of the incest taboo – but the old debates still remain. SSK has not only not eliminated the core theoretical debates within the philosophy of social science; it has actually put them in bold relief.

4   Economics and contemporary science studies

In this final section I would like to discuss the role of economics in the chicken debate and the surrounding science studies literature. Notice I did not say that I will be "applying" the chicken debate to the science of economics; it is not merely a matter of "application" since the economics is already contained within the various positions offered by those involved in the discussion. While economic theory is not explicitly discussed by the participants in the chicken debate, economic argumentation seems to be lurking immediately under the surface of all of the various contributions. Not only is such argumentation lurking under the surface, the reasons why certain authors allow it to surface, or allow one particular type of economic argument to surface, or keep it hidden altogether, turns on fundamental issues about the role of "the social" and "the individual" in the explanation of social phenomena: in this case the phenomenon of science.

As many authors have pointed out, a number of those writing in SSK use argumentation (sometimes explicitly and sometimes only implicitly) that sounds a lot more like the economics of science than the sociology of science.[4] More specifically, both of the critical responses to the chicken debate discussed above – Pickering (1995) and Barnes, Bloor, and Henry (1996) – consider the parallel between certain types of SSK and (certain types of) economics. Pickering's themes are broadly Marxist; he pays his respects to Marxist historians of science such as J. D. Bernal, but differentiates his own performative historiography from this earlier Marxist literature by stressing the nonteleological and contingent way that material and social agency interact within the mangle. The link here is to Marxian, not mainstream neoclassical economics, but it is economics, and it consistently informs Pickering's attempt to deal with the problems identified in the chicken debate.

Barnes, Bloor, and Henry also consider economics (in this case more mainstream economics), but it is in the context of criticizing other views rather than explicating their own. They argue that what is wrong with much of SSK is the general trend toward emphasizing "more and more strongly the standing of individuals as active agents in order to make sense of their actions or explain their provenance . . . consistent with an analogous shift in the social sciences generally" (Barnes, Bloor, and Henry, 1996, 114). In other words, rational-choice theory is now pervasive in the social sciences, and the use of "the 'economic' conception of the individual to understand what scientists did" (1996, 114) is just one – from the Strong Program's point of view, rather pernicious – example of this general theoretical trend. Again, this ultimately comes down to asserting a preference for one type of social theory (the Strong Program's interests sociology) over another type of social theory (rational-choice theory and microeconomics). As the comments by Barnes, Bloor, and Henry clearly indicate, the whole question of the role of "the individual" and "the society" and whether the problem of the social order can be understood in individualistic terms has been reopened within the literature of the chicken debate. It seems unlikely that the first generation of authors writing on SSK (including Barnes and Bloor twenty years ago) would ever have considered the problem of "the individual," or particularly the need to fight "the individual" usurping the role of "the social" within the literature that attempts to explain the social order of science, but it is now a serious issue within science studies.

Related to this last point, but separable from it, is the issue of how much the debates in SSK have altered our view of the role of society and nature in our conception of scientific knowledge. The problem is that there are not just two poles, nature and society, there are at least three – nature, society, and individual – and all three seem to be continually shape-shifting. According to mainstream neoclassical economics, agency resides neither in society nor in nature; it resides in individuals. Nature, in the form of production functions and resource endowments, is viewed as a constraint on economic behavior. Society, social things, like prices and economic institutions, are typically viewed as caused by, or explained by, the rational actions of individuals optimizing in an environment containing natural constraints. This is very different from the social vision that underpins most of SSK. SSK tends to replace the agency of nature with the agency of society, leaving the relationship between the individual and society relatively unexamined. A fully developed (neoclassical-based) economic approach to scientific knowledge would probably replace the agency of nature with the agency of individuals, while also leaving the relationship between the individual and the society relatively unexamined. In either case things are certainly much more complex than what was suggested by the first generation of SSK's basic insight that scientific beliefs are socially determined.

A good example of the complexity of the involvement of economics within science studies is the ANT of Latour and others. Chris McClellan (1996) has argued that ANT involves an analogy about competitive markets and capital accumulation that has been an ongoing source of tension within the ANT literature. For some ANT theorists scientists should be seen as entrepreneurs who build networks by enrolling actants through efficient investment of scarce resources; success is market success and knowledge, like capital, is accumulated in the process. Others involved in ANT accept some aspects of this market story but view it primarily as a critique of the encroachment of market rationality into every aspect of human life (including science). Thus, as McClellan explains, elements of ANT pull in both directions of "the great divide which separates *homo sociologicus* and *homo oeconomicus*" (McClellan 1996, 203).

5 Conclusion

This chapter has covered quite a lot of ground and it is useful to conclude by reviewing the main argument. The chapter started out by discussing the constructivist turn and the claim that recent changes in the general theory of science have rendered otiose various traditional debates within the philosophy of social science: such as those involving the character and relative explanatory status of "individuals" and "society." The chicken debate was then examined along with a few of the more recent responses to the initial exchange. It was discovered that the main point of contention among the various participants concerned the notion of the social – what social realism means, what it means to have a social cause, a social explanation, or social agency – and in particular how the social should be demarcated from both nature and the individual. No clear answers were found to these questions, but the point was made repeatedly that such questions are still (very much) relevant and have not been eliminated, and in fact have been reaffirmed, by the literature of the constructivist turn. Finally, it was argued that economics is directly involved in such debates, sometimes explicitly and sometimes only implicitly, and that how one views the relationship between the social and the individual (and the proper definition of these terms) is co-determined along with one's view about the proper way to do economics, and/or sociology, as well as the proper characterization of scientific knowledge.

The bottom line is that questions about social realism and the factors relevant in social explanation – the character of the individual–social–nature nexus – have not disappeared because of the demise of the Legend. Fundamental questions in the philosophy of social science are not only still alive, they have been given a new lease on life; social explanation is no longer just a topic for social studies, it is now relevant to the study of knowledge in general. Regardless of the reader's opinion about any of the particular positions represented in the chicken debate, I hope the debate has been a useful vehicle for exhibiting the relevant social questions. Not only are the core questions about the nature of the social order still with us, the role such questions play in current constructivist debates highlights the co-dependency of the social, economic, and epistemic orders much more clearly than it was exhibited by earlier approaches to science theory.

Notes

This chapter is based on my paper "Social realism and contemporary science theory," presented at the conference on "Fact or Fiction: Perspectives on Realism and Economics" at the Erasmus University, Rotterdam, November 14–15, 1997, published in translation as "Sociaal realisme binnen het huidige wetenschapsonderzoek," *Krisis*, 70 (1998, 38–54). Parts of the argument also draw on the discussion in chapter 5 of Hands (2001).

1. This controversy has been called "the most wide-ranging and seemingly radical debate" within SSK in recent years (Fuller 2000, 350). Some of the many commentaries on the debate include Friedman (1998), Fuller (1996), and Roth (1996).
2. Classic sources on the Strong Program include Barnes (1974, 1977) and Bloor (1976, 1991), while social constructivist classics include Collins (1985), Knorr Cetina (1981) and Latour and Woolgar (1979, 1986).
3. Latour and Woolgar's *Laboratory Life (1979)* was one of the major texts of the early social constructivist literature; during the 1980s; however, the work of the two authors diverged, with Woolgar becoming a major spokesperson for reflexivity and Latour becoming one of the founders of ANT.
4. Some of these include: Knorr Cetina (1991); Mäki (1992); Hands (1994, 1997, 2001); Callon (1995); Davis (1997); McClellan (1996); and Mirowski and Sent (2001). There is a rapidly growing literature that explicitly discusses the "economics of science" (Diamond 1996; Stephan 1996; Wible 1998; Sent 1999; Mirowski and Sent 2001) but that literature can be separated from the use of economic argumentation within SSK.

References

Ashmore, Malcolm (1989). *The Reflexive Thesis. Wrighting the Sociology of Knowledge*. Chicago: University of Chicago Press

Barnes, Barry (1974). *Scientific Knowledge an Sociological Theory*. London: Routledge & Kegan Paul

(1977). *Interests and the Growth of Knowledge*. London: Routledge & Kegan Paul

Barnes, Barry, David Bloor, and John Henry (1996). *Scientific Knowledge: A Sociological Analysis*. Chicago: University of Chicago Press

Bloor, David (1976). *Knowledge and Social Imagery*. London: Routledge
    (1991). *Knowledge and Social Imagery*, 2nd edn. Chicago: University of Chicago Press

Callon, Michel (1986). Some elements of a sociology of translation: domestication of the scallops and the fisherman of St. Brieuc Bay, in J. Law (ed.), *Power, Action and Belief: A New Sociology of Knowledge*. London: Routledge, 196–233
    (1995). Four models for the dynamics of science, in S. Jasanoff, G.E. Markle, J.C. Petersen, and T. Pinch (eds.), *Handbook of Science and Technology Studies*. Thousand Oaks, CA: Sage, 29–63

Callon, Michel and Bruno Latour (1992). Don't throw the baby out with the bath school! A reply to Collins and Yearley, in Andrew Pickering (ed.), *Science as Practice and Culture*. Chicago: University of Chicago Press, 343–368

Callon, Michel, John Law, and Arie Rip (eds.) (1986). *Mapping the Dynamics of Science and Technology: Sociology of Science in the Real World*. London: Macmillan

Collins, Harry M. (1985). *Changing Order: Replication and Induction in Scientific Practice*. Beverly Hills, CA: Sage

Collins, Harry M. and Steven Yearley (1992a). Epistemological chicken, in Andrew Pickering (ed.), *Science as Practice and Culture*. Chicago: University of Chicago Press, 301–326
    (1992b). Journey into space, in Andrew Pickering (ed.), *Science as Practice and Culture*. Chicago: University of Chicago Press, 369–389.

Davis, John B. (1997). New economics and its history: A Pickeringian view, in John B. Davis, (ed.), *New Economics and Its Writing*. Durham, NC: Duke University Press

Diamond, Arthur M. (1996). The economics of science, *Knowledge and Policy*, 9, 6–49

Friedman, Michael (1998). On the sociology of scientific knowledge and its philosophical agenda, *Studies in History and Philosophy of Science*, 29, 238–271

Fuller, Steve (1996). Talking metaphysical turkey about epistemological chicken, and the poop on pidgins, in P. Galison and D.J. Stump (eds.), *The Disunity of Science: Boundaries, Contexts, and Power*. Stanford, CA: Stanford University Press, 170–186
    (2000). *Thomas Kuhn: A Philosophical History for Our Times*. Chicago: University of Chicago Press

Hands, D. Wade (1994). The sociology of scientific knowledge: some thoughts on the possibilities, in Roger E. Backhouse (ed.), *New Directions in Economic Methodology*. London: Routledge, 75–106
    (1997). Conjectures and reputations: the sociology of scientific knowledge and the history of economic thought, *History of Political Economy*, 29, 695–739
    (2001). *Reflection Without Rules: Economic Methodology and Contemporary Science Theory*. Cambridge: Cambridge University Press

Kitcher, Philip (1993). *The Advancement of Science: Science Without Legend, Objectivity Without Illusions*. Oxford: Oxford University Press

Knorr Cetina, Karin (1981). *The Manufacture of Knowledge: An Essay on the Constructivist and Contextual Nature of Science*. New York: Pergamon

(1991). Epistemic cultures: forms of reason in science, *History of Political Economy*, 23, 105–122

Latour, Bruno (1987). *Science in Action*. Cambridge, MA: Harvard University Press

(1992). One more turn after the social turn, in E. McMullin (ed.), *The Social Dimensions of Science*. Notre Dame: University of Notre Dame Press, 272–294

(1993). *We Have Never Been Modern*. Cambridge, MA: Harvard University Press

Latour, Bruno and J. Johnson (1988). Mixing humans with non-humans: sociology of a door-opener, *Social Problems*, 35, 298–310

Latour, Bruno and Steve Woolgar (1979). *Laboratory Life: the Construction of Scientific Facts*. Beverly Hills, CA: Sage

(1986). *Laboratory Life: The Construction of Scientific Facts*, 2nd edn. Princeton: Princeton University Press

McClellan, Chris (1996). The economic consequences of Bruno Latour, *Social Epistemology*, 10, 193–208

Mäki, Uskali (1992). Social conditioning of economics, in Neil De Marchi (ed.), *Post-Popperian Methodology of Economics*. Boston: Kluwer, 65–104

Mirowski, Philip and Esther-Mirjam Sent (2001). Introduction, in Philip Mirowski and Esther-Mirjaim Sent (eds.), *Science Bought and Sold*. Chicago: University of Chicago Press, forthcoming

Pickering, Andrew (1990). Knowledge, practice and mere construction, *Social Studies of Science*, 20, 682–729

(ed.) (1992). *Science as Practice and Culture*. Chicago: University of Chicago Press

(1995). *The Mangle of Practice. Time, Agency, and Science*. Chicago: University of Chicago Press

Rosenberg, Alexander (1985). Methodology, theory, and the philosophy of science, *Pacific Philosophical Quarterly*, 66, 377–393

Roth, Paul A. (1996). Will the real scientists please stand up? Dead ends and live issues in the explanation of scientific knowledge, *Studies in History and Philosophy Science*, 27, 43–68

Sent, Esther-Mirjam (1999). Economics of science: survey and suggestions, *Journal of Economic Methodology*, 6, 95–124

Stephan, Paula E. (1996). The economics of science, *Journal of Economic Literature*, 34, 1199–1235

Wible, James R. (1998). *The Economics of Science: Methodology and Epistemology as if Economics Really Mattered*. London: Routledge

Woolgar, Steve (1992). Some remarks about positionism: a reply to Collins and Yearley, in Andrew Pickering (ed.), *Science as Practice and Culture*. Chicago: University of Chicago Press, 327–342

(ed.) (1988). *Knowledge and Reflexivity: New Frontiers in the Sociology of Knowledge*. London: Sage

18 Economists: truth-seekers or rent-seekers?

Jesús P. Zamora Bonilla

1 The conservative revolution meets reflexivity

Although a vast majority of economic theories assume that human agents are rational utility maximizers, some economic schools are more willing than others to carry this vision to its ultimate consequences. In particular, two of the leading schools of the so-called 'conservative revolution' of the 1970s are famous for having made an extensive use of the hypothesis of the *homo oeconomicus*. These approaches were the Public Choice school and the Rational Expectations school. Both theories launched demolishing attacks to a couple of basic ideas underlying interventionist economic policies: the idea that economists could discover the working of the economic system, and the idea that this knowledge could and should be used by politicians to "handle" or "fine tune" the system so as to maximize social welfare. Stated differently:

(1) Both the economists and the politicians were assumed to behave in an altruistic fashion, not influenced by personal interests
(2) The fundamental equations describing the functioning of the economic system would neither be affected by its discovery, nor by the government's intervention.

The Public Choice school directed its attacks mainly to the first of these assumptions, particularly against the standard view of the politicians' motivations. This school's fundamental thesis is that we cannot assume that economic agents are basically motivated by the maximization of their own income, and, at the same time, that public servants are simply benevolent incarnations of the general interest. The state should rather be seen, according to Buchanan and his followers, as a revenue-maximizing "Leviathan," integrated by politicians and bureaucrats who will use their discretionary powers only in their own interest, at least to the extent that the limits established in the constitution, or other constraining mechanisms, do not put stricter limits to that discretion. The power to tax, as well as the power to spend the revenue of these taxes, and the power *not* to tax some privileged activities, could also be used by other rent-seeking agents to distort the otherwise efficient working of the markets, in order to benefit from artificial monopoly rents. The powers of the politicians and bureaucrats should be, hence, severely limited at the constitutional level, as a means of protecting the freedom and the welfare of the citizens.[1]

But, if we were to generalize seriously the *homo oeconomicus* hypothesis, so as to include under its scope *all* economic agents, it should obviously be applied to *economists* as well. If we can not trust politicians and bureaucrats when they talk on behalf of "the public interest," can really we trust economists when they talk on behalf of "the truth"? My argument simply replicates the story that ancient Greeks knew as "the liar's paradox," or "the paradox of the Cretan," attributed to the philosopher Epimenides: "I'm a Cretan, and Cretans always lie." Public Choice theorists seem to be saying to us something like "I'm a disinterested truth-seeker *homo oeconomicus*, and *homini oeconomici* are never trustworthy when they pretend to serve some interests which are not those of themselves." The obvious moral is that, if individual greed is dangerous when it is not subjected to the discipline of the market or of the constitution, then economists' behavior should be constrained either by a market-like mechanism or by a constitution-like mechanism, if it is going to produce reliable knowledge at all.

Economists tend to assume that scientific disciplines, including economics, actually function like a "free market," in which competition entails that bad (i.e. false) ideas and theories are replaced more or less automatically by good (i.e. true) ones.[2] The lack of a broad consensus about very elementary topics in economics – and, more particularly, about the consequences of each kind of economic policy – shows that the working of such an "invisible hand" is not very quick and efficient, at least within economic science. But, even if a deeper and broader consensus around a theory were observed, consensus would not be by itself a proof of the theory's correctness (after all, a general agreement might also be due to a "monopoly" in the "market for ideas," i.e. to a lack of real competition). This means that it is not enough to *assume* that free competition of ideas would automatically lead to the truth; what we would like to have is a *proof* that this is the case, or at least we should have a plausible model showing that this can reasonably be the case.

The Rational Expectations school, in its turn, insisted more than other macro-economic theories in the rationality of economic agents: according to this school, people make unbiased forecasts of the consequences of economic policies. The Rational Expectations hypothesis does not entail, as some of its critics have believed, that agents have a "correct" model of the economy within their heads, only that they can learn to eliminate systematic errors in the ways they form expectations.[3] The "correction mechanism" is supposed to be of an evolutionary kind, although, as far as I know, it has not been developed as much as, for example, the Darwinian mechanism proposed by Alchian and Friedman to defend the hypothesis that those firms which do not learn to maximize profits will not "survive."[4] The possibility of devising a specific evolutionary mechanism leading to unbiased expectations is, in any case, doubtful. In general, "natural selection" does not guarantee that the equilibrium which is actually reached is an efficient one. In the case of expectations formation, if among the information-processing systems which have been *actually developed* there were one leading to "better" predictions than the rest, independently of which system the rest of agents had, then this system would be "selected," but this argument does not entail that the selected system is necessarily a "rational" one, in the sense of being the best one among all the *conceivable* systems. Even if a mechanism producing "perfect" predictions were discovered by some agents, it could be possible that an "imperfect" mechanism were not superseded by the first one if the second happened to be an evolutionarily stable strategy.[5] After all, how could Rational Expectation macroeconomics explain, for example, the fact that the ("inefficient") Keynesian orthodoxy existed at all for two or three decades?

In fact, rather than explaining the formation of expectations by an evolutionary mechanism working on the cognitive systems of *individual* economic agents, it is reasonable to assume that, in a complex economy, the ability to forecast macroeconomic variables would be possessed by some group of *experts*, who would sell their services both to private agents and to public institutions. Instead of searching for an equilibrium in the evolution of cognitive systems, more coherent with (new classical) economic theory would be the idea that actual macroeconomic theories, models, and predictions are the outcome resulting from an equilibrium *in the "market" for macroeconomic expertise*. More realistic macroeconomic models might contain, hence, an explicit description of that "market," in the same sense that they can include a description of the money market or the labor market. Stated a bit differently: *economic knowledge should be seen, in part, as an endogenous variable of economic models.*[6]

In the following sections I will briefly describe and discuss some ideas that could be used in the construction of an economic model of the production of scientific knowledge. Section 2 presents an application of constitutional economics to the study of scientific *norms*, an approach which is illustrated in section 3 by means of two examples. In section 4 I will comment on the relevance of collective decisions in the mechanism producing a consensus about scientific *statements*. Lastly, section 5 discusses to what extent the mechanisms formerly described are applicable to economics as a scientific discipline.

2   Scientific method: a constitutional approach

An economic model of the production of scientific knowledge must begin by making some assumptions about the utility function of scientists. I will assume that they mainly derive utility from getting their own theories or models accepted by their colleagues, and, in some disciplines, by the general public. Obviously, they also enjoy the production and possession of "knowledge," for if they simply desired popularity and wealth, they would surely do better by devoting their efforts to sports, music, or other forms of entertainment. We can also suppose that scientists prefer having more income and wealth to less, and, at least in the case of economists, that they also get satisfaction from the political power of putting their own theories into practice.[7]

The last two elements in the scientists' preferences (income and political power) can nevertheless be seen as dependent on the first two ("recognition" among colleagues and among the public): the more popular your theories are, the more probable it is that you get political power and a high rent. The basic problem for a scientist is, hence, how to reach the first two goals, and this is perhaps a Herculean work: if convincing lay people that your theories are right may be a more or less difficult task, convincing your own colleagues *would be impossible* if they simply wanted (as you also want) to maximize the popularity of their own theories: accepting other colleagues' theory would be like scoring a goal against their own goalkeeper! We do not need to assume that all scientists (nor even most of them) are absolutely reluctant to enhance their rivals' popularity; but I am trying to show that *even if scientists were so cynically motivated*, they could nevertheless reach an agreement on the norms of scientific method.

If each researcher within a scientific community intends basically to maximize the popularity of her own theories (both among her colleagues and among the general public), it follows that scientists only derive utility *in a direct way* from decisions taken by others. That is, each scientist does not receive her reward directly from *her* adoption of certain theories or statements, but from the theory choices made by *other* people. The only way of actively increasing her degree of recognition will be, hence, by exerting some influence on these choices. If we limit the choices under consideration to those made by scientists (not by the general public), this entails that science must be seen as a kind of *exchange*: in order to receive recognition, one has to offer something which fosters the recognition of others. A common line of thought among sociologists and economists of science is that scientists offer this recognition in exchange for the *information* provided by colleagues (especially by the person who has been the first in disclosing that piece of information),[8] but this common idea has some problems. It particularly takes for granted that scientists value (correct) "information," either *per se*, or because it serves them in their own pursuit of recognition. In the first case (right information is desired on its own), it would be unclear why researchers should worry about the "true cognitive value" of a piece of information if, as radical sociologists of science have pointed out, scientists' fundamental concern is recognition *instead of* "knowledge," and, more importantly, if the very idea of "cognitive value" is nothing but a meta-physical chimera.[9] In the second case (right information is valued because of its usefulness), accepting a piece of (right) information would be useful for a researcher in her pursuit of recognition only if (1) the other scientists also accepted that information, (2) it tended to "confirm" the propositions defended by the first scientist, and (3) her colleagues were willing to explicitly recognize point (2); what needs to be proved is, then, why scientists accept many times information that "disconfirms" their own theories, and why they devote effort to publicly recognize the "authorship" of the information they are using, instead of simply using it without indicating its source.

In order to answer these questions, I propose to consider that what scientists exchange is not "recognition for information," but the *mutual acceptance of constraints*: they offer the compromise of subjecting their own theory choices to some rules, in exchange for their colleagues' observance of the same constraints. These rules would function like the *methodological constitution* of a scientific discipline or of a scientific community, and they can be different for different groups of researchers, and even for the same group in different periods. This constitution is what makes "the game of persuasion" possible at all, for a scientist could try to persuade a colleague of accepting a theory only if the latter's theory choices obey some determinate pattern, a pattern allowing the former to know what kind of arguments or strategies to use in order to persuade the latter.

The most essential aspect of the constitutional approach is its methodological individualism: it does not assume that the outcome of the social *interaction* among scientists is a social *entity* which we could call "collective knowledge," and which would have the same analytical properties that knowledge, beliefs, or information have in the case of individual scientists. Instead, the constitutional approach suggests taking a piece of information as "public knowledge" among a group of scientists if *every* member of that group publicly acknowledges that this information is acceptable according to a set of methodological rules that have also been *unanimously* accepted by the members of the group. If there is disagreement among a group about the norms that must be applied, or about the outcome of their application, then our approach will simply identify a group's "public state of knowledge about a certain issue" with the indication of what proposition (if any) each member of the group has publicly accepted concerning that issue.[10] Another peculiarity of the constitutional approach is that we need not necessarily be interested in finding out an *absolutely optimal* system of norms; our modest goal is, instead, to discuss whether a group of rational agents could reach a unanimous agreement about a *particular* norm or set of norms once they have agreed on looking for a norm of a certain *kind*.[11]

In order to participate in a collective decision about the acceptance of a rule, each member of a scientific group will basically take into account the probability that her own theories would become accepted if a certain rule were adopted; note that many rules will usually be established *before* most theories, hypotheses, and models in the scientific field are devised, as if they were adopted "behind a veil of ignorance," and this will tend to make the choice of a rule more impartial; hence, the more uncertain the private benefits of alternative methodological norms are for a scientists, the stronger will be the influence of mere epistemic motivations in the choice of norms.

From the point of view of their role in the process of getting a theory accepted, these "constitutional rules" can be classified as follows:

(1) *Norms for theory comparison.* These rules tell under what circumstances a theory, hypothesis, or model can be considered better than another, or under what circumstances the epistemic value of a theory will have increased or decreased. For example, the norm indicating that having correctly predicted an unknown event increases the epistemic value of a model is a norm of this kind.[12]

(2) *Norms of inference.* These indicate that, *if you have accepted some statements, you must also accept (or reject) another specific statement.* In practice, however, some statement-connecting norms will only make some combinations of statements more or less *untenable,* especially when the norms of theory comparison are not easy to apply to those cases, and hence, when it is not easy to establish which theory is better under the circumstances indicated by the inference norm. In any case, a researcher can benefit from her colleagues' adoption of some statement-connecting rules in an obvious way: if they obey a rule which tells (or from which it follows) that "if you accept E, you must accept T_i," then, researcher i can increase the degree of acceptance of her own theory if she persuades many colleagues to accept E in the first place.

(3) *Action-related norms.* These tell scientists that, *if some people have performed certain actions in certain circumstances, and if they accept certain propositions, then they also must (or must not) accept another proposition, or they must (or must not) perform certain actions.* Rules of this kind entail that some statements must be accepted, not because other statements have been already accepted, but because of some additional reasons. These other reasons can be of a variety of types: they can be *results* of observations or experiments made by the researcher, or *reports* of observations or experiments made by others, or the *acceptance* of some statements by others (as in the case of many propositions one learns through textbooks, which in many cases are accepted as mere assertions of authority). Note that the individuals who have performed the actions stated in the antecedent of a rule of this kind need not be the same individuals who are pondering whether to apply the rule or not. Note also that action-related norms refer not only to the obligation of accepting or not accepting a statement, but also

to the appropriateness or inappropriateness of performing *other actions*; for example, some of these rules can indicate how experiments must be conducted. Action-related norms play an essential role in the game of persuasion, since rules of inference only allow us to persuade a colleague to accept a theory if she already accepts some propositions that "trigger" those inference norms.

(4) *Enforcement norms.* These establish the penalty that has to be imposed on a scientist who has disobeyed some rule. Two important points must be indicated here. The first one is that, since we have supposed that the fundamental source of utility for a researcher is the degree of popularity of the theories proposed by her, the only kind of penalties that can be introduced in our model are those establishing that (some of) these theories must *not* be accepted. The second point is that enforcement norms are not only addressed to the infractors of the other kinds of rules, but to all the members of the scientific community, who, according to these norms, *have the obligation of not accepting* the theories proposed by the infractors; as a consequence, there will be some norms establishing a penalty for those scientists who have failed to apply a sanction when they had to do it.[13]

What can be said about these four kinds of norms from an economic point of view (as opposed, for example, to a sociological one)? In the first place, the *process of establishing* a norm (or a system of norms) can be studied as a negotiation in which a mutually favorable agreement is sought. For example, figure 18.1 shows a situation where two scientists (or, perhaps, two different groups of equal size and power within a scientific community) have different preferences about the minimum degree of success that a theory or principle must have in order to be considered "acceptable," that is, a norm of type (2). I will briefly discuss, in the next section, a formal model allowing us to derive

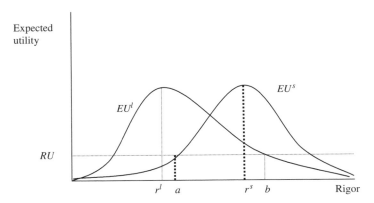

Figure 18.1   A norm of type (2)

the utility functions used in figure 18.1. For the moment, let us suppose that the "strict" preferred to establish r^s as the minimum acceptable level of success, while the "lenient" preferred r^l. RU represents the reservation utility: that which would be received if no agreement were reached and each scientist joined another community or found a different job. The "strict" would neither accept a rule lower than a, nor lower than r^l (since r^l is better for both groups than any other point to the left); equally, the "lenient" would not accept any point to the right of r^s or b. So, any rule between a and r^l would be a Nash equilibrium, and hence, a possible "contract."[14]

In the second place, we can also study the *efficiency* of a norm. In this context, the concept of "efficiency" has at least two different senses. In the first place, we can explore if the existing norms tend to produce situations where no scientist (or, by the way, other groups of citizens) can get a higher level of utility without someone else getting a lower one; i.e. we can study if the norms are "Pareto-efficient" (for example, a norm above point b or below point r^s in figure 18.1 would be inefficient in this sense). In the second place, we can investigate whether the existing norms of a scientific community tend to produce an optimum body of "knowledge," at least according to the epistemic values of the members of the community (for example, a norm above point b would be epistemically better than b itself, though the incentives faced by the researchers preclude reaching an agreement so strict – if we grant scientists the liberty of choosing the norm). Another example of this concept of "epistemic efficiency" would be the following: in the case of action-related norms, we can study the possibility of establishing "sincerity-promoting rules" (or "strategy-proof mechanisms"), e.g. ways of doing and reporting experiments, such that, if the agreement is obeyed by the others, each experimenter will find out that her best strategy is to report sincerely the result of her experiment even if this result goes against her own theory. These later kind of norms are of the highest importance, since they permit the construction of *intersubjective knowledge* out of the subjective experiences and private interests of each researcher. I will also succinctly present in the next section a mechanism having this property. The concept of epistemic efficiency will appear again in section 4.

Lastly, we can also study the *stability* properties of these norms, and especially the question concerning their self-enforceability. A minimum condition for a system of norms being self-enforceable is that it generates a coordination game, i.e. one in which the best strategy for each player is to do what the others do. Of course, a scientific community can also reach an equilibrium in which not every member adopts exactly the same rules as the others: if different groups adopt different compromises, each individual scientist will consider the pros and the cons of joining one group or another, and her decision will depend, among other things, on the size of each group. Another possible application of our approach would be to consider the rules existing in a given community, not as the result of a consensus among its current members, but as something which has been "inherited" by them from past generations, and that each generation can adapt to their own circumstances. The rigidity or flexibility of the norms may have a strong influence on their evolution, on the evolution of the scientific communities they regulate, and on the evolution of the knowledge produced by these communities. Hence, the study of scientific norms from an evolutionary perspective would also be of the greatest interest.

3 Two examples

In this section I will offer two examples of "constitutional methodological norms" that *could* be established among a scientific community. The first one refers to the choice of an inference rule, i.e. the choice of an epistemic quality level or "rigor" such that, if a theory happens to be the only one surpassing it, it should be accepted by all the community members; I will call this level "the acceptance standard." Let U be the utility one scientists gets if her own theory is unanimously accepted by her colleagues, and let us assume that the utility she receives if her theory is rejected is zero; let $F(x)$ be the prior probability she has of devising a theory whose quality level is of x at most; and finally, assume that this probability is the same for the n members of the community. It is possible to prove that the expected utility of establishing x as the acceptance standard will be:

$$EU(x) = (1 - F(x))F(x)^{n-1}U(N) + [1 - (1 - F(x))F(x)^{n-1}]U(0)$$
$$= (F(x)^{n-1} - F(x)^n)U(N). \tag{1}$$

The first-order condition for the maximization of this expected utility is:

$$EU'(x) = U(N)[(n - 1)F(x)^{n-2}f(x) - nF(x)^{n-1}f(x)] = 0, \tag{2}$$

and this entails that $F(x) = (n - 1)/n$, or, which is the same, $1 - F(x) = 1/n$. That is, the members of a scientific community, were they motivated basically by public recognition, would desire that an acceptance standard were established such that the prior probability each member has of devising an acceptable theory is just the inverse of the number of community members.

If the inference norm does not command us to suspend judgment if more than one theory happens to surpass the acceptance standard, but allows us to accept *any one* of those theories, it can be proved that the preferred standard would be lower. On the other hand, if scientists are motivated also by "knowledge," and they prefer *ceteris paribus* a stricter norm than a lower one (i.e. if U depends positively on x in (1) and (2)), then it can be proved that the preferred standard would be higher. So, it is possible that not all scientists prefer exactly the same standard, and a process of negotiation like that described in figure 18.1 can take place; the standard which is finally chosen will have no epistemic virtue *per se*, besides the fact that, if it happens to be around the one established by (2), it will be a relatively strong one. Its main virtue is, instead, of economic nature that: *it allows us to establish an incentive system which makes the effort of scientific research attractive enough for enough people.*

The second example I am going to present is a mechanism to allocate resources for the replication of experiments, one guaranteeing two things: (a) that each replicator reveals the datum actually observed by her, instead of the datum predicted by her own theory (if she has one[15]), and (b) that the resources are given precisely to the most skillful experimenters. I will suppose that the result of an experiment or observation can be summarized in a single magnitude, and that it is possible to define the "distance" between any two different values of that quantity. I will also assume that each researcher makes the experiment or observation a number of times, using the resources she has been endowed with, and derives a certain statistical distribution of the possible values of the quantity, as well as a distribution of the possible values of the mean of all announced results. Lastly, I will suppose that the two distributions are symmetric.[16] The proposed mechanism is the following:

(a) Each researcher decides whether to perform the experiment or not, and, if she decides to perform it, she has also to decide whether to reveal a result or not; all the researchers who decide to reveal a result do it at the same time.

(b) If the difference between the mean of all revealed data and the datum revealed by a researcher is bigger than d, then this scientist gets a "penalty" which decreases her utility level in V; if the difference is lower, then she receives a public recognition which increases her utility level in U; if a researcher does not reveal any result, her utility level does not change.

(c) The financial and material resources the community can devote to making the experiment are allocated in the following way: every researcher (or team) announces the minimum margin of error d she is able to accept (based on her previous experience as an experimentalist), and the resources are distributed beginning by the researcher who has announced the minimum d, until they are exhausted; the margin to which all researchers are submitted corresponds to the one announced by the last researcher who has been endowed with resources.

(d) All the members of the scientific community must accept as the value of the measured magnitude the mean of the revealed data, with a margin of error that depends on their variance.

It is possible to prove that the most rational strategy for each experimenter under this mechanism is to reveal sincerely both the minimum margin to which she is able to commit herself, and the true outcome of her replication of the experiment.[17] The first of these properties allows the scientific community to allocate the resources among the people who are most able to perform the experiment well, whereas the second one allows us to trust the experiment's revealed results.

The application of some constitutional norms such as the two commented on above can warrant that the knowledge produced by a scientific community is relatively "objective," both in the sense of being impartial and in the sense of having been subjected to some strong quality tests. I am not asserting that precisely these mechanisms exist in the "cognitively successful" scientific communities, nor that these "constitutional" rules should be established within an "assembly." But I would like to suggest that those disciplines which have managed to establish some norms with analogous properties are those which are also most successful as suppliers of reliable knowledge.

4   Collective decisions and the dynamics of scientific knowledge

The "constitutional" rules of scientific method described in the previous section tend, if they are well defined and enforced, to promote agreement about data, hypotheses, laws, or any other kind of scientific statements, even if the dominant (though not exclusive) desire of scientists were recognition. Nevertheless, we can not assume that actual methodological rules (particularly when we think about the norms of a concrete discipline or subdiscipline) are as well established as other types of legal rules are, since they are usually tacit, rather than encoded, and also because they are usually difficult to apply unambiguously to singular cases. This means that, even if the members of a scientific community have mutually agreed in constraining their choices of statements to some common rules, there is still the possibility that not all of them accept the same data, models or theories, although their methodological compromises may tend to reduce this variation, as compared to what would have been the case if those shared rules had not existed at all.

If methodological constraints are not enough for generating a full consensus around one solution to a scientific problem (or, more radically, if no unanimous agreement has been reached about methodological norms), we can legitimately ask what factors determine the actual degree of acceptance of each alternative solution among a scientific community. Elsewhere I have proposed a model which identifies three factors making a scientist more willing to accept a given statement:[18] the epistemic value the statement has for her (which will mainly depend on the interpretation she makes of the shared rules and of their application to that problem), the degree in which the statement is favorable to the theories proposed by her (again according to those rules), and the degree of acceptance of the statement within the scientist's community. The inclusion of this last factor needs some justification. In the first place, for many statements a scientist needs to use during her work, the "private" information she will have about them will be very poor, and she will simply be unable to perform her work without trusting what her colleagues assert; so, the more agreement they will show on a certain statement, the less probable it will be that all of them have misleading information about it.[19] In the second place, communication among scientists tends to be easier the more "knowledge" they share; hence, if communication is essential while trying to persuade a colleague, then you will need to accept a high proportion of the statements she accepts. In the third place, if you want others to accept the hypothesis you are proposing, then you will need to show that the methodological norms they accept entail that your hypothesis has an epistemic value high enough, *given the other statements they accept*; so, the more accepted a statement is among your community, the stronger will be the incentive you have to devise a hypothesis which is *supported* by that statement, and hence, the more interesting it will be for you to accept it.[20]

Since the details of this model of theory choice can be examined in the papers referred to in n. 18, I will indicate here only the more interesting consequences. In the first place, if the application of the constitutional constraints does not make it compulsory to accept a particular solution to a given scientific problem, there can be more than one stable equilibria (i.e. more than one vector $x = (x_1, \ldots, x_n)$, such that x_i is the degree of acceptance of the ith solution among the scientific community, and that x is a steady state in the dynamics generated by the mutual interdependence of the scientists' decisions, i.e. one where the desired decisions of all scientists are mutually consistent – a Nash equilibrium – and which is an attractor for other vectors which are not Nash equilibria). In the second place, under some circumstances, some of these steady states will be Paretian-inefficient, i.e. it is possible that x is a stable equilibrium but there is another distribution of degrees of acceptance under which no scientist would have a lower level of utility, but at least one of them would have a higher level. In the third place, it may also happen that every scientist believes solution i is epistemically better than solution j, but there is a stable equilibrium in which $x_i < x_j$ (we can refer to this situation as one of "epistemic inefficiency"). Lastly, the existence of multiple equilibria can make of the evolution of scientific knowledge a strongly *path-dependent* process, since the actual degree of acceptance of a scientific hypothesis will not only depend on epistemic factors (i.e. each researcher's beliefs about its scientific merits, given the information she has) and on social factors (i.e. the "conformity effects" described in the preceding paragraph, as well as each researcher's desire for recognition), but also on the *order* in which the relevant information has been produced and disseminated, and on the *order* in which the competing hypotheses have been devised and publicly proposed.

These four results are really bad news for those who would want to use economic theory as an instrument to show the "efficiency" or "rationality" of scientific research, since they confirm some of the main points defended by radically relativist sociologists of science, or so it might seem at first sight.

Nevertheless, I think that the problem only emerges owing to the fact that we have modeled scientists simply as passive automata myopically adjusting to the situation they confront. If we consider, instead, that researchers have the possibility of being conscious of the "problems" caused by their own decisions, as well as the capacity of "negotiating" a solution to those problems, we can show that *collective action* among scientists can help to make the production of scientific knowledge a much more rational enterprise. Obviously, the constitutional choices referred to in sections 2 and 3 were also collective decisions; the main differences between that case and the present one are the following: in the first place, the constitutional choice would be a unanimous decision of all the members of a scientific community, whereas I will now study collective decisions taken by groups smaller than the full community; in the second place, the objects of the constitutional choice were methodological *norms*, and we will now consider decisions about to accept or to reject a scientific *statement*.

Suppose, in the simplest possible case, that the members of a scientific community have to choose between accepting a hypothesis or rejecting it,[21] and assume that there are two possible stable equilibria, x and y, corresponding to two different degrees of acceptance of the hypothesis.[22] If each researcher just decided *individually* whether to accept or to reject the hypothesis, then any of the two equilibria could be reached (for example, x), depending on the situation from which they started. But if scientists realized that there is another stable equilibrium (what could be possible thanks to fluent communication among researchers), and if some of them realized that they would reach a higher utility level in y than in x (among those who reject the hypothesis in x but accept it in y), this group of scientists could form a "coalition" and change their former *individual* decisions of rejecting the hypothesis for a *collective* decision in the opposite sense. The last decision is "collective" in the sense that it is only interesting to adopt it for each member of the group if the other members do the same; i.e. the members of the group face a coordination problem in taking the decision. It can be proved that the collective compromise of accepting the hypothesis is self-enforceable iff the size of the coalition is bigger than the absolute difference between x and z (z being the unstable equilibrium lying between x and y; see n. 22). If the coalition is formed and its decision is self-enforceable, then other scientists who were rejecting the hypothesis in x would find it more interesting to accept it, which would induce more scientists to do the same, and so on, until equilibrium y is reached. This result also entails that there will be a possible coalition having enough power to "jump" from equilibrium x to equilibrium y iff there is no possible coalition with the power of doing the reverse.

The possibility of "jumping-at-once" from one stable equilibrium to another entails that, at least under the circumstances considered by the existing models, only one stable equilibrium remains, which eliminates the problems of underdetermination and path-dependence. Paretian inefficiencies are also eliminated, since those researchers who were better in equilibrium y than in x could form a coalition to "jump" to y, if the actual equilibrium were x. The only remaining problem is epistemic inefficiency, although this is only due to our assumption that researchers can take into account, in order to accept or reject a hypothesis, not only their private opinions about it and the public pronouncements of their colleagues, but also the degree of support the theories proposed by them receive from that hypothesis; in the absence of this motivation, epistemically inefficient equilibria would be eliminated as well (more formally, if every scientist thinks that hypothesis H is better in the epistemic sense than H', it cannot be the case that, in the equilibrium which is stable under collective decisions, H' has a higher degree of acceptance than H). Nevertheless, the formation of coalitions can have some *costs*: time must be devoted to talking and discussing with colleagues, and a risk is assumed by each member, for it is not sure that their collective decision will in the end be successful (for example, the size of the coalition might be too small). So, the possibility of a fluent communication among scientists is essential in permitting their collective decisions to solve the problems generated by conformity effects.[23]

5 Is economic knowledge efficiently produced?

Here we have considered science as an institution devoted to the production of "knowledge," but integrated by people who are not exclusively (and perhaps not fundamentally) motivated by the "pursuit of knowledge," but for the attainment of other personal goals. In a sense, society faces here a problem of the "principal–agent" type: how can the people whose money is employed to fund scientific research (the "principals") make scientists (the "agents") behave as if they were truth-seekers, instead of mere rent-seekers? Some authors have argued that something like the "invisible hand of the market" would also exist in the case of science, making it more interesting individually for each researcher to seek valid results than to present erroneous or fraudulent ones, and to defend those theories which she personally thinks are better justified than those which better help her to reach her own private goals. Perhaps some economic models showing this possibility can be devised, but I suspect (for reasons stated in section 2) that only an agreement about scientific *norms* i.e. an exchange of *constraints*, instead of a mere exchange of "actions" – can make the scientists' decisions be consistent with the pursuit of knowledge. In fact, even in the case of the market the "invisible hand" works only because there is a legal order which defines and enforces property rights. On the other hand, if we choose to model scientists as individual utility maximizers, and ignore the possibility of negotiation and collective decision-making, then all seems to indicate that equilibrium analysis will lead us to conclude that the production of scientific knowledge is not as rational and as efficient as the "invisible hand" metaphor might suggest.

In the case of science, "constitutional" rules would define what can, can not or must be taken as a solution to a problem, or as a better solution to another one, and hence, those norms *create* the game that scientists will later play, using either individual or collective strategies. From the point of view which is defended in the present chapter, the more freedom scientists have to establish a system of methodological norms (and the more severe the chosen norms are), and the more freedom scientists have to communicate, negotiate, or establish coalitions with colleagues, the more probable it will be that the "scientific knowledge" produced by them will be of a high quality *according to the epistemic criteria of scientists themselves*. I do not think there is, in general, any other criterion of epistemic value which could be more acceptable than consistency with the epistemic part of scientists' preferences, for the specialists in a scientific discipline have, after all, a deeper sense of what can be taken as "knowledge" within their own field. The main problem of an institutional organization of science *from the cognitive point of view* is, then, how to make scientists *strive* for reaching theories which have the highest possible epistemic value in their own opinion, and how to make them *sincerely reveal* their true opinions about the theories actually proposed.

The question is, hence, how does all this affect our discussion on economic knowledge? Is economics, as a scientific discipline, constituted in such a way that the mechanisms analyzed in the previous chapters apply to it? Instead of offering a list of possible "cognitive shortcomings" of economic science, I propose to take the fundamental elements of our collective-action model of scientific research and see whether they can be attributed to economics. In the first place, it is hard to deny that economics, particularly mainstream economics, is an activity regulated by norms, *severe* methodological norms. Papers published in "top" journals must have passed strong quality tests, perhaps no less strict than in the "harder" sciences, and in general there is little doubt among the profession about who are the most "eminent" practitioners, those who have produced the "best" theoretical or (less frequently) empirical work. But it is doubtful that the *aim* of those tests, and of the criteria used to identify who is a good economist, is specifically *to determine the compulsory acceptance of the content of published models or theories*. The main function of the methodological norms considered in sections 2 and 3 was simply to make it possible that a scientist could become the winner in a race for the solution to a problem, and *being* the winner entails that all (or almost all) your colleagues *explicitly accept you are right*. In economics, instead, accepting that a model or theory is terribly good (even much better than its rivals) does not force you to recognize that the model or theory is (even approximately) *right*. In the majority of cases, what makes of an economic model a "good" one (in terms of the quality rankings of the profession) is, instead, the mastery of analytical skills revealed by its creator. Economics is in this sense more similar to the fine arts or to sports than to other scientific disciplines: we will find in it severe norms, and fierce competition as well, but the losers in that struggle will not have the obligation of *adopting* the winners' work.[24]

In the second place, if methodological rules are not enough to promote scientific consensus in economics, will collective decision-making avoid, at least, that epistemic inefficiencies take place within the discipline? Two factors can make it difficult for this mechanism to function in economics as efficiently as it may do in natural sciences. The first factor is that the reasons to accept an economic theory, model, hypothesis, or datum may not only be the ones referred to in section 4: besides epistemic assessment, support of one's preferred theories, and conformity to others' decisions, an economic statement can also be accepted by an economist because it tends to promote in some way her economic, political or social interests. For example, usually the effects of economic policies on the general welfare are very uncertain for individuals, but *some* of their consequences for *some* agents are very clear: for example, the wealthy may not be sure about the *general* and *long-term* effects of a big cut in the marginal rates of the income tax, but they will be very sure about some *particular* effects of this policy, and they may tend to accept and disseminate a theory which proposes a measure of this kind. Even if a situation happened in which an epistemically inefficient equilibrium were actualized and a possible coalition existed which were interested in passing to an efficient equilibrium (i.e. if they were interested *for epistemic reasons* in "jumping-at-once" to the acceptance of, say, an heterodox theory), this "jump" would probably have *real* effects on economic policy, or on the working of the economic system, and the agents who thought that they were going to be harmed by this change might provide some incentives to economists in order to prevent them to "jump." Hence, since the consequences of economic theories almost always refer to interest-laden problems, it seems that a good strategy would be not to trust too much in those theories until a detailed argument is offered showing that the people who have produced and disseminated that "knowledge" have made it so under a system of incentives guaranteeing the neutrality and objectivity of their conclusions.

In economics there is perhaps a second factor which makes it more difficult for coalitions to eliminate epistemic inefficiencies. This is the fact that the "economic knowledge" which is more relevant to take into account is not only that of economists, but the economic beliefs, intuitions or expectations of *economic agents* (i.e. consumers, firm managers, politicians, and so on).[25] It is at least conceptually possible that some economists had discovered "the true laws of the economic system" (if such a thing existed at all), but no one else believed them. Since the evolution of the economy will depend more on the "opinions" each agent has than on the "truth" possessed by a minority within

an ebony tower, a truly "reflexive" economic theory (as, for example, Rational
Expectation Macroeconomics pretended to be) should not automatically assert
that people have true, unbiased knowledge of the relevant economic variables
and mechanisms; this could be accepted only after having shown why conformity effects and ideological biases *could not* lead to stable equilibria in which
some radically false economic beliefs survived and had a high degree of popularity. If these epistemically inefficient equilibria existed in the economy at
large (and not only within economics as a discipline), it would be much more
difficult to create a big enough coalition which could "jump" to an efficient
equilibrium, simply because it would probably involve millions of people, and
not only a few dozens (as in the case of scientific coalitions).

In conclusion, the credibility of economic knowledge depends basically on
the incentives faced by those people who produce it, disseminate it, and make
use of it. As this credibility is growingly contested from some quarters, I think
economists should devote more effort to justify the objectivity of their theories
and the reliability of their recommendations. It can be argued that "the burden
of proof" should be on the accuser's side, but actually no accusation is being
made here: only the conceptual possibility of epistemic inefficiencies is indicated. It would be interesting if economic theorists provided an account of how
an *objective* economic knowledge could be reached, as well as an empirical
determination of whether the actual practice of economics corresponds to that
theoretical account. In order to do so, the elaboration of an "economics of scientific knowledge" seems to be an essential previous stage. I believe that deep
and radical changes in economic theory can be expected if this program is taken
seriously by the profession.

Notes

Financial support from the Fundación Urrutia Elejalde, from Spanish government's
DGICYT research project PB98-0495-C08-01, and from the Department of Economics
of the Universidad Carlos III, has encouraged the writing of this chapter. Some preliminary versions of it were presented in the Permanent Seminar of Economic Methodology
of Universidad Autónoma de Madrid (November 1999), in the Seminar of Economics
and Philosophy of the Cátedra Sánchez-Mazas (San Sebastián, Spain, 1999), and in
the Seminar "Theoretization and Experimentation in Economics" (Rovaniemi, Finland,
December 1999). My thanks to Juan Carlos García-Bermejo, Andoni Ibarra, Uskali
Mäki, and Timo Tammi for inviting me to take part in them. I have also received helpful comments from Francisco Álvarez, Shaun Hargreaves Heap, Frank Hindriks, David
Teira, and especially Juan Urrutia.

1. See, for example, Brennan and Buchanan (1985).
2. See Colander (1989), and, in general, the papers contained in Colander and Coats
   (1989). See also Wible (1998) for a convincing criticism of the idea that "science is
   a free market."

3. Lucas (1987).

4. After all, in what sense would an economic agent not "survive" who was not able to predict the rate of inflation in an unbiased way?

   For a survey of the literature on economics and evolution, see Vromen (1995).

5. See, for example, Vega-Redondo (1996).

6. The same idea has been defended in Mäki (1999), where he proposes considering the applicability of an economic theory to itself (i.e. its capacity to explain its own degree of popularity and its – assumed – epistemic superiority with respect to alternative theories) as an additional test each theory should pass.

7. Of course, the mere fact that somebody pursues private benefits, among other things, does not make her automatically a "rent-seeker"; by "rent-seeking scientists" I would mean, rather, those who used (at least a part of) the resources devoted to science in a manner which was only profitable for them, and not for the other members of the society (as long as they are interested in funding science for producing reliable knowledge). So, the concept of "rent-seeking" refers only to the *behavior* of researchers, not to their motivations: the pursuit of a high income or of political power will not make a scientist a "rent-seeker" if she acts in a manner which is compatible with the pursuit of the highest amount of knowledge.

8. See, for example, Hull (1988, esp. chapter 10), and Dasgupta and David (1994, section 4).

9. See, for example, Latour and Woolgar (1979). Personally, I do not accept these radical assumptions, but I am trying to show that even if scientists were as depicted by those authors, they would be interested in establishing some "objectivity-promoting" methodological norms.

10. By recognizing this essential methodological individualism, the constitutional approach avoids the problems rightly detected by Wade Hands (1997) in other "naturalistic *cum* economic" explanations of scientific knowledge (such as Goldman and Shaked 1991, or Kitcher 1993): our approach does not "want something to emerge (a special type of belief) that is qualitatively different from the beliefs of the individual agents" (Hands 1997, S113), and it does not intend, as well, to construct a notion of "public knowledge" as a kind of "aggregate" having the same properties of individual beliefs.

11. It is almost certain that no human group can devise and study all *possible* kinds of norms they might adopt; but once some *type* of norm has been proposed within a group, it is much easier for its members to discuss what *specific features* they would desire the chosen norm to have.

12. I have defended elsewhere the notion that some prevailing methodological norms correspond to those that would be chosen by a group of scientists satisfying two conditions: (a) the epistemic element in their utility functions corresponds to what I have called "empirical verisimilitude of a theory given the existing data," and (b) they choose the rules without knowing what probabilities of success *their own* theories will have under those rules (i.e. they choose "under the veil of ignorance"). See Zamora Bonilla (1999a).

13. Enforcement norms are, in this sense, "meta-norms." Axelrod (1997, chapter 3), shows that introducing this kind of norms in computer "prisoner's dilemma"

tournaments drastically reduces the frequency of "defections." On the other hand, the justification of obeying a meta-norm is not clear from the point of view of instrumental rationality (see, esp., Elster 1989, chapter 3).

14. Of course, the positions of the four relevant points can change, depending on the shapes of the expected utility functions and on the reservation utility levels (which, in addition, need not be the same for each group).

15. Or if there is one datum that is more "favorable" for her in some sense.

16. The results depend essentially on the symmetry assumption; it would be an interesting analytical problem to show whether some mechanisms with the same properties exist if this assumption is relaxed.

17. A detailed proof is available from the author.

18. Zamora Bonilla (1999b). Brock and Durlauf (1999) also present a similar, though mathematically more sophisticated, model.

19. Cf., for example, Hardwig (1991).

20. See, for example, Banerjee (1992) for the economic modeling of conformity to others' behavior.

21. I am using the term "hypothesis" in the widest possible sense, as a proposition of any level of generality whose truth is not known with absolute certainty.

22. In this case it can be proved that there will also be an *unstable* equilibrium z, between x and y. For all the proofs referred to in this paragraph, see Zamora Bonilla (1999b, 470–471, 477–480). For the problem of stability, cf. also Brock and Durlauf (1999, 121), though they ignore the possibility of collective decisions, which is basic to my argument.

23. The change in the degree of popularity of a hypothesis owing to the collective decision of a coalition can be related to Bruno Latour's arguments about the role of "enrolling allies" to make a theory triumph (cf. Latour 1987). What Latour would probably not accept is the efficiency-promoting character of these collective decisions.

24. It is particularly sad that empirical evidence is used so little to actually *resolve* economic disputations. For a recent proposal of establishing a kind of empirical competition among economic models, as well as a recognition-allocation mechanism based on its results, see Slembeck (2000). I have tried to explain the relative lack of empirical testing in economic theory in Zamora Bonilla (1999a).

25. The relevance of this "everyday" economic knowledge has been emphasized in the articles contained in Garnett (1999).

References

Axelrod, R. (1997). *The Complexity of Cooperation*. Princeton: Princeton University Press

Banerjee, A.V. (1992). A simple model of herd behavior, *The Quarterly Journal of Economics*, 107, 797–817

Brennan, G. and J.M. Buchanan (1985). *The Reason of Rules. Constitutional Political Economy*. Cambridge: Cambridge University Press

Brock, W.A. and S.N. Durlauf (1999). A formal model of theory choice in science, *Economic Theory*, 14, 113–130

Colander, D. (1989). The invisible hand of truth, in D. Colander and A.W. Coats, *The Spread of Economic Ideas*. Cambridge: Cambridge University Press, 31–36

Colander, D. and A.W. Coats (1989). *The Spread of Economic Ideas*. Cambridge: Cambridge University Press

Dasgupta, P. and P.A. David (1994). Toward a new economics of science, *Research Policy*, 23, 487–521

Elster, J. (1989). *The Cement of Society: A Study of Social Order*. Cambridge: Cambridge University Press

Garnett, R.F. (Jr.) (ed.) (1999). *What Do Economists Know?*. London: Routledge

Goldman, A.I. and M. Shaked (1991). An economic model of scientific activity and truth acquisition, *Philosophical Studies*, 63, 31–55

Hands, D. Wade (1997). *Caveat emptor*: economics and contemporary philosophy of science, *Philosophy of Science*, 64 (proceedings), S107–S116

Hardwig, J. (1991). The role of trust in knowledge, *Journal of Philosophy*, 88, 693–700

Hull, D.L. (1988). *Science as a Process: An Evolutionary Account of the Social and Conceptual Development of Science*. Chicago: University of Chicago Press

Kitcher, P. (1993). *The Advancement of Science: Science without Legend, Objectivity without Illusions*. New York: Oxford University Press

Latour, B. (1987). *Science in Action: How to Follow Scientists and Engineers through Society*. Milton Neyhes: Open University Press

Latour, B. and S. Woolgar (1979). *Laboratory Life: The Social Construction of Scientific Facts*. London: Sage

Lucas, Robart E. (Jr) (1987). Adaptive behaviour and economic theory, in R.M. Hogarth and M.W. Reder (eds.), *Rational Choice: The Contrast between Economics and Psychology*. Chicago: University of Chicago Press, 217–242

Mäki, Uskali (1999). Science as a free market. a reflexivity test in an economics of economics, *Perspectives on Science*, 7(4), 486–509

Slembeck, T. (2000). How to make scientists agree: an evolutionary betting mechanism, *Kyklos*, 53(4), 587–592

Vega-Redondo, F. (1996). *Evolution, Games and Economic Behaviour*. Oxford: Oxford University Press

Vromen, J.J. (1995). *Economic Evolution*. London: Routledge

Wible, J.R. (1998). *The Economics of Science. Methodology and Epistemology as if Economics Really Mattered*. London: Routledge

Zamora Bonilla, J.P. (1999a). Verisimilitude and the scientific strategy of economic theory, *Journal of Economic Methodology*, 6, 331–350

(1999b). The elementary economics of scientific consensus, *Theoria*, 14(3), 461–488

Index